FROM THE LEFT BANK TO THE MAINSTREAM:
Historical Debates and Contemporary Research
in Marxist Sociology

THE REYNOLDS SERIES IN SOCIOLOGY

Larry T. Reynolds, *Editor*

by **GENERAL HALL, INC.**

FROM THE LEFT BANK
TO THE MAINSTREAM:
Historical Debates and Contemporary
Research in Marxist Sociology

Patrick McGuire
University of Toledo
and
Donald McQuarie
Bowling Green State University

GENERAL HALL, INC.
Publishers
5 Talon Way
Dix Hills, New York 11746

FROM THE LEFT BANK TO THE MAINSTREAM:
Historical Debates and Contemporary Research in Marxist Sociology

GENERAL HALL, INC.
5 Talon Way
Dix Hills, New York 11746

Publisher: Ravi Mehra
Composition: *Graphics Division,* General Hall, Inc.

LIBRARY OF CONGRESS CATALOG CARD NUMBER: **93–81354**

ISBN:1–882289–13–7 [paper]
1–882289–14–5 [cloth]

Manufactured in the United States of America

Contents

Part II Social Institutions

ACKNOWLEDGMENTS

The editors and authors would like to acknowledge the contribution of a number of colleagues and associates who provided us with critical commentaries on the chapters included in this volume. They include Julia Adams, Anthony Blasi, Johanna Brenner, Barbara Brents, Elizabeth Cass, Barbara K. Chesney, Pierre Clavel, Peter Dreier, Shelley Feldman, Walda Katz Fishman, Martha Gimenez, Muge Gocek, Jim Gregson, Pamela Bettis , Barbara Laslett, Seamus Metress, Roslyn Mickelson, Harvey Molotch, Jeffery Paige, Linda Pertusati, Joyce Rothschild, Stamatis Spirou, Randy Stoecker, Jim Thomas, Cornell West, and J. Allen Whitt. Completing this book would have taken much longer to put together were it not for the support we received from our respective universities, the University of Toledo and Bowling Green State University, and our respective sociology departments. We would also like to thank our series editor at General Hall, Larry Reynolds, for his suggestion that we put this book together as well as for his relentless red pen in copyediting. The editors also wish to acknowledge the efforts of our assistants Jennifer Accetolla and Karl Friedrich Smith who read each manuscript and provided commentary on spelling, writing style, clarity, and format. Thanks to Scott G. McNall for his help in working out the arrangement through which the proceeds from this book are dedicated to creating an American Sociological Association Marxist Section graduate student scholarship fund. We would especially like to thank the authors who contributed to this book and the publisher's series editor, Larry Reynolds, for contributing their share of the book's proceeds to this scholarship fund. These colleagues and friends have helped, through their work, to make creating this book a truly enjoyable and collective effort.

INTRODUCTION

U.S. SOCIOLOGY, THE AMERICAN DREAM, AND THE SPECTER OF KARL MARX

Patrick McGuire
and
Donald McQuarie

"Communism is dead." This judgment has come to be perceived as a universally accepted fact—a statement so obvious that it is simply repeated by one media announcer after another without argument or question. "Marxism was a complete and utter failure" is yet another judgment offered nightly by news analysts and other TV pundits. Students in several universities have challenged their professors by shouting, "Why should I bother reading Marx?"

And here you hold in your hands a book that professes to discuss the contributions made by Marxist theory and analysis to our understandings of contemporary social institutions and practices. So what is going on? Are we and the contributors to this book some bunch of left orthodox zealots who do not own TV sets and missed the news that Marxism is dead? Or, in fact, is Marxism not quite as defunct as is generally believed by the American public? Might there still be important insights for the social sciences and social praxis to be made from within the Marxist tradition?

Clearly we believe that the latter is the case. We and our contributors are convinced that Marxism offers important insights into how and why our society works the way it does, and that it is absolutely essential to the struggle for a more socially just and economically responsive society. One need not be a "Marxist" or even a radical to find value in the arguments presented by scholars working within this tradition. Indeed, even conservative academics begrudgingly acknowledge the importance of this approach to understanding society. They recognize that it renders important insights not gleaned by relying on the logic and methods of other approaches to the study of our society. And we believe that this book will show that this Marxist tradition, broadly defined, is not only alive and well but has made valuable contributions—in many instances, contributions of crucial importance—to all the varied subfields of sociology during the past two decades.

1

What Makes an Analysis a Marxist Analysis?

The field of Marxist theory has exploded over the past half century, so there is as great a variety of competing perspectives and viewpoints *within* Marxist theory as exist within the non-Marxist social sciences. Thus, to talk about the contributions of Marxist theory is somewhat misleading because there is not one Marxism, but many competing and sometimes complimentary versions of Marxism. (This is one reason why many contemporary Marxist theorists prefer the label neo-Marxism.) In our view, certain broad definitional elements of structure and content mark these contemporary theories and analyses as Marxist. That is, there is a common, irreducible core set of characteristics shared by all Marxist perspectives.

First, a Marxist analysis is class focused. It proceeds from the assumption that the relationship between people and property—between humans in the production process and the various relationships of exploitation and appropriation that arise from that process—is the fundamental sociological relation in society. Quickly and crudely stated, a Marxist analysis starts from the position that this is a capitalist society and that the interests of capitalists permeate the ideas of our culture and the structure of our social institutions, as well as shape the conditions of everyday life for all citizens. This is not to deny the crucial, and often determining, role played by gender, race, ethnicity, or sexual preference.

Second, a Marxist analysis recognizes that productive labor (physical and mental) is the source of all wealth in society. Third, a Marxist analysis is politically committed to a set of social goals. It argues that human needs should be placed above market needs, the needs of capitalists for profit, and the needs of any specific individual. Its aim is principally social, aimed at the realization of a conception of the public good.

Fourth, such an analysis sees conflict and change as natural and inevitable parts of social life. Marxist analysts understand that society changes through opposition and conflict; a process they refer to as dialectical change. Their analyses reject the liberal notion of a smooth, continuous (linear), evolutionary process of progress toward some inevitable goal.

Fifth, as Marx himself noted, a good analysis should be afraid neither of its own conclusions nor of the powers that be. Marxists tend to be critical of the status quo and existing structures of power. This has proven to be as true for Marxist dissidents under the old Soviet system (e.g., Bahro, Szelenyi, Rakovski, Medvedev, and Kagarlitsky) as for Marxists in the capitalist "West."

Sixth and finally, a Marxist analysis is committed to creating knowledge that can help inform the struggles for progressive and liberating social change. The point, as was argued a century ago, is not merely to interpret the world but to create the ideas and conditions necessary to change it in ways that liberate society and its members.

The Case for Marxist Analyses in American Society

The case against Marx and Marxism in the U.S. press is almost always based on equating Marx and Marxist thought with the political, economic, and cultural conditions in the former Soviet Union, Eastern Europe, and China. Yet significant elements of the left in this country and others have criticized the Russian and Chinese models literally since their inception. Many of the major thinkers of the twentieth century—George Orwell, Jean Paul Sartre, Herbert Marcuse, Charles Steinmetz, and Albert Einstein, to name but a few—were critical of Leninism and yet read and found value in the writings and analyses of Marx and subsequent Marxists.

The 1960's New Left in the United States and elsewhere grew from two strains: anticapitalism and antiauthoritarianism. Members of this movement in Western Europe and the United States continuously criticized the Leninist model and the organized communist parties as well as the Western capitalist nations. They actively criticized the efforts of the United States as a capitalist nation and its autocratic foreign policy. Yet they also provided some of the best critiques of the Russian model, describing it as a case of state capitalism. Since that government was an owner of the factories, acted like an owner—seeking to increase the level of profit, replacing economic democracy with an authority structure that exploited workers, and engaging in industrial production without consideration of the social and ecological costs of those acts—and produced goods for exchange in the capitalist world economy, the Soviet Union was argued to be an example of state capitalism. Among many New Left theorists the Soviet Union was twice cursed: It was both capitalist and authoritarian.

The implications of equating Russian communism and Marxism, and the impact of the state capitalist model were recently discussed on a nationally syndicated late-night news show. The conversation went largely as follows: The host asked a leading member of a Scandinavian socialist government what the collapse of the Soviet Union meant for socialism. Clearly this was a shot at socialism in general and at Marxism in particular. The Scandinavian coolly replied, "One down, one to go." When asked to explain further, he explained that the collapse of the Russian communist (state capitalist) model left only the U.S. private capitalist model as an obstacle to economic justice and social progress.

This gentleman proceeded to argue the importance of Marxist analysis for understanding why the Russian Leninist system had collapsed and then explained why that analytic framework had been crucial to avoiding the excesses of both private and state capitalism in his country. The host was completely befuddled. As he struggled to grasp the ideas being presented, his head twisted from side to side like one of those stuffed dogs on a spring that you see in the back window of an old car lurching through traffic. The expected correct answer and normally received truth were not forthcoming because elsewhere Soviet communism and Marxist theory are not conceptualized as synonymous. The host (and probably most of the audience) struggled to come to grips with a set of ideas and recognitions that would be obvious to a majority of citizens in a score of other industrial nations.

Two important questions arise from this brief introduction. Why would anyone think that Marxist thought had something to contribute to our understanding of society? And if it is important and can contribute to a better society, then why do we not know more about it?

Let's answer the initial question first. The United States had the highest standard of living in the world in 1965. Yet by 1980 we were eleventh and by 1990 we had the seventeenth highest standard of living in the world. The percentage of unionized workers has declined steadily since 1953. The purchasing power of workers' wages has decreased about 22 percent since 1956. This decrease occurred despite the fact that the average worker now works a forty-four hour workweek, rather than the forty hour average of 1956. The numbers of unemployed, coupled with "discouraged workers"—a euphemism for those who have run out of unemployment benefits and are still without work—are at their highest levels since the Great Depression. Foreclosures on farms and homes, as well as bank failures, are also at post-1940 records. Whereas ten years ago the homeless numbered perhaps 100,000, there are now 2 to 3 million homeless; a quarter of them in families and a quarter of them employed at least 20 hours per week. Thirty-seven million people (17 percent of the population) do not have any health insurance; a condition that contributes to America's having an infant mortality rate that is twenty-second in the world. At the extreme end, we have rates of infant mortality in inner cities which are higher than the average in Turkey or Pakistan, and the rate of mental impairment caused by malnutrition among our children is about the same as one finds in Honduras. Yet our leaders and many of our fellow citizens talk with a straight face about the triumph of the "free" market.

The same social and humanist criterion by which we judge the Russian economy as a failure should be used to evaluate the U.S. economy. Conservatives have historically condemned the breadlines and other queues for social necessities in Leninist societies, and rightly so. Yet here in the United States we have multiyear waiting lists for affordable low-income housing, year long waiting lists for entry into drug and alcohol programs, and multihour waits for emergency medical service often followed by a denial of admission to hospitals based on economic considerations rather than health needs. We face prolonged waits for mass transit vehicles in the very limited areas where they are available and how long we will wait for crime-free streets is anyone's guess.

Do societies exist in which basic housing, food, medical, and transportation service is provided? Yes. And they tend to share the same basic characteristics. Principal among them is a commitment to democratic participation in the economy. Sometimes this involves government ownership of banks and industry, sometimes government efforts to coordinate the economy while prioritizing social needs, sometimes worker ownership of corporate securities, and sometimes even democratic organization of the workplace. These societies have intellectual traditions, political parties, social movements, and unions that draw on Marxist theories and analyses. Many of them actively criticize the original work of Marx, in the same way that Americans criticize the excesses of Adam Smith and the social Darwinism of Herbert Spencer, but then build on the ideas of theorists who follow and modified those notions.

The Marxist theoretical tradition similarly builds on, modifies, and elaborates on Marx's original ideas. An article by Michael Burawoy (1990) details the growth of Marxist scholarship as a distinct body of scientific knowledge with ongoing propositions and hypotheses modified and refined over a hundred-year period—a progressive and reflective intellectual tradition and research program. In the course of those debates and in developing social practices that follow from those debates, other countries have fashioned societies that are more caring, more responsive to human need, and because of their multiparty systems and extension of direct election to the board room and the workplace, more democratic than our own. As the *Los Angeles Times* recently noted: "Socialism is alive and well in the economic policies of many of the democratic world's strongest political parties (even some conservative ones). Governments have embraced Marxist ideas of social obligation, even as they have fought Marxist political expansionism" (Messler and McManus 1991). These societies differ from us in one principal and fundamental manner—our belief in market solutions. They take control of their own lives, while we wait for things to improve. As the economist Robert Lekachman (quoted in Bowles et al. 1984:324) noted, "The American fixation upon private market solutions to public problems is an aberration even in other capitalist societies," a point verified in a recent poll by the Los Angeles Morrow Center for the People and the Press (Messler and McManus 1991).

Why do we not know more about such societies and their political practices and policies? As A.J. Liebling once noted: Freedom of the press is guaranteed only to those who own the presses (Parenti 1977:193). In the United States there are three major TV networks, two major press services, and daily newspapers (but few with competing ownerships) are published in most cities. Most of these are owned by corporations and depend on the goodwill and advertisements of other corporations. They are dominated by banks and multimillionaire owners, all of whom share a generally similar view of what matters, what should be part of the public debate, and what should be ignored. In other societies, political parties of various ideologies sponsor the publication of newspapers, and organized press unions have substantial influence on editorial policy. Each of these ensure a greater diversity of opinion than commonly exists in the United States.

Sociology in the United States has greater political diversity than other academic disciplines, and its members are more progressive than the majority of American citizens, as the conservative sociologist Seymour Martin Lipset and his coauthor Everett C. Ladd (1973) noted two decades ago. Sociologists have not been afraid to read and think about Marx and Marxism, and many have attempted to participate in international debates among Marxists. One-time U.S. presidential adviser and sociologist Amitai Etzioni goes so far as to argue that there are really only two paradigms in social science: "One is neo-classical—born in Adam Smith and expressed in sociology by exchange theory and rational choice theory, emphasizing individual actions and values." The second, "co-existing, neither driving it out nor being driven out by it" is the Marxist paradigm (1988:3). The Marxist paradigm has been expressed in sociology in critical theory, world systems theory, structural Marxist sociology, and much of contemporary historical sociology and feminist theory. In fact, as Lowell Hargens recently noted in an essay in *Contemporary Sociology,* among the most frequent citations in mainstream U.S. sociology are "Marx, Lenin, Weber, Parsons, Merton" (1991:373).

As the *Los Angeles Times* article cited above noted, "Much of the politics, sociology, and economics of the world is analyzed through a Marxist prism and described in a Marxist vocabulary" (Messler and McManus 1991). But progressive sociologists in the United States have had to pay a price for their use of Marxist citations, categories, and analyses, and their attempt to affect public debates with arguments arising from a Marxist framework. Upton Sinclair's (1923) book on academic censorship documented the repression of this political focus during the "red scare" of 1918-23. Ellen Schrecker's (1988) book on McCarthyism and the academy in the 1950s, and Richard Flacks' article (1988) in *Critical Sociology* on the academy in 1970s and 1980s documents a similar pattern of political censorship.

In our own time this effort continues. It takes a slightly different form today. Radical right-wing ideologues energetically argue the need to preserve free speech for themselves and at the same time hypocritically condemn the presence of leftists and Marxists on campus. They argue against the mere presentation of Marxist and other left ideas, claiming that there is no equal time for, or tolerance of, conservative ideas. Books such as Alan Bloom's *Closing of the American Mind* (1988), Roger Kimball's *Tenured Radicals* (1990), and Dinesh D'Souza's *Illiberal Education* (1991) claim that radicals and Marxists have taken over U.S. campuses and are busy subverting traditional standards of free speech in the name of "political correctness." Interestingly enough, these books are not themselves the product of any process of disinterested scholarship but have been commissioned and underwritten by conservative foundations such as the Olin Foundation and the Heritage Foundation (Lazare 1992). But, to return to the substance of the conservatives' complaint, we wonder, where are all these radical scholars? What campuses have they taken over? The argument seems exaggerated, at best. (Perhaps we are living the worst nightmare of a radical—we were preoccupied and missed the revolution!)

When we look out our windows at our campuses, we find the politics of university faculty members in general, and social scientists in particular, to be very supportive of the status quo. Instead of faculty being in control, we note the presence of university boards of trustees who are generally conservative business people who are actively promoting the adoption of the "corporate" model for university operations.

One cannot help but note the irony that there is no national organization of radicals and Marxist scholars. There is, however, a well-funded organization of conservative academics called the National Association of Scholars. There are several conservative pressure groups focused on suppressing left, progressive, Marxist, feminist, and other dissident ideas, and they receive support through foundations funded by Coors, Mobil, Olin, and other major corporations, as well as CIA-linked groups and organizations (Burris and Diamond 1991; Diamond 1991). They rail against politically correct speech, multiculturalism, cultural diversity, secular humanism, socialist theories, and affirmative action. In short, their efforts seem to be directed toward suppression of alternative ideas. While conservatives ostensibly argue for free speech and the importance of public debate on university campuses, at the same time they call for the elimination of the individuals and ideas with which they disagree (Diamond 1991). Reflecting on the efforts of these conservative intellectuals, we summarizeas their agenda as: Free speech for me, but not for you. In other words, political censorship.

Why are these people so afraid of alternative ideas and critical commentary? Can these ideas really be that powerful and so subversive that once you hear them you can never believe anything written by conservatives? Or is it that if you read and accept these ideas, you and people like you may start to change the world in ways that work against the interests of these people and their wealthy benefactors? Are they defending free speech, or are they defending private interests and so fear any alternative that challenges not only the intellectual but the economic and social status quo?

A Basis for Reflection

This book is a collection of essays that survey the state of academic Marxist sociology today. It also attempts to present the basic notions of a Marxist analysis to you in a readable manner. We also want you to understand that as American intellectuals have attempted to come to grips with the problems and dilemmas facing the United States, Marxist analyses, ideas, and insights have become part of their analytic frameworks. In the United States, Marxism has finally become one of the many strains of thought that affect the analysis and debate of scholars and, to a much lesser extent, the course of policy deliberations in the United States. With the collapse of the Soviet Union and its so-called "Marxism," Marxist ideas may increasingly effect policy-making. Certainly the impact of Marxist analyses varies significantly among disciplines (although many scholars using this framework even work in business schools). In sociology, Marxism has had a major impact on some disciplinary specializations and less impact on others.

To the extent that Marxist theory and analyses have begun to affect the course and content of debates in U.S. sociology, students seeking to understand and participate in these debates (and perhaps to effect social change) need to know the background of these ideas. If Marxist thought has something to teach us, we need to understand how those ideas originated, how debates proceeded and changed within various historical contexts, and what is the current state of those debates.

These concerns have shaped the structure of this book. For each chapter, we have asked experts to write an essay on their sociological field. For reasons of continuity, the essays are structured in a similar manner. The first part of the essay reviews the history of the debates over each subject among Marxists and other left theorists in various nations from the time of Marx to the 1960s. This lets us see the genesis and changing focus of the debates. We see the impacts of various cultures and how the ideas and struggles of people of various nations changed the ways in which Marxists looked at the world. It allows us to understand how a "tradition" is born and develops, and at the same time we learn that if a tradition is to survive, it must be self-critical and dynamic.

The second section of each essay is a discussion and analysis of the debates among Marxists and other left theorists from 1960 to now. These debates shaped the understandings of contemporary sociologists and are often reflected directly or indirectly in the development of modern sociology as a discipline.

The third section is a discussion and analysis of the contributions of Marxist analysis to mainstream U.S. sociology. By mainstream sociology we mean the issues and concerns discussed in established professional journals, textbooks, academic publications, and classroom lectures. We survey these developments to note both how Marxism has contributed to the advancement of sociology and to make clear that it is increasingly difficult to effectively explain or analyze the conditions of modern society without relying on a framework grounded in class analysis. In their conclusions, the authors suggest what they believe will be the next major debates within their specialty areas, and what they believe are the next important issues to be considered.

What about the commitment to social change that we noted at the beginning of this introduction? Some radical Marxists have wondered whether or not the "academization" of Marxist analytic framework and categories have taken away the organizing impact and revolutionary power of the theory. They fear that Marxist theory has become a mere debating forum and Marxist analysis merely a new tool for domination. Others, including most of the authors in this book, emphasize that what is important is wider distribution of radical ideas and concepts among the population, leading to a larger public discussion of basic problems of the society. This approach reflects the belief that academic theories and discussions can create the ideological basis for progressive social change.

For us, the answer to the question about academization is simple. In our everyday practice, we are educators. We are interested in making the debates on the subject accessible to people interested in these topics. We attempt to offer the best explanations and analyses possible to colleagues and interested readers.

One hundred years of analysis and practice suggest that hoarding crucial knowledge is counterproductive and that a monopoly on ideas benefits only an organized elite, whether that elite is state capitalist or private capitalist in form. The bases of real democratic change are knowledge and choice. And to choose knowingly, one must understand that several alternatives are available and what is entailed in the selection of each. One must also understand that the practice of democracy and the demand for accountability and justice need not be limited to the political sphere—although real democracy in politics would certainly be a step forward. Bringing forth the knowledge in this book is itself a political act and practice because, as Herbert Marcuse recognized almost three decades ago, in naming what is absent, we break the spell of things that are.

What will happen with the knowledge included in this book and the purposes to which it is put are up to you. And that is as it should be.

References

Bloom, Alan. 1988. *The Closing of the American Mind*. New York: Oxford University Press.

Bowles, Samuel, David Gordon, and Thomas Weisskopf. 1984. *Beyond the Wasteland*. New York: Anchor Books.

Burawoy, Michael. 1990. "Marxism as Science: Historical Challenges and Theoretical Growth." *American Sociological Review* 55:775–93.

Burris, Val, and Sara Diamond. 1991. "Academic Freedom, Conspicuous Benevolence, and the National Association of Scholars." *Critical Sociology* 18(3):125–42.

D'Souza Dinesh. 1991. *Illiberal Education: The Politics of Race and Sex on Campus*. New York: Free Press.

Diamond, Sara. 1991. "Readin', Writin', and Repressin'." *Z Magazine*, 45–49.

Etzioni, Amitai. 1988. *The Moral Dimension*. New York: Free Press.

Flacks, Richard. 1988. "The Sociology Liberation Movement: Some Legacies and Lessons." *Critical Sociology* 15: 9–14.

Hargens, Lowell. 1991. "Impressions and Misimpressions about Sociology Journals." *Contemporary Sociology* 20:343–49.

Kimball, Roger. 1990. *Tenured Radicals: How Politics Has Corrupted Our Higher Education*. New York: Harper & Row.

Lazare, Donald. 1992. "The Right Side of PC." *In These Times* May 27, 16.

Lipset, Seymour Martin, and Everett Ladd. 1972. "The Politics of American Sociologists." Pp. 67–105 in *Varieties of Political Expression in Sociology*. Chicago: University of Chicago Press.

Messler, Stanley and Doyle McManus. 1991. "Communism Failed but Influence Lingers." *Los Angeles Times*, reprinted *Toledo Blade,* September 29, E3.

Parenti, Michael. 1977. *Democracy For The Few*. New York: St. Martin's Press.

Schrecker, Ellen. 1988. *No Ivory Tower: McCarthyism and the Universities*. New York: Oxford University Press.

Sinclair, Upton. 1923. *The Goose Step—A Study of American Education*. Chicago: Privately published.

PART I:
SOCIAL STRUCTURE AND PROCESSES

CLASS STRUCTURE:

CLASS, NOT STRATA: IT'S NOT JUST WHERE YOU STAND, BUT WHAT YOU STAND FOR

Howard Kimeldorf

"No credit is due me for discovering the existence of classes in modern society and the struggle between them," Marx (1968a:679) confided to a friend in 1852. "Long before me bourgeois historians had described the historical development of this class struggle and bourgeois economists the economic anatomy of the classes." Yet all of the descriptive and anatomical detail so meticulously recorded by earlier "bourgeois" thinkers failed to produce an understanding of class as elegant and sophisticated as that of Marx. As such, his writings on class constitute what many sociologists regard as Marx's most important and enduring contribution to the discipline.

In this chapter, I review the topics of class and class structure as they have evolved within Marxist sociology. Given both the sheer volume of writing on the subject of class and the multitude of ways in which it has been deployed within Marxism, the following discussion can serve as no more than an introduction— necessarily somewhat selective—to the theory and practice of class analysis.

Classical Treatments of Class

Marx

Although Marx, by his own admission, did not discover the existence of classes, his work placed them on the intellectual agenda of sociology. Indeed, after Marx, it is no longer possible to think about modern society without attending to the questions of class conflict and social transformation that he posed so forcefully, often polemically, throughout his work. Many sociologists, of course, remain critical of what they regard as Marx's overreliance on the explanatory power of class. But there is no denying that the concept of class has become indispensable for understanding the trajectory of modern society.

Marx's influence here is especially remarkable since he wrote very little on the subject of class *per se*. In fact, nowhere in his voluminous writings did he even bother to define what he meant by class. The closest he ever came to doing so appears in the final volume of *Capital*. There, on literally the last page of what was to be his final work, he asks: "What constitutes a class?"—only to answer posthumously, in the words of Friedrich Engels, his friend and collaborator, that "here the manuscript breaks off" (Marx 1967b:886).

Fortunately, Marx left us not only with this nagging question but with various pieces of an answer scattered throughout the corpus of his work (Dahrendorf 1959). Assembling these fragments into a coherent theory has not been easy, however, in part because Marx himself employs the concept of class in radically different ways depending on his particular intellectual needs at the moment (see Ossowski 1963; Dos Santos 1970)

In general, his more theoretical investigations treat class in a highly abstract manner, as something of a disembodied social force. Explicating his approach to class analysis in the preface of *Capital*, Marx (1967a:10) writes that flesh and blood "individuals are dealt with only in so far as they are the personifications of economic categories, embodiments of particular class relations and class interests." When operating with this abstract model, Marx chooses to focus on the two "pure" classes that arise in each of the major historical epochs: slaves and masters under ancient society, lords and serfs under feudalism, and capitalists and workers under capitalism. The relationship between these classes, Marx (1967b:791) claims, "reveals the innermost secret, the hidden basis of the entire social structure."

Such theoretic grandeur rests on Marx's (1970:20) view of class as "the real foundation" of society over time. In each epoch, a subordinate class, so defined by its exclusion from the means of production, is compelled to produce over and above what is required for its own subsistence. This surplus is expropriated by a dominant class of nonproducers, whose ownership of productive property allows them to live off of the labor of those beneath them. The way in which this surplus "is pumped out of the direct producers," Marx (1967b:791) argues, "determines the relationship of rulers and ruled" and thus the basic classes in any society.

The transition from one class system to another is driven by the ever-developing forces of production, as advances in science and technology make it possible for society to greatly expand its social surplus. But whether or not this possibility is realized—and if so, how fully—depends on the relationship between classes. When in the course of history the prevailing logic of class relations comes into conflict with the forces of production, society faces a contradiction between what is technically possible given its level of productive forces and what is s[oci]ally allowable under its existing system of class domination. At such moments, the class relations reveal themselves to be nothing more than useless "fetters" on the productive forces. So exposed, they are "burst asunder," ushering in an era of social revolution that culminates in the transformation of the class structure itself (Marx 1970:21, 1968b:40).

The deterministic streak running through this account is tempered somewhat when Marx descends from his highly abstract model of society. Abandoning the search for "general laws of motion," which guided his theoretical explorations in *Capital*, Marx's empirical investigations of class structure are at once less teleological and more historically sensitive. In his analysis of mid-nineteenth-century French society, for example, it is neither the forces of production nor some inexorable law of history that occupies center stage; instead, Marx (1968c, 1968d) directs our attention to the conflict—pre-eminently political—waged between and within classes. At this concrete level of analysis, the class struggle appears rather more contingent and open-ended, involving not just two main actors but peasants, workers, the petty bourgeoisie, capitalists, and landowners, as well as different fractions within each of these classes. Clearly, then, Marx is aware that the class structure is infinitely more complex than is suggested by his simple dichotomous model. But, as he argues with respect to England, his paradigmatic case of capitalist development, the presence of "middle and intermediate strata" is "immaterial" to his analysis, since all such groupings ultimately will be swept aside by the "tendency and law" of capitalism to transform all "labour into wage labour and the means of production into capital" (Marx 1967b:885).

This prediction of growing class polarization resonated with the world of many mid-nineteenth-century observers. But Marx did not live long enough to see his vision realized. As he lay on his deathbed in 1883, it was apparent—if not to Marx himself, then certainly to many of his contemporaries—that a dichotomous model of class structure was already badly out of sync with changing sociological realities. By the turn of the century, the most obvious countervailing tendencies could no longer be ignored: first, that an intermediate category of nonmanual employees was growing daily under capitalism; second, that the traditional working class was still a long way from achieving majoritarian status in any capitalist country; and third, that many individual workers held views that betrayed their "true" proletarian interests.

Defending (and Revising) Marx: Kautsky, Lenin

These developments sparked a furious debate among Marx's followers. A minority, led by the German "revisionist" Edward Bernstein (1961), argued that increasing social differentiation coupled with the continuing "immaturity" of the working class had rendered Marx's revolutionary scenario both unlikely and unnecessary. But the majority of "scientific socialists" at that time disagreed, maintaining that the "laws of history" were still on their side. Representing this position, Karl Kautsky (1910), another prominent German socialist, argued that most "non-industrial wage earners"—in his day, civil servants, clerks, sales and service workers—would eventually be driven into the ranks of the proletariat. Such was the iron law of "proletarianization" under capitalism, which "causes the condition of the proletariat to become more and more that of the whole population" (Kautsky, quoted in Przeworksi 1977:360). If, as Kautsky readily conceded, individual members of this expansive working class did not always think like workers, it was simply because their consciousness of class lagged behind their objective location in the class structure.

Although defending the more orthodox position, Kautsky's intervention had the effect of nudging Marxism in a less deterministic direction by expanding the theoretical space available to class actors and their organizations. This can be seen, for example, in Kautsky's discussion of class consciousness. He begins by acknowledging that class location is never automatically translated into class consciousness—a formulation not unlike Marx's own distinction between class as an objective category ("class in itself") and class as a subjective social force ("class for itself"). But whereas Marx was content to let the laws of capitalist economic development bring subjectivity into line with objective class position, Kautsky (1910) called on the revolutionary party to help bridge this gap. Thus, while Kautsky remained confident that the locomotive of history continued chugging down the track as before, he insisted that the party could provide much-needed lubrication to the ideological rails, thereby accelerating the (inevitable) arrival of socialism.

Building on Kautsky's emergent critique of economic determinism, Vladimir Lenin developed a more politicized understanding of the class struggle, in particular emphasizing the role of political organization in helping constitute the proletariat. Writing in 1902, he argued that the economic laws that Marx identified as the motors of revolutionary consciousness had been nullified by the ideological incorporation of the working class under contemporary capitalism. To break the hold of bourgeois ideology, Lenin (1966) proposed "a party of a new type" consisting of professional revolutionaries who assumed primary responsibility for bringing the idea of socialism to the workers. By abandoning Marx's faith in the efficacy of economic laws, Lenin underscored the significance of both history and politics in the formation of social classes.

Western Marxism

Lenin's analysis was vindicated as much by the success of revolution in his native Russia as by its failure elsewhere in Europe. In trying to explain the crushing defeat of working-class movements in Germany, Austria, Italy and

Hungary after World War I, many West European Marxists returned to Lenin's earlier emphasis on ideological incorporation. Although generally agreeing with Lenin that the revolutionary party had an important role to play in class formation, the post-World War I generation of Marxists focused their attention on the ideological processes that made the vanguard party necessary in the first place (Korsch 1970; Luxemburg 1971; Anderson 1976). Their explorations, producing a rich and vast body of writing, suggested that bourgeois thinking was far more pervasive and powerful than previously granted; indeed, capital's ideological hegemony neither showed signs of weakening in the face of economic laws, as Marx had predicted, nor did it seem seriously threatened by the counterhegemonic mission of the vanguard party, as Lenin believed.

If economic exploitation remained the motor of class struggle, ideology was now seen as a powerful driving force whose significance, Hungarian Marxist Georg Lukacs (1971:51, 69) argued, "grows in proportion...as the decisive battle" approaches. Refusing to reduce the consciousness of the proletariat to "the average of what is thought or felt by the single individuals who make up the class," Lukacs, following Lenin's construction of false consciousness, simply "imputed" to the working class a consciousness that ideally reflected its "true" position in the production process. Unfortunately, Lukacs offered little practical advice for transforming the existing "psychological reality" of the masses into his utopian state of class consciousness.

This task of ideological purification was taken up by the Italian Marxist Antonio Gramsci (1971). Rejecting the categories of "true" and "false" consciousness, Gramsci insisted that the subjective conditions of the proletariat's existence under capitalism was a source not only of their subordination to bourgeois ideology but also of their own counterhegemonic ideology. Class consciousness, rather than representing an idealized state of cognition achievable only by intellectuals, was realized for Gramsci whenever the masses rejected the "common sense" worldview of their oppressors. The struggle in the streets was thus unwinnable without first winning the battle for workers' minds. Class war, Gramsci concluded, was ultimately decided on the ideological front.

By the 1920s, then, the concept of class had been to some extent pried loose from its economic foundation. The "laws of motion" that Marx—at least in his theoretical writings—saw propelling capital and labor forward into conflict began to lose their explanatory power around the turn of the century, as workers in one country after another failed to carry out their historic task of overthrowing capitalism (Abendroth 1972). Without ever abandoning the economic foundation of classes, early twentieth-century Marxists turned increasingly to political and ideological factors in attempting to explain the seeming quiescence of the Western working classes.

This period of creative rethinking, having been spurred by the resiliency of capitalism following World War I, came to an abrupt end with the economic crisis of the 1930s. Facing widespread unemployment, poverty, and hunger, hundreds of thousands of workers took to the streets, squaring off against an intransigent capitalist class. With pitched battles fought in major cities across Western Europe and the United States, the "workers of the world" seemed at long last destined to fulfill their revolutionary mission. Now that the proletariat was behaving as theorized, the need for problem solving disappeared, undermining the kind of self-reflective stance that had produced so many important innovations in the theory of class. Increasingly self-assured, many Marxists retreated to a more familiar orthodoxy, once again anchoring class firmly in the economy (e.g., Corey 1935; Bimba 1936). Some such form of economism—reinforced by intellectual conformity within the international Communist movement and later solidified by the Cold War—continued to guide Marxian thinking about class through the early 1960s.

Rediscovering and Rethinking Class

Containment of the 1930s working-class insurgency raised anew the question of the proletariat's revolutionary ambitions. But this time no answers were forthcoming, in large part because the anticommunist offensive following World War II placed Marxism off limits, making it difficult even to broach the subject of class in "polite" circles. In the United States, where the Cold War ushered in what C. Wright Mills aptly characterized as "the great American celebration," academics and popular pundits alike—echoing Bernstein's revisionism—argued that growing equality had transformed the basic contours of society. Writing in 1963, Kurt Mayer (1974) saw America's class structure evolving from the pyramid shape that Marx had described to something more closely resembling a diamond, in which both capital at the top and labor at the bottom were being absorbed into a bulging middle class.

Anti-Class I: Capitalism Without Capital

Capital's disappearance was traced to the socialization of corporate property and the concomitant rise of managerialism (Berle and Means 1932). With more and more companies "going public," it was argued, control of the nation's economy had been taken away from a few wealthy individuals and placed in the hands of countless stockholders, including many ordinary citizens of modest means (Bell 1961). This dispersion of stock ownership produced a corresponding democratization of corporate administration, marked by the ascendancy of a new managerial elite (Galbraith 1967). Being propertyless functionaries, corporate managers were presumably less profit oriented than their capitalist ancestors, thus allowing the mature corporation to behave in a more "socially responsible" manner (Bell 1973).

To make the capitalist class disappear, however, required a clever statistical sleight of hand. Critics pointed out that corporate ownership was still highly concentrated. While many Americans did indeed own small amounts of stock, well over half the shares of stock was held by 1 percent of all adults. The degree of concentration was even higher when families rather than individuals were taken as the unit of analysis. For families, the wealthiest .5 percent controlled over half of all privately held stock. However widespread the phenomenon of stock ownership, it was clear that a small group of investors—capitalists, if you will—remained the principal beneficiaries of corporate earnings (Domhoff 1983:58-59).

Arguments concerning managerialism and corporate responsibility were more difficult to nail down. There was never any doubt that managerial functions had increased in importance with the growing scale and complexity of the corporate form. But whether that gave managers effective control was not at all clear (Zeitlin 1974). What was clear was that managerial dominance—to whatever extent it existed—had utterly failed to steer the corporate economy in a more socially responsible, less profit-oriented direction (Herman 1983). In short, the American economy continued to be dominated by "the same old gang" of wealthy capitalists (Zeitlin 1978).

Anti-Class II: Bourgeois Workers

At the other end of the class structure, labor's disappearance was attributed to growing postwar affluence leading to the social decomposition of the working class. Suburbanization, economic security, and a more consumption-oriented lifestyle had supposedly undermined the distinctiveness of working-class culture and identity, giving rise to a "new bourgeois worker." Thus was born the thesis of "embourgeoisment"—a vaguely defined term meant to capture what many sociologists saw as a growing convergence between blue-collar workers and the white-collar middle class. "Large sections of the working class are moving up," observed Ferdynand Zweig (1960:404), "not only to higher standards of living, but also to new standards of values and conduct and new social consciousness." Materialistic and contented, illiberal and authoritarian, this "old working class" was now seen as a conservative defender of the status quo rather than as a vehicle for revolutionary change. By the mid-1960s this image of the "bourgeois worker" had hardened into an academic dogma, embraced not only by scholars on the political right but also, more significantly, by those on the left—from ex-socialists (Lipset 1960:chap. 4) to critical theorists (Marcuse 1964) to more traditional Marxists (Baran and Sweezy 1966).

Claims of embourgeoisment relied heavily on anecdotal accounts and unexamined attitudinal data that were frequently at odds with the reality of working-class life. If some unionized factory workers had achieved a measure of financial security, the vast majority remained trapped in a hand-to-mouth existence. Still, even for the economically secure, affluence represented freedom from want, not some kind of incipient status striving associated with the traditional middle class. A similar distinction in values could be found in homeownership. Whereas middle-class property owners typically viewed their homes as an integral part of the suburban lifestyle, working-class residents tended to see their housing investments in more practical terms, as a means of escaping the cycle of rent, landlords and urban decay. In focusing on such objective indicators as income levels and residential patterns, Zweig and others neglected the continuity in working-class values that helped to sustain a distinctive proletarian subculture (Lockwood 1960; Hamilton 1965; Goldthorpe et al. 1968). Later critics of embourgeoisement took a different tack, arguing that any convergence in class lifestyles merely reflected Kautsky's long-overdue "proletarianization" of white-collar workers (Jelin 1974; Braverman 1974; Oppenheimer 1985).

The New Left's Class Analysis

The Cold War image of a classless America had thus been seriously undermined by academic critics well before the social movements of the late 1960s arose to finish it off. With deep and divisive conflicts over foreign policy, race, gender, class, and culture threatening to tear the country apart, consensual arguments fell on deaf ears. Stepping out of the shadows of Cold War liberalism, a generation of radical activists rediscovered the relevance of Marxism as a tool for understanding and changing the world.

What many New Leftists found most useful in Marx were his youthful writings on philosophy, human nature, and alienation—themes that resonated with their own personal and political sensibilities. When the young Marx (1967c), himself attending college, wrote of capitalism distorting social life and in the process destroying our basic humanity, he struck a responsive chord with fellow students a continent away and more than a century removed. Living in a world of material abundance (or so it appeared), America's New Left argued that the struggle to overcome alienation, not exploitation, defined the revolutionary impulse under advanced capitalism (Oglesby 1969). In class terms, this meant privileging the struggle of educated professional and technical workers, whose strivings for creativity, personal autonomy, and self-realization could never be accommodated under the present system. Pointing to a deepening contradiction between their competency and the restrictions still imposed on them by capitalism, Andre Gorz (1964) and Serge Mallet (1975) argued that this "new working class" of educated labor was in the forefront of the struggle against capitalism.

But the "new" working class proved to be no more revolutionary than the "old." By the early 1970s, with the dampening of social protest, the time for reappraisal was at hand. Turning self-consciously to Marx for answers, many neo-Marxists were drawn by the promise of structuralism. Elaborating a theory of social structure in which real historical actors figured as mere "bearers" of underlying objective forces, structuralists claimed to be following the mature Marx in developing a scientific understanding of capitalism and of the class struggle. Alienation, having been consigned to the "humanist" or prescientific phase of Marxism, was replaced by exploitation at the center of the neo-Marxian discourse (Althusser and Balibar 1970).

Although mimicking the abstract mode of presentation found in *Capital*, structuralists were highly critical of what they regarded as the author's occasional lapses into economism. In particular, Marx's account of social change was ridiculed as "the theory of productive forces." As part of the escalating attack on economism, Marx himself was singled out for not fully appreciating how the class struggle shapes the introduction of new technology. Deeply influenced by Lenin, Gramsci, and other Western Marxists, and drawing inspiration from the emerging Maoist critique of the Soviet political elite, structuralists argued that classes occupied objective positions that were not reducible to economic location alone. In the words of Nicos Poulantzas (1975:16), a leading exponent of this view, "structural determination involves economic, political and ideological class struggle, and these struggles are all expressed in the form of class positions" within particular historical settings.

Putting his theory of structural determination to work, Poulantzas (1975) proceeded to map out the major classes under contemporary capitalism. Based on three criteria, he identified the working class as all those whose labor produced surplus value (economic), lacked any supervisorial responsibilities (political), and required no special knowledge (ideological). Such a definition might seem reasonable on paper, but in practice it meant reducing the working class to around one-fifth of the labor force in the United States (Wright 1976), thereby elevating the vast majority of Americans into a "new petty bourgeoisie" or middle class—just like mainstream sociology had argued in the early 1960s!

The debate over class boundaries was fueled by considerations of political strategy that were closely related to the size of the proletariat. With so much at stake, the "boundary question" remained a lively topic of discussion for years, as various theorists offered different, frequently competing criteria for working-class membership (Walker 1979; Abercrombie and Urry 1983). At the center of the controversy were low-level supervisors, professionals, and technicians—ironically, the very same occupations heralded as the core of the "new" working class less than a decade earlier, but now seen as quasi-proletarian, having one foot in the working class and another in the new middle class. The difficulties of locating this group in the class structure produced a dizzying array of arguments, with some theorists seeing professionals and technicians as appendages or "class segments" of either capital or labor (Szymanski 1972; Freedman 1975; Herkomer 1976), whereas others granted them greater autonomy, either as a separate intermediate class (Ehrenreich and Ehrenreich 1977; Carchedi 1975; Poulantzas 1975) or as occupying a "contradictory location" independent of the two major classes (Wright 1976).

The Present State of Class Analysis

The structuralist wave that crested in the mid-1970s was already beginning to recede by the end of the decade. Within many fields of Marxist inquiry, the intellectual tide had begun flowing in a more voluntaristic direction, prompted by the inability of structuralist analysis to account theoretically for the occurrence (or not) of collective action.

Class Formation

The relationship between structure and agency has of course been a long-standing concern of class theorists, beginning with Marx's early attempt to distinguish "class in itself" from "class for itself," through the various formulations of "lagged," "false," or "imputed" consciousness advanced by Kautsky, Lenin and Lukacs, and continuing down to the present in the distinction that is sometimes drawn between class structure and class formation. And yet, despite all this attention, the connection between structural location and collective action remains something of a black box within Marxism, representing what David Lockwood (1981) has termed "the missing link" within the theory of class (also see Russell 1980-81).

This theoretical lacuna has elicited a range of reactions from class theorists. Some have chosen to respond by reasserting the primacy of struggle in the determination of classes (Miliband 1989). Embracing the structuralist critique of economism, Adam Przeworksi (1977:343) writes that classes are determined "by objective conditions that are simultaneously economic, political, and ideological." At the same time, he actively repudiates the epistemological premises of structuralism, which, in privileging structure over agency, necessarily minimizes the significance of struggle in the constitution of classes. Przeworski thus rejects the notion that classes first exist as objective structures and only then enter into struggle. Instead, he maintains that classes are themselves products of earlier struggles, which have as their effects the organization and disorganization of social classes. "Precisely because class formation is an effect of struggles," Przeworksi (1977:343) argues, "outcomes of this process are at each moment of history to some extent indeterminant."

A similar move away from the determinism of *Capital* toward a more processual account of class formation can be found within Marxist historiography. Particularly influential here is the work of the British Marxist historian Edward Thompson. "Class," Thompson (1963:9) writes, is "something which in fact happens...in human relationships." In those few words, Thompson calls into question the reigning structuralist biases of both Marxism and mainstream sociology—for if class is "something which in fact happens," then it must be situated in historical time; and if what happens affects "human relationships," then class must be concerned first and foremost with the lives of real men and women. And that is just what Thompson argues, insisting that class formation is an irreducibly historical process reflecting the lived experiences of ordinary human beings. True to his Marxist roots, Thompson asserts that the most important class experiences are those that take place within the sphere of production. But his "productionism" is a far cry from that of classical Marxism with its rigid "laws" of economic determination (Sewell 1990). Positing instead a more flexible "logic" guiding the formation of classes, Thompson employs his concept of experience as the missing link between productive activity and consciousness. Building on this theoretical foundation, recent research on class formation displays a healthy regard for context, culture and contingency (see, among others, Katznelson and Zolberg 1986; Kimeldorf 1988; McNall 1988).

Neo-Weberianism

This turn toward a nonreductionist, experiential conception of class has opened the door to various neo-Weberian influences (Wenger 1987). The reaction has been somewhat mixed. European, especially British, class theorists have generally welcomed the growing rapprochement between Marx and Weber. Beginning with Weber's definition of class as market capacities, Anthony Giddens (1973) argues that such market locations are crystalized into cohesive social classes through the medium of shared experiences, including those that take place in production where labor is divided according to task, the exercise of authority, and the distribution of rewards. By synthesizing Weber's emphasis on the market with Marx's focus on production, Giddens's theory of "class structuration" neatly brings the two traditions together.

A similarly synthetic account of class formation has been advanced by another British sociologist, Frank Parkin. Although claiming to offer a "bourgeois critique" of neo-Marxism, Parkin (1979:46, 53) actually comes quite close to Marx when he argues that exploitation and property belong at "the centre of class analysis." Where he breaks with classical Marxism is in his attempt to identify classes based not on the mode of production but on what Parkin terms the "mode of collective action." Anchoring his analysis in Weber's concept of "social closure," he argues that competing logics of closure hold the key to class position, with those on top relying on a strategy of exclusion, while those on the bottom are forced to compete through usurpation. Similar Weberian influences can be seen in Pierre Bourdieu's (1987) writings on class, in which his concept of "social space" serves the same analytical ends as Parkin's notion of social closure.

Weberian influences have not always been so well received by Marxists. In the United States, where the two camps have traditionally occupied hostile theoretical ground, the reception has generally been much cooler. Thus, Erik Wright (1989), a leading figure in class theory, calls upon fellow Marxists to resist the "Weberian temptation" of defining class in terms of domination. Drawing a clear line of demarcation, Wright's (1985) larger theoretical project revolves around an elaborate and sustained defense of his class criteria as being consistent with a Marxian emphasis on exploitation. Yet, even Wright is unable to purge Weberian influences completely; they reappear throughout his argument, cloaked in the language of neo-Marxism (Burris 1989). After reviewing several such failed repudiations of Weber, it is hard to argue with Parkin's (1979:25) contention that "inside every neo-Marxist there seems to be a Weberian struggling to get out."

Post-Marxism

The critique of economic determinism, the turn to both history and experience, and the renewed dialogue with Weber have all come together around an emerging "post-Marxist" position that class is no longer the main axis of social change under capitalism (Hindess 1987). Contrary to Marx's theory of history, the progressive advance of the productive forces has created neither the material basis for socialism nor the social preconditions—in the form of a unified and class conscious proletariat—for its political realization (Gorz 1982). But even if both of these conditions were met, it remains doubtful whether workers in the United States and Western Europe would have a special interest in socialism. To believe otherwise not only flies in the face of history, it means adopting, in Chantal Mouffe's (1983:20) words, a "more sophisticated form of economism" in which interests are seen as objective and fully formed in the sphere of production.

The upshot of all this has been to resurrect many of the same themes that were originally put forward by Cold War sociology concerning the classlessness of American society. But what gives the poststructuralist critique its added sting is that it emanates from the left, being mainly promoted by academics who have in the past been closely identified with Marxism. In addition, their arguments carry a greater sense of urgency, as trends in class structure that were unclear forty years ago have become unmistakable today. Under the impact of accelerated capital flight, plant closings, and deindustrialization, the traditional blue-collar working class is for the first time beginning to decline in *absolute* numbers, and as it does, labor's organizational strength has fallen off accordingly. At the same time, new social movements not based on class have emerged to fill the political vacuum: women, people of color, environmentalists, antiwar activists, and others, whose diverse programs now represent the best hope for an extension of radical democracy (Hindess 1987; Laclau and Mouffe 1985).

This latest round of attacks on class appears at a time when the gap between rich and poor has never been greater. At present, the richest .5 percent of Americans control over 37 percent of our nation's total wealth, representing the highest concentration of economic resources since the dawn of corporate capitalism in the late nineteenth century. While this "new plutocracy" made out like bandits under Reagan's (counter) revolution—the number of millionaires, for example, increased several fold—the situation looks rather different from the other end of the class structure, where the share of earned income going to the poorest 40 percent continues to fall, hovering at around 15 percent (Phillips 1990). Such figures, far from suggesting the disappearance of class, point instead to its continuing significance as a fact of life under capitalism.

Conclusion

Class analysis, however firmly rooted in the writings of Karl Marx, has flourished on its own in the hot house atmosphere of real political struggle. Spurred by changes in class composition, organizing strategies, and intellectual life generally, contemporary theories of class bear little resemblance to the reductionist model found in the pages of *Capital*. Economic relations, while still privileged, have yielded significant ground to ideological and political factors, just as rigid conceptions of class structure have given way to more historically sensitive accounts of class formation. Dichotomous images of class structure, once the unassailable starting point, have been discarded in favor of a more complex mapping of class segments, intermediate groups, and contradictory locations. For contemporary students of class analysis, then, the question is not whether to go beyond Marx's basic model, but whether doing so "enriches the theory or simply adds confusion" (Wright 1989:348).

Our answer to this turns on a series of related questions. What, given the multitude of amendments and qualifications over the years, remains the specifically Marxian contribution to class theory? Put differently, in what sense can we even speak of a distinctly Marxian approach to class analysis? Is such an approach, however understood, limited to the most abstract level of analysis where classes appear as disembodied social forces? Or can it be profitably deployed, with certain refinements, at a more empirical level to elucidate actual patterns of class formation? If so, what is the appropriate arena of study? Is it advisable or even possible to investigate class formation within a single community or individual nation rather than as part of an integrated world system. And, finally, how are movements organized around class—in whatever arena—related to those based on gender, race, ethnicity, peace, or the environment, and how might the prospect of cross-class coalitions bear on the contest between capitalism and socialism? Such questions, which are currently on the agenda, promise to keep alive the rich tradition of theoretical innovation and political engagement that continue to define the Marxian project of class analysis.

References

Abendroth, Wolfgang. 1972. *A Short History of the European Working Class* . New York: Monthly Review Press.

Abercrombie, Nicholas and John Urry. 1983. *Capital, Labour and the Middle Classes*. London: George Allen & Unwin.

Althusser, Louis and Etienne Balibar. 1970. *Reading Capital.* London: New Left Books.

Anderson, Perry. 1976. *Considerations on Western Marxism*. London: New Left Books

Baran, Paul and Paul Sweezy. 1966. *Monopoly Capital: An Essay on the American Economic and Social Order*. New York: Monthly Review Press.

Bell, Daniel. 1961. *The End of Ideology*. New York: Collier.

———. 1973. *The Coming of Post-Industrial Society: A Venture in Social Forecasting* . New York: Basic.

Berle, Adolph, Jr., and Gardiner C. Means. 1932. *The Modern Corporation and Private Property* . New York: Macmillan.

Bernstein, Edward. 1961. *Evolutionary Socialism*. New York: Schocken.

Bimba, Anthony. 1936. *The History of the American Working Class* . New York: International Publishers

Bourdieu, Pierre. 1987. "What Makes a Social Class? On the Theoretical and Practical Existence of Groups." *Berkeley Journal of Sociology* 32:1–17.

Braverman, Harry. 1974. *Labor and Monopoly Capitalism: The Degradation of Work in the Twentieth Century*. New York: Monthly Review Press.

Burris, Val. 1989. "New Directions in Class Analysis." Pp. 157–67 in *The Debate on Classes,* Erik Wright et al. London: Verso.

Carchedi, G. 1975. "On the Economic Identification of the New Middle Class." *Economy and Society* 4:1–86

Corey, Lewis. 1935. *The Crisis of the Middle Class*. New York: Covici-Friede.

Dahrendorf, Ralf. 1959. *Class and Class Conflict in Industrial Society* . Stanford: Stanford University Press.

Domhoff, G. William. 1983. *Who Rules America Now? A View for the 80s* . New York: Simon & Schuster.

Dos Santos, Theotonio. 1970. "The Concept of Social Classes." *Science and Society* 34:166–93.

Ehrenreich, Barbara and John Ehrenreich. 1977. "The Professional-Managerial Class." *Radical America* 11:7–31.

Freedman, Francesca. 1975. "The Internal Structure of the American Proletariat: A Marxist Analysis." *Socialist Revolution* 5:41–83.

Galbraith, John K. 1967. *The New Industrial State*. New York: New American Library.

Giddens, Anthony. 1973. *The Class Structure of Advanced Societies*. New York: Harper & Row.

Goldthorpe, John H., David Lockwood, Frank Bechhofer, and Jennifer Platt. 1968. "The Affluent Worker and the Thesis of Embourgeoisement." Pp. 115–37 in *Comparative Perspectives on Stratification: Mexico, Great Britain, Japan*, ed. Joseph A. Kahl. Boston: Little, Brown

Gorz, Andre. 1967. *Strategy for Labor: A Radical Proposal*. Boston: Beacon Press.

———. 1982. *Farewell to the Working Class: An Essay on Post-Industrial Socialism*. Boston: South End Press.

Gramsci, Antonio. 1971. *Selections from the Prison Notebooks of Antonio Gramsci*, ed. Quintin Hoare and Geoffrey Nowell-Smith. London: Laurence and Wishart.

Hamilton, Richard F. 1965. "Affluence and the Worker: The West German Case." *American Journal of Sociology* 71:144–52.

Herkomer, Sebastian. 1976. "The Concept of Stratum in the Class Analysis of Advanced Capitalist Societies." *Marxism Today* 20:56–64.

Herman, Edward S. 1983. "Managerialism and Corporate Responsibility." Pp. 391–402 in *The Big Business Reader: On Corporate America*, ed. Mark Green, Michael Waldman and Robert K Massie, Jr. New York: Pilgrim Press.

Hindess, Barry. 1987. *Politics and Class Analysis*. Oxford and New York: Basil Blackwell.

Jelin, Elizabeth. 1974. "The Concept of Working-Class Embourgeoisement." *Studies in Comparative International Development* 9:1–19.

Katznelson, Ira and Aristide R. Zolberg, eds. 1986. *Working-Class Formation: Nineteenth-Century Patterns in Western Europe and the United States*. Princeton: Princeton University Press.

Kautsky, Karl. 1910. *The Class Struggle*. Chicago: Charles H. Kerr.

Kimeldorf, Howard. 1988. *Reds or Rackets? The Making of Radical and Conservative Unions on the Waterfront*. Berkeley: University of California Press.

Korsch, Karl. 1970. *Marxism and Philosophy*. New York: Monthly Review Press.

Lenin, V.I. 1966. "What Is to Be Done?" Pp. 54–175 in *Essential Works of Lenin*, ed. Henry M. Christman. New York: Bantam Books.

Laclau, Ernesto and Chantal Mouffe. 1985. *Hegemony and Socialist Strategy: Towards a Radical Democratic Politics*. London: Verso.

Lipset, Seymour Martin. 1960. *Political Man: The Social Bases of Politics*. New York: Doubleday.

Lockwood, David. 1960. "The New Working Class." *European Journal of Sociology* 1:248–59.

———. 1981. "The Weakest Link in the Chain? Some Comments on the Marxist Theory of Action." *Research in the Sociology of Work* 1:435–81.

Lukacs, Georg. 1971. *History and Class Consciousness: Studies in Marxist Dialectics*. Cambridge: MIT Press.

Luxemburg, Rosa. 1971. *Selected Political Writings of Rosa Luxemburg*, ed. Dick Howard. New York: Monthly Review Press.

McNall, Scott G. 1988. *The Road to Rebellion: Class Formation and Kansas Populism 1865–1900*. Chicago: University of Chicago Press

Mallet, Serge. 1975. *Essays on the New Working Class*, ed. Dick Howard and Dean Savage. St. Louis: Telos Press.

Marcuse, Herbert. 1964. *One-Dimensional Man: Studies in the Ideology of Advanced Industrial Society*. Boston: Beacon Press.

Marx, Karl. 1967a. *Capital*, Vol. I. New York: International Publishers.

———. 1967b. *Capital*, Vol. III. New York: International Publishers.

————. 1967c. *Writings of the Young Marx on Philosophy and Society*, ed. Loyd D. Easton and Kurt H. Guddat. New York: Doubleday.

————. 1968a. "Marx to J. Weydemeyer in New York." P. 679 in *Karl Marx and Frederick Engels: Selected Works*. New York: International Publishers.

————. 1968b. "Manifesto of the Communist Party." Pp. 31–63 in *Karl Marx and Frederick Engels: Selected Works*. New York: International Publishers.

————. 1968c. "The Eighteenth Brumaire of Louis Bonaparte." Pp. 97–180 in *Karl Marx and Frederick Engels: Selected Works*. New York: International Publishers.

————. 1968d. "The Civil War in France." Pp. 252–313 in *Karl Marx and Frederick Engels: Selected Works*. New York: International Publishers.

————. 1970. *A Contribution to the Critique of Political Economy*. New York: International Publishers.

Mayer, Kurt. 1974. "The Changing Shape of the Class Structure." Pp. 117–22 in *The Worker in "Post-Industrial" Capitalism: Liberal and Radical Responses*, ed. Bertram Silverman and Murray Yanowitch. New York: Free Press.

Miliband, Ralph. 1989. *Divided Societies: Class Struggle in Contemporary Capitalism*. Oxford and New York: Oxford University Press.

Mouffe, Chantal. 1983. "Working-Class Hegemony and the Struggle for Socialism." *Studies in Political Economy* 12:7–26.

Oglesby, Carl, ed. 1969. *The New Left Reader*. New York: Grove Press.

Oppenheimer, Martin. 1985. *White Collar Politics*. New York: Monthly Review Press.

Ossowski, Stanislaw. 1963. *Class Structure in the Social Consciousness*. New York: Free Press.

Parkin, Frank. 1979. *Marxism and Class Theory: A Bourgeois Critique*. New York: Columbia University Press.

Phillips, Kevin. 1990. *The Politics of Rich and Poor: Wealth and the American Electorate in the Reagan Aftermath*. New York: Random House.

Poulantzas, Nicos. 1975. *Classes in Contemporary Capitalism*. London: New Left Books.

Przeworksi, Adam. 1977. "Proletariat into a Class: The Process of Class Formation from Karl Kautsky's The Class Struggle to Recent Controversies." *Politics and Society* 7:343–401.

Russell, James. 1980–81. "Dialectics and Class Analysis." *Science and Society* 44:474–79.

Sewell, William H., Jr. 1990. "How Classes are Made: Critical Reflections on E.P. Thompson's Theory of Working-Class Formation." Pp. 50–77 in *E.P. Thompson: Critical Perspectives*, ed. Harvey J. Kaye and Keith McClelland. Philadelphia: Temple University Press.

Szymanski, Albert. 1972. "Trends in the American Class Structure." *Socialist Revolution* 10:101–22.

Thompson, Edward P. 1963. *The Making of the English Working Class*. New York: Vintage Books.

Walker, Pat, ed. 1979. *Between Labor and Capital*. Boston: South End Press.

Wenger, Morton G. 1987. "Class Closure and the Historical/Structural Limits of the Marx-Weber Convergence." Pp. 43–64 in *The Marx-Weber Debate*, ed. Norbert Wiley. Newberry Park, Calif.: Sage.

Wright, Erik Olin. 1976. "Class Boundaries in Advanced Capitalist Societies." *New Left Review* 98:3–41.

————. 1985. *Classes*. London: Verso.

————. 1989. *The Debate on Classes*. London: Verso.

Zeitlin, Maurice. 1974. "Corporate Ownership and Control: The Large Corporation and the Capitalist Class." *American Journal of Sociology* 79:1073–119.

————. 1978. "Who Owns America? The Same Old Gang." *The Progressive* 42(June):14–19.

Zweig, Ferdynand. 1960. "The New Factory Worker." *Twentieth Century* 167:397–404.

SOCIAL MOVEMENTS:

AN ARGUMENT FOR UNDERSTANDING SOCIAL MOVEMENT AS CLASS MOVEMENTS

Scott G. McNall

For Karl Marx there was only one social movement worthy of attention, that of class-conscious proletarians toward human freedom. As Marx said (1977:141), "A class must be formed which has radical chains, a class in civil society which is not a class of civil society, a class which is the dissolution of all classes, a sphere of society which has a universal character because its sufferings are universal." I here briefly examine Marx's ideas about how this universal class would be formed and the reasons why Marx thought it would usher in a new era. In doing so, I point to an apparent contradiction embedded within the heart of Marxist theory itself, a contradiction that significantly shapes all our debates about how social movements are formed.

A social movement is usually thought of as a large group of people who have come together either to speed up or to block the process of social change. Not surprisingly, because they seek to protect or alter existing power relations in society, social movements often produce conflict. Given this definition, we see that Marx's ideas about the formation of a worldwide proletarian movement can be extended to the study of collective behavior in general. That is, Marx's ideas are relevant to an understanding of class and social movement formation, union and labor struggles, and the elaborate processes whereby state policy gets made.

Marx and the Marxists

What did Marx actually say about why and how workers organized, and how were his ideas used by those who followed immediately in his steps? Marx painted a bleak picture of nineteenth-century capitalism and the toll it would take on those who had to sell their labor power. We know, from the *1844 Manuscripts,* that Marx believed capitalist society automatically produces a variety of forms of alienation. All forms of alienation flow from the fact that people must sell their labor power. They lose the use and control of the fruits of their labor and become impoverished. As May (1983:43) has noted, Marx depicts the human condition

29

under capitalism as "one of total alienation, utter nothingness, and complete loss of freedom." If freedom comes, it will be realizable only in one burst, when communism is established. We may ask, "How could people who were totally alienated strive to create a new order?" The answer, from Marx, is that it is in their nature to do so *and* it is in the nature of capitalist society.

Marx saw people as possessed of a projective consciousness, or the desire and ability to fashion their visions in nature (McMurtry 1978). Unlike the bee described in *Capital*, who can only erect the same repetitive structure, human beings have the ability to create a myriad of images in their mind, which they then build in the real world. They are dreamers, who become themselves through the accomplishment of unalienated labor. Marx takes great pains, however, to point out that people are both creators and creatures of their society. As he tells us in *The Eighteenth Brumaire of Louis Bonaparte* (1919:9): "Man makes his own history, but he does not make it out of the whole cloth; he does not make it out of the conditions chosen by himself, but out of such as he finds close at hand." People create a world, and then are confined by ideology and alienation, against which they struggle to realize their true natures.

They also struggle because of the very nature of capitalist society. In *A Contribution to the Critique of Political Economy* (1970), Marx says that capitalism represents the final contradiction between the social forces and social relations of production and that bourgeois society creates the conditions for a solution to this antagonism (1970:21-22). The tensions within capitalist society cause people to use their critical faculties to develop class consciousness, in order to bring about the very changes that capitalism necessitates. Marx places people at the center of his work and charges them with the task of realizing their own perfection through the use of their minds (Rubel 1981:Chap. 2). Socialism or communism is thus both an economic possibility and an ethical necessity. People, who are conscious, goal-directed actors, will act on the basis of the contradictions within capitalist society. They will act because the contradictions, which alienate and dehumanize them, drive them forward.

At one stage in his work, chiefly *The 1844 Manuscripts,* Marx emphasized the active, striving, purposive actor. In *The German Ideology* and particularly in *Capital*, he emphasized the inevitability of social change. This dualism—the tension between necessity and human freedom—is reflected in the debates following Marx's death about whether or not the demise of capitalism was at hand, and what role the working class was to play in the movement from a capitalist to a socialist society. Could the working class liberate itself, or would it need the help of a vanguard party?

On one side of the debate were the orthodox synthesizers of Marx's work, the scientific socialists of the Second International (circa 1889-1914), who developed an evolutionary view of capitalism's fall. Marx's friend and close collaborator, Friedrich Engels, began the process of turning Marx into a scientific socialist. At Marx's graveside, Engels said, "As Darwin discovered the law of development of organic nature, so Marx discovered the developmental laws of human history" (cited in Harrington 1976:45). The idea that Marx's texts contained universal laws that predicted the imminent demise of capitalism was enormously appealing to socialists and utopians of all stripes, who were trying to organize political parties.

One of the chief defenders of the new Marxist orthodoxy was Karl Kautsky, who entered the movement as a journalist. He, like Engels, was heavily influenced by Darwinist thought and believed that Marx had revealed the universal and unvarying laws of capitalism. For Kautsky, and others like him, human history was simply a continuation of natural history. This meant, of course, that deliberative human action took a back seat when it came to political change. Kautsky was a leader in the German Social Democratic party, but did not really believe that the party could bring about the overthrow of capitalism. It could help to create a class-conscious proletariat, but the proletariat should not act until the final contradictions of capitalism had been reached. It was never clear just how one would recognize that the final stage was at hand, but it was essential that workers not engage in political actions or strikes that were premature.

A somewhat different idea about the role that workers could and should play is revealed in the work of Rosa Luxemburg. Luxemburg was known in Marxist circles before World War I for her attacks on the revisionists and reformers— Marxists who believed in the possibility of reforming capitalism through parliamentary and democratic means. Luxemburg subscribed to the orthodox notion that capitalism was doomed and that a revolution was imminent. She was unclear, though, about whether capitalism would collapse of its own accord or whether it would collapse because of a proletarian revolution (Kolakowski 1978:81). She came to believe that all workers were incipient revolutionaries, who could act for themselves. Her position, which was regarded as an aberration by Kautsky and Lenin, was that spontaneous mass strikes were a means both to educate workers and to bring about change. This view set her on a collision course with Lenin and the Bolsheviks, who believed that systematic work by the party and trade unions was necessary to create a revolutionary proletariat.

In Lenin's view, a socialist party must provide leadership, vision, and direction. It must be the vanguard of change, composed of professional revolutionaries. In short, the working classes were incapable of formulating a revolutionary ideology. As Lenin said,

> Since there can be no question of an independent ideology formulated by the working masses themselves in the process of their movement, the only choice is—either bourgeois or socialist ideology. There is no middle course....But the spontaneous development

of the working-class movement leads to its subordination to bourgeois ideology...trade-unionism means the ideological enslavement
of the workers by the bourgeoisie. Hence our task, the task of social-
democracy, is *to combat spontaneity*. (1965:384)

With Lenin, the active class-conscious actor is replaced by the party, and the
nuanced dialectics of Marx, emphasizing the tension between freedom and
necessity, were dropped for a mechanical, positivistic worldview of historically
inevitable outcomes.

Marxism as a viable social theory waned. World War I caused a split among
the Marxist parties in different countries over the issue of whether they should
support the war, condemn it, or remain neutral. This limited their ability to extend
Marxist theory to an analysis of new phenomena. The war also sealed Soviet
Marxism off from the rest of the world, limiting debate. After World War I,
working-class revolutions and movements were crushed all over Europe. Capitalism was restabilized and Russia became increasingly isolated after the
Bolshevik Revolution. The result was that Marxism died in the Soviet Union to
be reborn in the form of Stalinism, which held sway until well into the 1980s.

The flame of Marxist thought continued to be nourished outside of the Soviet
Union, though it would take World War II to create a new theoretical focus. Of
immediate concern was the issue of why Nazism had triumphed. Members of
what was called the Frankfurt School, namely Horkheimer, Fromm, and Adorno,
set about trying to understand the origin of the beliefs and myths that supported
totalitarian systems. They also tried to understand why the proletariat, which was
supposed to have helped to usher in a humane revolution, had apparently done
just the opposite. The Frankfurt school, originally founded in the late 1920s, had
a well-developed theoretical framework on which to draw in analyzing the
detritus of World War II. Horkheimer, Fromm, and Adorno drew heavily on the
Hegelian roots within Marx's thought. In particular, they focused on culture and
the idea that consciousness matters; it can alter the course of history. On the
positive side, the Frankfurt school brought the active human agent back onto the
stage of history. On the negative side, many Frankfurt theorists were extremely
pessimistic. They argued that capitalism had taken a new form and that it
achieved its domination over the minds of humans in new, quiet, and insidious
ways. Writers such as Marcuse (1964) argued that capitalist ideology was so all
pervasive that the possibilities for liberation and change were limited, if not nil.

A much more optimistic view of human potential is to be found in the work
of the Italian theorist Antonio Gramsci, founder of the Italian Communist party.
His most important writings were completed while he was in prison, put there by
Mussolini. Gramsci (1971) is best remembered for his views of ideology and its
independent role, views that remain profitable for understanding collective
behavior today. Gramsci first sided with the Leninists against the revisionists, in

arguing that the capitalist state cannot be reformed: Instead, it must be replaced. He differed significantly from the Leninists, however, in the means by which this would take place. For Gramsci, militants were to work at three levels: trade unions, factory councils, and in political parties (Annunziato 1988:146). Worker ideology was shaped at, and could be changed at, the point of production. The chief mechanism for doing so was the factory council, the germ of a socialist worker's government:

> The dictatorship of the proletariat can only come to life in a new type of organization which is specific to the proper activities of producers and not of wage-earners, slaves of capital. The factory council is the first cell of this organization. Since in the council all the branches of labor are represented proportionally to the contribution which each craft and each branch of labor gives to the creation of the object which the factory produces for the collective, the factory council is of a class and social nature. Its *raison d'etre* is in labor and in industrial production, which is a permanent fact, and not in wages in the division of society in classes, in a transitory fact which will be overcome (Gramsci 1955:36)

Gramsci, then, gives heavy weight to proletarians becoming class conscious through the mechanism of the factory council and using their newfound awareness to improve their working conditions through trade unions and political parties. He assumes, as does Marx, that there is a moral component to action. Socialism grew out of an active spirit of revolt; this spirit or ideology would transform capitalism (Metcalfe 1988:11).

The history of early Marxism offers us two different emphases for understanding collective behavior. We can see worker movements as growing out of massive contradictions in the economic order, which lead to change. Or we can understand that conscious actors can create the conditions for change themselves. Whichever perspective one chooses, the event to be explained was the seizure of state power, as had occurred in the Soviet Union, or the failure of workers to seize the state, as had occurred everywhere else. Marxist theory was not really pressed into service as a means of understanding collective behavior until well into the 1960s and 1970s.

Structural-Strain and Resource Mobilization Theory

Massive social upheavals in the 1960s and 1970s provided a challenge to Marxist theory, as well as to social movement theory in general. The civil rights movement in the United States, the student movement that followed fast on its heels, the "May Revolution" in Paris in 1968, wars of national liberation in Cuba and Vietnam, as well as the peace movement, demanded an explanation.

Traditional sociological theory had little to offer. Collective behavior and social movement theory had been dominated by a tendency to see outpourings of human sentiment, strikes, riots, and like forms of behavior as unusual or irrational. Functionalist theory, derived from Emile Durkheim and elaborated by Talcott Parsons and his students, tended to encourage a view of conflict that saw it as aberrant behavior, rather than a normal means by which humans sought to alter intolerable conditions. Structural-strain theory, or Neil Smelser's (1963) valued-added theory, is merely a sophisticated variant of functional theory.

The structural-strain model developed by Smelser in the early 1960s argues that all forms of collective behavior represent a break with the past and are a new response to unusual conditions. This perspective says that social movements arise during periods of rapid change or conflict or are caused by such trends as urbanization and modernization. But social movements are far more complicated than this. The ghetto riots of the 1960s were not caused by the "strain" of urbanization but were the calculated decision on the part of participants to fight for political benefits. A second limiting tendency of this perspective is to assume that all forms of collective behavior are spontaneous and nonrational approaches to the problems people face (McNall and McNall 1992:507-8).

The major challenge to Smelser's theory was resource mobilization theory, developed by two organizational theorists, John McCarthy and Mayer Zald (1973 1977). McCarthy and Zald recognized that resources are necessary for both the initiation and success of movements. Resources are broadly defined to include interpersonal networks, leaders, money, and previously existing organizational structure. In others words, the ability of groups to mobilize and sustain interaction depends not on grievances so much as on resources (Morris 1984:279). From this perspective, one would look at the civil rights movement, as resource mobilization theorists have, and show how the tight linkage of demonstrators to the networks of the African-American community and its churches provided a resource that contributed to the success of the movement.

Resource mobilization theory asks different questions than structural strain theory. The question is not "Why do these people want social change so badly and believe it is possible?" but "How can these people organize, pool resources, and wield them effectively" (Fireman and Gamson 1979:9)? Protest is "the continuation of politics by other (disorderly) means" (Perrow 1979:200). This perspective assumes that movement actors operate in terms of a utilitarian logic, that people join a movement because they expect to get something. The strong form of this argument has been posed by Charles Tilly (1978:99), who sees collective actors carefully weighing the costs and benefits of their action:

1. Collective action *costs* something.

2. All contenders count costs.
3. Collective action brings benefits in the form of collective goods.
4. Contenders continually weigh expected costs against expected benefits.

Resource mobilization theory was *not* an extension of Marxist theories of collective mobilization, although Tilly claimed in his elaboration of the theory that he was offering a Marxist challenge to Durkheimian theories of collective behavior. Nevertheless, there are some similarities. In the first place, one strain of Marxist theory argues that rational human action is primary, just as resource mobilization theory does. Both resource mobilization theory and Marxist theory have a material focus. Movements may form because people are competing for scarce resources. New resources (e.g., welfare benefits, jobs, land) may create new movements. But there are some primary differences between the ways in which Marxists look at social movements and the ways in which resource mobilization theorists view them.

The key to Marxist theory is the focus on exploitation (McNall, Levine, and Fantasia 1991:1-14). Marxist theory sees collective action, primarily the worker's movement, as arising from contradictions in the economic system and actors' collective identities as growing out of a class struggle. That is, economic crises produce class consciousness, which in turn leads to action. Class consciousness is heightened and refined through struggle. Resource mobilization theorists are more interested in the question of what causes a movement than how a movement is sustained and unfolds. The issue of exploitation and class struggle as motivating forces is absent from traditional social movement theory and from resource mobilization theory.

As I argued earlier, Marx's ideas about why people mobilize cannot be understood without taking into account that they do so to realize their human nature. To repeat, socialism is seen as both an economic possibility and an ethical necessity. If workers join a movement, it is assumed that they do so to help other people. It is through *collective* action that universal goals are achieved. Contrast this with resource mobilization theory and the ideas of Marcur Olson. Olson (1965:2) says that people will not act on behalf of a collective. Instead, "unless the number of individuals in a group is quite small, or unless there is coercion or some other specific device to make individuals act in their common interest, *rational self-interested individuals* will not act to achieve their common or group interests." If this were true, there would be little reason to believe that people could act together. Resource mobilization theory tends, then, to concentrate on why individuals join movements, rather than the reasons that collectives act together and stick together (Cohen 1985:672). The need to reform social movement theory, to consider problems relating to the development of consciousness and solidarity, was recognized by two French theorists, Alain Touraine and Manuel Castells.

New Social Movement Theory

The impetus for the development of "action theory" by Touraine (1981, 1983a, 1983b) and a theory of urban movements by Castells (1976, 1977, 1983) was the "May Revolution" of 1968 in Paris. This was a movement, from their perspective, "without classes," one in which change resulted primarily from action in the streets. In a spate, new single-issue movements sprang up, which seemed to have in common a vision of a nonauthoritarian, decentralized, and self-managed society (Hannigan 1985:437). In order to understand the meaning and direction of this outpouring, Touraine and Castells combined elements of Marxist theory with traditional collective behavior theory. The blend has been referred to as new social movement theory, for it seeks to comprehend movements that are largely noninstitutional in character.

John A. Hannigan (1985) has sought to summarize the contributions of Castells and Touraine to social movement theory. First, Castells and Touraine see social movements as having a reality of their own. This assertion must be understood against the background of their critique of resource mobilization theory, which sees movements as extensions of institutionalized actions, or actions aimed at gaining entrance to dominant political forms. Instead, Castells and Touraine independently argue that movements are sources of innovation because they are not bound by the rules of the dominant society. In fact, the aim of movements may be to create or establish alternative sets of values.

Second, while movement actors are portrayed as rational, they are also seen as people who join for moral or purposive incentives. Actors are involved in a collective effort to reform the social order. To take Touraine's (1983b:2) example of Solidarity in Poland, he says that the movement is an "instrument for the reconstruction of a whole society, for the renewal of social institutions and even of those economic and social forces which may eventually enter into conflict with Solidarity itself." Social movements, contrary to structural-strain theory, are solutions, not symptoms.

In Touraine's view, movement actors are involved in a search for the meaning of their actions. Actors evaluate and reevaluate the purposes of the organization, its strategies, and the effect of their efforts on the larger society. In short, ideology grows out of the movement and develops as a result of the joint search for new values and the desire to craft a new vision of the future. As Hannigan (1985:442) says, movements are portrayed as do-it-yourself projects, without a vanguard party or organizational bureaucracy pointing out to people what they are to do or what the meaning of their actions is.

This focus on the meaning of action, while valuable, does obscure the importance of organization. Both Castells and Touraine, in fact, argue that organization gets in the way of success and may even be substituted for it. This notion stands in stark contrast to empirical reality (Gamson 1975, 1980;

Hobsbawm 1984) and to Marx's notion that without organization the working-class could achieve virtually none of its goals. As Marx says in the *Eighteenth Brumaire*, if there is no connection between people, "and the identity of their interests begets no unity, no national union, and no political organization, they do not form a class. They are...incapable of enforcing their class interest in their own name, whether through parliament or through convention" (1919:109).

There is another flaw in the work of both Castells and Touraine, which derives from a curious adaptation of the work of Louis Althusser (1969). Like many European intellectuals, Castells and Touraine were initially attracted to the evolutionary aspects of Althusser's model of capitalist society. Both were also intrigued by the possibility that something other than the economy, which appeared all powerful, would provide the contradictions that would drive society forward to a new era (Eyerman 1984; McKeown 1984).

Althusser, who has the dubious distinction of being known as the founding father of Marxist structuralism, tried to free traditional Marxist theory from its uniform concentration on the economic. Althusser says that we must think of modern capitalist society as being composed of three distinct, though interrelated spheres: the polity, the economy, and ideology (or personal sphere). Social change results from contradictions within and between the separate spheres. Althusser hedges his Marxist bets, however, by noting that although these spheres are autonomous, the economic sphere is "determinant in the last instance." Structures, then, not actors, predominate in Althusser's worldview and contradictions are inevitable (evolutionary), rather than necessarily the work of collectivities.

The way in which Castells uses Althusser is to see the major contradiction of modern society as occurring not at the point of production, as Marx would argue, but within the sphere of consumption (housing, education, health benefits). The problem with this perspective is that it simply claims that struggles over housing, or any other scarce good, are something other than class struggles. Class struggles are, as Marx long ago pointed out, about who will control the allocation of the surplus value created in a society. By automatically assuming that contemporary collective action has something other than a class base, we may limit our ability to understand the action. Let me hasten to add that I recognize that not all collective behavior is grounded in class. My argument is that we should not label consumption struggles, or what some have called lifestyle struggles, as nonclass until we examine them.

Touraine, too, sees the struggles of contemporary life as having transcended the traditional dispute between labor and capital. Touraine contends the struggle is between a populace fighting for self-expression and a highly centralized, authoritarian state. Touraine also believes that at any given historical moment, only one all-encompassing unifying movement is possible and that this movement replaces the working class as the historical agent of change. Whether or not this is true is subject to empirical testing.

Both Castells and Touraine have done well to grapple with new forms of social protest, but in doing so they have adopted some features of Marxist theory, and rejected others, which may limit our understanding of modern protest. They have held fast to Marx's notion that human liberation is a primary goal of all revolutions but have forgotten Marx's injunction that the potential for liberation takes place within and is limited by specific economic conditions. There is no theory of the state, grounded in the observation that state policy is shaped by class struggle, among their theoretical baggage. A theory of the state is important, of course, because state policy shapes the terrain within which social protest unfolds. Just what are the issues that drive new forms of collective behavior? Can Marxist theory provide the key we need for analyzing them?

New Social Movements

Jean L. Cohen emphatically dismisses Marxism as a means of understanding the peace, ecological, women's, or citizen initiative movements that have proliferated throughout the West. In her words, "an approach that stresses the primacy of economic contradictions, class relations, and crises in determining the collective identity of social actors can no longer be defended" (1983:97). (It should be noted that the version of Marxism she assumes should itself be challenged, for it is the vulgar economism of the Second International.) Cohen goes on to argue that traditional institutions have lost their capacity to motivate people, to provide them with collective identities. The shopworn notion that welfare statism can fix what is wrong will no longer wash. People no longer want a bigger state, they want a smaller one that does not intrude into their lives. New social movements, then, are about the need to create new meanings, traditions, and solidarities. Movements do this by staking out arenas in which people can actually practice democracy and liberate themselves from total domination. (Gramsci would be quite comfortable with Cohen's view, for he would see the factory council as the means by which to create the "space" for liberation.)

The German social theorist Jurgen Habermas also sees the old politics as dead. Conflict is no longer over distribution but arises in the area of cultural reproduction, social integration, and socialization. The new politics "entails problems of quality of life, equality, individual self-realization, participation, and human rights" (1981:33). The new social movements provide for the emancipation of the individual. Another way to say this, a la Marx, would be to argue that the new social movements are about the need to feel fully human.

The contested terrain for the new social movements is civil society, as opposed to the state (Scott 1990). In the realm of civil society, people are able to stake out a new identity and protect democratic freedoms: "The issues raised by feminist, ecological, peace, and local-autonomy movements are thus all connected to the shifting boundaries between public, private, and social life, and involve struggles against old and new forms of domination in these areas" (Cohen 1985:701). Of course, theoretical frameworks such as those offered by Touraine and Castells, which focus on the creation of meaning and the mechanisms by which solidarity is created and maintained, are very helpful for understanding the new social movements.

But let us take a more critical look at the new social movements. It seems to me that people are claiming more for the new social movements than is reasonable, and that they do so because they suffer from the same pessimism that infected members of the Frankfurt School. They believe a new historical subject must be found—which may be true—and they believe that capitalism is so dominant, politically and economically, that the only grounds on which to stand and fight involve the personal sphere. The problem with this perspective, as I have already suggested, is that it largely ignores the political and economic systems that constrain behavior. Touraine himself warned that the main risk for the new social movements was a potential separation between these movements and the state: "In such a situation, social movements can easily become segmented, transform themselves into defense of minorities or search for identity, while public life becomes dominated by pro- or anti-State movements" (1985:780). In short, people forget that the state counts. The result is that movements of "change" are seldom directed against the constraining ligaments of capitalist society. The result is confusion of purpose, eventual frustration, and impotence.

The new social movements are middle-class movements (Elder 1985:882), with a limited vision, do-good politics, and a set of lifestyle concerns (Denitch 1982:57). Civil society and bourgeois individualism are celebrated, and the chance for real political and economic change recedes into the background. Those who argue that the new social movements provide liberatory potential also turn a blind eye to the world at large. Throughout Africa, Asia, and Central and Latin America, the struggle for democracy is primary, which means that the economic/political terrain is still the ground upon which the struggle is played out. Even if there were a postmodern world outside the minds of French and American academics, in the rest of the world people must deal with the reality of political and economic coercion (Barros 1986).

New social movement theory is a dead end because it disconnects people's feeling of alienation, translated into lifestyle movements, from the larger political and economic world from which it stems. It is not easy to understand the complex relationship between social class, the polity, the economy, and people's miseries. In general, social movement theory has not, until very recently, been informed by Marxist theory. And Marxist theorists traditionally found little of use in social movement theory, driven as it was by functionalism. Two things had to happen before a meaningful synthesis could occur. First, Marx's ideas about how social classes were formed needed to be clarified. Second, resource mobilization theory, with its focus on organization and resources, needed to be elaborated.

A Marxian Theory of Collective Behavior

Marx never wrote systematically about the development of social classes, though at varying points in his work he provided many important insights. These ideas have been drawn together by myself and my colleagues Rhonda Levine and Rick Fantasia (1991:1-12). We claim no primacy for the insights, for they draw together the ideas of Marxian class theorists working throughout the 1970s and 1980s. The purpose of offering them here is to show that classes are formed over time and that the process of class formation is very similar to the process by which any social movement is formed. I also wish to argue that many social movements are best understood as class movements, which means that Marxian theory is particularly relevant to understanding the conflicts of modern society. I further wish to suggest that many of the class-formation issues that Marxists have had to come to grips with are relevant for an understanding of how social movements form. I will not argue that all collective action is motivated by class interests. As Roy (1984:497-98) has pointed out, this would be foolish, since "the historical record is too full of examples of collective action propelled by religious, ethnic, regional, nationalistic, and other cross-class relationships to sustain such an assertion."

The essential feature of a Marxian analysis of class is that classes are defined in relationship to other classes within a given system of production. It is assumed that within a capitalist society classes stand in contradictory and antagonistic relationship to one another. The central struggle is over surplus value or the rate of exploitation. Labor movements, then, as well as strikes and riots can often be seen as a struggle over surplus value.

Class, from a Marxian perspective, is simultaneously an objective and a subjective phenomenon. It is a lived reality, independent of what people think about it, and it is a part of people's consciousness. What this means, empirically, is that classes are historically contingent. As Zeitlin (1980:3) has said, "[classes] are determined by their place in a historically specific ensemble of production relations and by their self-activity, which constitutes and reconstitutes these relations and their place within them." To illustrate, in the late nineteenth century, England had a far greater concentration of industrial workers than did the United States. Because of this objective fact, class formation took a different form in the United States than it did in Great Britain. More U.S. workers than

British ones came into contact with members of the middle class, which muted class conflict in the United States. In addition, the subjective conditions of workers differed because of divergent objective conditions. As workers developed an understanding of their relationship to the means of production and created ways to respond to their world, they developed a variety of ideological and political practices. In short, they became class conscious.

Eric Hobsbawm (1984:18) has defined class consciousness as a group's awareness and understanding of itself that grows out of opposition to other groups. People may act to protect a way of life, a way of working and living. In organizing and confronting the world in which they live, people develop class consciousness; it grows out of action. Nevertheless, this consciousness is not created entirely anew but is refined (McNall 1987:226). Here Marxist and social movement theory easily join hands because traditional social movement theorists (Turner and Killian 1987:Chap. 1) have long understood that new norms grow out of involvement in a movement. The action theory called for by Castells parallels Marx's understanding of how classes form and how meaning (class consciousness) develops.

Marxists have also given attention to the important role of organization, as have resource mobilization theorists, in sustaining movements. Organization, as Hobsbawm (1984:28) has said, also plays a central role in creating class consciousness, the moral glue that holds class movements together. One of the ways that people learn about the nature of their oppression and how to articulate the values they wish to protect is through participation in class organizations. In mobilizing, in trying to change the political and economic system, people create themselves as a class. No contemporary Marxist believes that class grows simply out of changed relations of production. It is created through organization and it is actively created through time. Though Marxists have had a tendency to focus on the working class, it is recognized that elites are created in the same manner (Roy 1991).

Both Marxists and resource mobilization theorists see humans as rational actors, but acting rationally does not mean acting selfishly, as Marx understood. People do, of course, count benefits and losses, but that is not all they do. By virtue of their involvement in movements, people develop a sense of group solidarity and moral commitment to the broad group in whose name the movements acts (Hirsch 1990; Jenkins 1983:537-38). Workers who strike often make many personal sacrifices, not the least of which are lost wages and the possibility that they will lose their job, either to a strikebreaker or because an irate employer decides to move the plant to another country. Even when people do return to work at the same plant for higher wages, the wage increases may never make up for what they lost while out on strike. They make an individual sacrifice so that the larger collective (all workers) may benefit.

Why do people mobilize, and why do they stick together? People do not mobilize, as vulgar economic determinists suggest, merely because of economic distress. From Marx's perspective, they mobilize because they have become so alienated that in order to realize their humanity, they must act. That is, alienation, by stimulating the development of class consciousness, causes people to come together to form organizations, and these organizations in turn heighten class awareness and a desire for action.

Social movement theorists put the matter somewhat differently. People mobilize because of challenges to traditional values and a sense of community. But this mobilization to protect values stems from economic dislocations. For example, in the 1880s and 1890s, hundreds of thousands of farmers in the North and South joined the Farmers Alliance in a attempt to halt the growing power of corporate America over their lives. The historian Steven Hahn (1983), in his study of yeoman farmers from the Georgia Upcountry who joined the Alliance, argued that they did so because of changed social relations. Upcountry farmers were angry about a new law that required them to keep their livestock penned rather than let them roam freely, as they had for decades. This new law, which would have cost them a great deal of money for fencing, led farmers to take political action, to form a movement. The proposed changes in grazing rights led to the fear that their whole lives were being subordinated to the dictates of an impersonal market. The Alliance—and then the Populist party that grew out of it—provided a means by which farmers could articulate threatened values and stand against challenges to their traditional ways of life. I have argued elsewhere (1988) that it is important to understand that a way of life was threatened because farmers were involved in a struggle over who would control the fruits of their labor. Thus, this great mass-democratic movement was at its heart a class movement because the battle was about exploitation. People mobilize when they are economically exploited; it is exploitation that threatens traditional values.

The reasons why people stick together, and whether or not they will be successful can best be understood from a resource mobilization perspective. The community networks in which people are embedded are a primary resource in determining the potential success of a movement. The Upcountry farmers were bound together by ties of kinship. The men and women who were part of the Montgomery, Alabama boycott that started the civil rights movement were connected through the African-American churches of Montgomery. Labor unions, especially those that were democratically constituted, were dense networks that made it possible for people to sustain long and bitter strikes (Offe 1985). Strong networks are an important resource in movement formation.

A Marxian perspective on social movements effectively solves the dilemma of whether or not one must focus on human agents or the structures that constrain them, as well as whether or not one considers micro-level rather than macro-level factors. In a Marxian view of the world, both agency and structure receive their due—people create their own history, but are constrained by it. Rational actors struggle against the bonds of dominant political and economic realities. State structure, as noted in our critique of new social movement theory, is of the utmost importance in determining whether or not a movement—any movement—is likely to achieve its goals. Traditional social movement theorists have not often given sufficient attention to the material world within which movements unfold.

A Marxist perspective on social movements can serve as a general checklist of things to consider when examining any form of collective behavior.

1. People mobilize as a result of alienation and economic exploitation to protect traditional values and a sense of community.

2. People act rationally, to achieve collective benefits.

3. Organization is key in sustaining movement growth and development, and in developing people's (class) consciousness.

4. New norms and values are created as a result of participation in a movement.

5. Class and social movement formation has both an objective and a subjective component. Real material conflicts bring about a desire for change.

6. Movement development takes place within a specific historically contingent political and economic context. State policy plays a role in determining the context within which movements unfold, affects the resource base of movements, and shapes class struggle.

The Legacy

Many scholars have simply given up trying to understand the complexities of the modern world. Or if they try to understand them, they offer theoretical models that portray the world as fragmentary and indeterminant. Consider Laclau and Mouffe (1985), who criticize Marxist theory in terms of the new social movements, which they believe offer a new vision and hope of radical democracy. In rejecting the view that the working class is the primary agent of change, they adopt a postmodernist view of the world. They subscribe to the notion that "discourse is all," which means that the world can be whatever we wish to make (speak) of it. The problem with this view, and all such theories, is that they randomize history, to use Perry Anderson's term (1983:48). Nothing is primary, which means that scientific explanation is impossible. The second thing such a view does is to eliminate the historical subject, for if everything is contingent, then the conscious, striving, goal-directed actor disappears from the scene. Finally, this view dismisses economics, class, and politics (Hunter 1988). Now, one may dislike capitalist society, but that is not really a reason to ignore it. We must still understand how people's life chances are shaped by the primary struggle to survive.

How we think about the world and about social movements also has important political implications. We might well give our attention to the process by which class movements are created. If we see the formation of a class as similar to the formation and development of a social movement, we see that a uniform ideology develops from a sustained attempt at change and that people come to act in the name of the collective, rather than for themselves,*through the movement*. People must learn to act and speak as one, and this comes about by creatively escalating the battle. This means that class, not lifestyle, organizations loom large: they are the means by which information is exchanged and new strategies are developed (McNall 1987:23). We need some way to sort out our political priorities and decide whether or not a movement can help protect civil society from the encroachments of the state and the economy. Marxist social movement theory offers that possibility.

References

Althusser, Louis. 1969. *For Marx*. New York: Vintage.

Anderson, Perry. 1983. *In the Tracks of Historical Materialism*. London: Verso.

Annunziato, Frank R. 1988. "Gramsci's Theory of Trade Unionism." *Rethinking Marxism* 1:142–64.

Barros, Robert. 1986. "The Left and Democracy: Recent Debates in Latin America." *Telos* 68:49–70.

Castells, Manuel. 1976. "Theoretical Propositions for an Experimental Study of Urban Social Movements." Pp.147–173 in *Urban Sociology: Critical Essays*, ed. C.G. Pickvance. London: Tavistock.

———. 1977. *The Urban Question: A Marxist Approach*. London: Edward Arnold.

———. 1983. *The City and the Grassroots: A Cross-Cultural Theory of Urban Social Movements*. London: Edward Arnold.

Cohen, Jean. 1985. "Strategy or Identity: New Theoretical Paradigms and Contemporary Social Movements." *Social Research* 52:663–716.

Denitch, Bogdan. 1982. "Social Movements in the Reagan Era." *Telos* 53:57–66.

Elder, Klaus. 1985. "The 'New Social Movements': Moral Crusades, Political Pressure Groups, or Social Movements?" *Social Research* 52:869–90.

Eyerman, Ron. 1984. "Social Movements and Social Theory." *Sociology* 18:71–82.

Fireman, Bruce and William A. Gamson. 1979. "Utilitarian Logic in the Resource Mobilization Perspective." Pp.8–44 in *The Dynamics of Social Movements*, ed. Mayer N. Zald and John D. McCarthy. Cambridge, Massachusetts: Winthrop.

Gamson, William. 1975. *The Strategy of Social Protest*. Homewood, Illinois: Dorsey.

———. 1980. "Understanding the Careers of Challenging Groups: A Comment on Goldstone." *American Journal of Sociology* 85:1043–60.

Gramsci, Antonio. 1955. *Ordine Nuovo 1919–1920*, Vol. 9. Torino: Einaudi.

———. 1971. *Selections from the Prison Notebooks*. New York: International Publishers.

Habermas, Jurgen. 1981. "New Social Movements." *Telos* 49:33–7.

Hahn, Steven. 1983. *The Roots of Southern Populism: Yeoman Farmers and Transformation of the Georgia Upcountry 1850–1890*. New York: Oxford University Press.

Hannigan, John A. 1985. "Alain Touraine, Manuel Castells and Social Movement Theory: A Critical Appraisal." *The Sociological Quarterly* 26:435–54.

Harrington, Michael. 1976. *The Twilight of Capitalism*. New York: Simon and Schuster.

Hirsch, Eric L. 1990. "Sacrifice for the Cause: Group Pressures, Recruitment, and Commitment in a Student Social Movement." *American Sociological Review* 55:243–54.

Hobsbawm, Eric. 1984. "Should Poor People Organize?" Pp. 282–96 in *Workers: Worlds of Labor*, ed. Eric Hobsbawm. New York: Pantheon.

Hunter, Allen. 1988. "Post-Marxism and the New Social Movements." *Theory and Society* 17:885–900.

Jenkins, J. Craig. 1983. "Resource Mobilization Theory and the Study of Social Movements." *Annual Review of Sociology* 4:527–553.

Kolakowski, Leszek. 1978. *Main Currents of Marxism: The Founders*, Vol. II. Oxford: Clarendon Press.

Laclau, Ernesto, and Chantal Mouffe. 1985. *Hegemony and Social Strategy: Towards a Radical Democratic Politics*. London: Verso.

Lenin, V.I. 1965. *Works*, Vol. 5. London: International Publishers.

McCarthy, John D., and Mayer Zald. 1973. *The Trend of Social Movements in America: Professionalism and Resource Mobilization*. Morristown, N.J.: General Learning Press.

———. 1977. "Resource Mobilization and Social Movements: A Partial Theory." *American Journal of Sociology* 82:1212–39.

McKeown, Kieran. 1980. "The Urban Sociology of Manuel Castells: A Critical Examination of the Central Concepts." *Economic and Social Review* 11:257–80.

McMurtry, John. 1978. *The Structure of Marx's World View*. Princeton: Princeton University Press.

McNall, Scott G. 1987. "Thinking about Social Class: Structure, Organization, and Consciousness." Pp. 223–46 in *Recapturing Marxism: An Appraisal of Recent Trends in Sociological Theory*, ed. Rhonda F. Levine and Jerry Lembcke. New York: Praeger.

———. 1988. *Road to Rebellion: Class Formation and Kansas Populism 1865–1900*. Chicago: University of Chicago Press.

McNall, Scott G., Rhonda F. Levine and Rick Fantasia, eds. 1991. *Bringing Class Back In: Contemporary and Historical Perspectives*. Boulder: Westview.

McNall, Scott G., and Sally A. McNall. 1992. *Sociology*. Englewood Cliffs, N.J.: Prentice-Hall.

Marcuse, Herbert. 1964. *One Dimensional Man*. Boston: Beacon.

Marx, Karl. 1919. *The Eighteenth Brumaire of Louis Bonaparte*. Chicago: Charles H. Kerr.

———. 1970. *A Contribution to the Critique of Political Economy*. New York: International Publishers.

———. 1977. *Critique of Hegel's "Philosophy of Right,"* ed. Joseph O'Malley. New York: Cambridge University Press.

May, John A. 1983. "The 'Master-Slave' Relation in Hegel's 'Phenomenology of Spirit' and in the Early Marx: A Study in One Aspect of the Philsophical Foundations of Marxism." University of Toronto, Department of Geography.

Metcalfe, Andrew W. 1988. "The Struggle to be Human: The Moral Dimension of Class Struggle." *Critique of Anthropology* 8:7–42.

Morris, Aldon D. 1984. *The Origins of the Civil Rights Movement: Black Communities Organizing for Change*. New York: Free Press.

Offe, Claus. 1985. *Disorganized Capitalism*. Cambridge, Mass.: MIT Press.

Olson, Mancur. 1965. *The Logic of Collective Action: Public Goods and the Theory of Groups*. Cambridge, Mass.: Harvard University Press.

Perrow, Charles. 1979. "The Sixties Observed." Pp. 192–211 in *The Dymanics of Social Movements*, ed. Mayer N. Zald and John D. McCarthy. Cambridge, Mass.: Winthrop.

Roy, William G. 1984. "Class Conflict and Social Change in Historical Perspective." *Annual Review of Sociology* 10:483–506.

———. 1991. "The Organization of the Corporate Class Segement of the U.S. Capitalist Class at the Turn of this Century." Pp. 129–63 in *Bringing Class Back In: Contemporary and Historical Perspectives*, ed. Scott G. McNall, Rhonda F. Levine, and Rick Fantasia. Boulder: Westview.

Rubel, Maxmilien. 1981. *Rubel on Karl Marx: Five Essays*, ed. and trans. Joseph O'Malley and Keith Algozin. Cambridge: Cambridge University Press.

Scott, Alan. 1990. *Ideology and the New Social Movements*. London: Unwin & Hyman.

Smelser, Neil J. 1963. *Theory of Collective Behavior*. New York: Free Press.

Tilly, Charles. 1978. *From Mobilization to Revolution*. Reading, Mass.: Addison-Wesley.

Touraine, Alain. 1981. *The Voice and the Eye: An Analysis of Social Movements*, trans. Alan Duff. London: Cambridge University Press.

———. 1985. "An Introduction to the Study of Social Movements." *Social Research* 52:749–87.

Touraine, Alain, Zsuzsa Hegedus, Francois Dubet, and Michael Wieviorka. 1983a. *Anti-Nuclear Protests: The Opposition to Nuclear Energy in France*. Cambridge: Cambridge University Press.

Touraine, Alain, Francois Dubet, Michael Wieviorka, and Jan Strzelecki. 1983b. *Solidarity: Poland 1980–1981*. Cambridge: Cambridge University Press.

Turner, Ralph H., and Lewis M. Killian. 1987. *Collective Behavior*. 3rd ed. Englewood Cliffs, New Jersey: Prentice-Hall.

Zeitlin, Maurice. 1980. "On Classes, Class Conflict, and the State: An Introductory Note." Pp. 1–37 in *Classes, Class Conflict, and the State*. Cambridge, Mass.: Winthrop.

GENDER

MARXIST THEORY AND THE OPPRESSION
OF WOMEN

Marietta Morrissey
and
Randy Stoecker

The work of social scientists who would call themselves Marxist feminists is significant and has had a growing impact on the discipline of sociology. Marxism and feminism meet in the consideration of domestic work, wage work, sexuality, the reproduction of the labor force, and divisions among women. This array of concerns has challenged conventional Marxist categories of analysis and stimulated the growth of feminist thought.

This essay begins with a definition of Marxist feminism and other basic terms: gender, patriarchy, social reproduction. We then suggest that the earliest period in Marxist feminist analysis, from Marx to 1960, established the two critical issues that would come to define Marxist feminist theory: the place of women's domestic work in the reproduction of the labor force; and the role of women in the paid labor force.

Next we consider issues addressed from 1960 to the present. Contemporary Marxist feminists follow earlier theories in examining domestic labor and the reproduction of the labor force. They analyze the position of women in the segregated labor market, especially as racial and ethnic divisions among women influence their ability to bargain with capital. The "patriarchal state," controlling both women's wage and nonwage labor, has also become an important focus of Marxist feminist analysis. Finally, contemporary Marxist feminists offer various theories of the impact of gender ideology on women's continued subordination as material constraints to women's labor force participation diminish, but women's rights to free sexual expression and reproductive choice are assaulted.

We conclude by considering the impact of Marxist feminism on American sociology. As the voices of women and minorities are more often heard in academic and political arenas, Marxist categories of analysis are invoked to explain their exploitation and oppression. But theoretical advances in the Marxist treatment of women's experience constantly need testing in the political arena. It is here that Marxist feminism meets its greatest challenge—to generate effective social programs and policies at a time when U.S. radical politics are threatened by the strength of conservative forces, and once invisible groups take the stage and redefine the terms of social transformation.

Important Terms

We begin by explaining key terms in the Marxist feminist literature: Marxist feminism, patriarchy, social reproduction, and gender.

1. We define *Marxism feminism* broadly in order to capture the developing character of this theoretical framework and the evolving political consciousness of its contributors. Marxist feminism utilizes Marx's categories of mode, means, forces, and relations of production to explain social conflict, including gender inequality. Marxist feminists differ in the degree to which they consider gender inequality to be independent of capitalist production, but all claim that gender inequality is integrally related to the dynamics of capitalist accumulation and production wherever gender inequality accompanies capitalism. In this essay, we will also discuss socialist feminists who share with Marxist feminists the political goal of a radically more egalitarian society, but reject one or more essential characteristics of Marx's historical materialism in their analysis of gender inequality.

2. *Patriarchy* is the control by men, as individuals or as extended family or kinship heads, of the labor of women. This control may be manifested in legally sanctioned ownership of women themselves or simply in the authority to assign women particular tasks. Patriarchy still exists in some parts of the world, particularly in rural areas. However, its legacy endures in other settings, including domestic and interpersonal relations.

3. *Gender* is the set of social expectations associated with maleness and femaleness. By using the word "gender," sociologists suggest that the social construction of male and female behavior is as important to collective experience and action as biologically based sexual characteristics.

4) *Social reproduction* refers to the work done, mostly by women, to prepare the future workforce. In narrow terms this work includes the birth and socialization of children for future work. Marxist feminists remind us, however, that many other tasks are required to generate a well-disciplined and compliant workforce, including housework, consumption of goods and services, and the care of adult household members (Laslett and Brenner 1989).

Marx and Engels

The first attempts to combine a critique of capitalism with an analysis of the oppression of women began, not with Marx and Engels, but with French utopian socialists of the 1830s and 1840s, including Saint-Simon, Fourier, and especially Flora Tristan (Moon 1978; Boxer and Quataert 1978). It was Karl Marx and Friedrich Engels, however, who would have a lasting influence on later Marxist and socialist theories of women's position. They would also make the first theoretical distinction between the *production* of goods and services and the *social reproduction* of labor. This section shows how Marx and Engels's thinking about the family and social reproduction, and its relationship to the family, developed and changed.

Marx's and Engels's earliest work focused on the family as the locus of social reproduction, by analyzing the family as independent of the economy in early society. Marx argued for the material separation of the family from civil society and its importance as a material force, asserting that "family and civil society constitute *themselves* as the state. They are the driving force" (Marx 1978a:17— italics in original).

Engels's early work concentrated on the trauma and destruction visited on families by capitalism. But he differed from Marx in two ways. First, Engels's interest (1958:29) was not to portray the family as a social force but "to discuss [the workers'] condition and to discover how they have been influenced by life and work in the great factory towns." Second, Engels (1958:160-64) considered women both as family members and as wage workers, although he emphasized the effect of women's wage work on the family: "When women work in factories, the most important result is the dissolution of family ties...the total death rate for small children is increased by the fact that their mothers go out to work....It deprives the husband of his manhood and the wife of all womanly qualities."

Marx's *Economic and Philosophic Manuscripts of 1844* and Marx and Engels's *German Ideology* bring gender and sex into their analysis. In the 1844 manuscripts, the analysis of sex and gender is grounded in the biological differences between men and women, suggesting a passivity of both nature and women in relation to men (Vogel 1983). In the *German Ideology*, Marx and Engels (1978a:159) argued that all divisions of labor arise out of "the natural division of labor in the family...where wife and children are the slaves of the husband." As families are separated from one another, *private* property develops and class inequality follows. This undermines the family as an independent institution. "The family, which to begin with is the only social relationship, becomes later, when increased needs create new social relations and the increased population new needs, a subordinate one" (Marx and Engels 1978a:156). Nevertheless, Marx and Engels (1978a:157) implied that social reproduction still may influence the course of history, since they argued that "a certain mode of production, or industrial stage, is always combined with a certain mode of co-operation, or social stage, and this mode of co-operation is itself a 'productive force.'"

In *The Communist Manifesto*, Marx and Engels moved away from analyzing social reproduction as a system independent of capitalist production. Instead, they argued that capitalism had so completely infiltrated and commodified social life that it had "torn away from the family its sentimental veil, and has reduced the family relation to a mere money relation" (Marx and Engels 1978b:476). They argued that "the bourgeois sees in his wife a mere instrument of production," and male infidelity ultimately makes bourgeois marriage "in reality a system of wives in common." Marx and Engels (1978b:488) imply that a class-transcendent "community of women" may be possible. Their desire is to abolish women as property objects, apparently across classes. The economy is still the single driving force in this analysis, subordinating social reproduction to its will, since the abolition of "the community of women" (the collective "prostitution" of women) will occur only with "the abolition of the present system of production."

The theoretical transition from the family and social reproduction as a primary social force, to the subsumption of all under capitalism, is completed in the first volume of *Capital*. The family became at most a unit of analysis, as in the calculation of the value of labor power to include not only "the labour-time necessary to maintain the individual adult labourer, but also by that necessary to maintain his family" (Marx 1978b:404). Marx went on to discuss the depreciation of the *man's* labor power as machinery allowed women and children to enter the labor market, rather than discuss its implications for women.

It would be left to Engels's *Origin of the Family, Private Property, and the State (1972)*, written after Marx's death, to present a comprehensive explanation for the historical oppression of women. Engels argued that early societies were matrilineal and that the original condition of men and women was a state of "promiscuous intercourse." Over time, social rules excluded blood kin from sexual relations, men took over the domestication and herding of animals, and an economic surplus was created. As a result, inheritance of wealth and certainty of paternity became important concerns in the community. Monogamy was imposed on women through the "overthrow of mother right" and the establishment of patriarchy—an epochal transformation that Engels (1972:68) labeled "the world-historic defeat of the female sex."

As capitalism develops, the oppression of women under monogamous marriage is modified by class relations. Engels (1972:79) argued that "marriage is determined by the class position of the participants, and to that extent always remains a marriage of convenience.... This marriage of convenience often enough turns into the crassest prostitution—sometimes on both sides, but much more generally on the part of the wife, who differs from the ordinary courtesan only in that she does not hire out her body, like a wageworker, on piecework, but sells it into slavery once and for all." However, because the proletarian woman is typically forced into the labor market, she has a measure of economic independence, allowing for a greater chance that her marriage will be based on love. Thus, Engels argued, the liberation of women would come only through their entry into "productive" labor. Here, for the first time, was a shift in focus to women as wage workers, the subject of much of the later socialist work.

Engels's argument and evidence have come under scrutiny (Leacock 1972; Redclift 1987). Some contemporary theorists see *The Origin of The Family, Private Property, and the State* as a return to the focus on the dual processes of production and reproduction first proposed in *The German Ideology* (Vogel 1983). Others, however, argue that while Engels presents production and reproduction as "analytically equivalent," reproduction takes a back seat to production "in the actual analysis" (Humphries 1987:11; Reed 1972). A third interpretation goes even further in arguing that only an economic determinist theory can be derived from Engels (Gimenez 1987; Maconachie 1987).

Those who followed Marx and Engels, then, were left with a Marxist theory that was ambiguous on whether the source of women's oppression might be independent of the source of capitalism and whether that oppression could be ended by ending capitalism alone. It is the latter issue that occupied late nineteenth and early twentieth century theorists who were also engaged in socialist movements of the day.

Marxist Feminism in the Late Nineteenth and Early Twentieth Centuries

Turn-of-the-century Marxists were committed to political action as much as to theoretical development. With Marx's and Engels's help, socialist parties had been organizing vast numbers of workers around the world and were agitating for political and economic rights and workplace protections. The emphasis in socialist circles on revolutionary workers' actions contrasted starkly with that of the day's feminism. The movement of middle- and upper-class women for suffrage and the right to develop economic independence through professional employment was regularly derided as "bourgeois feminism" in socialist circles. Those who strayed from party analysis of the working class were suspect. Even the famous Rosa Luxemburg, thought by contemporary feminists to have had little to say about women (Dunayevskaya 1981), was criticized by Lenin for attempting to organize prostitutes (Zetkin 1973). There were separate women's sections of the Socialist and Communist parties, and national and international women's conferences, for a time, but they were seldom long lived (Honeycut 1981).

Socialists who did focus on women pursued one of two routes of analysis and political strategizing. The path most respected in Socialist party circles was to analyze women as *wage workers*, following the economic analysis of the late Marx. Those advocating this perspective, such as V.I. Lenin, Clara Zetkin, Sylvia Pankhurst, and Anna Kuliscioff, were skeptical of the suffrage movement as a panacea. Instead, they argued that women could be truly liberated only through their entrance into wage work. They contended that women's participation in the wage labor force would eliminate their economic dependence on men and expand the working class movement.

Lenin, for example, strongly opposed women devoting time to issues that could not be reduced to their roles as wage workers, and he objected to sexuality and marriage issues occupying a central place in communist women's groups, even when those issues were analyzed using Marxist terminology and categories (Zetkin 1973). Instead his overriding concern was to bring women into public life: "If we do not draw women into public activity, into the militia, into political life; if we do not tear women away from the deadening atmosphere of house and kitchen; then it is impossible to secure real freedom, it is impossible even to build democracy, let alone socialism" (Lenin 1973:42). Lenin did contend that wage-working and peasant women were faced with double oppression, as proletarians and as domestic slaves. Consequently, the initial Soviet constitution passed revolutionary reforms in family law and women's rights, legislating equality in both the public and private spheres. He was also a strong advocate of increased representation of women in Soviet government (Lenin 1973), an international communist women's movement, and men's involvement in domestic work (Zetkin 1973).

Clara Zetkin, a leader in the German Social Democratic party, Sylvia Pankhurst, a British suffragist turned communist party member, and Anna Kuliscioff, an Italian Socialist party leader, argued, like Lenin, that the principal source of women's oppression was economic dependence on men, overcome by entering "productive" work. But each also moved beyond Lenin to examine dimensions of social reproduction. Zetkin emphasized that women were not only to become wage workers. They must develop as *mothers* as well, not isolated at home without rights, but as empowered public citizens (Honeycut 1981). Sylvia Pankhurst similarly argued that women who remain at home deserve political representation (Edmondson 1981). Anna Kuliscioff argued, much like the early Marx, that the original source of women's oppression was biological but that capitalism had made biological differences irrelevant. And while Kuliscioff was reluctant to criticize the traditional family, she did support immediate women's suffrage arguing against the party's formal position. (Springer 1981).

Elizabeth Gurley Flynn provided a rare case of a socialist who extended Marxist analysis to address family and reproductive work fully. Flynn, a central figure in the militant Wobblies labor movement and a founder of the American Civil Liberties Union, was the first woman chair of the Communist party USA. In many respects Flynn was quite orthodox. She opposed a separate woman's suffrage movement, believing that women's freedom could best be gained through economic independence. But Flynn was among the first Marxist feminists to develop a theory of housework, using the Marxist category of labor value. She argued that housework produced value and advocated that unpaid domestic women be organized in the same way as other workers (Baxandall 1987).

The second path socialists of the time pursued was to analyze the oppression of women, expanding Marxist class analysis to understand women's roles as sexual beings, childbearers, parents, and wives under capitalism. Despite being labeled Revisionists, theorists such as August Bebel, a German Social Democratic party leader; Alexandra Kollontai, a cabinet minister in the new Soviet government; Aline Valette, secretary of the National Council of the French Workers' party; and Madeleine Pelletier, a leader in the French section of the Workers' International, all broke in varying degrees from mainstream socialist thinking of the day. While agreeing with Marxist analyses of the economic oppression of women, they re-emphasized Marx and Engels's early work on the alienation of women in the family. Indeed, socialist feminist Lily Braun went so far as to use the commonality of family experience to argue for organizing women across classes.

Most of these "revisionist" socialist feminists ultimately blamed capitalism for women's oppression, but advocated women's liberation through changes in the social organization of reproduction as well as through economic transformation. August Bebel's (1971) *Women under Socialism*, as influential at the time as the work of Engels, argued that men's oppression of women is parallel to the capitalists' oppression of the proletariat. Bebel shied away from a complete break with Marxism, however, claiming that socialism would accomplish the overthrow of both oppressions (Vogel 1983). Alexandra Kollontai attacked "class feminism," asserting that it was impossible for women to be free under capitalism, but she also supported the struggle for woman's personality, unalienated sexual intimacy, and fulfilling man-woman relations.

Kollontai emphasized maternity as both a natural and a communist moral duty—motherhood was to be both protected and promoted (Stites 1981), moving further from party orthodoxy. Aline Valette offered the first attempt within socialism to explore the social position of women *across class* through her theory of "sexualism." Valette argued that mothering should be the most important and highest-status work in society and should be provided with community support (Boxer 1978). Socialist-feminist Madeliene Pelletier followed Valette in addressing marriage and sexuality. For her, women's oppression was rooted in dependence on marriage for economic security. And, following Freud, she focused on sexuality and the family. Pelletier advocated a complete dismantling of sex roles, access to abortion and contraception, and collectivized state-sponsored child care (Boxer 1981).

These theorists stretched the boundaries of Marxist theory, but still emphasized the economic foundations of social relations. The German socialist Lily Braun came the closest to combining a critique of capitalism with a critique of patriarchy. Braun was a suffragist who retained her interests in women's issues within the German Social Democratic party. First, she argued that while socialism was a necessary condition for the liberation of women, it was not sufficient. Second, Braun considered the liberation of sexuality and dealienation of love as *feminist* issues (Meyer 1987). Third, Braun believed that the socialist movement should cooperate with middle class feminists, and that there should be a feminist movement transcending class. Fourth, she revived the analysis of the *German Ideology* by arguing that sexuality, *along with* work, was a means of self-actualization, and she added a theory of alienated sexuality to Marx's theory of alienated labor. Finally, at the center of Braun's analysis was not the woman as *wage worker*, but the woman as *mother*. Mothers, Braun argued, should be supported by maternal insurance, communal housekeeping, and the absolute destruction of the monogamous family as society's economic unit (Meyer 1985). Braun was convinced "that ultimately the human species could be saved from self-destruction only through the de-alienation of femininity and motherhood" (Meyer 1987:xvi-xvii).

These ideas troubled members of the Socialist party of the time. After a bitter and divisive thirteen-year struggle with Clara Zetkin, Braun's influence narrowed in the party, and she withdrew from party work (Quataert 1979). The marginalization of the revisionists was soon followed by the marginalization or demotion of most of the turn-of-the-century women leaders and a reduced emphasis on women's issues in party socialism. Alexandra Kollontai, Sylvia Pankhurst, Madeleine Pelletier, and Clara Zetkin were all either demoted within the party or, disillusioned, left the party (Waters 1989). Turn-of-the-century Marxist thinkers, then, split along lines of the early and late Marx on the oppression of women. Socialist party orthodoxy emphasized the late Marx's more singularly economic analysis, while others emphasized the early Marx and Engels's conceptualization of social reproduction as a separate system. The debate between these two perspectives would resurface in the contemporary period.

Contemporary Marxist Feminism

In the 1960s, students and workers in Europe and North America turned again to Marx for a theoretical basis for explaining political struggle. The resulting social movement, generally called the New Left, emerged after two decades of Cold War inattention by activists and academics to Marxist thought. At every stage of its theoretical and political evolution, feminist challenges have shaped

Marxism of the contemporary era. The problems of women in the family, as wage workers, and victims of ideological as well as economic and political constraints have been the major themes of contemporary Marxist feminism.

Domestic Work and Social Reproduction

The first area of contemporary Marxist feminist discourse relevant to American sociology addresses domestic work and social reproduction. Scholars and activists have developed theoretical statements on these dimensions of the problem: the changing functions of the family in social reproduction; the contradiction between capital's need for reproduction of the labor force and increased production of goods and services; and women's oppression as house-wives and mothers and contending strategies for liberation.

The contemporary Marxist consideration of the family in social reproduction started with a rigorous and lengthy reappraisal of Engels's *The Origin of the Family, Private Property, and the State* (Vogel 1983; Weinbaum 1978; Eisenstein 1979). There is broad agreement about the strength and weaknesses of Engels's analysis in the light of both recent anthropological findings and the changed economic circumstances of advanced capitalism. But the emphasis on Engels's theories of the family and social reproduction, to the virtual exclusion of turn-of-the-century Marxist and socialist writing on women, suggests the power of his analysis for the contemporary era (Zaretsky 1976).

Marxist feminists looked first at Engels's understanding of the historical evolution of the family. In a widely cited essay, Gayle Rubin (1975) responds to Engels by noting that stratified gender relations have clearly existed independent of capitalist relations of production (see also Leacock 1972; Tong 1989; Vogel 1983). Using anthropological findings more accurate than Engels could command in the late nineteenth century, Rubin suggests that a "sex/gender system" exists in all societies to regulate sexual relations and reproduction. The creation and monitoring of kinship is in the interest of lineage preservation and other economic and social goals associated with particular modes and systems of production. Drawing on the work of Claude Levi-Strauss and Freud, Rubin illustrates further how, through the "traffic" or exchange of women, males have in most social formations ordered and dominated kinship, which in turn rein-forces gender differentiation.

Contemporary Marxist feminists also criticize Engels's characterization of the working-class family as the most egalitarian family form. Whatever its class basis, contend today's Marxist feminists, the nuclear family oppresses women (Vogel 1983). They argue further that as the family ceases to be a locus of production, its functions in the socialization of children and expansion of the individual's personal life have grown. Thus, the family's oppression of wives and mothers thus grows as women are increasingly isolated in the home. Their work in nurturing new generations of workers is neither socially valued nor rewarded. And as the sexual and other emotion related dimensions of social reproduction have become more important, women's responsibility for other family members has increased (Smith 1987; Zaretsky 1976).

Some Marxist feminists claim that it is capital's increased demands for a disciplined, well-educated, and emotionally stable labor force that has fueled nuclear family formation long after Engels and other early Marxists expected its demise and made more profound women's domestic isolation and oppression. Marxist feminist Eli Zaretsky contends that the contradiction between women's historically expanding work in reproduction and growing participation in the workforce and other public spheres must deepen. Hence, women's liberation cannot be separated from women's freedom from privatized and ever expanding domestic work (Zaretsky 1976; see also Smith 1987; Vogel 1983). Nor can socialism ignore individual needs for personal and sexual development, made possible in part by capitalist industrialization and the historically shortened wage-work day.

The tension between social reproduction and capitalist production is the second important theme in the contemporary Marxist feminist treatment of domestic labor and social reproduction. British Marxist feminist Juliet Mitchell contributes significantly to discourse on this question, basing her analysis on the principle that within capitalism are several invisible "structures" that shape class struggle (Mitchell 1971; Gimenez 1982). Mitchell argues that women's place has historically rested on participation in three structures of social life: reproduction, socialization of children, and sexuality. Today women engage as well in a fourth structure, production. Groups of women have mobilized to challenge their position in *each* of the four structures, with particular issues and movements dominant in different eras. The transformation of women's overall position will result only from the diminution of gender inequality in all four structures, but progress may be uneven and may heighten contradictions between structures. Mitchell expands greatly the scope of Marxist inquiry into women's position beyond the strictly material, and she frees subsequent Marxist feminist theorists of the need to link all of women's varied work, needs, and experiences directly back to relations of production.

Other Marxist feminist theorists have broadened Marxist thinking about reproduction in relation to production, while adhering more closely to Marx's historical materialist methodology. Barbara Laslett (1981) argues that there is a "struggle over the surplus" between capitalists and families, since families require resources to care for dependent family members. Meg Luxton (1980) studied the scope of domestic labor performed by three generations of women. She claims that domestic work contributing to social reproduction had a direct impact on class struggle. For example, Luxton argues, increased domestic production by women, such as sewing clothes for the family instead of buying ready-made ones, supported labor actions against capital by reducing social reproduction costs and reliance on men's wages.

Finally, contemporary Marxist feminists exploring domestic work and social reproduction have examined the oppressive nature of work in the home and attempted to develop a meaningful political response. Canadian Marxist feminist Margaret Benston (1969) asserts that housework and childrearing create use value that allows for the production of a surplus by wage workers outside the home. Its oppressive nature is a function of demands for greater household productivity, organically related to capital's demands for greater productivity by the paid labor force. Benston argues that women's liberation must eliminate the isolated, individualized, and burdensome tasks of housekeeping and child care. The maintenance of daily life for workers and their families can better be achieved through collective efforts, by both men and women (see also Barrett and McIntosh 1982).

Selma James and Mariarosa Dalla Costa (1973) extend Benston's premise that domestic work creates use value by arguing that housewives ultimately produce surplus value through the provision of domestic services to wage workers in their households. For this, women should be paid, argue James and Dalla Costa. In contrast to the more commonly held Marxist feminist position that women's interests are most fully satisfied through public wage labor, James and Dalla Costa recall some turn-of-the-century socialists in arguing that women's work in the home should be publicly valued and supported.

Women's Wage Work

The second major area of Marxist feminist concern is women's incorporation into the wage labor force. Although women often engaged in factory work in the late nineteenth and early twentieth centuries, early Marxists wrote little about it. By the 1970s, however, women's labor force participation increased markedly throughout the industrial world. Indeed, feminists chastised Marxists for their inattention to women's wage work (Hartman 1981), for women not only worked in increasing numbers but earned less than men for the same jobs and were restricted to particular job sectors. And some, notably African-American women, often worked in more degraded and isolated labor-market segments than other women (Davis 1981; Glenn 1985).

Marxist feminist analysis of women's labor force experience has focused on four areas: women's relative disadvantage in wages and working conditions; their segregation into particular jobs, often in service to others and as an extension of earlier domestic work in the reproduction of the labor force; women's place in the reserve army of the unemployed, the marginally employed, part-time, temporary workforce, and in the informal economy; and their victimization by an increasingly repressive welfare state. Uniting all these concerns for Marxist feminists is the conviction that women's skill and experience levels are less successful predictors for women (than men) of their eventual labor-market success. Instead, capital's exploitation of labor in the interest of accumulation and expansion has led to differentiations within the labor force, with women and ethnic minorities both relatively disadvantaged and set against white males for labor-market privileges.

Marxist feminist writings on labor-market segmentation suggest that women are excluded from some jobs. The work of Reich, Gordon, and Edwards (1973; see also Edwards 1979) and others suggests that good jobs—those with high wages, good benefits, union protection—are restricted to white males. Such jobs are frequently found in the so-called monopoly and state sectors where the lack of competition allows capital to accumulate and wages to rise. Smaller firms in the "competitive" sector, in contrast, are under the threat of absorption by larger, more technologically sophisticated firms, and seek to keep labor costs low to preserve themselves. Women constitute an especially attractive labor pool for these firms. Generally restricted from entry to monopoly firms, women may be desperate for work, demand relatively low wages, and show little inclination to form unions or engage in other kinds of collective action (Fernandez-Kelly 1989).

While women are frequently restricted to competitive sector positions, the evidence suggests that the labor market is segmented by gender in several additional ways (Bradly 1989; Walby 1988). Women's office work, for example, is often found in the monopoly and state sector. Women's other service-sector work also cross-cuts the monopoly/competitive sector dichotomy. Indeed, many areas of work, formerly the province of women in the home, are now socialized in production. Hospital work, food preparation, cleaning and maintenance are all jobs now done for pay by women (Glazer 1984). The sector in which they work is largely irrelevant to their position as laborers in a capitalist economy.

Edna Bonacich (1972, 1976) advances our understanding of women's relatively low wages by suggesting that any labor market can be segmented by gender or race. Capital seeks the segment of the labor pool willing to work for the least pay, under the harshest conditions. The feminization of clerical work over time suggests a tendency for women to work for less. The deskilling of clerical work through "feminization" suggests as well the abandonment by males of labor-market segments that provide neither training nor decent wages. Thus, capital pits working groups against each other, rewarding those least able to fight for more (Bonacich 1972, 1976; Beneria 1989; Fernandez-Kelly 1989). The result today is a complex system of competition among ethnic/gender/income groups for access to a declining number of good jobs.

The remedy for women in these circumstances is some form of collective action. Union and other political organizers have often ignored women in low-paying jobs or claimed that their responsibilities in the home after work make it difficult for women to participate in formal organizations (Glazer 1984; Walby 1986). Attitudes toward the mobilization of working women have changed, however, as their presence in the labor force has increased. But recent economic restructuring has worsened women's position in the labor force, driving them into the growing number of part-time, temporary jobs (Beechey 1987; Smith 1990). The ghettoization of women and minorities in occasional or "contingent" work and the rise in unreported "informal" sector earnings by women has diminished their political power.

Finally, women's disadvantage in the labor market has increased their dependence on welfare state programs over the twentieth century. These forms of assistance have traditionally provided less than women could earn in decent jobs and, in the United States, have penalized women for additional income seeking. Where these programs have been targeted to single mothers, the formation of conjugal relationships has threatened continuing receipt of benefits. The "patriarchal state" controls women's labor and labor-market access (Ambramovitz 1988; Gordon 1990; Walby 1990), as well as dimensions of their sexuality and their reproductive rights (Barrett and McIntosh 1982).

Contemporary Disputes in Marxist Feminist Sociology

Sociologists have developed a broad commitment in recent years to the study of women and gender. Marxist feminism has had a profound effect on the sociological study of gender by stressing the economic roots of gender roles and gender role socialization, and the systemic nature of gender oppression.

Many feminist sociologists have resisted Marxism's emphasis on the capitalist origins of inequality. Like other scholars sympathetic to historical materialism and the construction of a socialist economy, they contend that sexism and gender discrimination do not necessarily end with the transition to a more egalitarian society. Indeed, American economist Heidi Hartmann has described "the unhappy marriage between marxism and feminism." In a now classic treatise, Hartmann (1981:2) argued: "The 'marriage' of marxism and feminism has been like the marriage of husband and wife depicted in English common law: marxism and feminism are one, and that one is marxism." Hartmann and other socialist feminists (see Tong 1989; Jagger 1983; Eisenstein 1981) have argued further that Marxist feminist analysis underestimates the depth of patriarchy in the domestic realm, and they suggest that patriarchal relations in the home and in our collective ideology will endure long after capitalism has passed.

Sociologist Lise Vogel (1983) reviews both the inadequacies of Marxist feminism and the socialist feminist response. While frustrated with elements of the former, Vogel finally questions the analytical power of a socialist feminism stripped of Marxist categories of analysis. She notes, for example, that while "dual systems" theory, granting equal conceptual significance to capitalism and patriarchy, seems to extend the too-limited grounds of Marxist feminist analysis, it provides neither a dynamic for change nor a systematic mode of analysis (see also Vogel 1981). Within any social formation, patriarchy and capitalism are joined in an integrated and dynamic fashion, the root of which remains unclear in some socialist feminist analysis. Young (1981) argues similarly, along with many Marxist feminist anthropologists, that gender and class intersect in social divisions of labor and are not separate in any given setting. Vogel contends further that not only are patriarchy and capitalism integrated, but other forms of oppression (e.g., racism) are also joined in the mix that defines a social formation (see also Flax 1990; Jagger 1983; Walby 1990).

Some Marxist feminists have also questioned feminists' use of "patriarchy" (Beechey 1987; Bradly 1989). While male control of women's and children's labor existed in preindustrial societies (Rubin 1975; Barrett 1988; Bradly 1989), women now exercise considerably more freedom in the use of their labor. Nevertheless, inequality in gender relations exists in the labor market and in the domestic arena. To what extent must this inequality today be explained independent of capitalism?

The debate has led Marxist feminist sociologists to think more comprehensively about the impact of social beliefs concerning gender inequality and differentiation on the capitalist ordering of social relations. Martha Gimenez (1982) asserts the profound and enduring impact of gender ideology on class formation and conflicts, even while maintaining that our consciousness about gender is ultimately derived from society's economic base. Other Marxist feminist sociologists explain the impact of sexism on class relations in different terms. Michele Barrett (1988) defines gender ideology as a primarily cultural phenomenon, produced by a complex conjunction of material and ideological forces, rather than being rooted in the capitalist mode of production (see Brenner and Ramas 1984 for further discussion of this view). Harriet Bradly (1989) posits a "gendered work culture" that assigns men and women to particular job and income categories. British sociologist Sylvia Walby (1990, 1986) has developed a theory of patriarchy that includes both materially and ideologically based structures: the patriarchal mode of production; patriarchal relations in paid work; patriarchal relations in sexuality; male violence; patriarchal relations in cultural institutions; and patriarchal relations in the state. Patriarchal and capitalist modes of production are articulated, or joined, in the current era, with capitalist relations generally dominating, but not eliminating patriarchy. In sum, contemporary Marxist feminists attempt to integrate materialist and idealist interpretations of gender inequality and to incorporate into the Marxist framework the understanding that "all social relations are gendered" (Acker 1989:77; see also Acker 1988 for discussion of gendered "distribution of the means of survival in industrial capitalist societies").

The Future of Marxist Feminism

Marxist feminism has influenced American sociology in three major ways. First, many of the major feminist sociologists in the United States and Western Europe identify themselves as Marxist feminists or acknowledge the influence of Marxism on their work. Joan Acker, Nona Glazer, Barbara Laslett, Edna Bonacich, for example, have all made significant contributions to the development of Marxist feminism and are sociologists of high repute.

Second, major sociological conceptualizations of significant dimensions of gender relations derive from Marxist feminist discourse (Acker 1989). For example, sociology's widely applied understandings of gender in relation to segmented and split labor markets, nonwage labor, the reserve army of the unemployed, deskilled jobs, and the role of state in the reinforcement of women's oppression are based in part on Marxist feminist analysis.

Finally, feminism constantly informs sociology that gender inequality is systematic and deeply rooted in the capitalist system. Most sociological work on women and gender may not ultilize Marxist categories of analysis, but much takes the position that only radical changes in our system of economic production and distribution will alleviate gender inequality. Whether these changes are sufficient to end gender inequality remains an area of conflict between Marxist feminists and others who advocate radical social transformation.

Two areas of challenge remain for Marxist feminist studies in sociology. First, the danger of a detachment of Marxist feminism from political action grows as radical social movements become more difficult to sustain. American feminism has in recent years found itself part of a coalition of liberal rather than radical forces. Marxist feminism needs a movement to sustain its creativity and its relationship to the political economy and culture it seeks to describe. Second, the challenge of ethnic minority concerns to sociology finds an important expression in feminism generally and more critically in Marxist feminism. As Marxism must accommodate to interests of women to render the dynamics of capitalism accurately, so must it explain the oppression of ethnic minorities (hooks 1984, 1982; Joseph 1981; Morgen 1989). The category "women" cross-cuts many levels of economic stratification and racial oppression within advanced capitalism and in poor countries. The systematic understanding of how gender intersects with class and ethnicity has only begun. Without the successful completion of this project by Marxist feminists, the liberation of women cannot be realized.

References

Abramovitz, Mimi. 1988. *Regulating the Lives of Women: Social Welfare Policy from Colonial Times to the Present.* Boston: South End Press.

Acker, Joan. 1988. "Class, Gender, and the Relations of Distribution." *Signs* 13:473–97.

———. 1989. "Making Gender Visible." Pp. 65–81 in *Feminism and Sociological Theory*, ed. Ruth Wallace. Newbury Park: Sage.

Barrett, Michele. 1988. *Women's Oppression Today: The Marxist/Feminist Encounter.* rev. ed. London: Verso.

Barrett, Michele and Mary McIntosh. 1982. *The Anti-Social Family.* London: Verso.

Baxandall, Rosalyn Fraad. 1987. *Words on Fire: The Life and Writing of Elizabeth Gurley Flynn.* New Brunswick, N.J.: Rutgers University Press.

Bebel, August. 1971. *Women under Socialism*, trans. Daniel DeLeon. New York: Schocken Books.

Beechey, Veronica. 1987. *Unequal Work.* London: Verso.

Beneria, Lourdes. 1989. "Gender and the Global Economy." Pp. 241–58 in *Instability and Change in the World Economy*, ed. Arthur MacEwan and William K. Tabb. New York: Monthly Review Press.

Beneria, Lourdes, and Martha Roldan. 1987. *Industrial Homework, Subcontracting and Household Dynamics in Mexico City.* Chicago: University of Chicago Press.

Benston, Margaret. 1969. "The Political Economy of Women's Liberation." *Monthly Review* 21:13–27.

Bonacich, Edna. 1972. "A Theory of Ethnic Antagonism: The Split Labor Market." *American Sociological Review* 37:536–47.

———. 1976. "Advanced Capitalism and Black/White Race Relations in the United States: A Split Labor Market Interpretation." *American Sociological Review* 41:34–51.

Boxer, Marilyn J. 1978. "Socialism Faces Feminism: The Failure of Synthesis in France 1879–1914." Pp. 19–50 in *Socialist Women: European Socialist Feminism in the Nineteenth and Early Twentieth Centuries*, ed. Marilyn Boxer and Jean Quataert. New York: Elsevier.

———. 1981. "When Radical and Socialist Feminism Were Joined: The Extraordinary Failure of Madeleine Pelletier." Pp. 51–74 in *Socialism, Feminism, and the Problems Faced by Political Women 1880 to the Present*, ed. Jane Slaughter and Robert Kern. Westport, Conn.: Greenwood Press.

Boxer, Marilyn J., and Jean H. Quartaert. 1978. "The Class and Sex Connection: An Introduction." Pp. 1–18 in *Socialist Women: European Socialist Feminism in the Nineteenth and Early Twentieth Centuries*, ed. Marilyn Boxer and Jean Quataert. New York: Elsevier.

Bradly, Harriet. 1989. *Men's Work, Women's Work.* Minneapolis: University of Minnesota Press.

Brenner, Johanna, and Maria Ramas. 1984. "Rethinking Women's Oppression." *New Left Review* 144:33–71.

Davis, Angela. 1981. *Women, Race and Class.* New York: Random House.

Delphy, Christine. 1977. *The Main Enemy.* London: Women's Research and Resources Center.

Dunayevskaya, Raya. 1981. *Rosa Luxemburg, Women's Liberation, and Marx's Philosophy of Revolution.* Atlantic Highlands, NJ: Humanities Press.

Edmondson, Linda. 1981. "Sylvia Pankhurst: Suffragist, Feminist, or Socialist?" Pp. 75–100 in *European Women on the Left: Socialism, Feminism, and the Problems Faced by Political Women 1800 to the Present*, ed. Jane Slaughter and Robert Kern. Westport, Conn.: Greenwood Press.

Edwards, Richard C. 1979. *Contested Terrain: The Transformation of the Workplace in the Twentieth Century.* Lexington, Mass: Lexington.

Engels, Friedrich. 1958. *The Condition of the Working Class in England*, trans. W.O. Henderson and W.H. Chaloner. New York: Macmillan.

———. 1972. *The Origin of the Family, Private Property, and the State*, ed. Evelyn Reed. New York: Pathfinder Press.

Eisenstein, Zillah R. 1979. *Capitalist Patriarchy and the Case for Socialist Feminism*. New York: Monthly Review Press.

———. 1981. "Reform and/or Revolution: Toward a Unified Women's Movement." Pp. 339–62 in *Women and Revolution*, ed. Lydia Sargent. Boston: South End Press.

Fernandez-Kelly, Maria Patricia. 1989. "International Development and Industrial Restructuring: The Case of Garment and Electronic Industries in Southern California." Pp. 147–65 in *Instabilty and Change in the World Economy*, ed. Arthur MacEwan and William K. Tabb. New York: Monthly Review Press.

Flax, Jane. 1990. *Thinking Fragments: Psychoanalysis, Feminism and Postmodernism in the Contemporary World*. Berkeley: University of California Press.

Folbre, Nancy. 1984. "The Pauperization of Motherhood: Patriarchy and Public Policy in the United States." *Review of Radical Political Economics* 16:72–88.

———. 1986. "A Patriarchal Mode of Production." In *New Directions in Political Economy*, ed. R. Albelda. New York: M.E. Sharpe.

Gimenez, Martha. 1982. "The Oppression of Women: A Structuralist Marxist View." Pp. 292–323 in *Structural Sociology*, ed. Ino Rossi. New York: Columbia University Press.

———. 1987. "Marxist and Non-Marxist Elements in Engels's Views on the Oppression of Women". Pp. 37–56 in *Engels Revisited: New Feminist Essays*, ed. Janet Sayers, Mary Evans and Nanneke Redclift. New York: Tavistock.

———. 1990. "The Dialectics of Waged and Unwaged Labor: Waged Work, Domestic Labor and Household Survival in the U.S." Pp. 25–45 in *Work Without Wages: Domestic Labor and Self-Employment within Capitalism*, ed. J. Collins and Martha Gimenez. Albany: SUNY Press.

Glazer, Nona Y. 1984. "Servants to Capital: Unpaid Domestic Labor and Paid Work." *Review of Radical Politial Economics* 16:61–87.

Glenn, Evelyn N. 1977. "Degraded and Deskilled: The Proletarianization of Clerical Work." *Social Problems* 25:52–64.

———. 1985. "Racial Ethnic Women's Labor: The Intersection of Race, Gender and Class Oppression." *Review of Radical Political Economics* 17:86–108.

Gordon, Linda. 1990. "The New Feminist Scholarship on the Welfare State." Pp. 9–35 in *Women, the State and Welfare*, ed. Linda Gordon. Madison: University of Wisconsin Press.

Hartmann, Heidi. 1981. "The Unhappy Marriage of Marxism and Feminism: Towards a More Progressive Union." Pp. 2–42 in *Women and Revolution*, ed. Lydia Sargent. Boston: South End Press.

Holt, Alix, trans. 1977. *Selected Writings of Alexandra Kollontai*. London: Allison and Busby.

Honeycutt, Karen. 1981. "Clara Zetkin: A Socialist Approach to the Problem of Women's Oppression." Pp. 29–50 in *European Women on the Left: Socialism, Feminism, and the Problems Faced by Political Women 1880 to the Present*, ed. Jane Slaughter and Robert Kern. Westport, Conn.: Greenwood Press.

hooks, bell. 1982. *Ain't I a Woman?* London: Pluto Press.

———. 1984. *Feminist Theory: From Margin to Center*. Boston: South End Press.

Humphries, Jane. 1987. "The Origin of the Family: Born of Scarcity not Wealth". Pp. 11–36 in *Engels Revisited: New Feminist Essays*, ed. Janet Sayers, et al. New York: Tavistock.

Jagger, Allison M. 1983. *Feminist Politics and Human Nature*. Totowa, N.J.: Rowman and Allenheld.

James, Selma, and Mariarosa Dalla Costa. 1973. *The Power of Women and the Subversion of the Community*. Bristol: Falling Wall Press.

Joseph, Gloria. 1981. "The Incompatible Menage a Trois: Marxism, Feminism and Racism." Pp. 91–107 in *Women and Revolution*, ed. Lydia Sargent. Boston: South End Press.

Kern, Robert. 1981. "Margarita Nelken." Pp. 147–62 in *European Women on the Left: Socialism, Feminism, and the Problems Faced by Political Women 1880 to the Present* , ed. Jane Slaughter and Robert Kern. Westport, Conn.: Greenwood Press.

Laslett, Barbara. 1981. "Production, Reproduction, and Social Change: The Family in Historical Perspective." Pp. 239–58 in *The State of Sociology: Problems and Prospects* , ed. James F.

Laslett, Barbara, and Johanna Brenner. 1989. "Gender and Social Reproduction: Historical Perspectives." *Annual Review of Sociology* 15:381–404.

Leacock, Eleanor Burke. 1972. "Introduction." Pp. 7–66 in *Frederick Engels's The Origin of the Family, Private Property, and the State*, ed. Eleanor Leacock. New York: International Publishers.

Leacock, Eleanor, and Helen Safa. 1986. *Women's Work: Development and the Division of Labor by Sex.* South Hadley, Mass.: Bergin and Garvey.

Lenin, V.I. 1973. "There Can Be No Socialist Revolution Unless Women Take Part in It". Pp. 42–3 in *Women and Communism: Selections from the Writings of Marx, Engels, Lenin and Stalin* . Westport, Conn.: Greenwood Press.

Luxton, Meg. 1980. *More Than a Labour of Love: Three Generations of Women's Work in the Home* . Toronto: Women's Press.

Maconachie, Moira. 1987. "Engels, Sexual Divisions, and the Family." Pp. 98–112 in *Engels Revisited: New Feminist Essays*, ed. Janet Sayers, et al. New York: Tavistock.

Mann, Susan A. 1989. "Slavery, Sharecropping, and Sexual Inequality." *Signs* 14:774–98.

Marx, Karl. 1978a. "Contribution to the Critique of Hegel's 'Philosophy of Right.'" Pp. 16–25 in *The Marx-Engels Reader*, 2nd ed., ed. Robert C. Tucker. New York: Norton.

———. 1978b. "The Economic and Philosophic Manuscripts of 1844." Pp. 66–125 in *The Marx-Engels Reader*, 2nd ed., ed. Robert C. Tucker. New York: Norton.

———. 1978c. "Capital, Vol. I." Pp. 294–438 in *The Marx-Engels Reader*, 2nd ed., ed. Robert C. Tucker. New York: Norton.

Marx, Karl and Frederick Engels. 1978a. "The German Ideology." Pp. 146–200 in *The Marx-Engels Reader*, 2nd ed., ed. Robert C. Tucker. New York: Norton.

———. 1978b. "The Communist Manifesto." Pp. 469–500 in *The Marx-Engels Reader*, 2nd ed., ed. Robert C. Tucker. New York: Norton.

Meyer, Alfred G. 1985. *The Feminism and Socialism of Lily Braun* . Bloomington: Indiana University Press.

———. 1987. "Introduction." Pp. ix–xviii in *Lily Braun: Selected Writings on Feminism and Socialism*, trans. Alfred G. Meyer. Bloomington: Indiana University Press.

Mitchell, Juliet. 1971. *Woman's Estate*. New York: Random House.

Molyneaux, Maxine. 1979. "Beyond the Domestic Labour Debate." *New Left Review* 116:3–28.

Moon, S. Joan. 1978. "Feminism and Socialism: The Utopian Synthesis of Flora Tristan." Pp. 19–50 in *Socialist Women: European Socialist Feminism in the Nineteenth and Early Twentieth Centuries*, ed. Marilyn Boxer and Jean Quartaert. New York: Elsevier.

Morgen, Sandra. 1989. "Making Connections: Socialist-Feminist Challenges to Marxist Scholarship." Pp. 140–63 in *Women and a New Academy: Gender and Cultural Contexts* , ed. Jean F. O'Barr. Madison: University of Wisconsin Press.

Morrissey, Marietta. 1989. *Slave Women in the New World: Gender Stratification in the Caribbean* . Lawrence: University Press of Kansas.

Quataert, Jean H. 1979. *Reluctant Feminists in German Social Democracy 1885–1917* . Princeton: Princeton University Press.

Redclift, Nanneke. 1987. "Rights in Women: Kinship, Culture and Materialism." Pp. 113–44 in *Engels Revisited: New Feminist Essays*, ed. Janet Sayers, et al. New York: Tavistock.

Reed, Evelyn. 1972. "Introduction". Pp. 7–22 in *The Origin of The Family, Private Property, and the State by Frederick Engels*, ed. Evelyn Reed. New York: Pathfinder Press.

Reich, Michael, David M. Gordon, and Richard C. Edwards. 1973. "A Theory of Labor Market Segmentation." *American Economic Review* 63:359–365.

Rubin, Gayle. 1975. "The Traffic in Women: Notes on the Political Economy of Sex." Pp. 157–210 in *Toward an Anthropology of Women*, ed. Rayna Reiter. New York: Monthly Review Press.

Smith, Dorothy. 1987. "Women's Inequality and the Family." Pp. 23–54 in *Families and Work*, ed. Naomi Gerstel and Harriet Engel Gross. Philadelphia: Temple University Press.

Smith, Joan. 1990. "All Crises Are Not the Same: Households in the United States during Two Crises." Pp. 128–41 in *Work without Wages*, ed. J.L. Collins and Martha Gimenez. Albany: SUNY Press.

Springer, Beverly Tanner. 1981. "Anna Kuliscioff: Russian Revolutionist, Italian Feminist." Pp. 13–28 in *European Women on the Left: Socialism, Feminism, and the Problems Faced by Political Women 1880 to the Present*, ed. Jane Slaughter and Robert Kern. Westport, Conn.: Greenwood Press.

Stites, Richard. 1981. "Alexandra Kollontai and the Russian Revolution." Pp. 101–24 in *European Women on the Left: Socialism, Feminism, and the Problems Faced by Political Women 1880 to the Present*, ed. Jane Slaughter and Robert Kern. Westport, Conn.: Greenwood Press.

Tong, Rosemarie. 1989. *Feminist Thought: A Comprehensive Introduction*. San Francisco: Westview.

Vogel, Lise. 1983. *Marxism and the Oppression of Women: Toward a Unitary Theory*. New Brunswick: Rutgers University Press.

Vogel, Lise. 1981. "Marxism and Socialist Feminist Theory: A Decade of Debate," *Current Perspectives in Social Theory* 2:209–231. Greenwich, Ct.:JAI Press.

Walby, Sylvia. 1986. *Patriarchy at Work: Patriarchal and Capitalist Relations in Employment*. Minneapolis: University of Minnesota Press.

———. 1988. "Segregation in Employment in Social and Economic Theory." Pp. 14–28 in *Gender Segregation at Work*, ed. Sylvia Walby. London: Open University Press.

———. 1990. *Theorizing Patriarchy*. Oxford: Basil Blackwell.

Waters, Elizabeth. 1989. "In the Shadow of the Comintern: The Communist Women's Movement 1920–1943." Pp. 29–56 in *Promissory Notes: Women in the Transition to Socialism*, ed. Sonia Kruks, Rayna Rapp, and Marilyn B. Young. New York: Monthly Review Press.

Weinbaum, Batya. 1978. *The Curious Courtship of Women's Liberation and Socialism*. Boston: South End Press.

Yeatman, Anna. 1990. "A Feminist Theory of Social Differentiation." Pp. 281–99 in *Feminism/Postmodernism*, ed. Linda J. Nicholson. London: Routledge.

Young, Iris. 1981. "Beyond the Unhappy Marriage: A Critique of the Dual Systems Theory." Pp. 43–69 in *Women and Revolution*, ed. Lydia Sargent. Boston: South End Press.

Zaretsky, Eli. 1976. *Capitalism, the Family and Personal Life*. New York: Harper & Row.

Zetkin, Clara. 1973. "Lenin on the Women's Question." Pp. 89–104 in *Women and Communism: Selections From the Writings of Marx, Engels, Lenin and Stalin*, with Introduction by Harry Pollitt. Westport, Conn.: Greenwood Press.

RACE:

CLASSICAL AND RECENT THEORETICAL DEVELOPMENTS IN THE MARXIST ANALYSIS OF RACE AND ETHNICITY

James A. Geschwender
and
Rhonda F. Levine

Although a plethora of sociological writing has concerned itself with analyses of race, theories of racial stratification have never been a priority in social science. Classical social theorists, such as Marx, Durkheim, and Weber, were more concerned with the transition from feudalism to capitalism and the structural relationships shaping the new capitalist order. For classical Marxism, the emphasis was on the new class order, and questions of race were subsumed within class analysis. Classical Marxism implicitly addressed issues of race when considering the problem of divisions within the working class and the nature of "national oppression." As a consequence, contributions of Marxist social theory have been primarily in the areas of class-based and nation-based theories of race (Omi and Winant 1986:9–31).

This chapter briefly reviews classical views on the "national question," class-based and nation-based theories of race, and concludes by proposing a Marxist theoretical approach to the study of race that builds on positive aspects of both class-based and nation-based theories. This analysis locates the analysis of race in the class struggle that results from the twin contradictions of capitalism—that between capital and labor and that between the capitalist core and the periphery.

Classical Marxism and the National Question

Perhaps the most stimulating theoretical discussions of the national question have been located in debates over political strategy for achieving change (Davis 1976; Lowy 1976). So much so that the heated debate over whether nations did or did not have the right to self-determination took center stage, while pushing to the periphery questions as to the nature and composition of nations. It was not at all uncommon to see protagonists' conclusions as to whether a particular

66

people constitute a nation largely determined by their position as to the political desirability of self-determination for that people at the given historical moment. Although in the *Communist Manifesto* Marx and Engels argued that national differences and antagonisms were to become increasingly meaningless as capitalism developed on a world scale, Marx contradicted this point in other writings from the same time. For instance, Marx came to favor independence for Ireland after initially having supported the notion of autonomy for Ireland within a British federation. He came to this point because he concluded that:

> 1. only the national liberation of the oppressed nation enables national divisions and antagonisms to be overcome, and permits the working class of both nations to unite against their common enemy, the capitalists; 2. the oppression of another nation helps to reinforce the ideological hegemony of the bourgeoisie over workers in the oppression nations...; 3. the emancipation of the oppressed nation weakens the economic, political, military and ideological bases of the dominating class and the oppressor nation and this contributes to the revolutionary struggle of the working class of that nation. (Lowy 1976, p. 83)

This was not basically different from the rationale that underlay the support given by Marx and Engels to independence in Poland (Lowy 1976:83–84). They saw tsarist Russia as being the main bastion of reaction and impediment to the socialist transformation in Europe. Thus, any action that weakened Russia would be a progressive step furthering the cause of socialism.

Polish independence was desirable precisely because it would weaken the Russian empire. These initial concerns set the tone for Marxist analyses of the national question up to the present. It is perfectly understandable that theorists writing during the last quarter of the nineteenth century and the first quarter of the twentieth century should have an overriding interest in the breakup of empires, the rise of national movements for self-determination, and the creation of nation-states. It is equally understandable that they would be concerned with analyzing how all of this had an impact on the potential for achieving socialism. This led ultimately to the acceptance of the belief that nations had a "right to self-determination." This view, however, caused great problems of consistency within Marxist theory, especially inasmuch as many Marxists believed that the creation of independent nation-states in certain instances would be an error.

One of the concerns that led to this self-contradictory position was the question of the potential viability of small states. Luxemburg believed that Poland could not exist as a separate nation-state because it lacked the potential for a viable economy. She argued that Poland was in fact an intricate part of the Russian economic system. Even though different opinions were taken held on the relevance of their argument for the specific case of Poland, her general concern was shared by many others, and Lenin acknowledged it when he laid the basis for his theoretical support of the right to self-determination:

> Ever in favor of petty states, or the splitting up of states in general, or the principle of federation, Marx considered the separation of an oppressed nation to be a step towards federations, and consequently, not towards a split, but towards concentration, both political and economic, but concentration on the basis of democracy. (quoted in Davis 1976:18)

This is a position that Lenin more or less held to throughout the building of the Soviet ˙ nion. While he did not anticipate that the right to secession would be exercised, he was willing to defend the right of a small nation to secede because he thought that the economic advantages of the larger unit, and especially the advantage of belonging to a workers' state, would bring it back into the fold.

A second major concern expressed by many was that nationalism would be exploited to make national identity more important than class membership, thus creating patriotism and perpetuating class privilege. Luxemburg believed that in a capitalist society, the right to self-determination often meant the self-determination of the ruling class, while workers, lacking the power to do otherwise, would remain in a subordinate position. The belief that workers would thus be manipulated led Lenin to conclude in 1919 that the "self-determination" paradox could not be resolved through resorting to an advocacy of self-determination for the proletariat of a nation—a formulation he had previously supported (Davis 1976:12).

The debate over the "national question" had a significant impact on the analysis of African Americans in the United States. It had less impact on the analysis of Mexican Americans and Native Americans. The dominant position within Marxist circles until 1928–29 was that the primary contradiction of capitalism was between classes, and that "race" was a device used by capitalists to divide the working class. Hence, analyses of race were subsumed within class analysis. Discussions within the international communist movement between 1928 and 1930—often stimulated by African American communists who were formerly associated with the African Blood Brotherhood—resulted in the Communist Party U.S.A. adopting the view that African Americans residing in the southern region of the United States, known as the Black Belt, constituted a submerged nation and were entitled to the right to self-determination (Geschwender 1978:70–80). This view remained the official party position until the end of World War II (Omi and Winant 1986:46; Outlaw 1987:109). The "national question" or the view that racial solidarities constitute separate nations did not resurface as a major issue until the late 1960s and early 1970s.

Class-Based Theories of Race

Oliver Cox (1948) presented the classic formulation of a class analysis of racial exploitation by viewing the development of racism as an intrinsic part of the development of capitalism on a world scale (1948:985–88). Race prejudice originated with European expansionism, but race antagonisms did not reach full maturity until the latter half of the nineteenth century when European nations used a theory of racial superiority to justify economic aggression against people of color. The origin of modern race relations in America was marked by the slave trade. The slave trade itself was simply a means of recruiting labor to develop a profit out of American resources (1948:333).

Thus, for Cox, racial antagonisms began in Europe and were carried throughout the world. Everywhere Europeans went, they disrupted indigenous cultures. The very nature and efficiency of capitalist culture was sufficient to ensure the breakup of preexisting social structures. Cox insisted that all groups were capable of prejudice but that capitalism first developed among Europeans, consequently producing race prejudice among them. People of color who develop capitalism at the point of imperialism would be expected also to develop a sense of racial superiority to justify their expansion.

Although Cox wrote his book in 1948, it was not until some fifteen years later that class-based theories of race began to take hold within American sociology. The assimilationist perspective dominated U.S. sociology in the 1950s and 1960s (for a critique of this perspective, see Geschwender 1978:39–69). The assimilationists tended to view race and ethnicity as primordial categories, with race physiological and ethnicity cultural in nature. In their view, each minority group entered U.S. society in a disadvantaged position because of a lack of knowledge of U.S. culture and deficiency of skills and competencies that would enable them to compete successfully in U.S. society. The "failure" of the assimilationist perspective to explain persistent racial inequality in the United States became all too evident as the struggle for racial equality swept throughout the country in the mid to late 1960s. The civil rights movement, Black Power movement, and numerous other social movements of the time impressed young sociologists who would soon provide a radical critique of mainstream sociological analyses of race. Influenced by Marxist theory, many of them questioned how one could analyze race without understanding the nature of exploitation and oppression (for an extended discussion of class-based theories, see Geschwender 1978:93–105, 1987:138–141; Omi and Winant 1986:25–37).

Most of the work done from the perspective of a class-based theory of race has focused on race relations and racial oppression in the United States. The thesis (Baran and Sweezy 1966; Leggett 1968; Braverman 1974; Oppenheimer 1974; Wilhelm 1970; Winston 1973) usually viewed the members of a racial group as an especially disadvantaged sector of the working class. This sector can serve as a "reserve army," and when employed, can be more intensively exploited because of its relative powerlessness. Those who hold to this thesis tend to view capitalists as conscious and deliberate stimulators of racism within the working class in order to keep the class divided, weak, and, exploitable.

Specific theoretical formulations have been developed to understand the position of racial groups within the labor market. Segmented labor-market theory (Gordon 1972; Doeringer and Piore 1971; Edwards 1975, 1979; Edwards, Reich, and Gordon 1975; Gordon, Edwards, and Reich 1982; Piore 1975; Wachtel and Betsy 1973; Vietorisz and Harrison 1973; Bluestone 1971) argues that advanced industrial capitalist economies are segmented into monopoly (also called "primary" or "core") and competitive (also called "secondary" or "peripheral") sectors. Firms in the monopoly sector tend to be large, profitable, and capital intensive; to produce consumer durable goods; to be characterized by internal labor markets; and bureaucratic control, and to be oligopolistic. Consequently, their labor force tends to be highly skilled and productive; unionized; earns high wages; and exhibits stable career patterns. Firms in the competitive sector tend to be small, marginally profitable, and labor intensive; to be characterized by direct supervision and external labor markets; and to produce nondurable goods. Consequently, their labor force tends to be unskilled, unorganized, and poorly paid; to exhibit low levels of productivity; and to be characterized by unstable employment patterns. This notion of a segmented labor market provides the key determinant of racially based inequalities in production relations, since racial groups tend to be concentrated in the competitive sector, indicating a "divide and rule" tactic of the capitalist class.

Whereas segmented labor-market theory may describe the position of subordinate racial groups within the labor market, the theory advances little understanding as to why certain racial groups dominate certain economic sectors. Edna Bonacich (1972, 1975, 1976, 1979, 1980a, 1980b) has written a series of articles that critique the "divide and rule" implications of segmented labor-market theory and develop a theoretical foundation for split-labor market theory. Bonacich argues that much of the work in the segmented labor-market tradition has the tendency to attribute the origin of labor market characteristics to characteristics of firms themselves, when in fact the opposite is the case: The pattern of employment characteristic of the segmented labor market is the direct result of split-labor market dynamics.

Three key classes or class fractions are involved in split labor markets: capital or individual capitalists, higher-priced labor, and cheaper labor. The division between these latter two categories often corresponds to that between dominant and subordinate racial solidarities. Subordinate racial solidarities are disadvantaged because of institutionalized patterns of discrimination. Class conflict takes place between capital and dominant racial groups that seek to maintain their higher wage levels. Racial conflict occurs between dominant and subordinate workers as dominant workers attempt to prevent subordinate workers from pushing down the price of labor. For example, Bonacich (1980b) argues that labor has often attempted to solidify its position by pressing the state for protective legislation. When it achieves this, capital counterattacks by attempting to create as many loopholes in the rules as it can. The tendency is for the protective laws to come to be applied in the monopoly sector and not in the competitive sector. Consequently, the competitive sector remains an area in which capital can continue to employ cheap, powerless, and readily exploitable workers who often come from minority racial communities, while the more organized and powerful workers from the majority group dominate the jobs in the monopoly sector.

While split-labor-market theory may indeed add an important corrective to segmented labor theory, both perspectives ultimately reduce an understanding of racial dynamics to that of class dynamics. What remains untheorized is the origin of race and the differential allocation of groups to sectors of the economy.

Nation-Based Theories of Race

Not all Marxist scholars have reduced racial analysis to an analysis of class. C.L.R. James (1947), while recognizing the significance of class, also stressed the importance of racial struggle for the ending of racial and class oppression. For James, racial struggle is a constituent part of the struggle for socialism that may influence the revolutionary proletariat. James utilized a Marxist methodology, but he paid more attention to racial aspects of oppression than other Marxist scholars in the class-based tradition.

Most nation-based theories of race within a Marxist perspective understand racial oppression in terms of class exploitation *and* national domination (see West 1987:82–85 for a critique of this view). Some nation-based theories take as their starting point the Communist party's formulation of the Black Nation Thesis (see, for example, Hayward 1948; Perry 1978; Forman 1981). Although this perspective gained little acceptance within academic debates on racial oppression, a variant of the Black Nation Thesis surfaced in the mid-1960s, shifting focus from African Americans in rural areas to African Americans in urban areas (for an extended discussion, see Geschwender 1978:80–91). All variants of nation-based analyses of race discuss race in terms initially developed to analyze race relations under conditions of European colonialism. They typically are concerned with the situation of African Americans in poor urban areas. Stimulated by African American urban revolts in the mid-1960s, these views see African Americans as dominated and exploited by white Americans. Whites benefit from this form of exploitation and some concessions are made to the African American community to maintain the overall system of exploitation.

The early Communist party analysis of African Americans in the Black Belt as a submerged nation with a right to self-determination was developed in relation to an African American population that was largely southern, rural, and engaged in quasi-peasant agriculture. When African Americans migrated to industrial cities, mainly in the North after World War II, the Communist party dropped the submerged nation model and replaced it with a class model. Clark (1965), Carmichael and Hamilton (1967), Allen (1970), Tabb (1970), and Blauner (1972) examined the situation of African Americans in urban America and disagreed with the communist interpretation of the significance of migrations. For these scholars, African Americans in the poor urban areas represented an internal colony. As an internal colony, African Americans provide for the dominant white society similar functions to those that external colonies do for the mother country. The urban area becomes a cheap labor reserve for the dominant society. Unlike class-based theories, nation-based theories see the need to stress the question of national domination to explain racial oppression in the United States. In the case of African Americans, Africans were brought to the United States because it was profitable for whites. African culture was undermined. At all times in American history, African Americans have lived under conditions of white domination. This domination is, and always has been, economically profitable to whites.

Barrera and his collaborators (Barrera, Munoz, and Ornelas 1972) analyzed the barrio from the perspective of the internal colonial model. He (Barrera 1979) later extended the model to include all Mexican Americans in the Southwest. The internal colony was created as a result of American conquest that brought the Southwest into the United States. Over time, Chicano lands were expropriated, their economy was disrupted, all attempts at political organization were severely restricted, and their culture was undermined. Class segmentation evolved in such a manner as to bind Chicanos into a structurally subordinate position. Waves of immigration increased the numbers of Chicanos in the Southwest, but did little to improve their position in American society. Dominance was initially retained through violence and coercion, but it later became more subtle as neocolonial forms of control emerged. Moore (1970) rejected the internal colonial model and argued that the classic colonial model served quite well to describe the situation of Mexican Americans in New Mexico, while slight variations could be used for Texas (conflict colonialism) and California (economic colonialism). It appears that nation-based theories have much to offer in helping us to understand the situation of Chicanos in American society.

There have also been some less successful attempts to apply the internal colonial model to Native Americans (Hagen, 1962; Jorgenson 1971; Patterson 1971; Thomas 1966–67). They all note the process through which Native Americans were subjugated by conquest, had their land taken from them, and were then controlled by the Bureau of Indian Affairs and the reservation system.

Anders (1979) arrived at a very similar conclusion from his historical study of the Cherokee. But an analysis of federal attempts at termination led him to modify this position (Anders 1980). Ending the colonial relationship did not improve the situation but appeared to increase the dependence and underdevelopment of Native Americans. Consequently, he abandoned the internal colonial model and adopted dependency theory.

Moore (1976) argues that the internal colonial model fits best for the Native Americans that remain on the reservations (a minority) and applies least well to the urban dwellers (see Bee and Gingrich 1977 for a similar position). Jacobson (1984) argues that the internal colonial model does not apply to Native Americans because one of its essential features, the exploitation of minority labor— does not apply. Indian workers were, for the most part, ignored rather than exploited. Jacobson argues that what was really involved was a form of corporate colonialism in which Indian lands, but not Indians, were desired. Ward Churchill (1983:202) says that the totality of Marxist theory has nothing to offer the Native American, although he feels that Marxists can learn much from studying Native Americans and their history. He is certainly correct in the last point; however, it would appear that nation-based theories of race also could do much to help us understand the conquest and near extermination of Native Americans.

While these views are certainly important in viewing the specifics of racial oppression, there is a view that all whites benefit equally from a system of racial oppression. What is needed is a theory of racial oppression that can fully explicate just exactly at whose expense and to what degree they benefit or lose, along with an explication of the process of historical change in these relations.

New Directions in Theories of Race

Only within the past decade has new work begun to speak to the so-called race-class debate. Prior to this, most work on theories of race within the Marxist tradition attempted to speak to one side of the debate. Only recently are scholars attempting to theorize the interaction of race and class into a coherent theory of racial oppression (see, for example, Robinson 1983; West 1987; Outlaw 1987; Harris 1987; Omi and Winant 1986). Nevertheless, new work is either pitched at such a high level of abstraction that it is difficult to apply it to social reality, or it is so empirically based that it is difficult to generalize from the specific analysis. What follows is a step toward historically grounding a theory of race and racial oppression that draws on insight from both class-based and nation-based theories of race and racial oppression.

Capitalism's Twin Contradictions

The primary contradiction within capitalism is between capital and labor. In its pure form, capitalism requires a portion of the population to have been stripped of all means of earning a livelihood except for the sale of its labor power to capital (i.e., it has been proletarianized). While in principle an exchange of equal values takes place, the terms of the sale actually work to capital's advantage and labor's disadvantage. Capital purchases labor power at a cost (wage) sufficient to ensure the reproduction of labor as determined, in part, by current standards of socially defined needs. The labor so purchased is used by capital in the production of commodities. The value produced through the application of labor is greater than the price paid by capital and the remainder, after subtracting costs of equipment and raw materials, is surplus value appropriated by capital. Some of the surplus value is reinvested to feed the expansion of the productive process, and some takes the form of profit and is consumed. It is worth noting at this point that this is an idealized picture of a more complex reality. It is never true in any given society, regardless of the extent of economic development or the location in the global division of labor, that all of labor is fully proletarianized. There is always a segment of the working class that through a variety of means, provides some portion of the costs of its own reproduction. This reduces capital's labor costs and lowers its cost of production.

A second key contradiction within the capitalist world economy is the relation of core to periphery. As the capitalist world economy expands from its centers of capital accumulation, it incorporates more and more areas into the system and simultaneously develops a global division of labor. The newly incorporated areas tend to become producers of primary products and/or suppliers of labor power, while the core areas become the centers for the most advanced technological applications to manufacturing processes. Exchange between core and peripheral areas tends to be unequal to the disadvantage of the periphery. Just as capital extracts surplus value through the labor process, the core extracts surplus from the periphery through unequal exchange. Different standards for wage levels develop in the core and the periphery. Workers in the periphery tend to be paid a great deal less for their labor than do workers in the core. It is also typically the case that a significantly higher proportion of peripheral labor is only partially proletarianized. Peripheral regions, while incorporated into a capitalist world economy, also tend to be less often characterized by capitalist relations of production. Much of the surplus is often created by peasant producers and extracted through unequal exchange.

These two contradictions are not unrelated. It is precisely the struggle between capital and labor in one or another of its forms that generates the contradiction between core and periphery. It is clear that it is impossible for capitalism to be kept within the bounds of that region in which it initially develops, although there is not a clear consensus on the precise mechanisms that force expansion (Weiskopf 1978; Bonacich and Cheng 1984).

The Reproduction of the World Division of Labor

Thus the processes through which external areas are brought within the expanding world economy are touched off by core capital in its search for markets, cheap labor, and ultimately raw materials. Newly incorporated regions are introduced into the world economy in a disadvantaged position that tends to be reproduced over time. Frank (1967, 1969) dramatized this with the colorful phrase "the development of underdevelopment." The extraction of surplus from periphery to core is perhaps the most significant factor inhibiting the economic development of peripheral geopolitical formations (Frank 1969, 1978; Emmanuel 1972; Chase-Dunn 1975). This extraction may take place through a variety of forms, one of which involves the direct exploitation of the proletariat in the periphery by core capital. A second pattern involves peripheral capital exploiting peripheral labor and then losing the major portion of surplus value so extracted to core capital through unequal exchange.

The peasantry has historically been a more significant source of surplus in the periphery than has the classic proletariat. In many situations, representatives of core merchant capital have directly extracted surplus from peasant producers through unequal exchange. In other situations, this first level of unequal exchange takes place between peasants and a merchant class located in the periphery and composed either of persons indigenous to that peripheral geopolitical formation or of an immigrant people who are racially/ethnically different from both the peasant producers and the core capitalists. These merchants then lose the major portion of the surplus so extracted to core capital through unequal exchange. The net impact of any of these forms of surplus extraction is that surplus is removed to the core and is not available to fuel development in the periphery.

The Creation of Race and Core-Peripheral Relations

The formation (creation, emergence) of what has traditionally been referred to as racial groups may be located within the analysis of the growth, expansion, and development of a capitalist world system. Such solidarities (groups) have been created as a consequence of both the flow of capital from core to periphery and labor from periphery to core. Robert Park (1950) pointed the way for this analysis. European capital found it necessary to explore various regions of the world in a search for new markets and, to a lesser extent, raw materials. These early attempts to establish trading relations brought Europeans into contact with non-European populations of people with whom they differed in a number of recognizable characteristics. European society was capitalist society, possessing relatively advanced technology and relatively strong state structures.

The non-European societies with whom they came into contact were noncapitalist, possessing significantly less advanced technology and significantly weaker state structures. The non-Europeans were at a considerable disadvantage vis-á-vis the Europeans. Stronger state structures and advanced technology were translated into military superiority, which in turn ensured that terms of exchange would work to the disadvantage of non-Europeans and the advantage of Europeans. Relations of unequal exchange were established. Those goods received by the Europeans embodied far more labor time than did those they gave in exchange.

These are not precisely the terms used by Park in his description. He preferred to refer to contact between diverse groups that escalated into competition and conflict and was resolved through accommodation. The latter was simply the process of development of institutionalized structures of superordination-subordination. While the terms are different, however, the essence of his analysis is captured above. Park went on to note that all of this involved two populations differing in physical characteristics and behavioral practices. He suggested that these differences became the basis for the development of ethnocentrism and the tendency to think in "we-they" terms. Europeans saw in physical and behavioral differences an explanation for "backwardness" and a rationalization for relations of superordination-subordination and unequal exchange. Certainly people who were "biologically inferior" or who were culturally backward because of the fact that they were never exposed to the "stimulating effect of a temperate climate" could not be allowed to make decisions controlling their own or others' destiny.

Here, then, we may see the origin of the definition of groups in the incorporation of physical or cultural characteristics into an emerging ideology of racism in the context of unequal power relations. The ideology then served as a rationalization for domination and exploitation. For the most part, the dominated solidarities were already in existence as functioning societies, but the terms of their collective definition were newly created. It was often true that this process was set in motion by trading contacts that predated the incorporation of external areas into the world economy. Thus Winthrop Jordan (1968) is quite correct when he argues that racism and the tendency to think in racial categories became entrenched in Europe prior to the establishment of slavery or the creation of capitalist labor relations involving racially different people. He is correct in the statement of fact, but wrong in the implications he derives. Racism is not produced because of any intrinsic cultural predisposition to reject, or need to degrade, non-Europeans. Instead, racism and the economic extraction of surplus developed more or less hand in hand.

Racial categories and racist ideologies then were already existant and helped shape the manner in which external populations were incorporated into the expanding world economy. Stereotypes and prejudices developed in trading relations influenced the definition that Europeans formed of the capacity of the various racial or ethnic solidarities to play different roles within the larger economic system. There was a previously developed rationale for the incorporation of Africans, Asians, and Pacific Islanders in a subordinate capacity. The "truth" of this rationale is proven to Europeans time and time again by the inability of non-European people to alter their status within the system—an inability that is created by the extraction of surplus through unequal exchange. Thus we have a very short but tight circle. Initial inequalities between two people leads simultaneously to the creation of patterns of domination-subordination and to the emergence of a set of beliefs that form the intellectual rationale for an ideology of racism. In conjunction, these two maintain and intensify the initial inequalities and demonstrate the validity of the belief system.

The Creation of Race and Ethnicity in the Core

Park argued that there was no basic difference between the creation of races (and ethnicities) during the course of expansion of the world system and of later migrations of people from peripheral to core areas. We believe that there are strong parallels between the two processes, but there are also significant areas of difference. Park's analysis suggests that immigrant populations migrate from the periphery to the core in response to labor needs created by an expanding economy. On arrival, they tend to be located in those areas of the economy undergoing the most rapid expansion at the time. Thus persons from the same region of the world tend to become disproportionately concentrated in certain occupations and industries. This combines with a tendency toward regional (geographic) concentration and, in very many cases, ghettoization, to create conditions conducive to the development of self-perpetuating solidarities that are prone to be stereotyped and stigmatized by the members of the host population. The coincidence of physical and/or cultural distinctiveness with class, industrial, occupational, and geographic concentration encourages others to view members of the immigrant population in stereotypic fashion and to explain their location in the social organization of production and exchange in terms of either physical and/or cultural inferiority—in short, in terms of an emerging racist ideology.

It is important to note that the process of group definition in the course of migration does not always begin with a clear slate. Migrations tend to follow paths created by current or past societal relations. Some of the more obvious examples include the historical movement of colonized people from areas of surplus population to areas of labor shortage within the British Empire, migration from colonies to the mother country, and the more recent migration from former colonies to the former mother country (e.g., from the West Indies to Great Britain). In each instance, there already exists within the receiving society some set of images of the immigrant peoples that were formed in the course of earlier contacts. The stereotypic images and associated attitudes that members of the receiving society have of immigrants have an impact on the opportunity structure confronting them at time of arrival. They help to bring about the concentrations described earlier as producing new stereotypes. Stereotypic images may be modified in the course of the migration experience, but they do influence the subsequent development of additional stereotypes. Consequently, it may be more accurate to describe the migration process as modifying existing racial definitions and current racist ideology, rather than giving rise to new ones.

An Evaluation of the Concept of Race

It is clear from the foregoing that race is a social construct—a label applied to emerging solidarities within certain social-historical conjunctures. What is not clear is whether it also constitutes a useful scientific concept. Let us first consider the concept of "race." The popular definition of a solidarity as a "race" is not at all a function of its genetic composition, despite popular belief to the contrary. It is often true that the very same solidarity has been variously labelled a "race" or an ethnic group at different points in its history without any apparent change in its biological makeup (e.g., Irish Catholics in America, Jews). It is equally clear that the genetic composition of a solidarity does not determine the position occupied by that solidarity in the social organization of exchange. This position is the consequence of the manner and timing of the incorporation of a region into the capitalist world system and/or the introduction of the solidarity into the core during the peopling process (Williams 1990; Nordyke 1977).

Yet the physical characteristics of the solidarity come to be related to the position that the solidarity occupies in the social organization of production and/or exchange. The collective position occupied in the social structure is generative of stereotypes that form the underpinning for a collective social evaluation of the solidarity and the ultimate development of an ideology of racial superiority/inferiority. This ideology thus reinforces structural constraints which serve to keep the 'racial' solidarity in a disadvantaged position. We must be aware of the role played by an ideology of racism in legitimizing and maintaining a particular stratification order, but we must also be aware that, inasmuch as this ideology is not a product of actual genetic differences between people, the existence of the ideology may not be used as an argument for retaining the concept of "race" as a useful scientific concept for the study of processes within core regions.

There is also very little purpose to be served in retaining the concept of "race" to be used in the analysis of core-periphery relations. Wallerstein (1972) argues that race is an international status-group category that is a "blurred collective representation for an international class category, that of proletarian nations" (1972:181). "Racism, therefore, is simply the act of maintaining the existing international social structure" (1972:180). We believe that this analysis is faulty in that it leads to a confusion between objective reality and social consciousness—a confusion between concepts used by the people themselves in certain social-historical conjunctures and those that are useful for purposes of scientific analysis. It is true that there was once a congruence between core-peripheral relations and relations between European and non-European (white and non-white) people. The emergence of Japan as a world imperialist power has altered that considerably, but even if Japan had never become a major power, it would be a mistake to analyze this contradiction in racial terms. Nor may this problem be resolved by following Genet's suggestive lead in the manner done by Wallerstein (1979:165–221) and arguing that the content of a racial group is altered as the group changes its position in the international division of labor. That smells too much of the White Rabbit in *Alice in Wonderland* who lets words mean what he wishes them to mean. At any rate, it introduces a circularity of meaning by saying oppressed people constitute a race and when a people cease to be oppressed, they are no longer part of that race.

The essence of the contradiction between core and periphery is economic despite the fact that it has often been defined in racial terms. The relation of superordination-subordination has been buttressed by an ideology of racism and racial consciousness that have served as a basis for anti-imperialist struggles. Yet race, per se, was never an essential part of the social reality. Extraction of surplus from the periphery to the core through unequal exchange can take place between two groups that are socially defined as being of the same broad racial group— e.g., core-peripheral relations between North and South in the United States between the Civil War and World War II. Our theories and concepts must make it possible for us to analyze the important role played by racism as an ideology and racial consciousness as a facilitator of the development of political struggles, but they must not mislead us into thinking that genetic differences between groups somehow lay at the root of economic relations. We believe that retention of the concept of "race" has exactly these connotations, and for this reason it must be scrapped.

The phenomenon previously analyzed with the concept of race is important, and we must have an appropriate concept to be used in its analysis. We argue that we should return to the classical Marxist tradition and use the concept of nation to refer to people who are incorporated into the capitalist world system in a subordinate (peripheral) position and from whom surplus is extracted. These people normally constituted differentiated societies before incorporation and usually remain so after incorporation. Frequently, their current class or authority structure is exploited as the vehicle for their domination. We may also use the concept "submerged nation" to refer to people who have been incorporated into a core geopolitical formation as an entity through conquest or border change (e.g., Native Americans, Mexican Americans in the Southwest, Hawaiians). Neither of these concepts is appropriate for use with people who previously constituted a submerged nation but who have become dispersed throughout the larger core society, but who continue to be more intensively exploited than other workers or to experience unequal exchange (e.g., African Americans). For these people, we propose to use the concept of national minority. We also use the term national minority to refer to people who migrated from periphery to core in a relatively voluntary fashion.

Nevertheless, we must not make the error of assuming that any of these concepts refer to people who are internally homogeneous. There is little question that both the dominant people and national minorities in core societies are class differentiated and that unequal exchange has differential impact on the different classes within that entity. In some cases, the proletariat in the core may benefit in the manner described by Rodney (1974); in other instances, it may suffer through loss of jobs as capital is displaced to the periphery or through reduced wages as core capital reduces its costs of production to compete with goods produced in the periphery (Bonacich 1980). Peripheral societies are similarly differentiated by class, and the relations of unequal exchange have a differential impact on the different classes within these entities. Wallerstein (1975) notes that the process of expropriation of surplus value often involves the development of a three-tiered format within which the middle tier both participates in the exploitation of the lower tier and is exploited by the upper tier.

The term *comprador bourgeoisie* is used to describe this tier when it is both located in peripheral societies and shares a common sense of historical identity with the lower tier. This stratum occupies a position analogous to that attributed to the proletariat in the core by Rodney. Unequal exchange between the periphery and the core siphons off a substantial portion of the surplus that they would otherwise retain for themselves if—and this is a big if—they were able to retain their position of advantage without the political and military support received from the core. Yet they are allowed to retain for themselves a portion of the surplus that they might lose entirely if the ending of unequal exchange between periphery and core were to be accompanied by a social transformation within the peripheral geopolitical formation.

We cannot accept classes and status groups in the global division of labor as identical, nor even as two manifestations of the same phenomenon, because they stand in different relations to the process of accumulation. The essential point in our argument is not at all the simple fact that the boundaries of the two classifications do not coincide. That is a minor matter. Far more important is the fact that the internal composition of classes is differentiated to include segments having different positions in the relationship of unequal exchange (e.g., core and peripheral capitalists) and the internal composition of status groups includes a variety of persons bearing different relations to the generation of surplus (i.e., the creation of value).

The essence of class has to be the relationship between a stratum that creates value and a stratum that expropriates it. It matters little for our purposes whether value is created by the proletariat and expropriated through the wage relationship or if value is created by the peasantry and expropriated through unequal exchange. In either event, class positions are defined by the relationship between strata creating value and those expropriating it from its creators. If a status group can be demonstrated to include both those creating value and those expropriating it from them, then it clearly includes two distinct classes that stand in relation to one another. It is overly simplistic—no, it is more than that, it is simply incorrect—to select for analytic purposes concepts that ignore that distinction and reduce all to members of a single category.

It is absolutely true that everything we have described here is located within a capitalist world economy and that it feeds the process of capital accumulation. But classes and status groups are integrated into the world economy in different manners and play different roles in the accumulation process. By and large, classes are located in the social organization of production and status groups in the social organization of exchange. The two are intricately linked within a unitary capitalist world economy, but they are not the same. Certain analytic tasks may allow us to treat them as an integrated whole, but others, particularly the analysis of social change, demand that they be kept analytically distinct. The important distinction between extraction of surplus value through production and extraction of surplus via unequal exchange may be maintained only by avoiding concepts that reduce classes and status groups (and thus production and exchange) to two manifestations of the same thing.

Bonacich (1980a) reduced racism to an ideological adjunct to class exploitation. Wallerstein came very close to eliminating the concept altogether by stripping it of any meaning independent of the exploitation process. Willhelm (1970, 1983) makes the opposite error. He relies on racism as an independent cause for this continued oppression. We do not at this point wish to take issue with his basic analysis, although we believe it to be a bit too sharply drawn. We do, however, wish to state our strong objection to Willhelm's tendency to leave racism as a "free-floating" phenomenon—a prime cause. We do not dispute the existence of racism. Nor do we disagree with his argument that racial oppression cannot be reduced to a simple functional need of capitalism. But we do insist that whenever we attribute an independent causal efficacy to racism, we must still explain that very racism.

Racism may take on a life of its own once created, but it initially arises somewhere, and our entire argument to date has been built around the premise that we can locate the origin of racism in the creation and expansion of the capitalist world economy. Furthermore, we insist that despite the fact that racism, like all ideological systems, may take on a life of its own and exhibit independent causal influences that, nevertheless, it changes in response to changes in capitalist relations of production and/or modifications in the structure of the world economy.

As capitalism evolves, the structure of the world economy is modified, and, inevitably, this has an impact on the evolution of ideological systems (e.g., the association between the rise of anti-Japanese sentiment in the United States and the decline of the American auto and steel industries). This impact does not appear in the form of one-to-one strict determination of changes. But, in the long run, ideological belief systems do change in a manner reflecting the impact of changing economic relationships. We must locate our analysis of racism as an ideology in a larger context that takes into account both class and national (that is either core-peripheral or dominant group-national minority) relations. But we must not lose sight of the fact that national (racial) oppression is real and that it exists separately from class exploitation. The two may be linked, but neither is reducible to the other.

References

Allen, Robert. 1970. *Black Awakening in Capitalist America: An Analytic History*. New York: Doubleday (Anchor Books).

Anders, Gary. 1979. "The Internal Colonization of Cherokee Native Americans." *Development and Change* 10:41–55.

———. 1980. "Theories of Underdevelopment and the American Indian." *Journal of Economic Issues* 14:681–701.

Baran, Paul A. and Paul M. Sweezy. 1966. *Monopoly Capital: An Essay on the American Economic and Social Order*. New York: Monthly Review Press.

Barrera, Mario. 1979. *Race and Class in the Southwest: A Theory of Racial Inequality*. Notre Dame: University of Notre Dame Press.

Barrera, Mario, Carlos Munoz, and Charles Ornelas. 1972. "The Barrio as an Internal Colony." Pp. 465–98 in *People and Politics in Urban Society*, ed. Harlan Hahn. Beverly Hills: Sage.

Bee, Robert, and Ronald Gingrich. 1977. "Colonialism, Classes, and Ethnic Identity: Native Americans and the National Political Economy." *Studies in Comparative International Development* 12:70–93.

Blauner, Robert. 1972. *Racial Oppression in America*. New York: Harper & Row.

Bluestone, Barry. 1971. "The Tripartite 'Economy' Labor Markets and the Working Poor." *Poverty and Human Resources* 5:15–36.

Bonacich, Edna. 1972. "A Theory of Ethnic Antagonism: The Split Labor Market." *American Sociological Review* 37:547–559.

————. 1975. "Abolition, the Extension of Slavery, and the Position of Free Blacks: A Study of Split Labor Markets in the United States 1830-1863." *American Journal of Sociology* 81:601-28.

————. 1976. "Advanced Capitalism and Black/White Race Relations in the United States: A Split Labor Market Interpretation." *American Sociological Review* 41:34-51.

————. 1979. "The Past, Present, and Future of Split Labor Market Theory." Pp. 17-64 in *Research in Race and Ethnic Relations*, Vol. I, ed. Cora Bagley Marrett. Greenwich, CT: JAI.

————. 1980a. "Class Approaches to Race and Ethnicity." *Insurgent Sociologist* 10:9-24.

————. 1980b. "The Creation of Dual Labor Markets." Paper presented at conference, "The Structure of Labor Markets," Athens, Georgia.

Bonacich, Edna, and Lucie Cheng. 1984. "Introduction: A Theoretical Orientation to International Labor Migration." Pp. 1-56 in *Labor Migration Under Capitalism: Asian Workers in the United States Before World War II*, ed. Edna Bonacich and Lucie Cheng. Berkeley: University of California Press.

Braverman, Harry. 1974. *Labor and Monopoly Capital: The Degradation of Work in the Twentieth Century*. New York: Monthly Review Press.

Carmichael, Stokely and Charles V. Hamilton. 1967. *Black Power: The Politics of Liberation in America*. New York: Vintage.

Chase-Dunn, Christopher. 1975. "The Effects of International Economic Dependencies Upon Development and Inequality: A Cross-National Study." *American Sociological Review* 40:720-38.

Churchill, Ward, ed. 1983. *Marxism and Native Americans*. Boston: South End Press.

Clark, Kenneth B. 1965. *Dark Ghetto*. New York: Harper & Row.

Cox, Oliver C. 1948. *Caste, Class and Race: A Study in Social Dynamics*. New York: Doubleday.

Davis, Horace B. 1976. *The National Question: Selected Writings by Rosa Luxemburg*. New York: Monthly Review Press.

Doeringer, Peter B., and Michael J. Piore. 1971. *Internal Labor Markets and Manpower Analysis*. Lexington, Mass.: Lexington.

Edwards, Richard C. 1975. "The Social Relations of Production in the Firm and Labor Market Structure." Pp. 3-26 in *Labor Market Segmentation*, ed. Richard C. Edwards, Michael Reich, and David M. Gordon. Lexington, Mass.: Lexington.

————. 1979. *Contested Terrain. The Transformation of the Workplace in the Twentieth Century*. Lexington, Mass.: Lexington.

Edwards, Richard C., Michael Reich and David M. Gordon, eds. 1975. *Labor Market Segmentation*. Lexington, Mass.: Lexington.

Emmanuel, Aghiri. 1972. *Unequal Exchange: A Study of the Imperialism of Trade*. New York: Monthly Review Press.

Forman, James. 1981. *Self-determination and the African-American People*. New York: Open Hand Press.

Frank, Andre G. 1967. *Capitalism and Underdevelopment in Latin America*. New York: Monthly Review Press.

————. 1969. *Latin America: Underdevelopment or Revolution*. New York: Monthly Review Press.

————. 1978. *Dependent Accumulation and Underdevelopment*. New York: Macmillan.

Geschwender, James A. 1978. *Racial Stratification in America*. Dubuque: William C. Brown.

————. 1987. "Race, Ethnicity, and Class." Pp. 136-60 in *Recapturing Marxism: An Appraisal of Recent Trends in Sociological Theory*, ed. Rhonda F. Levine and Jerry Lembcke. New York: Praeger.

Gordon, David M. 1972. *Theories of Poverty and Unemployment*. Lexington, Mass.: Lexington.

Gordon, David M., Richard Edwards, and Michael Reich. 1982. *Segmented Work: Divided Workers: The Historical Transformation of Labor in the United States*. Cambridge: Cambridge University Press.

Hagen, Everett. 1962. *On the Theory of Social Change*. Homewood, Ill.: Dorsey.
Harris, Leonard. 1987. "Historical Subjects and Interests: Race, Class and Conflict." Pp. 91–106 in *The Year Left 2*, ed. Mike Davis, Manning Marable, Fred Pfeil, and Michael Sprinker. London: Verso.
Haywood, Harry. 1948. *Negro Liberation*. New York: International.
Jacobson, Cardell K. 1984. "Internal Colonialism and Native Americans: Indian Labor in the United States from 1871 to World War II." *Social Science Quarterly* 65:158–71.
James, C.L.R. 1947. "The Revolutionary Solution to the Negro Problem in the United States." *Facing Reality* 4:12–18.
Jordan, Winthrop D. 1968. *White Over Black: American Attitudes Toward the Negro 1550–1812* . Baltimore: Penguin.
Jorgenson, Joseph. 1971. "Indians and the Metropolis." Pp. 66–113 in *The American Indian and Urban Society*, ed. Jack Wadell and O.M. Watson. Boston: Little Brown.
Leggett, John C. 1968. *Class, Race and Labor: Working Class Consciousness in Detroit* . New York: Oxford University Press.
Lowy, Michael. 1976. "Marxists and the National Question." *New Left Review* 98:81–100.
Luxemburg, Rosa. 1976. "The National Question and Autonomy." Pp. 101–287 in *The National Question: Selected Writings by Rosa Luxemburg* , ed. Horace B. Davis. New York: Monthly Review Press.
Moore, Joan. 1970. "Colonialism: The Case of Mexican Americans." *Social Problems* 17:463–72.
———. 1976. "American Minorities and 'New Nation' Perspectives." *Pacific Sociological Review* 19:447–67.
Nordyke, Eleanor C. 1977. *The Peopling of Hawaii*. Honolulu: University of Hawaii, East-West Center.
Omi, Michael, and Howard Winant. 1986. *Racial Formation in the United States: From the 1960's to the 1980's*. New York: Routledge and Kegan Paul.
Oppenheimer, Martin. 1974. "The Sub-proletariat: Dark Skins and Dirty Work." *Insurgent Sociologist* 4:6–20.
Outlaw, Lucius. 1987. "On Race and Class, Or, On the Prospects of 'Rainbow Socialism'." Pp. 107–21 in *The Year Left 2*, ed. Mike Davis, Manning Marable, Fred Pfeil, and Michael Sprinker. London: Verso.
Park, Robert Ezra. 1950. *Race and Culture*. New York: Free Press.
Patterson, Palmer. 1971. "The Colonial Parallel: A View of Indian History." *Ethnohistory* 18:1–17.
Peery, Nelson. 1978. *The Negro National Colonial Question*. New York: Workers Press.
Piore, Michael J. 1975. "Notes for a Theory of Labor Market Stratification." Pp. 125–50 in *Labor Market Segmentation*, ed. Richard Edwards, Michael Reich, and David M. Gordon. Lexington, Mass.: Lexington.
Robinson, Cedric J. 1983. *Black Marxism: The Making of the Black Radical Tradition* . London: Zed Press.
Rodney, Walter, 1974. *How Europe Underdeveloped Africa* . Washington: Howard University Press.
Tabb, William K. 1970. *The Political Economy of the Black Ghetto* . New York: Norton.
Thomas, Robert K. 1966–67. "Colonialism: Classic and Internal." *New University Thought* 4:36–44.
Vietorisz, Thomas, and Bennett Harrison. 1973. "Labor Market Segmentation: Positive Feedback and Divergent Development." *American Economic Review* 63:366–76.
Wachtel, Howard and Charles Betsy. 1972. "Employment at Low Wages." *Review of Economics and Statistics* 54:121–29.
Wallerstein, Immanuel. 1972. "Social Conflict in Post-Independence Black Africa: The Concepts of Race and Status Group Reconsidered." Pp. 165–84 in *The Capitalist World-Economy*, ed. Immanuel Wallerstein. Cambridge: Cambridge University Press.

————. 1975. "Class Formation in the Capitalist World-Economy." Pp. 222–30 in *The Capitalist World-Economy*, ed. Immanuel Wallerstein. Cambridge: Cambridge University Press.

————. 1979. *The Capitalist World-Economy*. Cambridge: Cambridge University Press.

West, Cornell. 1987. "Race and Social Theory: Towards a Geneological Materialist Analysis." Pp. 74–90 in *The Year Left 2*, ed. Mike Davis, Manning Marable, Fred Pfeil, and Michael Sprinker. London: Verso.

Willhelm, Sidney M. 1970. *Who Needs the Negro?* New York: Doubleday.

————. 1983 *Black in White America*. Boston: Schenkman.

Williams, Richard. 1990. *Hierarchical Structures and Social Values: The Creation of Black and Irish Identities in the United States*. New York: Cambridge University Press.

Winston, Henry. 1973. *Strategy for a Black Agenda: A Critique of Theories of Liberation in the United States and Africa*. New York: International.

SOCIAL CHANGE AND DEVELOPMENT:

"A WORLD AFTER ITS OWN IMAGE": THE MARXIST PARADIGM AND THEORIES OF CAPITALIST DEVELOPMENT ON A WORLD SCALE

Martin J. Murray

Classical Marxism bequeathed an historical legacy that seems to rest on an apparent paradox. On the one hand, classical Marxist theorists, particularly Marx and Engels, but also Lenin, Luxemburg, et al., believed that capitalism was an historically progressive force compelled by its own intrinsic logic eventually to transform into its own image all regions of the world brought under its sway. On the other hand, empirical investigation seems to suggest otherwise; namely, the geographical spread of capitalism did not set in motion a chain reaction whereby the so-called Third World, as it was progressively incorporated into the capitalist world economy, travelled along the same path to capitalism that had been forged by the early Western European pioneers.

Over at least the past three decades, Marxist-influenced and Marxist-inspired scholars have been faced with an intellectual challenge. The historical process of capitalist development taking place in the peripheries of the capitalist world economy did not seem to resemble the "European model." Was it possible to explain economic stagnation, or "persistent poverty," as George Beckford (1972) put it, within the conceptual framework of classical Marxism, or was it necessary to jettison this theory altogether and create an alternative?

Classical Marxism: Its History and Legacy

Classical Marxism rested upon a dual premise: on the one hand, capitalism was an historical source of material progress on an ever-widening scale; on the other hand, capitalism was, as Marx eloquently put it, "a refined and civilised method of exploitation" (1965:394), a class-bound historical system with real limits to growth and expansion. For the classical Marxists, this twofold character of capitalism did not present any theoretical problems. Capitalism would, they confidently forecast, not only establish the material foundations for socialism and communism but also create its own gravediggers, namely, the progressively powerful proletarian class with nothing to lose but its chains.

The founders of the classical Marxist tradition, Marx and Engels, never systematically addressed the question of how the geographical spread of capitalism on a world scale would be expressed in spatial terms. What they did say on the subject cannot be found in their principal theoretical writings except in highly schematic form, but is mainly scattered in numerous newspaper articles and private correspondence. Nevertheless, the general tone of what Marx and Engels (1939:21) appeared to believe was originally laid out in 1848 in the*Communist Manifesto*:

> The bourgeoisie, by the rapid development of all instruments of production, by the immensely facilitated means of communication, draws all, even the most barbarian nations into civilisation. The cheap prices of its commodities are the heavy artillery with which it batters down all Chinese walls, with which it forces the barbarians' intensely obstinate hatred of foreigners to capitulate. It compels all nations, on pain of extinction, to adopt the bourgeois mode of production; it compels them to introduce what it calls civilisation into their midst—i.e., they become bourgeois themselves. In one word, *it creates a world after its own image.*

Marx followed a similar line of reasoning in many of his historical writings on India, on colonialism, and on other non-European areas of the world (see Avineri 1969; Kiernan 1967, 1974). In 1867, in the Preface to the first volume of *Capital*, Marx (1965:8-9) returned once again to this theme. He spoke of the "natural laws of capitalist production...working with iron necessity toward inevitable results," concluding with the oft-quoted passage: "The country that is more developed industrially only shows to the less developed the image of its own future."

The essence of the classical Marxist paradigm was that capitalism contained by its very nature an expansionist impulse, that is, the production of capital to produce more capital. In explaining capitalist development and expansion, Rosa Luxemburg (1951:43) elaborated and refined these basic premises. Her central thesis was that only by invading primitive (i.e., "natural" or nonmarket) economies through trade, force, and guile was the capitalist system able to stay alive. She stressed that "the imperialist phase of capitalist accumulation, which implies competition, comprises the industrialization and capitalist emancipation of the hinterland." Luxemburg thus followed one of Marx's main arguments that noncapitalist modes of production standing in the path of capitalist expansion would be forced to give way to the capitalist mode of production. As a consequence, industrialization of the hinterlands was the eventual outcome of capitalist competition. She also argued that simple market competition was unable by itself to dissolve precapitalist 'natural' economies. As a result, only force was capable to breaking down the barriers to penetration (see Bradby 1980).

Classical Marxist Theories of Imperialism

Nickolai Bukharin (1966), Rudolph Hilferding (1910), and V.I. Lenin (1939) shifted the terrain of classical Marxism away from the immanent logic of capitalist social relations to the construction of plausible explanations for the intense international rivalries leading to the outbreak of World War I. These classical Marxist theories of imperialism built on the "capital logic" impulses characterizing Marx's theoretical work in particular to contextualize the understanding of world capitalism. From the late nineteenth century to World War I, world capitalism underwent a profound transformation. In particular, the evolution of the organization and structure of capitalist business enterprises was accompanied by the wholesale transformation of the capitalist state apparatuses. State agencies became huge bureaucracies both shaping and enabling particular patterns of capital accumulation.

Hilferding's (1910) main contribution was the introduction of the concept of *finance capital*, the product of the fusion of industrial and banking/financial capital into huge interlocking groups that elevated capitalist competition to a higher plane. Instead of price cutting, these groups enlisted state support in their efforts to gain control of whole industries by financial and political means. Bukharin (1966) transformed Hilferding's analysis by situating it within the framework of an evolving world economy in which two tendencies were at work: the tendency to monopoly and the formation of groups of finance, and the acceleration of the geographical spread of capitalism and the integration of a single capitalist world economy. Bukharin (1966) also stressed the necessary linkage between imperialism and the changing character of the world economy. "The entire structure of world economy in our times," he concluded (1966:141–42), "forces the bourgeoisie to pursue an imperialist policy." Although he emphasized the importance of the concentration and centralization of capital, and the rivalry among imperialist capitals "for increased competition in the sales markets, in the market of raw materials, and for spheres of capital investment" (1966:122), he did not analyze what deleterious effects these tendencies of the world economy would have on dependent economies.

The starting point for Lenin's analysis of imperialism was the onset of European rivalry over far-flung colonial empires. Lenin's main contribution was to insist that the imperialist expansion taking place in the decades before World War I signalled the emergence of an entirely new stage of capitalism. Lenin's description of the chief characteristics of the new colonial era—monopolistic privileges and preferences, seizure of territories, plunder of raw materials, enslavement of local peoples, nationalism, racism, militarism—is largely accurate. Lenin agreed with Hobson (1938) that the prime cause of capital exports was the vast increase in the supply of capital in the metropolitan countries. Yet this explanation for how and why imperialist expansion took place when and where it did depends on establishing a causal linkage between the drive for colonies with the super-abundance of capital in the hands of monopolists seeking fresh investment outlets.

This thesis has remained the subject of considerable debate. In the main, Marxists and non-Marxists alike have questioned Lenin's thesis on both theoretical and empirical grounds. Is it intellectually possible, many observers have asked, to establish a single, all-encompassing theoretical paradigm that can be imposed on the complex sequence of events that revolutionized the capitalist world economy between the 1880s and World War I (Semmel 1970; Gallagher and Robinson 1961; O'Connor 1973; Owen and Sutcliffe 1972)? Other observers have raised doubts not only about the relative amount of capital pouring into the newly colonized territories, but also the directionality of capital flows (see Cairncross 1953; Dobb 1937; Strachey 1960; Brewer 1980; Emmanuel 1972a, 1972b; O'Connor 1973; Owen and Sutcliffe 1972; Kemp 1967; Barratt Brown 1963, 1973, 1974).

Postwar Capitalist Expansion and the Modernization Paradigm

The "long boom" of unprecedented capitalist growth and expansion that characterized the post-World War II period provided the historical setting for the birth of the modernization perspective. By the 1960s, this conceptual framework had become the dominant paradigm within mainstream social science literature on social change (Bendix 1967; Huntington 1971). The proximate origins of the modernization paradigm can be traced to the response of American political elites and intellectuals to the prevailing international climate, particularly the rise of the Cold War and the simultaneous emergence of so-called Third World nation-states as prominent political actors in world politics in the wake of the disintegration of the European colonial empires. During at least the first two decades after World War II, American social scientists, with the generous support of governmental and private agencies, turned increasing attention to the problems of economic development, political stability, and social and cultural change in Asia, Latin America, and Africa (Tipps 1973; So 1990; Kesselman 1973). Confident forecasts of growing material prosperity in the West created fertile ground within intellectual circles for a paradigmatic framework that would celebrate the triumph of Western capitalism over Soviet-style communism and provide a political strategy for transporting material prosperity to the emergent Third World.

Evolutionary theory and twentieth-century functionalism were particularly influential in shaping the modernization paradigm. Scholars operating within this intellectual framework made frequent use of dichotomous-type constructions (e.g., "tradition" versus "modernity"); relied on concepts such as "integration," "social differentiation," and "social system"; and emphasized evolutionary, gradual, and continual change as the normal condition of stability. In general, the modernization paradigm conceived of social change as a unilinear, directional process and defined development as the end point of the transformation of "traditional" social structures into "modern" ones (Levy 1953, 1966; Lerner 1957; McCord 1965; Banfield 1958; Eisenstadt 1960, 1965, 1970; Pye 1966; Hoselitz and Moore 1963).

Within this evolutionary framework, each of the social sciences constructed elaborate theories that were quite elegant in their simplicity. Thus, for example, "stages of growth" theories confidently predicted that, given the proper mix of factors, all national economies were poised to "take off into self-sustained economic growth" (Rostow 1952, 1960). Similarly, social psychologists contrasted the authoritarian or traditional personality types with creative, achievement-oriented, modern personality types (McLelland 1960; Hagen 1962). Finally, political scientists constructed elaborate classification schemes that purported to distinguished between traditional and modern forms of government (Almond and Coleman 1960; Shils 1962; Huntington 1969; Apter 1965; Banfield 1958; Pye 1962, 1966; Pye and Verba 1965; LaPalombara 1964); and sociologists traced the growing complexity of divisions of labor in social organizations (Smelser 1963; Hoselitz 1952, 1960). Beyond these general sorts of attributes associated with modernization theory, the task of identifying "characteristic" features of the perspective was not an easy one. The heterogeneous meanings attached to the concept of modernization embodied a wide range of substantive interests, levels of abstraction, and degrees of attentiveness to definitional issues (Pye 1966; So 1990).

The modernization perspective pictured evolutionary change in terms of a linear path along which all "national societies," with perhaps some minor variations, progressed over time. Rostow's (1960:54) colorful metaphor, the "take-off" into the never-never land of "high mass-consumption," epitomized this starry-eyed vision of worldwide progress. What was taken as axiomatic was that contact between "traditional" and "modern" "national societies" was a necessary condition for development of the former (see Chodak 1973). The intellectual energy expended on the modernization enterprise is legendary. "The popularity of the notion of modernization," Tipps argued, must be sought not in its clarity and precision as a vehicle of scholarly communication, but rather in its ability to evoke vague and generalized images which serve to summarize all the various transformations of social life attendant upon the rise of industrialization and the nation-state in the late eighteenth and nineteenth centuries. (1973:199)

The whole body of modernization literature tended to be deductive and often amounted to little more than abstract-definitional exercises. The tendency to reduce politics to socioeconomic variables was widespread where the state in so-called developing countries primarily functioned to help maintain the basic patterns of the social system (Kohli 1986).

The "Dependency" Response to the Modernization Paradigm

Modernization theory came under considerable criticism. Weberian scholars such as Bendix (1967) found the theoretical impulses too evolutionary, overgeneralized, and reductionist. Kesselman (1973) expressed grave reservations about the inherent conservative bias in the modernization paradigm. But it was Andre Gunder Frank (1967, 1969a, 1969b, 1972) who mounted the most direct challenge to the basic postulates underpinning the modernization paradigm. In Frank's view, the conditions of "Third World" impoverishment and deprivation cannot be understood as an *original state*, characterized by "backwardness" or "traditionalism," through which "the now developed countries passed long ago" (1969a:4). On the contrary, this condition of underdevelopment was "the result of "centuries-long participation in the process of world capitalist development" (1969a:7).

In short, "underdevelopment is not due to the survival of archaic institutions and the existence of capital shortage in regions that have remained isolated from the stream of world history....Underdevelopment was and still is generated by the very same historical process which also generated economic development: the development of capitalism itself" (1969a:9). Capitalist penetration, Frank suggested, made the economies of the underdeveloped countries dependent on those of the developed nations. The consequence was "a satellite development which [is] neither self-generating nor self-perpetuating" (1969a:8). Frank buttressed his thesis with empirical support, drawn mainly from an historical survey of Latin America indicating that "satellites experience their greatest economic development and especially their most classically capitalist industrial development if and only when their ties to their metropolis are weakest" (1969a:9–10).

The basic premises of the dependency model were originally elaborated by a group of Latin American social scientists, particularly Raul Prebisch, Teotonio

Dos Santos (1970), Fernando Cardoso (1972a, 1972b), Enzo Faletto, Anibal Quijano, Osvaldo Sunkel, Jose Luis Reyna, Edelberto Torres, Tomas Vasconi, Marcos Kaplan, Rui Mauro Marini (1969), and Pablo Gonzales-Casanova. The dependency paradigm was a response to the perceived failure of "import substitution" industrialization and to a growing disillusionment with the conventional economic explanations for Latin American backwardness (see Valenzuela and Valenzuela 1978; O'Brien 1975; Booth 1975; Roxborough 1979; So 1990). The intellectual roots for the ideas that evolved into dependency theory originated with the UN Economic Commission for Latin America (ECLA). ECLA took the view that conventional economic theory as expounded in the developed capitalist countries was inadequate for confronting the problems of underdevelopment. In explaining underdevelopment in Latin America, ECLA's first general secretary, Raul Prebisch (1950), advocated a "structuralist" perspective, that is, an appreciation of different historical situations and national contexts. He contended that Latin American underdevelopment was the result of Latin America's position in the world economy and its adoption of liberal capitalist economic policies. Prebisch's views were a continuation of a strong anti-imperialist, non-Marxist tradition in Latin American political and intellectual circles (O'Brien 1975:9–11).

The critique of the modernization paradigm gained widespread popularity in English-speaking academic circles and contributed greatly to a revitalization of Marxist thinking (Bernstein 1971, 1973; So 1990). Frank coined the phrase "the development of underdevelopment," and this catchall slogan became a point of departure for the rapid proliferation of historically grounded studies of underdeveloped regions of the globe carried out under the generic rubric of the dependency model (Bodenheimer 1970, 1971; Cockcroft, et al. 1972; Rhodes 1970; Szentes 1971). On balance, dependency theorists shared broad agreement on two main points: first, development and underdevelopment are polarized parts of a single whole, or, put another way, interdependent structures of one global system (Sunkel and Paz 1970; Sunkel 1962, 1969; Furtado 1964, 1970; Cardoso 1972a, 1972b, 1977; Cardoso and Faleto 1972). "Underdevelopment and development," Sunkel (1973:133) eloquently put it, "[are] simply the two faces of a single universal process."

Second, the condition of underdevelopment is the direct consequence of interaction between the center and the periphery of this unified system. As Sunkel and Paz (1970) argued, development is a global, structural process of change, and underdeveloped countries lack an autonomous capacity for change and growth; as a result, they are dependent for those on the center. In other words, the point of departure for the dependency perspective was that the structure of the world economy is a totality within which underdeveloped countries are subsystems so that the theory of underdevelopment becomes essentially a theory of dependence (see O'Brien 1975:12–14; Bath and James 1976; Blomstrom and Hettne 1984; Gulalp 1978). As Dos Santos (1973:76) argued:

> Dependence is a conditioning situation in which the economies of one group of countries are conditioned by the development and expansion of others. A relationship of interdependence between two or more economies or between such economies and the world trading system becomes a dependent relationship when some countries can expand through self-impulsion while others, being in a dependent position, can only expand as a reflection of the expansion of the dominant countries.

Despite its rapid rise to popularity during the late 1960s and early 1970s, the dependency perspective did not advance much beyond an "orienting framework," a heuristic device that operated as a broad umbrella under which all those who rejected the modernization paradigm could seek shelter. The *dependencistas* split into several different currents. One current stemmed from the ECLA structuralist perspective, emphasizing core-periphery relations, dependent development, and blocked growth (Sunkel 1962, 1969, 1973; Furtado 1964, 1970). Another stemmed from a more clearly defined Marxist perspective, emphasizing the theory of dependency as a subordinate field within a general Marxian theory of capitalism and, in particular, a complementary part of the theory of imperialism (Cardoso 1972a, 1972b, 1977; Marini 1969).

Dependency Theory: Refinements and Elaborations

The modernization perspective was premised on a linear and unidirectional theory of historical development where "underdevelopment" was simply the manifestation of a time lag in the realization of the natural tendency toward a homogeneous level of development through the capitalist regions of the world (Stuckey 1975:94). In other words, modernization presupposed that capitalism was the principal source of human progress and hence was not responsible for underdevelopment. What the dependency theorists accomplished was to demonstrate conclusively that these claims were patently false (Frank 1957, 1969) and, as a consequence, the dualist models for understanding economic development possessed limited utility.

Yet what cogent alternative explanation for the relationship between capitalist development and underdevelopment did dependency offer? Critics of the dependency model (and, along with it, the "development of underdevelopment" perspective) concentrated on three main weaknesses. First, the reliance on the imagery of metropolis and satellite (and core and periphery) as hermetically sealed opposites was so rigid and static that dependency theorists were unable to account for qualitative changes in the structure of the world economy over time (Kaufman, et al. 1975; McHenry 1976; Jackman 1982; Haggard 1986). Second, the dependency model over-emphasized "externally generated" world "trade-and-aid" relations at the expense of virtually ignoring "internally grounded" class relations (Smith 1986). Third, and related to the first two, the dependency perspective was not only too broad in scope but also confused and contradictory. In short, it lacked conceptual rigor (Booth 1975; Foster-Carter 1973, 1976, 1978; Chilcote 1974; Leys 1977; DeKadt and Williams 1974; Ray 1973; Nove 1974; Palma 1978; Halperin-Donghi 1982; Seers 1981; Warke 1973; Kiljunen 1989; Laite 1988). Lall (1975:808–809) argued:

> The concept of dependence is impossible to define and cannot be shown to be causally related to a continuance of underdevelopment. It is usually given an arbitrarily selective definition which picks certain features of a much broader phenomenon of international capitalist development, and its selectivity only serves to misdirect analysis and research in this area.

As O'Brien (1975:24) contended, "One looks in vain through the theories of dependency for the essential characteristics of dependency. Instead one is given a circular argument: dependent countries are those which lack the capacity for autonomous growth and they lack this because their structures are dependent ones."

A host of scholars valiantly attempted to preserve the spirit of the dependency framework and simultaneously overcome its theoretical weaknesses and conceptual deficiencies. Cardoso and Faletto (1970), for example, shared the *dependencista* point of view that "underdevelopment" could be grasped only by situating the whole development process within a globally defined historical context. Yet they emphasized that dependence was not an external variable imposed, by definition, from outside, but instead the condition of dependence was part of a whole system of social relations. They stressed that social and political aspects of the development process need to be concretely connected with the economic aspects, not just juxtaposed with them. Others, like Sunkel (1969), stressed that the perceived causes of underdevelopment were in reality the symptoms or results of the normal function of the total system; that is, underdevelopment with all its generally understood characteristics was a normal part of the whole process of capitalist development on a world scale (see O'Brien 1975:15; Fitzgerald 1983; Limqueco and McFarlane 1983). This "revised dependency" perspective differed significantly from the original *dependencista* view that "underdevelopment" signified "distorted growth," "lumpendevelopment," or, in other words, a deviation from normal, genuine, and "real" capitalist development (Baran 1957; Amin 1974, 1976).

In contrast to Frank's (1969) notion of "the development of underdevelopment," Cardoso (1972:89) suggested that "in fact, *dependency, monopoly capitalism* and *development* are not contradictory terms: there occurs a kind of dependent capitalist development in the sectors of the third world integrated into the new forms of monopolistic expansion." This idea of dependent capitalist development challenged the stagnationist theories of underdevelopment advanced by Frank (1969a, 1969b), Emmanuel (1972a, 1972b, 1974), and others (Amin 1974, 1976; Wallerstein 1974a, 1974b), which argued that contact between metropolis and satellite *necessarily* enriched the former at the expense of the latter. In contrast, this idea of dependent capitalism suggested that the world economy was governed by structural dynamics that allowed for the historical possibility of selected industrialization in regions of the globe otherwise considered "underdeveloped" (Sutcliffe 1972; Petras 1979; McMichael, Petras, and Rhodes 1974; Evans 1979).

Bill Warren (1973, 1980) offered the flip-side of the dependency paradigm. He challenged what he called the "fiction and illusion of underdevelopment" by suggesting that incorporation into the world economy offered the real possibility of capitalist growth and expansion. He also equated the dependency paradigm with "nationalist mythology," thereby hinting broadly that these ideas served the interests of the Third World petty bourgeoisie. His iconoclastic point of view provoked considerable criticism and debate (McMichael, Petras, and Rhodes 1974; Emmanuel 1974; Ahmad 1983; Gulalp 1986; Petras and Brill 1985).

Beyond Dependency: Globalist Paradigms

Critics subjected the modernization paradigm to such severe, unrelenting criticism that it simply unravelled (Bernstein 1971, 1973). All those pressing for an alternative formulation agreed that the "developed" and "underdeveloped" economies were not separate and unconnected spheres but formed parts of an integrated whole. The view that underdevelopment could be understood only as an integral part of the capitalist world economy was, of course, not a novel idea. All classical Marxist theorists recognized this point. But what was novel in the dependency model was the attempt to start from the structure of the world economy as a whole and then develop laws of motion of the dependent parts. One common theme uniting the diverse currents of the dependency theorists was that the classical Marxian theory of imperialism was Eurocentric, that is, Lenin, Bukharin, Luxemburg, and Hilferding were principally concerned with analyzing the characteristic stage of capitalism that resulted in imperialism and its effects on the European class struggle, and simultaneously overlooked the dynamics of capital accumulation in the underdeveloped regions (O'Brien 1975:20–21).

Perhaps more than anyone else inspired by the dependency model, Samir Amin (1974, 1976, 1977) carried this line of reasoning to its logical conclusion. Taking the center/periphery metaphor as his analytic point of departure, Amin contrasted normal, expanded reproduction (1974:374) with distorted development in the periphery (1974:391). For him, accumulation on a world scale spawned two polar opposite variants of capitalist development. On the one side, "normal" capitalist development (as formally outlined by Marx in *Capital*) was autocentric, characterized by a dynamic relationship between producer goods and consumer goods sectors (Marx's Departments I and II) and propelled by home-market demand. On the other side, "peripheral capitalism" was, from the outset, extroverted and externally oriented where the key sectors were export production and import consumption (1974:607). The periphery, which is characterized by blocked growth, pays tribute to the center (1974:393). Most significantly, Amin conceived of "peripheral" capitalism as a reality *sui generis*, defining it as a distortion of standard or normal development (Bernstein 1979; Smith 1980; Foster-Carter 1978:48).

The origins of the world-systems approach can also be traced to the intellectual ferment that arose out of the opposition to the modernization perspective. The insistence of world systems theorists that the global division of labor, not the individual nation-state, was the proper "unit of analysis" was a welcome conceptual advance over not only conventional developmental economics but also rigid 1930s-style orthodox Marxism. Borrowing from Polanyi (1944), Frank (1969a), Emmanuel (1972b), and the French *Annales* school, Wallerstein (1974a, 1974b, 1979, 1980, 1989) constructed a tripartite model of the functioning world system: core, periphery and semiperiphery. Others, notably Bergeson (1983) and Chase-Dunn (1989), have pushed the world-systems approach in a more structuralist direction. The well-rehearsed criticisms of the world-systems approach are legion and need not be repeated in detail here (Brenner 1977; Murray 1977; Dupuy and Truchil 1987; Thompson 1983; Brewer 1980:158–181; Gulalp 1981).

Suffice it to say that the main objections to the world-systems approach have concentrated on three areas. First, the all-encompassing definition of capitalism in world-systems theory leads necessarily to conflating all forms of capital (e.g., industrial, finance, merchants', circulating, money) and ignoring qualitative differences in the way in which dominant classes exploit subordinate classes. Without a precise and theoretically specific understanding of capitalism, class analysis falls by the wayside. Second, by assuming that because the whole (in this instance, the global system) is greater than the sum of its parts (the constituent states), the parts lead no significant existence separate from the whole, but operate simply in functionally specific ways entirely as a consequence of their place in the world system. This "tyranny of the whole," as Smith terms this way of thinking (1986:30) means that "it is sufficient to know the properties of the system as a whole to grasp the logic of its parts; no special attention need be paid to specific cases insofar as one seeks to understand the movement of the whole." The theoretical shortcoming of this methodological holism is that "it deprive[s] local histories of their integrity and specificity, thereby making local actors little more than the pawns of outside forces" (Smith 1986:35–36). Third, and related to the first two points, the world-systems perspective rests on an underlying functionalist bias in explaining the dynamics of the system over historical time where changes in parts are understood as necessary to the continual operation and reproduction of the whole system (Skocpol 1977). In addition, the world-systems model relies on Emmanuel's notion of unequal exchange in order to explain the mechanisms through which surplus generated in the periphery is siphoned to the core. Bettelheim (1972) and Pilling (1973) have raised serious theoretical objections to uncritical and undue reliance upon this notion of unequal exchange.

The Ongoing Debate with Classical Marxism

The dependency school reached the high point of its popularity during the 1960s and 1970s. To be sure, scholars influenced by the guiding threads of the *dependencista* framework (namely, that the structure of the globally integrated economic system was the key variable to be studied in order to understand the form that development had taken in the so-called Third World) were not a monolithic group. By challenging the validity of the modernization paradigm, many *dependencistas* were led inevitably to a rethinking of all existing perspectives. In particular, a growing number of scholars questioned the capacity of classical Marxist theories of imperialism to explain the evolution of the world economy in the post-World II era (Barratt Brown 1963, 1973, 1974; Kemp 1967; Brewer 1980; Owen and Sutcliffe 1972). These debates prompted some to insist upon the development of new theories to explain the new conditions. Amin (1974:20), for example, contended: "Undoubtedly, the fundamental concepts produced by Marxist analysis constitute the necessary equipment needed for a theory of accumulation on a world scale. This, however, is all that can be said, for the theory itself has not yet been created."

Yet not everyone shared Amin's bold proclamation, paraphrasing Lenin, that "everything in this field still remains to be done' (1974:21). Other scholars interpreted the collapse of the modernization paradigm as a vindication of classical Marxism. Diverse groups of scholars actively attempted to preserve the integrity of classical Marxist theories of imperialism and simultaneously recognized that global relations had changed considerably since the time of Lenin, Bukharin, and Hilferding. Paul Baran's *The Political Economy of Growth*(1957) anticipated many of the criticisms of neoclassical development economics in vogue in the 1960s and was a forerunner of the Monthly Review school, a perspective that inspired an entire generation of Marxist scholars in the United States. Borrowing from the orthodox Marxist premises of both Dobb (1937) and Sweezy (1942), Baran launched a detailed investigation of the whole "morphology of backwardness" (1957:163ff). Baran's work marked a significant shift in Marxist theory, both in its theoretical content and in the problems it addressed. Baran identified monopoly capital as the cause of economic stagnation in the advanced as well as the underdeveloped countries. He broke from the prevailing Marxist conventional wisdom by arguing that the development of capitalism in the underdeveloped countries was an essentially different process from that which the advanced countries had experienced in an earlier period of history. He argued that instead of expanding and deepening the further development of industrial capitalism, the "main task of imperialism [was] to slow down and to control the economic development of underdeveloped countries" (1957:197).

In contrast to the dependency model, which explained the process of underdevelopment in terms of the structural dependence of the underdeveloped economies upon the developed economies, Baran (1957:194) explained the origins and reproduction of the process of underdevelopment in terms of the "hardening and strengthening [of] the sway of merchant capitalism, in slowing down and indeed preventing its transformation into industrial capitalism." The result of the flow of foreign investment into the underdeveloped countries was "a political and social coalition of wealthy compradors, powerful monopolists, and large landowners dedicated to the defense of the existing feudal-mercantile order" (1957:195).

A large number of scholars, notably Magdoff (1969, 1978), Baran and Sweezy (1972), and O'Connor (1972), contributed significantly to the revitalization of intellectual interest in classical Marxist theories of imperialism. The principal accomplishment of the Monthly Review school was to demonstrate that the trade relationships and flow of investment capital from the developed countries to the periphery led to the progressive subordination of the weaker areas. Some theorists, notably Mandel (1973), charted a bold new course, seeking to incorporate the insights of the dependency model into a classical Marxist framework. Mandel's theory—developing Trotsky's earlier insights— of combined and uneven capitalist development on a world scale established a promising grand synthesis. Others (Jalee 1968, 1969, 1972) tended to ignore theories of dependence and underdevelopment altogether in constructing a model of the dynamics of world economic process.

In advocating a return to the Marxian orthodoxy of the "law of value," Geoffrey Kay (1975:103–04) roundly criticized the dependency model for its reliance upon "an eclectic combination of orthodox economic theory and revolutionary phraseology, seasoned with supposedly self-explanatory facts."

Because they "turn[ed] their backs on the law of value," Kay (1975:104) pressed the point of view that the best these "radical development economists" could achieve "was a historical account of the process of underdevelopment elaborated through empirical categories, such as *dependence, metropole* and *satellite*, which collapse into hopeless contradiction in the face of close investigation." Kay (1975:104) conceded that the dependency theorists, "in contradistinction to the classical Marxist view that capital breaks down all non-capitalist modes of production and creates 'a world after its own image,'" have shown that "capital, despite its corrosive effects, has bolstered up archaic political and economic forms through a series of alliances with powerful elements in the pre-capitalist orders." Kay's main argument was that independent merchant capital, because it failed to generate self-sustaining economic growth and development, was the principal cause of underdevelopment. His view that capital created underdevelopment, not because it exploited the underdeveloped world but because it did not exploit enough, echoed Emmanuel's (1972a 1974) argument, but without borrowing the theory of unequal exchange *toot court.*

Beyond Dependency: Modes of Production

The critique of dependency theory and the "development of underdevelopment" approach inspired the growth of "modes of production" approaches (Foster-Carter 1978). Laclau's broadside against Frank's "underdevelopment" (1969a, 1972) model can be seen, in retrospect, as the opening wedge in a wholesale attack on the postdependency globalist perspective epitomized by Frank, Wallerstein, and Amin. As Laclau (1971:24–25) saw it, Frank defined capitalism as "(a) a system of production for the market in which (b) profit constitutes the motive of production and (c) this profit is realized for the benefit of someone other than the direct producer who is thereby dispossessed of it." This conception "totally dispenses with *relations of production*" in the definition of both feudalism and capitalism (1971:25). Laclau offered an orthodox Marxist solution, but with a new twist. Unlike the classic Dobb-Sweezy debate on how the transition from feudalism to capitalism occurred in sixteenth- and seventeenth-century Europe, Laclau suggested that in the subsequent centuries the capitalist mode of production neither evolved mechanically from what preceded it nor did it necessarily dissolve it. Indeed, far from discarding and transcending precapitalist forms, capitalism not only coexisted with them but even depended on them.

The introduction of the modes of production discussion into the sociology of development literature originated with debates in economic anthropology (Clammer 1975). Scholars such as Meillassoux, Godelier, Terray, Dupre, and Rey drew their inspiration from structuralist Marxism, particularly the work of Althusser and Balibar (1970). These writers discovered, mainly from their own historically grounded field research, that as capitalism penetrated noncapitalist milieux it did not simply sweep away all archaic, backward forms of production lying in its path. Instead, as Meillassoux (1980:199) put it, pre-capitalist forms of production were "undermined and perpetuated at the same time." Others spoke of "conservation and dissolution effects" (see Poulantzas 1974:125; Bradby 1980). Thus, the idea of the articulation of modes of production was born to express the contradictory nature of hybrid forms of production containing both capitalist and noncapitalist elements (Long 1975; Taylor 1979; Wolpe 1980; Alavi, et al. 1982; Chilcote and Johnson 1983). Rey (1971, 1973) carried this line of reasoning even further. He contended that capitalism never immediately nor thoroughly eliminated the precapitalist modes of production it confronted; on the contrary, it depended upon noncapitalist forms of production and exploitation for its own reproduction and survival (see Brewer 1980:261ff).

The Marxist *Problematique* and Capitalist Development

These ongoing debates regarding the nature of capitalist development originate with the classical Marxist paradox, namely, how to explain why capitalist development did not unfold in identical fashion everywhere that capitalism penetrated. The effort to transform Lenin's conjunctural analysis of intra-imperialist rivalry around World War I into a general theory of imperialism *tout court* produced a range of insoluble riddles for Marxism. Leninist-inspired perspectives fail on two main counts: first, their false separation between imperialism and capitalism, thereby giving solace to the misplaced idea that nation-states are the principal carriers of imperialist and capitalist relations; and, second, the monocausal explanation for capitalist expansion (the "export of capital" thesis) is too simplistic to account for historical variation. By taking the world economy as its analytic starting point, the dependency perspective successfully differentiated itself from the faulty "stages" and "national economy" mind-set prevailing within Marxist-Leninist thinking in the 1960s.

Yet in their effort to build a formal theory of underdevelopment, the dependency theorists place undue reliance on one-sided schemes that identify capitalist penetration of the periphery with economic stagnation. These mechanistic models fail to fit with existing historical evidence. Similarly, the globalist paradigm, particularly the world-systems perspective, not only reproduces the errors of the dependency school but also falls into the trap of methodological holism; that is, it explains the dynamics of core-periphery relations solely in terms of the functional requirements of the whole capitalist system. Finally, the "modes of production" framework correctly points to historical specificity, yet suffers from an undue dependence on structural determination and mechanistic rigidity.

What remains to be explained is how and why capitalist development takes shape in a highly heterogeneous and uneven fashion on a world scale. The starting point for the Marxist *problematique* is the proposition that capitalism is an exploitative system where the particular structural mix of social-property relations enables the owning classes to siphon surplus labor from the propertyless classes. The central organizing principle of Marxist theory is that capitalist development entails both structural and class dynamics, where the unfolding of the historically specific structural and class contradictions ensures that the pattern of combined and uneven capitalist development leaves the appearance of "rich" and "poor" nations, regions, and areas on a world scale (Palloix 1971, 1973; Murray 1971; Hymer 1972; see Radice 1975).

References

Ahmad, Aijaz. 1983. "Imperialism and Progress." Pp. 33–73 in *Theories of Development: Mode of Production or Dependency?*, ed. Ronald Chilcote and Dale Johnson. Beverly Hills: Sage.

Alavi, Hamza, et al., ed. 1982. *Capitalism and Colonial Production*. London: Croom Helm.

Almond, Gabriel, and James Coleman, ed. 1960. *The Politics of the Developing Areas*. Princeton: Princeton University Press.

Althusser, Louis, and Etienne Balibar. 1970. *Reading Capital*. London: NLB.

Amin, Samir. 1974. *Accumulation on a World Scale: A Critique of the Theory of Underdevelopment*. Vols. I and II. New York: Monthly Review Press.

———. 1976. *Unequal Development*. New York: Monthly Review Press.

———. 1977. *Imperialism and Unequal Development*. New York: Monthly Review Press.

Apter, David. 1965. *The Politics of Modernization*. Chicago: University of Chicago Press.

Avineri, Shlomo, ed. 1969. *Karl Marx on Colonialism & Modernization*. New York: Doubleday Anchor.

Banfield, Edward. 1958. *The Moral Basis of a Backward Society*. New York: Free Press.

Baran, Paul. 1957. *The Political Economy of Growth*. New York: Monthly Review Press.

Barratt Brown, Michael. 1963. *After Imperialism*. London: Merlin Press.

———. 1973. "A Critique of Marxist Theories of Imperialism." Pp. 35–70 in *Studies in the Theory of Imperialism*, ed. Roger Owen and Bob Sutcliffe. London: Longman.

———. 1974. *The Economics of Imperialism*. Harmondsworth, England: Penguin.

Bath, C. Richard, and Dilmus James. 1976. "Dependency Analysis of Latin America: Some Criticisms, Some Suggestions." *Latin American Research Review* 11(3):3–54.

Beckford, George. 1972. *Persistent Poverty: Underdevelopment in Plantation Economies in the Third World*. New York: Oxford University Press.

Bendix, Reinhard. 1967. "Tradition and Modernity Reconsidered." *Comparative Studies in Society and History* 9 (April):292–346.

Bergeson, Albert. 1983. *The Crises of the Capitalist World Economy*. Bervely Hills: Sage.

Bernstein, Henry. 1971. "Modernization Theory and the Sociological Study of Development." *Journal of Development Studies* 7(2):141–160.

———, ed. 1973. *Underdevelopment and Development: The Third World Today*. Harmondsworth, England: Penguin.

———. 1979. "Sociology of Underdevelopment versus the Sociology of Development?" Pp. 77–106 in *Development Theory: Four Critical Studies*, ed. David Lehmann. London: Frank Cass.

Bettelheim, Charles. 1972. "Theoretical Comments." Pp. 271–322 in Arghiri Emmanuel, *Unequal Exchange*. New York: Monthly Review Press.

Blomstrom, Magnus, and Bjorn Hettne. 1984. *Development Theory in Transition*. London: Zed Books.

Bodenheimer, Suzanne. 1970. "The Ideology of Developmentalism: American Political Science's Paradigm Surrogate for Latin American Studies" *Berkeley Journal of Sociology* 15:115–127.

———. 1971. "Dependency and Underdevelopment: The Roots of Latin American Underdevelopment." Pp. 155–182 in *Readings in U.S. Imperialism*, ed. K.T. Fann and Donald Clark Hodges. Boston: Porter Sargent.

Booth, David. 1975. "Andre Gunder Frank: An Introduction and Appreciation." Pp. 50–85 in *Beyond the Sociology of Development*, ed. Ivar Oxaal, Tony Barnett, and David Booth. London: Routledge and Kegan Paul.

Bradby, Barbara. 1980. "The Destruction of Natural Economy." Pp. 93–127 in *The Articulation of Modes of Production*, ed. Harold Wolpe. London: Routledge and Kegan Paul.

Brenner, Robert. 1977. "The Origins of Capitalism: A Critique of Neo-Smithian Marxism." *New Left Review* 107(July–August):25–87.

Brewer, Anthony. 1980. *Marxist Theories of Imperialism: A Critical Survey*. London: Routledge and Kegan Paul.

Bukharin, Nikolai. 1966. *Imperialism and World Economy*. New York: Howard Fertig.

Cairncross, John. 1953. *Home and Foreign Investments 1870–1913* Cambridge: Cambridge University Press.

Cardoso, Fernando. 1972a. "Dependent Capitalist Development in Latin America." *New Left Review* 74(July–August):83–95.

———. 1972b. *Estado y Sociedad en America Latina*. Buenos Aires: Ediciones Nueva Vision.

———. 1973. "Associated Dependent Development: Theoretical and Practical Implications."In *Authoritarian Brazil: Origins, Policies, and Future*, ed. Alfred Stepan. New Haven: Yale University Press.

———. 1977. "The Consumption of Dependency Theory in the United States." *Latin American Research Review* 12(3):7–24.

Cardoso, Fernando Henrique, and Enzo Faletto. 1972. *Dependencia y Desarrollo en America Latina*. Mexico, D.F.: Siglo Veintiuno Editores.

Chase-Dunn, Christopher. 1989. *Global Formation: Structures of the World-Economy*. London: Basil Blackwell.

Chilcote, Ronald. 1974. "Dependency: A Critical Synthesis of the Literature." *Latin American Perspectives* 1(1):4–29.

Chilcote, Ronald, and Dale Johnson, eds. 1983. *Theories of Development: Mode of Production or Dependency?* Beverly Hills: Sage.

Chokak, Szymon. 1973. *Societal Development: Five Approaches with Conclusions from Comparative Analysis*. New York: Oxford University Press.

Clammer, John. 1975. "Economic Anthropology and the Sociology of Development: 'Liberal' Anthropolgy and Its French Critics." Pp. 208–228 in *Beyond the Sociology of Development*, ed. Ivar Oxaal, Tony Barnett, and David Booth. London: Routledge and Kegan Paul.

Cockcroft, James, Andre Gunder Frank, and Dale Johnson, eds. 1972. *Dependence and Underdevelopment*. New York: Doubleday Anchor.

De Kadt, E., and E. Williams, eds. 1974. *Sociology and Development*. London: Tavistock.

Dobb, Maurice. 1937. *Political Economy and Capitalism*. London: Routledge and Kegan Paul.

Dos Santos, Theotonio. 1973. "The Crisis of Development Theory and the Problem of Dependence in Latin America." Pp. 57–80 in *Underdevelopment & Development: The Third World Today*, ed. Henry Bernstein. London: Penguin.

———. 1970. "The Structure of Dependence." *American Economic Review* 60 (2):231–36.

Dupuy, Alex, and Barry Truchil. 1987. "The Limits of the World Systems Perspective." Pp. 117–35 in *Recapturing Marxism*, ed. Rhonda Levine and Jerry Lembcke. New York: Praeger.

Eisenstadt, S.N. 1960. *Modernization: Protest and Change*. Englewood Cliffs: Prentice Hall.

———. 1965. *Essays on Comparative Instituitions*. New York: Wiley.

———, ed. 1970. *Readings in Social Evolution and Development*. Oxford: Pergamon Press.

Emmanuel, Arghiri. 1972a. *Unequal Exchange: A Study of the Imperialism of Trade*. New York: Monthly Review Press.

———. 1972b. "White Settler Colonialism and the Myth of Investment Imperialism." *New Left Review* 73 (May–June):35–57.

———. 1974. "Myths of Development versus Myths of Underdevelopment." *New Left Review* 85 (May–June): 61–82.

Evans, Peter. 1979. *Dependent Development: The Alliance of Multinationl, State, and Local Capital in Brazil*. Princeton: Princeton University Press.

Fitzgerald, F.T. 1983. "Sociology of Development," Pp. in *Neo-Marxist Theories of Development*, ed. Peter Limqueco and Bruce McFarlane. London: Croom Helm.

Foster-Carter, Aidan. 1973. "Neo-Marxist Approaches to Development and Underdevelopment." *Journal of Contemporary Asia* 3(1):7–33.

———. 1976. "From Rostow to Gunder Frank: Conflicting Paradigms in the Analysis of Underdevelopment." *World Development* 4(3):167–80.

———. 1978. "The Modes of Production Controversy" *New Left Review* 107(January–February):47–78.

Frank, Andre Gunder. 1967. *Capitalism and Underdevelopment in Latin America: Historical Studies of Chile and Brazil*. New York: Monthly Review Press.

———. 1969a. "The Development of Underdevelopment." Pp. 3–20 in *Latin America: Underdevelopment or Revolution*, ed. Andre Gunder Frank. New York: Monthly Review Press.

———. 1969b. "Sociology of Development or Underdevelopment of Sociology." Pp. 21–94 in *Latin America: Underdevelopment or Revolution*, ed. Andre Gunder Frank. New York: Monthly Review Press.

———. 1972. *LumpenBourgeoisie: Lumpendevelopment: Dependence, Class, and Politics in Latin America*. New York: Monthly Review Press.

———. 1977. "Dependence Is Dead, Long Live Dependence and the Class Struggle: An Answer to Critics." *World Development* 5(4):355–70.

Furtado, Celso. 1964. *Development and Underdevelopment: A Structural View of the Problems of Development and Underdeveloped Countries*. Berkeley: University of California Press.

———. 1970. *Economic Development of Latin America: A Survey from Colonial Times to the Cuban Revolution*. Cambridge: Cambridge University Press.

Gallagher, John, and Ronald Robinson, with Alice Denny. 1961. *Africa and the Victorians: The Climax of Imperialism*. New York: St. Martin's Press.

Gonzalez-Casanova, Pablo. 1965. "Internal Colonialism and National Development." *Studies in Comparative International Development* 1(4):27–37.

Gulalp, Haldun. 1978. *Imperialism and Underdevelopment*. Development Studies Occasional Paper No. 26. School of Development Studies, University of East Anglia.

———. 1981. "Frank and Walllerstein Revisited: A Contribution to Brenner's Critique." *Journal of Contemporary Asia* 11(2):169–88.

———. 1986. "Debate on Capitalism and Development: The Theories of S. Amin and B. Warren" *Capital and Class* 28(Spring):139–59.

Haggard, Stephan. 1986. "The Newly Industrializing Countries in the International System." *World Politics* 38(January):343–70.

Hagen, Everet. 1962. *On the Theory of Social Change*. Homewood, Ill.: Dorsey Press.

Halperin-Donghi, Tulio. 1982. "'Dependency Theory' and Latin American Historiography." *Latin American Research Review* 17(1):115–30.

Hilferding, Rudolph. 1910. *Finanzkapital*. Vienna: Vorwarts.

Hobson, J.A. 1938. *Imperialism: A Study*. London: Allen and Unwin.

Hoselitz, Bert, ed. 1952. *The Progress of Underdeveloped Areas*. Chicago: University of Chicago Press.

———. 1960. *Sociologicial Factors in Economic Development*. Glencoe: Free Press.

Hoselitz, Bert, and Wilbert E. Moore, eds. 1963. *Industrialization and Society*. Paris: UNESCO.

Huntington, Samuel. 1969. *Political Order in Changing Societies*. New Haven: Yale University Press.

———. 1971. "The Change to Change." *Comparative Politics* 3(April):283–322.

Hymer, Stephen. 1972. "The Multinational Corporation and the Law of Uneven Development." Pp. 113–140 in *Economics and World Order from the 1970s to the 1990s*, ed. J. Bhagwati. New York: Collier-Macmillan.

Jackman, Robert. 1982. "Dependence on Foreign Investment and Economic Growth in the Third World." *World Politics* 34(January):175–98.

Jalee, Pierre. 1968. *The Pillage of the Third World*. New York: Monthly Review Press.

———. 1969. *The Third World in the World Economy*. New York: Monthly Review Press.

———. 1972. *Imperialism in the Seventies*. New York: Joseph Okpaku Press.

Kaufman, Robert, H.I.Chernotsky, and B. Geller. 1975. "A Preliminary Test of the Theory of Dependency." *Comparative Politics* 7(3):303–30.

Kay, Geoffrey. 1975. *Development and Underdevelopment*. London: Macmillan.

Kemp, Tom. 1967. *Theories of Imperialism*. London: Dobson.

Kesselman, Mark. 1973. "Order or Movement? The Literature of Political Development as Ideology." *World Politics* 26(October):139–54.

Kiernan, Victor. 1967. "Marx and India." Pp. 159–190 in *The Socialist Register 1967*, ed. Ralph Miliband and John Saville. London: The Merlin Press.

———. 1974. *Marxism and Imperialism*. London: Edward Arnold.

Kiljunen, Kimmo. 1989. "Toward a Theory of the International Division of Industrial Labour." *World Development* 17(1):109–38.

Kohli, Atul. 1986. "Introduction." Pp. 3–21 in *The State and Development in the Third World*, ed. Atul Kohli. Princeton: Princeton University Press.

Laclau, Ernesto. 1971. "Feudalism and Capitalism in Latin America." *New Left Review* 67(May–June):19–38.

Laite, J. 1988. "The Sociology of Development." Pp. 13–49 in *Perspectives on Development*, ed. P.F. Leeson and M.M. Minogue. Manchester: Manchester University Press.

Lall, Sanjaya. 1975. "Is 'Dependence' a Useful Concept in Analyzing Underdevelopment?" *World Development* 3(11–12):799–810.

LaPalombara, Joseph, ed. 1964. *Bureaucracy and Political Development*. Princeton: Princeton University Press.

Lenin, V.I. 1939. *Imperialism: The Highest Stage of Capitalism*. New York: International Publishers.

Learner, Daniel. 1957. *The Passing of Traditional Society: Modernizing the Middle East*. Glencoe: Free Press.

Levy, Marion. 1953. "Contrasting Factors in the Modernization of China and Japan." *Economic Development and Cultural Change* 2(3):161–179.

———. 1966. *Modernization and the Structure of Societies*. Vols. I and II. Princeton: Princeton University Press.

Leys, Colin. 1977. "Underdevelopment and Dependency: Critical Notes." *Journal of Contemporary Asia*, 7(1):92–107.

Limqueco, Peter, and Bruce McFarlane, eds. 1983. *Neo-Marxist Theories of Development*. London: Croom Helm.

Long, Norman. 1975. "Structural Dependency, Modes of Production and Economic Brokerage in Rural Peru." Pp. 253–82 in *Beyond the Sociology of Development*, ed. Ivar Oxaal, Tony Barnett, and David Booth. London: Routledge and Kegan Paul.

Luxemburg, Rosa. 1951. *The Accumulation of Capital*. London: Routlege and Kegan Paul.

McClelland, David. 1960. *The Achieving Society*. Princeton: Van Nostrand.

McCord, William. 1965. *The Springtime of Freedom: Evolution of Developing Societies*. New York: Oxford University Press.

McHenry, D.E. 1976. "The Underdevelopment Theory: A Case-Study from Tanzania." *Journal of Modern African Studies* 14(1):621–36.

McMichael, Philip, James Petras, and Robert Rhodes. 1974. "Imperialism and the Contradictions of Development." *New Left Review* 85(May–June):83–104.

Magdoff, Harry. 1969. *The Age of Imperialism*. New York: Monthly Review Press.

———. 1978. *Imperialism: From the Colonial Age to the Present*. New York: Monthly Review Press.

Mandel, Ernest. 1973. *Late Capitalism*. London: New Left Books.

Marini, R.M. 1969. *Subdesarrollo y Revolucion*. Mexico, D.F.: Siglo XXI Editores.

Marx, Karl. 1965. *Capital*. Vol. I. Moscow: Progress Publishers.

Marx, Karl, and Friedrich Engels. 1939. *The Communist Manifesto*. Moscow: Progess Publishers.

Meillassoux, Claude. 1980. "From Reproduction to Production: A Marxist Approach to Economic Anthropology." Pp. 189–201 in *The Articulation of Modes of Production*, ed. Harold Wolpe. London: Routledge & Kegan Paul.

Murray, Martin J. 1977. "Recent Views on the Transition from Feudalism to Capitalism." *Socialist Revolution* 34(July–August):64–91.

Murray, Robin. 1971. "The Internationalisation of Capital and the Nation State." *New Left Review* 67(May–June):84–109.

Nove, Alec. 1974. "On Reading Andre Gunder Frank." *Journal of Development Studies* 10(3–4):445–55.

O'Brien, Philip. 1975. "A Critique of Latin American Theories of Dependency." Pp. 7–27 in *Beyond the Sociology of Development*, ed. Ivar Oxaal, Tony Barnett, and David Booth. London: Routledge & Kegan Paul.

O'Connor, James. 1972. "The Meaning of Economic Imperialism." Pp. 23–68 in *Readings in U.S. Imperialism*, ed. K.T. Fann and Donald Clark Hodges. Boston: Porter Sargent.

Owen, Roger, and Bob Sutcliffe, eds. 1972. *Studies in the Theory of Imperialism*. London: Longman.

Palliox, Christian. 1971. *L'Economie mondiale Capitaliste*. Paris: Maspero.

———. 1973. *Les Firmes Multinationales et le Proces d'Internationalisation*. Paris: Maspero.

Palma, G. 1978. "Dependency: A Formal Theory of Underdevelopment or a Methodology for the Analysis of Concrete Situations of Underdevelopment?" *World Development* 6(7–8):881–924.

Petras, James, eds. 1979. *Critical Perspectives on Imperialism and Social Classes in the Third World*. New York: Monthly Review Press.

Petras, James, and Howard Brill. 1985. "The Tyranny of Globalism." *Journal of Contemporary Asia* 15(4):403–20.

Pilling, Geoffrey. 1973. "Imperialism, Trade and 'Unequal Exchange': The Work of Aghiri Emmanuel." *Economy and Society* 2(2):164–85.

Polanyi, Karl. 1944. *The Great Transformation: The Political and Economic Origins of Our Time* . New York: Rinehart.

Poulantzas, Nicos. 1974. *Classes in Contemporary Capitalism* . London: New Left Books.

Prebish, Raul. 1950. *The Economic Development of Latin America and its Principal Problems* . New York: United Nations.

Pye, Lucian. 1962. *Politics, Personality, and Nation Building* . New Haven: Yale University Press.

———. 1966. *Aspects of Political Development*. Boston: Little, Brown.

Pye, Lucien, and Sidney Verba, eds. 1965. *Political Culture and Political Development* . Princeton: Princeton University Press.

Ray, D. 1973. "The Dependency Model of Latin American Underdevelpment: Three Basic Fallacies." *Journal of Interamerican Studies and World Affairs* 15(February):4–20.

Rey, Pierre-Philippe. 1971. *Colonialisme, Neo-colonialisme, et Transition au Capitalisme* . Paris: Maspero.

———. 1973. *Les Alliance de Classes*. Paris: Maspero.

Radice, Hugo, ed. 1975. *International Firms and Modern Imperialism* . London: Penguin.

Rhodes, Robert, ed. 1970. *Imperialism and Underdevelopment: A Reader* . New York: Monthly Review Press.

Rostow, Walt Whitman. 1952. *The Process of Economic Growth*. New York: Norton.

———. 1960. *The Stages of Economic Growth: A Non-Communist Manifesto* . Cambridge: Cambridge University Press.

Roxborough, Ian. 1979. *Theories of Underdevelopment*. London: Macmillan.

Seers, Dudley. 1981. *Dependency Theory: A Critical Reassessment* . London: Francis Printer.

Semmel, Bernard. 1970. *The Rise of Free Trade Imperialism: Classical Political Economy, the Empire of Free Trade, and Imperialism 1750–1850* . Cambridge: Cambridge University Press.

Shils, Edward. 1962. *Political Development in New States* . 'S-Gravenhage: Mouton.

Skocpol, Theda. 1977. "Wallerstein's World Capitalist System: A Theoretical and Historical Critique." *American Journal of Sociology* 82(5):1075–90.

Smelser, Neil. 1963. "Mechanisms of Change and Adjustment to Change." Pp. 32–54 in *Industrialization and Society*, ed. Bert Hoselitz and Wilbert E. Moore. Paris: UNESCO.

Smith, Sheila. 1980. "The Ideas of Samir Amin: Theory or Tautology?" *Journal of Development Studies* 17(1):7–21.

Smith, Tony. 1986. "The Underdevelopment of Development Literature." Pp. 25–66 in *The State and Development in the Third World*, ed. Atul Kohli. Princeton: Princeton University Press.

So, Alvin. 1990. *Social Change and Development: Modernization, Dependency, and World-Systems Theory*. London: Sage.

Strackey, John. 1960. *The End of Empire*. New York: Praeger.

Stuckey, Barbara. 1975. "Spatial Analysis and Economic Development," *Development and Change* 6(1):89–101.

Sunkel, Osvaldo. 1962. *Capitalismo Transnacional y Desintegracion Nacional en America Latina* . Buenos Aires: Nueva Vision.

———. 1969. "National Development Policy and External Dependence in Latin America." *Journal of Development Studies* 6(1):34–57.

———. 1973. "Transnational Capitalism and National Disintegration in Latin America." *Social and Economic Studies* 22(1):132–76.

Sunkel, Osvaldo, and P. Paz. 1970. *El Subdesarrollo Latinoamericano y la Teoria del Desarrollo* . Mexico, D.F.: Siglo XXI editores.

Sutcliffe, Bob. 1972. "Imperialism and Industrialisation in the Third World." Pp. 171–192 in *Studies in the Theory of Imperialism*, ed. Roger Owen and Bob Sutcliffe. London: Longman.

Szentes, Tomas. 1971. *The Political Economy of Underdevelopment* . Budapest: Akademiai Kiado.

Taylor, John. 1979. *From Modernization to Modes of Production: A Critique of the Sociologies of Development and Underdevelopment*. New York: Macmillan.

Tipps, Dean. 1973. "Modernization Theory and the Study of National Societies: A Critical Perspective." *Comparative Studies in Society and History* 15(2):199–226.

Thompson, William. 1983. *Contending Approaches to World Systems Analysis*. Beverley Hills: Sage.

Valenzuela, Samuel, and Arturo Valenzuela, "Modernization and Dependency: Alternative Perspectives in the Study of Latin American Underdevelopment." *Comparative Politics* 10(July):535–57.

Wallerstein, Immanuel. 1974a. "The Rise and Future Demise of the World Capitalist System: Concepts for Comparative Analysis." *Comparative Studies in Society and History* 15(4):387–415.

———. 1974b. *The Modern World System I: Capitalist Agriculture and the Origins of the European World-Economy in the Sixteenth Century*. New York: Academic Press.

———. 1979. *The Capitalist World-Economy*. Cambridge: Cambridge University Press.

———. 1980. *The Modern World System II: Mercantilism and the Consolidation of the European World-Economy 1600–1750*. New York: Academic Press.

———. 1989. *The Modern World System III: The Second Era of Great Expansion of the Capitalist World-Economy 1730–1840s*. New York: Academic Press.

Warke, Thomas. 1973. "The Marxian Theory of Underdevelopment: A Review Article." *Journal of Developing Areas* 7(4):699–710.

Warren, Bill. 1973. "Imperialism and Capitalist Industrialization." *New Left Revew* 81(September–October):3–45.

———. 1980. *Imperialism: Pioneer of Capitalism*. London: Verso.

Wolpe, Harold. 1980. "Introduction." Pp. 1–44 in *The Articulation of Modes of Production*, ed. Harold Wolpe. London: Routledge and Kegan Paul.

LABOR:

LABOR'S CRISIS AND THE CRISIS OF LABOR STUDIES:TOWARD A RETHEORIZED SOCIOLOGY OF LABOR

Jerry Lembcke,
Art Jipson,
and
Patrick McGuire

Advancing the interests and improving the lives of working people have been at the heart of Marxism since its inception. From the first joint writings of Marx and Engels through the 1960s, radical intellectuals (including academics) have analyzed the course and implications of the ongoing struggles between owners and workers. Such efforts have provided tactical insights and strategic guidance to protect and advance the interests of workers, the unemployed, and the unemployable—in other words, the interests of the vast majority of society.

About thirty-five years ago in the United States, unions represented about one-third of all workers. They now have reached an all-time low, representing only 12 percent of industrial workers and only 16 percent of all workers if one includes public-sector workers. If the decline in the rate of membership continues, by the year 2000 unions may represent only 5 percent of all workers (Editors 1990).

Reflecting on the decline in union membership and the political image and power of labor, Gordon, Edwards, and Reich (1982) asked: Why have workers become so quiescent? As the decay of economic and social life accelerated during the era of Reagan and Bush, bankers, academics, and think tanks analyzed the nature of U.S. economic problems and offered suggestions about how to resolve the economic crisis. Everyone, that is, except labor. The magnitude of the problems and the implications of the proposed solutions made the absence of an articulated labor perspective all the more serious. After a hundred years of labor activism, we reach a point in history where one must ask: Is labor capable of playing a role in resolving this crisis? The impotent response of organized labor to this crisis seems to imply that there is a crisis both of activism and of theory within the labor movement (Arnesen 1990).

After reviewing Marxist theorizing on labor before 1960, we examine the Marxist-influenced labor theories from 1960 through the early 1980s. We show that the "radical political economists" and "new labor historians" failed to break with the theoretical and methodological assumptions of neoclassical economics and pluralist sociology. This failure is at the heart of the crisis of labor studies. Ironically, these same assumptions were a crucial factor in these new theories receiving significant attention from mainstream sociologists because they resonated with the pluralistic assumptions of academic sociology. Finally, we analyze the strands of an emerging Marxist-influenced approach to labor studies that we believe can provide new starting points for a sociology of labor, as well as new insights into the origins of, and potential responses to, the crisis of labor.

Classical Marxist Contributions to the Labor Question

A review of Marxist labor studies is more than a history of that approach. It lays the basis for allowing us to understand how and where the analysts of labor began to become detached from labor and the labor movement. Thus, we are both reviewing the paths that led to the present state of analysis and detailing how analysts—in part because of concrete conditions in the society and the labor movement and in part because of academic methods and theories that limited their analyses—contributed (by their actions and inactions) to a breakdown of this otherwise progressive interchange. By identifying the missteps of analysts, we hope to help reframe the sociology of labor so that it may contribute to a more dynamic labor movement and help address the current economic crisis in ways that are beneficial to society at large. The first step in this process involves reviewing the basic principles in the classical Marxist framework and the initial debates about the role of workers in the society.

For Marx, humanity survives through labor and meets its needs by transforming its environment: "By producing their means of existence men indirectly produce their material life" (1976:17). People adapt to their environment by forming complex social groups including the development of divisions of labor. These divisions of labor yield differential access to scarce resources, differential relations to the means of production, and thus lead to the formation of classes and class fractions. As Marx argued: "With the division of labour is given simultaneously the...unequal distribution, both quantitative and qualitative of labour and its productions, hence property" (1976:56).

Thus, for Marx, each specific mode of production has its own division of labor. The capitalist mode of production is characterized by workers who have only their labor power and skills to sell and by capitalists who own the means of production—the land, factories, and equipment—and who develop these resources for their own benefit. According to Marx and subsequent Marxists, all value is created by labor power, and in securing a profit the capitalist withholds part of the value of the worker by paying a wage less than the full value of that labor (1964:25).

While Marx expressed this theory in a humanistic manner, it is not a theory grounded in ethical imperatives. Instead, beginning as an insight in *Wages, Price, and Profit* (1975), it was subsequently refined and extended through Marx's life, culminating as a fully articulated scientific theory of economic life in Marx's multivolume *magnum opus Capital* (1978).

Marx described the dichotomy between the interests of owners and workers as resulting in class antagonisms. Those antagonisms became both the basis of new worker exploitation by owners and the seed of progressive and possibly revolutionary change. Trade unions were seen as the key to sowing that seed more widely. Marx understood that as trade unions initially arose within specific industries, they were an organized expression of workers forced to combine in response to and against capitalists who had already combined in the collective pursuit of greed. In *The Communist Manifesto* (1968), Marx and Engels noted that while unions were sometimes effective in combatting the actions of the capitalist, their effectiveness was often limited by their fragmented and localized nature. Nevertheless, they recognized that workers' experiences in unions were crucial to creating a sense of classwide agency (1968:18–9).

Marx and Engels were critical of worker's political parties, which they felt all too often distracted workers from the pursuit of class interests. They were also critical of unions which sought only wage increases. Nevertheless, they recognized the positive behavioral impact of the trade union's apprenticeship system in teaching discipline and knowledge of collective interests and in promoting worker's self-government and autonomy. Union-led strikes served the structural role of clarifying class interests. By bringing together workers from various nations, regions, and industries, unions served to increase class consciousness and class power. They also served as a site of organized class opposition during periods of repression (1965:140, 411, 477, 215, 174, 176, 261).

For Marx and Engels, unions constituted the centralized organizational form needed to challenge the organized capitalist class successfully. Unions constituted an agency that in the immediate context functioned to challenge capitalist initiatives and attract new members, and simultaneously to create the material and ideological basis for a structural transformation of society.

Marx and Engels attacked their conservative critics within the socialist movement who argued that unions were destructive combinations that undermined worker skills (1965:140, 215, 293). Rejecting Marx's call for the revolutionary overthrow of capitalism as extreme, and claiming that workers would not willingly leap into the unknown, these critics posed simplistic notions of evolutionary change based on moralism and a belief in progressive evolution— factors Marx believed functioned to pacify and disempower workers. Marx's recognition of the radical potential of trade unions was an important break with these functionalist analyses, which were predicated on economic, political, social, biological, or moral determinism.

Marx also criticized the anarchist Proudhon, who argued that wage increases were simply passed along to worker/consumers; that strikes only led to mechanization which displaced workers (1973:145–49); and that trade unions should seek to become self-management societies (Woodcock 1956). Later anarchists such as Bakunin worked from the assumption that humans have a "natural instinct" that makes them desire freedom and liberty. They argued that such instincts lead to a "natural organization" of people founded on equality. Because organized authority structures run counter to these "instincts," the masses will rise up and smash the state and all other institutional sources of domination and establish a new social order organized around these "instincts" (Guerin 1970).

While Marx and Bakunin disagreed on the motives and goals of the anti-capitalist revolution, they agreed that the most desirable forum for mobilizing worker's consciousness and capacity for organized action was the trade union. Bakunin placed more faith in the worker's own appraisals of the possibilities and potential for change. He and his supporters argued that the discipline and hierarchy of established trade unions were counterproductive and that Marx's emphasis on the industrial working class divided the "natural enemies" of capitalism. Seeking a more inclusive organization, anarchists argued for a single union embracing millions of producers opposed to the capitalists, who only stole from the productive efforts of others (Kropotkin 1899). Anarchists perceived the trade unions as both the "combat unions in the class struggle for better working conditions, and associations of producers which serve to transform capitalist society" (International Anarchist Congress 1907:1).

These disagreements over whether unions were a forum for defining consciousness or one in which consciousness was taught, the desirability of centralized authority, and the class composition of those allying to resist capitalism resulted in a fight over control of the First International that ultimately destroyed the International. These basic differences between Marxists and anarchists have continued into this century (in various forms) and have continuously weakened the trade union movement. Indeed, aspects of the anarchists' critique were reflected in several important debates that occurred*within* Marxism during the early years of this century.

Reflecting on the experience of the revolutionary movement in the backward conditions of the Russian Empire, V.I. Lenin argued that the labor movement must be guided by a disciplined cadre of revolutionaries that would provide workers with the intellectual leadership needed to achieve a more radical outlook (1905). Left to their own devices, he argued, labor movements came to reflect a "trade union consciousness" that limited the revolutionary potential of workers by producing only reformist ideas. He argued that without guidance workers would lose sight of the real goals of working-class struggles and become preoccupied with wage issues and attempts to influence the government into promoting their general welfare (Lenin 1970).

Rosa Luxemburg, however, argued that a "true" revolution required the support of the masses. She criticized Lenin for not paying sufficient attention to creating and promoting the norms of democracy within the working class, a practice that was to lead to disastrous consequences for the Bolshevik party and Russian communism. Starting from an economic analysis that demonstrated the tendency of the capitalist economy to breakdown (1963), she argued that workers' consciousness resulted from their recognizing the existence and consequences of the on-going and destructive contradictions of capitalism. For Luxemburg, class consciousness was the direct product of class struggle. The type of class struggle that best highlighted class issues and class contradictions for workers and that broke through the barriers and illusions erected by the capitalist state, she argued, was the mass strike.

Luxemburg believed that trade union participation was an important stage in the creation of worker consciousness and the establishment of unity among worker groups. In supporting mass strikes and helping to identify the contradictions of capitalism, the revolutionary socialist program could become infused into the daily struggle of the masses, and the ultimate goal of revolution would become part of their immediate concerns (Waters 1970:202–07). She argued that the movement toward socialism must be expressed in the will of the people learned in trade union struggles, not the inculcation of ideas by a centrally organized revolutionary elite.

While Luxemburg has falsely been called an anarchist, it is clear that her thought was influenced by anarchism (Geras 1967). Emphasizing the importance of democratic values and mass consciousness, she opposed Lenin's vanguard approach and criticized Lenin's actions and the potential totalitarian effects of the Russian Revolution in key pamphlets (Luxemburg 1972).

Other Marxists also argued that the focus of revolutionary activity should be based in the real life of workers. Whereas the anarchists believed in "a movement without a head," the Council Communists saw the labor movement and shop-floor life as the basis for revolutionary activity. Anton Pannekoek, a Dutch theorist, argued that the working class must organize itself first in conflict with its employers and then (as such struggles developed) in the construction of a system of social production controlled by the workers (1975:377). He asserted that socialism was the direct non-mediated control of production by workers and that mass action (including but not limited to trade unionism) could help develop the solidarity and understanding necessary to transform society.

Building upon this emphasis on self-management, Pannekoek argued that workers did not need to have a fully formulated idea of socialism before beginning to struggle against capitalism. He saw trade unions, spontaneous wildcat strikes, and general strikes consuming industries and nations. Revolutions would lead to workers' councils, which would manage each factory. These developments would eventually culminate in the creation of representative assemblies of workers, directly elected from the shop floors of factories around the world.

Synthesizing these debates, the Italian Marxist Antonio Gramsci accepted Lenin's criticism of trade unions as inherently conservative and unsuited for mobilizing worker consciousness. Yet he joined Luxemburg in rejecting Lenin's emphasis on party discipline and the development of a vanguard, emphasizing instead the importance of democratic practices and consciousness formation. He built on the insight of Luxemburg and the Council Communists that revolutionary activity arose directly from the content of work and from shop-floor struggles. Gramsci adapted the ideas of the Council Communists and helped form workers' councils in factories—organizations he viewed as the model and training ground for a future proletarian state. Yet elements of Lenin's concerns were also present in Gramsci's formulation. Reflecting on the rising tide of fascism in Italy from 1917 to 1922, he rejected the notion of consciousness arising from spontaneous uprisings and emphasized the role of the Communist party in actively encouraging the development of class consciousness. He believed that ultimately workers' councils must be linked into a central hierarchy (1971).

Both the presence and absence of Marxist theory has profoundly influenced the development of U.S. trade unions in the twentieth century. In 1905, U.S. socialists and syndicalists created the Industrial Workers of the World (IWW), a movement for a single union to include all workers. The IWW was formed in reaction to the political conservatism of the American Federation of Labor leadership and the AFL's interest in organizing only skilled labor (Dubofsky 1969). Competition between socialists and antisocialist trade unions permeated almost all union activities. Socialists almost captured the leadership of the AFL in 1912, and the radical IWW was involved in several major labor and popular uprisings from 1910 to 1920. During World War I and the "Red Scare" of 1918–20 that followed, a flurry of nationalism and xenophobia was mobilized by the U.S. government against foreign radical thought and influence. This quickly escalated into a war against both immigrant and native American radicalism, which was pursued by the government with great ruthlessness and an utter disregard for constitutional rights. Socialists—within and outside trade unions— were jailed or deported, and their meetings and organizations broken up. By 1921 the AFL was the principle organization of trade unions in the United States as many socialists, including those promoting labor's interests, turned to political action including attempts to create a labor party (Weinstein 1967).

As Marxist influence waned in the United States, the institutionalist theory of John R. Commons and Selig Perlman (1979) established both the ideological basis for union actions and the dominant paradigm for labor studies for the next fifty years. Grounded in assumptions about human behavior and individualism, this approach focused on contractual relationships and negotiation. It exhibited no concern for the sociostructural position of labor in general and espoused no pervasive or unifying labor ideology.

In the 1930s and 1940s, the Communist party played a major role in forming the Congress of Industrial Organizations (CIO), which mobilized unskilled laborers principally in mass-production industries and organized unemployed workers in many American cities. Leninist-influenced organizers helped form and expand the United Auto Workers, the United Electric, Radio and Machine Workers Union, and the longshoremen and seamen's unions (Kimeldorf 1988). Yet after the postwar strike flurry and amidst the reaction of McCarthyism, the CIO and AFL merged, and the radical elements of the CIO were purged. The conservative ideology and business unionism of the institutionalists became the predominant philosophy in the new AFL-CIO.

In the 1950s, labor studies focused on analyses of "labor problems." Concerns with the historical context and theoretical context of labor disappeared from analyses of labor, and analyses of radical contribution were stigmatized as politically motivated. Economic analyses were reduced to measuring changes in wage and benefit increases and alteration of institutional size, as labor scholars increasingly shifted to using quantitative analyses of individual-level data (Brody 1989:9–10). Fixated on quantitative methods, William Form voiced the belief of many pluralist sociologists studying labor that it was time to "abandon attempts to explain macrosociological events with broad theories" (1979:22).

Detached from the concerns of labor, labor studies began to recede from the intellectual scene, principally becoming a professional area for training union officials and negotiators. Within sociology, labor issues were separated into focuses within specialty areas such as the sociologies of occupations, organizations, and social movements.

Marxist Social History and Labor Process Studies, 1960–90

In 1970 the editors of *Radical America* heralded a new school of historiography that rejected the celebrationist accounts of U.S. history and that critically reevaluated "Old Left" political practice (O'Brien 1970). Many of these radical historians had been strongly influenced by E.P. Thompson and William Appleman Williams. Thompson's *The Making of the English Working Class* (1963) emphasized the subjective aspects of history and encouraged young scholars to frame historical questions in terms of "shared experiences" and to view history as an interactive process that occurred within a cultural context.

These radical social historians challenged the institutionalist theory of labor relations, claiming it could not explain the dynamics of monopoly capitalism and was preoccupied with trade unions as the sole vehicle through which working class history unfolded. By limiting their analyses to accounts of union function-aries, company negotiators, and government arbitrators, institutionalists were seen as depicting workers as having neither class consciousness nor a part to play in their own history. Reflecting their "New Left" ideals, the new social historians argued that trade unions were inherently conservative institutions—a position that allowed them to attack both the conservative institutionalists and the U.S. socialists who had emphasized unions as agents of social change. Instead, they emphasized the role of mass movements, general strikes, spontaneous worker rebellions, and the syndicalist tradition in U.S. working-class experience (Brecher 1972; Aronowitz 1973).

Yet, the social historians were unable to address the deepening crisis of the U.S. labor movement during the 1970s for several reasons. First, they drew their research questions from the turn-of-the-century period of immigrants and syndicalist movements, rather than their own time. Second, they had an additive notion of class power based on the association of sovereign individuals in the production process. Third, their antipathy toward established political traditions and organizations influenced their interpretations of key events. Finally, as a result of equating working-class capacity with control of production, they had problems explaining the successful organizing efforts of unskilled industrial workers during the 1930s.

In rejecting institutionalism, social historians took a step forward. Yet, embedded in their analytic assumptions was a double political bias—the anti-communism of the postwar labor establishment and the anticommunist bias of traditional academic labor history. As the crisis of labor deepened, social historians retreated further into the nineteenth century, producing case studies that were increasingly less relevant to the contemporary crises of labor.

A second impact of the social history focus was the disintegration of labor as a subject area (Gutman 1977; Brody 1979). Absent the unity provided by the functionalist assumptions of the institutionalists, labor history became a compi-lation of race, ethnic, gender, community, and work studies with little relation-ship to one another and little relevance to modern labor. It was even suggested that the relationship between disparate cases of working-class formation in different countries had ceased to be important (Katznelson and Zolberg 1986; Lembcke 1987), and there were hints of a depoliticized postmodernist future for labor history (Buhle 1989).

Another radical approach, and a reaction to the deskilling of labor, was the emphasis on the labor process. Stone (1974) built on an in-depth historical analysis of wage incentive schemes in the steel industry to show how institu-tional programs allowed employers to maximize power over workers and introduce new technology (1974). She challenged the then dominant "model of a free and open labor market allocating labor according to comparative marginal costs and distributing income according to respective marginal productivity" (Stone 1974:23).

In a parallel insight, built on an analysis of the macroeconomic changes of the twentieth century, Braverman made visible the class conflict that had pervaded the workplace since the introduction of scientific management early in the twentieth century (1974). He has been credited with reviving the Marxist tradition of labor studies, and his followers have produced copious studies attempting to specify the relationships between technological change and job displacement, skill level, and other variables.

While radical in its focus and findings, Braverman's approach shared epistemological assumptions with the conservative pluralist studies of S.M. Lipset, et al. (1956). It fragmented workers, worklife, and unions into atomistic bits and imposed causality running from the parts to the whole in a homogenized social matrix, and it equated working-class power with aggregated individual sovereignty. Braverman's work has come under criticism from other Marxists for its empiricism and decomposed research agenda (Hakken 1988) and for its inability to understand the relationship between the workplace and other social and cultural spheres (Benenson 1982; Clawson 1982).

Despite these shortcomings, the labor-process approach offers an explanation of the contemporary crisis of labor. Yet, due in part to its methodology, it locates the crisis at the interface between monopoly and competitive forms of production, and elevates the importance of skilled labor and the petty bourgeoisie in the process of history—hardly an approach compatible with the working-class centered assumptions of classical Marxism.

Drawing on two different elements of the Marxist tradition—the focus on economic dynamics and on ideological formation—U.S. labor studies had advanced beyond the institutional theories that emphasized the inabilities of the working class. By the mid-1980s, however, many Marxists felt that each theory had become a victim of its assumptions, the ideology of its historical milieu, and the epistemology of its practitioners.

Mainstream American Sociology of Labor and Work, 1970–85

As Granovetter and Tilly noted in the *Handbook of Sociology*: "The shadow of Marx falls long over any discussion of connections between labor processes and inequality (in modern sociology)" (1988:176). Research on the "dual labor market" and on "labor-market segmentation"—outgrowths of Braverman's labor-process emphasis (Kalleberg and Sorenson 1979:356–58)—has been one of the most thoroughly explored subjects in modern sociology.

Scores of articles and books have examined the ability of this approach to explain conditions in different sectors of the economy, parts of the country, and different nations. It has been used to explain the changing effects of economic life on different racial and gender groups and on the changing composition of occupations, occupational mobility, and careers (Kalleberg and Sorenson 1979:364–71; see Cornfield 1991:38–40).

Appropriated and denuded of its class context, labor-process theory (in the guise of dual labor markets and labor segmentation) has principally been used by mainstream sociologists to describe and explain micro processes of the *status quo*, including occupational characteristics, income inequality, and limits on individual social mobility. Individuals become the sources of social mobility in a system that (by analytic inference) is magically void of systematic exploitation and institutional structures dedicated to increasing that exploitation. Most often, union membership is treated only as an indicator of corporate size or form, and unions are reduced to a unit of the monopoly corporate environment.

Several labor-process-focused studies of unionization and unions have appeared in mainstream sociology. More often, however, unions have been treated as a variable like any other in the socioeconomic matrix and analyzed as a factor affecting income and occupational advancement (Cornfield 1991:38–39). Thus the malaise, routinization, and narrow "apolitical" focus of labor unions have been reflected in labor studies.

The sociology of labor borrowed from the labor process and social-history approaches. It generally accepted the epistemological flaws and ideological biases of these two approaches. This includes the assumptions that long-term capitalist development involves the erosion of working-class capacity and that class struggle has the effect of disempowering the working class. Such assumptions have led even radical scholars virtually to write off the working class. Both the "class analysis" (Wright 1985) studies that redefined the boundaries of class and the "state-centered" theories (Skocpol and Finegold 1982) that emphasized managers and bureaucrats have minimized the role and capacity importance of the working class (Levine 1988; McNall, et al. 1991). Even ethnographic studies have exhibited an anti-working class and anticommunist bias (see Sennet and Cobb 1972; Rubin 1976; Aronowitz 1973).

The absence of a coherent Marxist perspective in mainstream sociology studies of labor through 1980 arose from a preoccupation with methodology and an unreflective acceptance of the dominant epistemology. This preoccupation distorted the Marxist insights borrowed from other disciplines, and it has contributed to the marginalization of labor as a focus of study and a perceived factor in explaining social change.

From the Ashes of the Old: Class Capacity and the Sociology of Labor

Retheorizing the sociology of labor means focusing on class rather than atomized individual workers as the unit of analysis. It means we must understand the contradictory, rather than the normative, implications of proletarianization. It also means avoiding the fragmented and atomized discourses common to both the social-history and labor-process frameworks that undergird recent work in the sociology of labor. Finally, it means clearly stating the composition and the importance of class capacity.

During the late 1980s, an emerging trend within the sociology of labor promised both to redress these problems and to provide a new point of departure. This "class formation and class capacities" trend restores the centrality of working-class efficacy. It affirms working-class culture and does not shy away from the tough ideological questions that post-1945 labor politics skirted. It explores the dialectical relationships between social consciousness and social organization, treats class capacities as an inter- as well as an intraclass phenomenon, and recognizes the historical and spatial dimension of class power.

These characteristics are evident in several recent sociological studies. Rick Fantasia (1988) uses participant observation studies of recent strikes to show that working-class capacity was not destroyed by deskilling, bureaucratization, cooptation, and cultural diversification. Howard Kimeldorf (1988) begins with the observation that the U.S. working class exhibits both business-union conservatism and class-conscious militancy, and he uses historical-comparative methods to study under what conditions each of these arises and is reproduced. Lembcke (1988) combines case histories of CIO unions with organizational analysis to show that proletarianization enhanced working-class capacity but that the unevenness of that process produced a divided working class. These and other studies (see Oestreicher 1988; Trotter 1985) make a case for an affirmative concept of working-class culture based on the collectivity. In many ways, this approach is an extension of Gramsci's criticisms of Lenin regarding issues of strategy, intellectual allegiance, and class capacity.

Earlier mainstream sociology approaches either ignored working-class culture or defined it relative to middle-class culture and values (see Lipset 1956; Rosen 1956; Renshon 1974). Because the analytical categories and methodological assumptions of pluralist theory were widely accepted (even by neo-Marxists—MacLeod 1987), few studies have cast working-class traits and values in a positive light. Further, anticommunism was a crucial factor in the treatment of working class culture. Communists within the CIO unions had emphasized workers' culture and the importance of unskilled workers (Piven and Cloward 1977). Reacting to these communist initiatives and the repressive setting of McCarthyism, liberal pluralist sociology constructed a fictitious authoritarian working-class personality to explain the link between the workers and their communist leaders (which was real), as well as a link between workers and fascism (which was not real). New Left scholars were sufficiently ambivalent about communists in the labor movement that they either reproduced the pluralist interpretation or avoided the subject altogether.

Nonconformity with this Cold War code could be risky for academics. When Keeran (1980) wrote the first scholarly study of the purge of communists from the United Auto Workers, he lost his job at Cornell University. There were no other major U.S. attempts to challenge the Cold War mythologies until the mid-1980s. In 1984, Zeitlin and Kimeldorf edited a book with materials from authors who, as labor historian Robert Zieger sarcastically noted, "appear untroubled by association intellectually with a Popular Front (Communist party) world view" (1984:298).

Marxist theory and method returned to labor studies by way of sociology. Wright's (1979) distinction between relational and gradational definitions of class, and Offe and Wiesenthal's (1980) demonstration that class capacities are class specific, each broke new ground. "Capacity" refers to the capability of the working class to act in its own interests in ways that transform the social relations of capitalism; it is those *means* available to the working class to liberate itself from its subordination to the capitalist class. According to Offe and Wiesenthal (1980), capitalist-class power is based on its accumulation of capital, while working-class power is based on the association of workers.

Therborn (1983) further specified the notion of class capacities by distinguishing between petty bourgeois and working-class sources of power. The power of the petty bourgeois is based on its pursuit of individual autonomy within the labor process, while the source of working-class power is in its collectivity. This distinction suggests a resolution to the long-standing debates between Marx and the anarchists by showing that the origins and goals of the class capacity of these two groups differ.

Therborn also distinguished between the *intrinsic capacity* that classes have—their respective resources—and their *hegemonic capacity*—the ability to deploy their intrinsic capacity against opposing classes. Yet he also points out that class power is not a zero-sum game wherein the power of one class weakens another. Therefore, as capitalist-class power increases through capital accumulation, it simultaneously and contradictorily collectivizes the working class and thus empowers it. Thus, capitalist-class power depends on its ability to engage in capital accumulation while blocking the contradictory effects of that accumulation on the working class—that is, to exercise hegemonic capacity. One way of doing this is for the capitalists to displace collectivizing organizations indigenous to the working class with those intrinsic to the capitalist class. For example, if capitalists can convince workers that labor unions that rely on large treasuries and high-paid legal experts are more effective than rank-and-file mobilization, it will have placed class struggle on terms most favorable to it.

Therborn also introduces a *spatial* dimension which explains both the U.S. working-class' capacity and labor's current crisis. He argues that a key determinant of which class will hold sway at any historical moment is "the extent to which the public practices of the working class are coextensive with the territorial range of the supreme political power which the class must confront" (Therborn 1983:41). Thus the history of class relations under capitalism can best be understood as a series of flanking actions, with the capitalist class first attempting to expand its geographical options and then attempting to block working-class efforts to keep pace.

The class-capacities approach makes a significant methodological break with the dominant academic approaches to labor studies because it asks questions at the level of class. It does not reduce analysis of class relations to the level of individuals, and thus it provides a basis for the criticism of survey research methods in class analysis (Fantasia 1988:8). And it places labor studies in a time-space matrix that creates possibilities for more dialectical analyses of the labor movement.

The temporal dimension of class capacities have been examined in several recent studies. Montgomery (1979), Nelson (1984), and Rosenzweig (1983), have noted the tenacity of the working-class culture of collectivity, while Fantasia (1988), Kimeldorf (1988), and Bensman and Lynch (1987) suggest that this collective culture is even an intergenerational phenomenon.

The contribution of the family to political socialization is well documented (Jennings and Niemi 1968), including opinions, attitudes, and values regarding social mobility and party identification (Rosen 1956; Renshon 1974). Yet there are many impediments to the intergenerational transmission of collective culture (Rosenzweig 1983; Anyon 1979). The role of families in shaping attitudes and values toward unions is complex, since families exist across all classes. If it is true that families transmit culture, what is the class specificity of the family role (Howe 1987:20) and how is it related to the intergenerational transmission of collective culture? Surprisingly, little of the literature on working-class formation and class consciousness addresses this important question.

As Pilcher (1973) showed in his study of West Coast longshoremen's communities, unions play an important role in the transmission of working-class culture. The intergenerational transmission of culture and class capacity is demonstrated most clearly in Benenson's (1985) analysis of the intersection of workplace and family life. Reexamining the skill degradation thesis, he found that the gender specificity of industrial changes taking place made the working class family central to the way changes occurred. He pointed out that the

> importance of the family economies, is that they encompassed in microcosm, the skill range of their respective industries. Work place issues affecting one occupational group had direct bearing on the welfare of family members employed in other job categories, industrial conflicts, refracted through the family, mobilized working class communities *en bloc.* (1985:118)

The generational distance between unionized, skilled male workers and nonunion, unskilled (mostly) female workers in the garment, mining, and shoe industries was often bridged by father-daughter family bonds. In the meat packing industry, the grievances of young female workers "commanded support among the better-organized, skilled male butchers" when workplace relations were mediated by family ties. Finally, organizing skills appear to have been transmitted from one generation to another. Newcomers to the world of industrial work—often daughters of male craft or skilled workers—"learned about organizing from their fathers who already belonged to craft unions and mutual aid societies" (Benenson 1985:128). Thus the creation and promotion of proletarianization seems to be mediated by family.

The spatial dimension of the formation of class capacities also needs to be taken into account. As David Harvey (1989:201–13) argues, economic development is always regionally specific. Economic periods, and periods when certain kinds of technology and skill levels are dominant, are also regional periods. This implies that we would expect to find that lower-skilled industrial labor developed not only at a later time than craft-oriented production but also in a different geographic region. Thus, typically, the generation entering the emergent, mass production, economic sector was physically separated from the generation steeped in the class-based organizational experience of an earlier era of economic development. In such cases, the "daughters" (from Benenson's study) employed in the new plants would have relocated from their family residence, in which case the mediating role of the family would be greatly diminished. Or, as was more often true, the new workforce would be immigrant workers whose "inherited beliefs" (Gutman 1987:15–18) would be consistent with the preindustrial work experience of their families.

If this is an important insight, it should also effect upward social mobility— a logical correlate of Benenson's thesis. Goldthorpe's (1968) study on the upward social mobility (*embourgeoisment*) among the working class has received significant attention in sociology. But Bensmen and Lynch (1987), and Ryan and Sackrey (1984) find that, just as proletarianization was mediated by family, so too is *embourgeoisment.* When family ties keep upwardly mobile professionals in touch with their working-class roots, they retain a greater commitment to the needs and values of that class. In such cases, academically acquired skills of, say, a lawyer or teacher can enhance the capacity of the working-class community. If upward social mobility occurs simultaneously with geographic mobility, the intergenerational ties may be broken and class-based allegiances lessened. Not surprisingly, as Storper and Walker (1989:10) show, the opening of new economic sectors typically occurs through the expansion of economic space, which means that social mobility presumes spatial relocation.

Thus, Braverman's deskilling argument captures only part of the multifaceted relationships. Deskilling *does* diminish the autonomy of individual workers and, by extension, diminishes working-class capacity. But, viewing the U.S. working-class experience in its most comprehensive dimensions, we can see that class capacity has not been diminished by skill degradation *per se*. Instead, skill degradation created the possibility for capitalists to own and control through their managers, which in turn permitted them to move assets while maintaining a relatively stable existence for themselves as a class (Dunn 1980). Meanwhile, workers, pulled hither and yon by the increasing rapidity of capital's mobility, have their capacity to produce and reproduce a collective culture constantly diminished.

Historically, it appears that the control of space has been as important as the control of skill in creating class capacity. Further, it seems that the class advantages of spatial movement have changed in the last ninety years. Before 1900, capital was largely locally owned and unable to afford the cost of strategic relocations. Adams and Kasakoff (1984:29–37) found that in colonial New England, families with property and wealth tended to stay in one community (as did their property), while workers tended to move. Further nineteenth-century craftsmen were "honor bound" to walk out of a shop if the traditional rules of employment were broken—a pattern that continued into the twentieth century (Montgomery 1979). Thus, in the nineteenth century, labor's ability to move was a source of class power.

After the separation of ownership and management, capital could move without the capitalist having to move. Thus, by the turn of the century, spatial mobility began to weaken the influence of labor within cities by dispersing workers and disrupting solidarity (Gordon 1984). As Bluestone and Harrison (1982) and Richard Peet (1987) have argued, capital's mobility in the mid- to late twentieth century destroyed unions and weakened working-class communities, thereby diminishing working-class power. When skills were more valued, mobility benefited the working class. When ownership and management were separated, however, the complexity of production fragmented (and work deskilled), the cost-benefit advantages of geographical mobility shifted to the capitalists. Owners could stay in a community, keeping their social (including intergenerational) networks in place.

The effects of cultural and geographic changes on labor were reflected in the characteristic form of union organization. The (AFL-affiliated) craft unions were located principally in the eastern United States. They adopted a protectionist posture toward new technical developments, refusing to organize the unskilled immigrant and western U.S. workers, or to restructure their organizations along industry lines. These biases might have been mitigated by a union organizational structure that took such changing historical conditions into account. Instead, disinclined to counterbalance the spatial effects and cultural-historical factors, these workers adopted forms of organization that actually amplified the imbalances of class power (Lembcke 1988).

The importance of studying the link between temporal and spatial dimensions of class formation can be seen in Stephen Thernstrom's study of socialism and social mobility (1984). He argues that the length of time a group of workers resides in a particular place is a crucial variable in the formation of social solidarity. His study suggests that not only does the group share common experiences but that the group's process of reflection about these commonalties takes time. Yet culture (collective or otherwise) is something more than experience. It includes symbols (language) and an interpretive framework by which the group knows and understands that experience; it is the combination of the "inherited belief" component and the experience itself. Moreover, the notion of inheritance presumes the presence of more than one generation in the process by which a class becomes conscious of itself. The bridge to full working-class consciousness has seldom been crossed because, in part, capital has been able to destroy working-class community and disrupt the intergenerational process of class formation.

Returning to the current crisis and applying this class-capacity framework, we note that the current wave of expansion began after 1945. Corporate managers in basic industry "found themselves confronting an unprecedented profit squeeze," and they responded by creating "an unprecedented wave of total plant shutdowns" (Bluestone and Harrison 1982:34–35). The class logic of this course of action is made more clear in Peet's (1987) study, which shows that capital moved from states and regions that ranked high in class struggles to locations that ranked low. Similarly, as noted in Perrucci, et al. (1988:24): "The level of unionization was the best predictor of capital flight, such that in the 1970s corporations tended to move to states without powerful trade unions." Workers who stayed in the declining regions have been pushed to the margins of the economy, while those who have moved have broken ties with one or more generations of their families (Bluestone and Harrison 1982:99–104).

Deindustrialization has amounted to a "class war on workers" (Bluestone and Harrison 1982:19) and more particularly against the communities "where the great worker organizing drives of the 1930's and 1940's were most successful and which also retained their industrial structures virtually intact until recently" (Peet 1987:51). The deindustrialization of the past two decades was the completion of a forty year class war against the radical working-class movements of the 1930s. Capital flight was the last step in a series of efforts that included antilabor legislation; Cold War purges of labor leaders with broad visions of unionism; and limiting labor activities to negotiations over wages, hours, and work conditions.

Conclusion

The United States is undergoing a period of political and economic devastation seldom seen in its history. Unemployment, underemployment, homelessness, hunger, the decline in health and educational systems, and the resurgence of racism and national chauvinism have combined to portend a future ridden with crises. The suffering of large numbers of working people and others who have been economically discarded has continued to increase.

The prospect of a meaningful, effective response to those conditions by the labor movement and its traditional left-wing allies appears distant. These crises result not simply from the failure of capitalism but from the failure of unions and the socialist movement to respond effectively. By comparison, ten years into the Great Depression of the 1930s, the U.S. left was mobilized and playing a central role in the resolution of the crisis. *Class* was central to the strategic vision of that movement, and the working class was the social base on which the movement was built.

To contribute to the creation of a movement able to lead our society out of the present crisis, the sociology of labor has to be reconceptualized in ways that do not devalue the role of the working class or fragment the study of class relations. We have argued for an analysis that stays at the level of class and that uses organizations (family, union, etc.) as the empirical referents for levels of class capacity. We have argued for an analysis that understands class capacity as a relational phenomenon that has intraclass and interclass dimensions, is historical, has spatial dimensions, and comprehends the dialectical relationship between social relations and class consciousness. Toward that end, we have highlighted some recent developments in the discipline that offer new and promising points of analytic departure, and that may provide a framework for beginning to respond to our current crisis.

References

Adams, John W. and A.B. Kasakoff. 1984. "Migration and the Family in Colonial New England: The View from Genealogies." *Journal of Family History* 9:24–42.

Anyon, Jean. 1979. "Ideology and United States History Textbooks." *Harvard Educational Review* 49:361–86.

Arnesen, Eric. 1990. "Crusades Against Crisis: A View from the United States and the 'Rank and File' Critique and Other Catalogues of Labour History's Alleged Ills." *International Review of Social History* 35:106–27.

Aronowitz, Stanley. 1973. *False Promises*. New York: McGraw-Hill.

Benenson, Harold. 1982. "The Reorganization of U.S. Manufacturing Industry and Worker's Experience 1880–1920: A Review of 'Bureaucracy and the Labor Process' by Dan Clawson." *Insurgent Sociologist* 11(3):65–75.

————. 1985. "The Community and Family Bases of U.S. Working Class Protest 1880–1920: A Critique of the 'Skill Degradation' and 'Ecological Perspectives." Pp. 109–32 in *Research in Social Movement, Conflicts and Change*, ed. Louis Kriesberg. Greenwich, Conn.: JAI.

Bensman, David, and R. Lynch. 1987. *Rusted Dreams: Hard Times in a Steel Community*. New York: McGraw-Hill.

Bluestone, Barry, and Bennett Harrison. 1982. *The Deindustrialization of America*. New York: Basic Books.

Braverman, Harry. 1974. *Labor and Monopoly Capital*. New York: Monthly Review Press.

Brecher, Jeremy. 1972. *Strike!* Greenwich, Conn.: Fawcett.

Brody, David. 1979. "The Old Labor History and the New: In Search of an American Working Class." *Social History* 20:111–126.

————. 1989. "Labor History, Industrial Relations, and the Crisis of American Labor." *Industrial and Labor Relations Review* 43:7–18.

Buhle, Mary Jo. 1989. "Gender and Labor History." Pp. 55–79 in *Perspectives on American Labor History: The Problems of Synthesis*, ed. J. Carroll Moody and A. Kessler-Harris. DeKalb: Northern Illinois University Press.

Clawson, Dan. 1982. "Reply to Benenson." *Insurgent Sociologist* 11(3):76–80.

Cornfield, Daniel. 1991. "The U.S. Labor Movement: Its Development and Impact on Social Inequality and Politics." *Annual Review of Sociology* 17:27–49.

Dubofsky, Melvin. 1969. *We Shall Be All: A History of the IWW*. New York: Quadrangle.

Dunn, Marvin. 1980. "The Family Office as a Coordinating Mechanism Within the Ruling Class." *Insurgent Sociologist* 9(2–3):8–23.

Editors. 1990. "Trends in Organizing: Alarming Projection—5% by 2000." *Economic Notes* 58(5–6): 11–12.

Fantasia, Rick. 1988. *Cultures of Solidarity: Consciousness, Action, and Contemporary American Workers*. Berkeley: University of California Press.

Form, William. 1979. "Comparative Industrial Sociology and the Convergence Hypothesis." *Annual Review of Sociology* 5:1–25.

Geras, Norman. 1976. *The Legacy of Rosa Luxemburg*. London: Verso.

Goldthorpe, John. 1968. *The Affluent Worker*. Cambridge: Cambridge University Press.

Gordon, David. 1984. "Capitalist Development and the History of American Cities." Pp. 22–47 in *Marxism and the Metropolis: New Perspectives in Urban Political Economy*, 2nd ed., ed. William Tabb and Larry Sawyers. New York: Oxford University Press.

Gordon, David, Richard Edwards, and Michael Reich. 1982. *Segmented Work, Divided Workers*. Cambridge: Cambridge University Press.

Gramsci, Antonio. 1971. *Selections from the Prison Notebooks*. New York: International Publishers.

Granovetter, Mark and Charles Tilly. 1988. "Inequality and Labor Processes." Pp. 175–221 in *The Handbook of Sociology*, ed. Neil Smelser. Beverly Hills: Sage Publications.

Guerin, David. 1970. *Anarchism*. New York: Monthly Review Press.

Gutman, Herbert. 1977. *Work, Culture, and Society*. New York: Random House.

————. 1987. *Power and Culture: Essays on the American Working Class*. New York: Pantheon.

Hakken, David. 1988. "Studying New Technology After Braverman: An Anthropological Review." *Anthropology of Work Newsletter* 1(1):17–24.

Harvey, David. 1989. *The Condition of Postmodernity: An Inquiry into the Origins of Cultural Change*. Cambridge: Basil Blackwell.

Howe, Carolyn. 1987. "Class Analysis and Political Socialization: The Production and Reproduction of Class Consciousness." Paper, Society for the Study of Social Problems, Chicago.

International Anarchist Congress. 1907. *Statement of Principles*. Chicago: International Anarchist Congress.

Jennings, M. Kent and R.G. Niemi. 1968. "The Transmission of Political Values from Parent to Child." *American Political Science Review* 62:169–84.

Kalleberg, Arne and Aage Sorensen. 1979. "The Sociology of Labor." *Annual Review of Sociology* 5:351–79.

Katznelson, Ira, and Aristide Zolberg, eds. 1986. *Working Class Formation: Nineteenth Century Patterns in Western Europe and the United States*. Princeton: Princeton University Press.

Keeran, Roger. 1980. *The Communist Party and the Auto Workers Unions*. Bloomington: Indiana University Press.

Kimeldorf, Howard. 1988. *Reds or Rackets? The Making of Radical and Conservative Unions on the Waterfront*. Berkeley: University of California Press.

Kropotkin, Peter. 1899. *Memoirs of a Revolutionist*. Boston: Houghton, Mifflin.

Lembcke, Jerry. 1987. "Working Class Formation: Nineteenth Century Patterns in Western Europe and the United States by Ira Katznelson and Aristide Zolberg." *Labor History* 28:559–61.

———. 1988. *Capitalist Development and Class Capacities: Marxist Theory and Union Organization*. Westport, Conn.: Greenwood Press.

Lenin, V.I. 1905. *What Is to Be Done?*. New York: International Publishers.

———. 1970. *On Trade Unions*. Moscow: Progress Publishers.

Levine, Rhonda. 1988. *Class Struggle and the New Deal: Industrial Labor, Industrial Capital, and the State*. Lawrence: University of Kansas Press.

Lipset, Seymour M., Martin Trow, and James Coleman. 1956. *Union Democracy*. New York: Doubleday Anchor.

Luxemburg, Rosa. 1963. *The Accumulation of Capital*. London: Monthly Review Press.

———. 1972. *The Russian Revolution and Leninism or Marxism?* Ann Arbor: University of Michigan Press.

MacLeod, Jay. 1987. *Ain't No Makin' It: Leveled Aspirations in a Low-Income Neighborhood*. Boulder: Westview Press.

McNall, Scott, Rhonda Levine, and Rick Fantasia. 1991. *Bringing Class Back In: Historical and Contemporary Perspectives*. Boulder: Westview Press.

Marx, Karl. 1964. *The Economic and Philosophic Manuscripts of 1844*. New York: International Publishers.

———. 1973. *The Poverty of Philosophy*. Moscow: Progress Publishers.

———. 1975. *Wages, Price, and Profit*. Peking: Foreign Language Press.

———. 1976. *The German Ideology*. Moscow: Progress Publishers.

———. 1978. *Capital; A Critique of Political Economy*. Moscow: Progress Publishers.

Marx, Karl, and Friedrich Engels. 1965. *Karl Marx and Friedrich Engels: Selected Correspondence*. Moscow: Progress Publishers.

———. 1968. *The Communist Manifesto*. New York: Monthly Review Press.

Montgomery, David. 1979. *Worker's Control in America*. London: Cambridge University Press.

Nelson, Bruce. 1984. "Pentecost' on the Pacific: Maritime Workers and Working Class Consciousness in the 1930's." *Political Power and Social Theory* 4:141–82.

O'Brien, James, et al. 1970. "New Left Historians of the 1960s." *Radical America* 4(8–9):1–4.

Oestreicher, Richard. 1988. "Urban Working-Class Political Behavior and Theories of American Electoral Politics 1870–1940." *Journal of American History* 74(4):1257–86.

Offe, Claus, and Helmut Wiesenthal. 1980. "Two Logics of Collective Action: Theoretical Notes on Social Class and Organizational Form." Pp. 67–115 in *Political Power and Social Theory*, Vol. 1., ed. Maurice Zeitlin. Greenwich, Conn.: JAI.

Pannekoek, Anton. 1975. "Workers' Councils." Pp. 384–500 in *Root and Branch*. New York: Fawcett.

Peet, Richard, ed. 1987. *International Capitalism and Industrial Restructuring*. Boston: Allen and Unwin.

Perlman, Selig. 1979. *A Theory of the Labor Movement*. Philadelphia: Porcupine Press.
Perrucci, Carolyn, Robert Perrucci, Dena Targ, and Harry Targ. 1988. *Closings: International Context and Social Costs*. New York: Aldine De Gruyter.
Pilcher, William. 1972. *The Portland Longshoremen: A Dispersed Urban Community*. New York: Holt, Rinehart, and Winston.
Piven, Frances Fox, and Richard Cloward. 1977. *Poor People's Movements*. New York: Pantheon.
Renshon, Stanley. 1974. *Psychological Needs and Political Behavior: A Theory of Personalilty and Political Efficacy*. New York: Free Press.
Rosen, Bernard. 1956. "The Achievement Syndrome: A Psychocultural Dimension of Social Stratification." *American Sociological Review* 21(2):203–11.
Rosenzweig, Roy. 1983. *Eight Hours for What We Will: Workers and Leisure in an Industrial Community 1870–1920*. Cambridge: Cambridge University Press.
Rubin, Lillian. 1976. *Worlds of Pain: Life in the Working Class Family*. New York: Basic Books.
Ryan, Jake, and C. Sackrey. 1984. *Strangers in Paradise: Academics From the Working Class*. Boston: South End Press.
Sennett, Richard, and Jonathan Cobb. 1972. *The Hidden Injuries of Class*. New York: Knopf.
Skocpol, Theda, and Kenneth Finegold. 1982. "State Capacity and Economic Intervention in the Early New Deal." *Political Science Quarterly* 97:255–78.
Stone, Katherine. 1974. "The Origins of Job Structures in the Steel Industry." Pp. 27–84 in *Labor Market Segmentation*, ed. Richard Edwards, et al. Lexington, Mass.: Lexington Books.
Storper, Michael and R. Walker. 1989. *The Capitalist Imperative: Territory, Technology and Industrial Growth*. New York: Basil Blackwell.
Therborn, Goran. 1983. "Why Some Classes are More Successful Than Others." *New Left Review* 138:37–55.
Thernstrom, Stephen. 1984. "Socialism and Social Mobility." Pp. 408–451 in *Failure of a Dream?: Essays in the History of American Socialism*, ed. John Laslett and Seymour M. Lipset. Berkeley: University of California Press.
Thompson, E.P. 1963. *The Making of the English Working Class*. New York: Vintage Press.
Trotter, Joe. 1985. *Black Milwaukee*. Urbana: University of Illinois Press.
Waters, M.A., ed. 1970. *Rosa Luxemburg Speaks*. New York: Pathfinder Press.
Weinstein, James. 1967. *The Decline of Socialism in America*. New York: Vintage Press.
Woodcock, George. 1956. *Pierre-Joseph Proudhon*. London: Routledge and Keegan Paul.
Wright, Eric. 1979. *Class Structure and Income Determination*. London: Verso.
———. 1985. *Classes*. London: Verso.
Zieger, Robert. 1984. "The Popular Front Rides Again." *Political Power and Social Theory* 4:297–302.

PART II:

SOCIAL INSTITUTIONS

STATE AND POLITICS:

FROM THE KING OF PRUSSIA TO THE NEW WORLD ORDER: MARXIST THEORIES OF STATE AND POWER

Donald McQuarie
and
Patrick McGuire

Marxists think about state and power in a fundamentally different way from traditional sociologists. The latter use a concept of power akin to that used by Max Weber; power is the ability to achieve one's goals despite the resistance of others. Their analysis is predicated on the assumption that all groups have access to, and can gain control of, the government. Their studies focus on the attempts of various social actors and agencies to influence government policy and structures through direct or symbolic participation in governmental processes.

The Marxist concept of power operates on a structural and relational level at the same time (McQuarie and Spaulding 1989). Power is structurally grounded in property relations as the position of one class relative to the other—owners to workers. Property confers power, and the state, by acting to protect property, is a structure that necessarily defends the interests of owners. Rather than the state being neutral and all groups having equal access to policy making, Marxists argue that the state is class biased and is the institutionalized form of capitalist power.

Power is also a relationship. It is an attribute pursued by both classes as they attempt to create or alter policy. In this context, Marxists discuss the attempt of the ruling class to use the state to manage the affairs of the class as a whole and the attempt of workers to pursue their own class interests. Thus the state is both a biased structure of class domination and an arena in which the opportunities for improving working-class life are created or constricted. These different concepts of power and the state (coupled with a view of the world as riddled with contradiction and conflict, rather than ebbing and flowing forces) have resulted in a different set of concerns and unique insights.

Marxist Theory to 1960

Marx's early political works were abstract critiques emphasizing a contradiction between the public and private spheres of life. He saw political emancipation—guarantees of voting, assembly, party membership—as a step forward. Yet he recognized that these political rights also made people more dependent on the state (which guaranteed those rights) and thus obscured the pursuit of social emancipation. Marx also argued that the state was unable to address "social ills" such as unemployment, poverty, and exploitation, because it was dominated and occupied by the individuals and organizations that caused the social ills. Further, even if well intended people came to govern, the state could not create "social remedies" because it relied on the economic resources of the affluent who caused those ills. For these reasons, Marx's early writings rejected political rights and parliamentary government as inadequate to met the social and economic needs of the people (Marx 1975).

Working alone, Marx's future coauthor and lifelong companion, Friedrich Engels had written *The Condition of the Working Class in England*(1973). In this study, he outlined how private property owners had historically dominated state policy making, and had created the various social ills that permeated the fabric of social life. Engels showed that by protecting the rights of private property owners, the state created, maintained, and worsened the conditions of life for the nonproperty-owning majority. Engels identified private property as the source of state bias and as the spring from which human misery flowed.

Marx had identified the contradictions in state structures and goals and those of the society at large. Engels had shown it was private property that had both caused social ills and that dominated state structure and operation. Integrating these insights suggested that only a revolution that included the overthrow of the state and of private property relations could eliminate social ills and create human emancipation. The wedding of these distinct insights first appeared in *The Communist Manifesto*, written by Marx and Engels in 1848 (Marx 1973a:62–98).

For thirty years, socialists had been organizing in Europe, drawing inspiration from such early socialist thinkers as Pierre Joseph Proudhon, August Blanqui, and Henri St. Simon, a man often referred to as the "Father of Sociology." The *Manifesto*, written as a statement of principle for a group to which Marx and Engels belonged, was published at the same time as uprisings erupted in France, Italy, Germany, and Austro-Hungary. The *Manifesto* argued that workers needed to identify their class interests, seize the state, and "centralize all instruments of production in the hands of the state" (Marx 1973a:86). State power, they argued, should be used to sweep away class antagonisms by abolishing private property and therein the existence of social classes. Before the workers could implement these principles, their uprisings were crushed.

In analyzing the aftermath of this defeat, Marx offered his most systematic statement of his theory of the state. *The 18th Brumaire of Louis Bonaparte* (Marx 1973b:143–240) was a study of how class bias becomes structurally embedded in the state. Arguing that domination of the workers was the first priority of the capitalist state, Marx showed how capitalists used cross-class alliances and crises to outlaw worker organizations and undermine more democratic forms of government in France from 1848 to 1851. For capitalists to consolidate their power, they had to coalesce with other groups. After domination over the workers was established, however, the power of noncapitalist groups—the unemployed, intellectuals, retailers, and clerics—who had coalesced with the capitalists was diminished by legislation.

Marx noted divisions within classes and among fractions of classes. And he noted that the state reflected these divisions (and contradictions) within its structure—in parties, and within and among legislative, executive, and judicial organs. Thus, while the state is a source of class domination, it is not a monolithic bloc. State actors, policies, and even structures can exhibit some autonomy from specific class actors and fractions, and can violate some aspects of capitalist class interests. As noted in *The 18th Brumaire*, capitalists will even accept political dictatorship which reduces their participation in state processes, as long as the state protects private property, assures ongoing exchange and trade processes, and prevents labor strikes.

In protecting such basic "order," the state becomes an institutionalized form of class siege dominating the rest of the society, according to Marx. By creating different opportunities and constraints that benefit capitalists more than other groups, the "normal" state acts as both the instrument of class domination and the organizer of the ongoing capitalist revolution as it restructures the economy and society, consistent with the classwide needs of private interests.

After the Paris Commune of 1870–71, Marx modified his theory of the state. Reacting to war and economic desperation, Parisian workers (and a large section of the middle class) had revolted and formed a new government that enacted many social reforms. In response, the French and German armies (which had been at war) signed an armistice, released prisoners, and cooperatively crushed the uprising. After the surrender, the French army executed thousands of men, women, and children, and tens of thousands more were exiled to overseas prison camps (Horne 1965).

Reflecting on the larger pattern of national and international armies burning or bombarding cities and then executing workers, and on the thwarted working class electoral efforts during the previous twenty-five years, Marx reformulated his theory of the state in *The Civil War in France*. He noted that class rule was structurally assured at the nation-state level by an international constellation of capitalist states. He argued that violent repression was but the extreme end of a continuum of class domination by the state. What is "exceptional" about the response of the capitalist state to direct class challenge is the clarity of its class bias, not that it is repressive, since the state is "normally" engaged in ensuring the civil war of daily life. These insights led Marx to conclude that the state could not be simply captured and power and economic decision making centralized and used for the good of the workers. Rather, the machinery of the military and the state bureaucracy must be shattered.

Following Marx's death, Marxists continued to debate and develop both Marx's insights into the functioning of the capitalist state and his strategies of socialist revolution. Three major debates arose in response to different aspects of his theory, including debates over (1) revolution and state structure, (2) reform of the state, and (3) centralization of state bureaucracy.

In the most famous extension of Marx's theory, Lenin built on Marx's themes of the exceptional state. *Imperialism* (Lenin 1971:169–263) emphasized the increasingly international content of capitalism and the role of the state in aiding and protecting capital accumulation. Lenin also compared the 1917 uprising in Russia to the Paris Commune. In *State and Revolution* (1971:264–351), he extended and reframed Marx's ideas in *The Civil War in France*. While noting the class-biased structure of the state, Lenin emphasized the role of the bureaucracy and the military as repressive agencies of class power. Believing that world revolution was imminent and that structural power between classes was the key issue, Lenin advocated crushing the capitalist state and creating a workers' state to shepherd the process of social change. Yet his proposed workers' state was merely an inverted image of Marx's repressive capitalist state. (Marx saw the capitalist state enforcing the domination of the capitalist class over the working class, while Lenin's worker's state existed to suppress the industrialists and financiers.) It was to institutionalize working class power structurally above, and relationally in opposition to, capitalist power. This workers' state was necessary because, as Lenin recognized, international capitalist power would be mobilized in an armed conflict and an economic struggle against the workers' state.

International pressure, bureaucratic inertia, party procedures and conspiracies, and the suppression of workers' power by the Bolshevik party (Siriani 1982) created a state opposed to both capitalist power and workers' power. What emerged was a state capitalist nation wherein the state acted as the capitalist and in which state actors sought self-interest, in part by suppressing electoral democracy and internal dissent. There were significant objections to and critiques of these developments by other Marxists, including Karl Kautsky and Rosa Luxemburg—leaders of German socialist parties (Kautsky; 1964, Luxemburg 1961; for Lenin's reply, see Lenin 1975).

A second debate asked whether the state could be reformed and worker power increased through political participation. While Marx and Engels rejected reform during Marx's lifetime, Engels later noted the importance of voting by class-conscious workers, and the potential of using an elected government to increase class power peacefully (Engels 1978).

Engels's secretary, Eduard Bernstein, and German socialist Karl Kautsky advocated evolutionary socialism, or Social Democracy, a political approach built upon Marx's concept of the "normal state." While continuing to emphasize class struggle and Marx's two-level theory of power, it argued that workers' parties could use the ballot to gain control of the state apparatus and increase working-class power relative to the capitalists. By limiting the production of opportunities that benefit capitalists, and by occupying and dominating the bureaucracy and military, the class-biased structure of the capitalist state could be challenged and altered by elected socialists. By practicing electoral democracy, and creating and operating publicly owned enterprises, the conditions of workers' daily lives could be improved and their structural power increased, as a result of their (expanding) collective ownership of the productive property of the society (Tudor and Tudor 1988).

Kautsky and the Social Democrats rejected Lenin's theory of the state, and they repudiated the Russian Revolution. A gulf emerged between socialists and communists. While receding from prominence in Marxist theory, the socialist parties pursued the Social Democratic strategy and were intermittently elected in France between 1936 and the present and in Britain during each decade from 1920 through 1980, and constantly in Scandinavia from 1920 through now (except during Nazi occupation). These actors, motivated by these goals, created the structures of the modern social welfare state.

The third debate focused on centralized class power and a centralized state and asked where and how prerevolutionary consciousness and postrevolutionary governance should occur. This debate was initially between the socialists Marx and Engels and the anarchists Proudhon and Bakunin, who argued that centralized authority prevented human liberation and that the state, which made capitalism possible, was the enemy of humanity. They criticized Marx, Engels, and others who proposed creating a centralized workers' state.

Anarchists proposed eliminating the state and all other bureaucracies and replacing them with autonomous, self-coordinating communal societies organized on the principle of mutual aid. They created alternative economic and political organs to provide members with the ideological and experiential skills needed to participate in the democratic society that was to be formed after the revolution. Because they saw the centralized state, rather than private property, as the main social problem, they welcomed peasants and professionals into their movement. Anarchists were involved in major nineteenth century and early twentieth-century class struggles in Europe (especially Spain, Italy, and Russia) and in the United States. Anarchists, such as Emma Goldman (1923), critiqued Leninism because it ignored the peasants, substituted a centralized hierarchical party for democracy, created a centralized state that used its authority to suppress dissent, and established a centrally directed economy.

Similar criticisms were voiced by Marxists. But their analyses focused on private property, the capitalist state, and class power, rather than authority structures as such. These criticisms emphasized that Lenin failed to provide institutional opportunities for workers to raise consciousness and gain the skills needed for political and economic self-governance. Beginning in 1919, Antonio Gramsci offered a systematic analysis of the link between mass culture and the rise of class-based revolutionary ideology in Italy. He helped form "workers' councils," local institutions of economic and political power that paralleled capitalist institutions but were democratically run by the workers (1977).

In the 1880s the Belgian and Dutch socialists had created alternative cultural organizations (athletic leagues, choirs, literary groups, etc.). Pursuing Social Democratic electoral policies and focusing on local governance, they pursued a policy called "municipal socialism." Anton Pannekoek helped form and lead workers' councils, transforming the municipal socialist program toward a revolutionary workers' councils program after 1909. Their goal was to create a workers' state, not above existing classes, but as a replacement for the class-biased political structures of the capitalist state and as an alternative to state capitalism (Strikwerda 1991; Pannekoek 1975; Smart 1978).

Lenin railed against this approach in *Left-Wing Communism* (1971:516–91). Yet the Council Communists' emphasis on promoting worker consciousness and political and economic self-governance, and the unceasing class-based, power-focused critique of the party and state, challenged Lenin's centralism. Additional workers' councils were formed in Germany, Russia, and elsewhere. Lenin (and, under quite different conditions, Mussolini and Hitler) found it necessary to crush these groups and jail their leaders.

This brief review has provided insights into the structures and biases of the capitalist state and has offered an explanation of the rise both of the social welfare state and of state capitalism. It allows us to see the creation and operation of the latter two state forms as arising from rational concerns (rather than authoritarian fanaticism, self-interest, or indecision and compromise—themes frequently voiced by mainstream American academics). It also provides insight into the concepts and motives that guided generations of individuals collectively making their own history and seeking (with varying success) to avoid the biases and limits of capitalism.

Marxist Theory, 1960 to the Present

The late 1960s saw a rebirth of interest in the Marxist theory of the state. Two factors encouraged this increased interest in the state and Marxist theory generally. First, struggles between powerful Western nations and Third World people seeking to determine their own fate—such as the wars between France and Algeria or between the United States and Vietnam—led some people to question the relationship between the state and powerful multinational corporations. Second, as racial minorities and women found themselves fighting to gain the human rights supposedly guaranteed to them, many began to wonder why the state existed, if not to protect the rights of its citizens. This new interest in state theory contrasted sharply with the near-total neglect of the state by Marxist theorists between 1925 and 1965. Open rebellions and class struggle in North America, Western Europe, and Eastern Europe refocused attention on the role of the state. The growing role of the state in economic planning and the growth of the state's welfare functions from the 1930s to the present led many Marxists to posit a new and expanded role for the state in response to the power of multinational corporations and the crises that this new monopoly capitalist economy had precipitated (see Baran and Sweezy 1966; Gough 1979).

Undoubtedly the most important contribution in this reappraisal was Nicos Poulantzas's development of a complex and evolving theory of the state in capitalist society, as well as the debate between Poulantzas and Ralph Miliband (Poulantzas 1969, 1973, 1975, 1976, 1978; Miliband 1970, 1973). In his 1969 *The State in Capitalist Society*, Miliband presented a Marxist critique of liberal-pluralist theory by identifying various capitalist constraints on state policy making. These constraints include the economic power of the capitalist class, the requirements of private capital accumulation, the social processes that mold the ideological commitments of the state elite, and the role of big business and business-organized interest groups in the formation of state policy. Miliband argued that an especially crucial role is played by elite members of the capitalist class who exercise direct personal influence on government policy makers through their role as influential business elites and as occupants of crucial positions inside government. Thus, Miliband argued, the capitalist class, by virtue of its economic power is able "to use the state as its instrument for the domination of society" (Miliband 1969:23).

This position was rejected by Poulantzas, who argued instead that the capitalist state should not be viewed as an instrument of the ruling class but should be understood *functionally* in terms of the role that it plays in the capitalist mode of production:

> The relation between the bourgeois class and the State is an *objective relation*. This means that if the *function* of the State in a determinate social formation and the *interests* of the dominant class in this formation *coincide*, it is by reason of the system itself: the direct participation of members of the ruling class in the State apparatus is

not the *cause* but the *effect*, and moreover a chance and contingent one, of this objective coincidence. (Poulantzas 1969:73)

According to Poulantzas, direct participation by members of the capitalist class is largely irrelevant and at times could even be detrimental because the policies pursued by individual capitalists will always be parochial, reflecting the interests and needs of particular firms. Therefore, in order for the state to organize the dominance of the capitalist class *as a whole*, it must have a "relative autonomy" that prevents it from being subordinated to the demands of any particular fraction (or part) of the capitalist class. For Poulantzas, promoting the long-range interests of the capitalist class may even entail the state granting various concessions to subordinate classes. Nevertheless, he argued, such concessions or reforms are always made in the interests of organizing the long-term dominance of capital. Finally, the state bureaucracy does not in itself exercise power. Instead, the state and its institutions are "power centres" that act to concentrate and focus class interests into class power (Poulantzas 1973:335–36,104). Specifically, the capitalist state plays three interlocking functions: (1) to ensure the *political organization* of the dominant capitalist class; (2) to ensure the *political disorganization* of the working class; and (3) to organize the *political support* of the middle class (Poulantzas 1973:287–88).

This debate between Poulantzas and Miliband proved to be crucial for the development of contemporary Marxist theories of the state. Their approaches became the poles between which all other Marxist (and many Marxist-influenced) theories of the state have navigated. Poulantzas's position became known as the *structuralist* approach. Nonstructuralists such as Miliband view the state as an institutional entity including the state bureaucracy, political parties, lobbyists, and policy-making institutions, which are occupied by elected, appointed, and civil service officials. They argue that whatever class occupies the state apparatus can manipulate state policy in its own behalf and against its opponents.

Structuralists, by contrast, view the *mode of production* as the structural basis of capitalism and the state as one of three spheres of domination constricting and shaping actions and behaviors in ways that create and maintain that structure (the other two being the ideological and economic spheres). Thus the state takes a particular form reflecting the capitalist mode of production; regardless of who occupies the state apparatus, it will operate to benefit capitalists. It is a *capitalist state*, rather than a *state in capitalist society*, as nonstructuralists would argue. As a result, structuralists perceive a relative autonomy of the state from active control by class actors.

A second and quite distinct effort to derive a theory of the state from the logic of capital accumulation was undertaken by the German *capital logic* or "derivationist" school during the 1970s (see Holloway and Picciotto 1979).

Attempting to derive or develop a theory of the state from the logic of capital accumulation, these theorists argued that Poulantzas was correct in approaching the study of the capitalist state from the perspective of a structural analysis of its function. But in placing the theory of the state at the analytical level of the "political" and separating it from the "economic," they claimed that Poulantzas had *overstressed* the state's political functions and *understressed* its economic functions. Furthermore, in ignoring the laws of motion of capital—most especially the tendency of the rate of profit to fall—Poulantzas could not appreciate the *limitations* imposed on state actors by the necessary role of the state in assuring capital accumulation.

The capital-logic school argued that the capitalist state was determined by its necessary economic functions. This point, stated in a more determinist and dogmatic form, had been a staple of orthodox Leninist political theory for many years. Leninist "state monopoly capitalism" theorists had argued that state intervention and an increasingly politicized economy are consequences of the general crisis of capitalism. Powerful monopoly capitalists use the state to disadvantage their weaker capitalist rivals and to redistribute capital to the monopoly capitalist sector. In this way, the monopoly capitalist sector and the state are fused into a single mechanism of exploitation and oppression (Jessop 1982:32–47). This formulation was part of the traditional Marxist heritage originally rejected by Poulantzas because of its naive instrumentalism.

Capital-logic theorists such as Elmar Altvater and Joaquim Hirsch also rejected the instrumentalism of the state monopoly capitalist approach. But their work shares an essential continuity with that older model in their insistence that any successful theory of the capitalist state must be derived from an analysis of both the changing political constraints and the needs imposed by the capital accumulation process. According to these theorists, competition between individual capitalists inevitably undermines the capacity of the capitalist system to reproduce itself. This incapacity can be expressed in terms of a number of basic system needs or requisites that cannot be met by individual capitalists—material infrastructure, education of the labor force, regulation of trade, and so on. Thus there is a need for a state that can function as an "ideal collective capitalist" in order to secure these external conditions of capitalist reproduction (see Altvater 1973).

In attempting to identify those needs of capitalism, capital-logic theorists extended or "grounded" the abstract ideas of Poulantzas by adding a historical dimension to his analysis. Their research indicated that these system "needs" change over time, reflecting the changing process of capital accumulation and its unfolding internal contradictions. Chief among the influences causing these changes in state form and function is the effect of the falling rate of profit—the tendency for the rate of profit to decline as a result of competition—which constitutes the ultimate horizon or limit of capital accumulation in Marxist economic theory. Capital-logic theorists noted that these economic needs eminate from a general imperative grounded in the mode of production and that the maintenance of the economy requires that the state act to guarantee commodity production, a legal system, the private property relationship, and the wage-labor process (Blanke, et al. 1978; Aumeeruddy, et al. 1978).

Does this mean that, for capital-logic theorists, state officials are more insightful, knowledgeable, or perspicacious than individual capitalists, as the structuralist position seemed to imply? The answer is no. Capital-logic theorists argue that the capitalist state attempts to cope with threats to the accumulation process, but it does so "blindly." That is, the capitalist state (as is the case with individual capitalists) is blinded by its adherence to bourgeois ideology. Thus it is able to act only in a defensive or reactive manner, and it creates policy within a framework that assumes (and therefore supports) business success (and therefore capital accumulation) as an essential feature of the economic and social "health" of a nation.

Historically, they argue, this state intervention has taken different specific forms in response to different capitalist crises. First, the state intervened to impose capitalism as a structure and to make its citizenry dependent on the capital accumulation process. Later, the state intervened to help centralize and monopolize capital. Then it formed the imperialist world market in response to the crises of national markets and the technological transformation of the labor process. Finally, the state has promoted the process of technological revolution (in the means of production) to cope with crises brought on by the tendency for the rate of profit to fall (Hirsch 1979:83). Because each of these courses of intervention is reactive, however, they have produced contradictory effects, and these effects have occurred unevenly throughout the system. Ultimately, Hirsch argues, the state cannot successfully regulate the process of capital accumulation and its recurring deep-seated crises (1979:97).

This form of theorizing is not unique to Europe. James O'Connor (1973) has developed a different version of this theory, set within an American context. For O'Connor, the growth of the monopoly (or corporate) sector in the economy creates a number of social strains that the state attempts to mitigate through increased state spending. But this step creates another set of crises around state taxation and the state budget. Ultimately, O'Connor concludes, the state is unable to resolve the stresses that arise from monopoly capital's utilization of the state budget to socialize the costs of private capital accumulation, such as educating and training the workforce, cleaning up corporate pollution, establishing and maintaining lines of business communication and transportation and other "infrastructure," providing pensions for retired workers, health care for injured workers, and so on.

O'Connor extends the German derivationists' discussion of state fiscal crisis by showing how these struggles over the state budget and taxation have an impact on the field of class struggle. As the burden of taxation falls primarily on the working class, one might expect the fiscal crisis of the state to sharpen class struggle. The working class is politically disorganized, however, in part because many workers (e.g., teachers, social workers, police, soldiers) depend on and support the state. As a result, the American working class is politically divided even over issues with "clear" class divisions and implications (O'Connor 1973:42–44).

O'Connor's emphasis on the theme of class struggle around the institutions of the state and the state budget is also reflected in the work of an eclectic group of theorists who have focused their work on the topic of the political legitimation of the state. For these theorists, there is a fundamental contradiction between the two primary tasks of the capitalist state. On the one hand, it must sustain the process of private capital accumulation or, put more directly, it must act in the interests of capital. On the other hand, the state must also preserve the loyalty of the dominated classes in society. This means that it must appear as a *neutral arbiter* of class (and all other) conflicts. "Legitimation" theorists Offe (1984), Habermas (1975), and Wolfe (1977) see these two goals as incompatible in the long run.

Like the derivation theorists, legitimation theorists believe that the capitalist state has shouldered increasing economic and social welfare functions during the twentieth century in order to avoid economic crises. But they do not believe that these state actions have been based on purely—or even largely—economic criteria. Instead, the general thrust of the twentieth-century welfare state has been to ensure an acceptable level of "mass loyalty." Moreover, as the state expands its actions into areas previously considered to belong to the "private" sphere of capital, increasing public attention and debate is drawn to issues of public choice, planning, and control, which reveal the state's preference for capital and the one-sided nature of its functioning (Habermas 1975:68–73; Offe 1984:155–57).

Different legitimation theorists have emphasized different aspects of this crisis. Some have argued that the growth of the welfare state has derailed anti-capitalist politics to the extent that workers may find it "rational" to choose to struggle within capitalism for further reforms rather than seek to overthrow it as a system (Przeworski 1985; Offe 1984). Others have emphasized the degree to which the legitimation crisis of the modern state has displaced struggles for socialism to the level of struggles for democracy (Bowles and Gintis 1986; Wolfe 1977). All these theorists agree that the state can no longer be assumed to act solely and unambiguously in the interests of capital. Instead, state agencies and policies have become part of the field of class struggle, subject to cross-cutting and contradictory class-based pressures and influences.

By the late 1970s, the ongoing conversation over the nature of the capitalist state had brought about a fundamental reassessment of the terms of the original debate about structuralism. In response to the criticisms and extensions of his work, Poulantzas moved away from the strict structuralist position that had characterized his earlier work and recognized the state as an arena of class struggle. He increasingly modified his original concept of the capitalist state as an integrated institution over which the ruling class exercises unquestioned control. Poulantzas had come to realize that if the state is a condensation of contending class forces (1975:24–26), then the "class nature" of the state—that is, the amount and extent of class bias present in the state structure—is subject to change with the shifting balance of class forces. In his last published work (1978), Poulantzas conceded that the state must be seen as an arena of class struggle, with different class forces and alliances struggling for influence throughout the state bureaucracy. He had come to recognize the state as a fractious and divided body where localized power struggles take place among and within the various state apparatuses. While Poulantzas still occasionally reiterated that the specifically "capitalist" nature of the state apparatuses guarantees that the various class microstruggles within the state and its bureaucracies must eventually result in the long-term political interest of the bourgeoisie (see Jessop 1982:183), the implication of his final work on the state seems quite clear: It might be possible for subordinate classes to struggle for control of the state through democratic political struggles.

Yet successful class struggle within the state and the realization of democratic change was not seen by Poulantzas as inevitable. Writing in the late 1970s, he warned that as the capitalist state took on more economic and ideological roles, the displacement of class conflict could initiate a struggle by the capitalist class to establish a more "authoritarian" form of state power. For the near future, Poulantzas concluded, working-class struggles would center on the fight for democracy, not only to establish direct democracy in the workplace but also to defend the institutions of electoral democracy in the state. In taking this position, Poulantzas became one of the first orthodox Marxist state theorists to break with Leninism and specifically endorse the institutions of electoral "bourgeois" democracy in any future socialism (Poulantzas 1978:203–65; see also Altvater 1973; Therborn 1978).

Yet other Marxist theorists had taken up this theme of democratic renewal. The theorist whose work has been most closely identified with the reevaluation of parliamentary democracy and its role in any transition to socialism is the Italian scholar Norberto Bobbio (1987a, 1987b). For Bobbio, bourgeois democracy does not represent the political form of the capitalist state most responsive to capitalist power and suppression of the proletariat. Instead, the achievement of bourgeois democracy in every country has been the result of real working-class struggles for political representation and power (for a somewhat different assessment on this point, see Therborn 1977). Furthermore, economic democracy (i.e., socialism) cannot exist in the absence of full political democracy. Therefore, full parliamentary or representative democracy is for Bobbio the precondition of any advance toward socialism. Bobbio explicitly rejects the Leninist doctrine of the dictatorship of the proletariat. "A dictatorship, even one with the trappings of socialism, never achieves anything more, as far as the mass of the population who has to endure it is concerned, than a change in the ruling elite" (Bobbio 1987a:76).

For Bobbio, the state is the key arena for the struggle for socialism, which is conceptualized as the extension of political democracy to the economy. In adopting this argument, Bobbio comes close to the "revisionist" social democratic position articulated by Bernstein, in which socialism itself is seen as the culmination of a long process of democratic reform. This position has been embraced, however, by a growing number of Marxist political theorists who rejected the Soviet experience as a guide and who were soured by the failure of the radical movements of the 1960s and 1970s (Cunningham 1987; Keane 1988; Bowles and Gintis 1986; Held 1987). For some Marxists, this rethinking of the Marxist theory of the state has also led to a rejection of what is seen as traditional Marxism's "labor metaphysic" or the emphasis on the industrial working class as a revolutionary subject (Laclau and Mouffe 1985; Hindess 1987).

Increasingly, the new consensus of the "post-Marxism" of the late 1980s and the 1990s is that the traditional Marxist political project of the emancipation of the working class can be accomplished only through a broad collaboration with the "new" social movements (feminism, antiracism, antinuclear, antimilitarism, ecology, etc.) that have emerged over the past two decades. Working-class struggles must become part of a broader project of social emancipation in which no one position or theory is "guaranteed" a universal explanatory place. While Marxists increasingly recognize that class is not a universal explanation for all conditions within capitalism, they continue to argue that class-focused analyses and struggles remain key components of any successful movement for social liberation.

The Marxist Impact on Mainstream Sociology

The Marxist literature on the state gained entry in political sociology through a series of debates between pluralists (Dahl 1961, 1967; Rose 1967) and "critical," or neo-Marxist, elite theorists (Mills, 1956; Domhoff, 1967, 1978; Dye, 1976), which focused on the U.S. national, state, and regional governments. In their more sophisticated forms, both pluralism and elite theory are concerned with the struggle of organized groups within and around the state. Both theories see a multitude of interest groups and associations competing to press their various (and often conflicting) interests on state bureaucracies and agents. Often such pressure is wielded indirectly through the mediation of political parties and the electoral process. At other times pressure is exercised directly on state regulatory agencies and lawmaking bodies.

The two theories disagree over the extent to which they see the political process being organized or dominated by particular groups, economic sectors, or institutional actors. For pluralists, the political structure of capitalist democracies is an open "marketplace" in which a wide variety of interest groups compete for access to and influence over state policy makers. State policies are created through a process of pressure, negotiation, and compromise in which these interest groups form shifting coalitions and bargain with both government agencies and one another in order to reach outcomes in which the interests of all concerned parties are (ideally) represented. Pluralists conclude that no single ruling group or "elite" will always or even usually prevail.

While pluralists argue that political power in capitalist democracies is *diffuse*, elite theorists see power as *concentrated* in the hands of the "elites" who staff and manage the top positions in dominant economic, political, and social institutions. Furthermore, they believe that there is a *community of shared interest* among elite members of the pinnacle institutions of society, which results in a dominant, consolidated, and hierarchical social order. Acting in a self-conscious, collaborative fashion, these elites make up the ruling body of any society.

It is difficult to summarize the impact of the Marxist contribution to this mainstream debate over the past two decades. For one thing, as we have shown in the preceding section, there is no single theoretical position to which all Marxist political sociologists subscribe. Consequently, as various Marxists have intervened in the debate within mainstream political sociology, they have established a number of sometimes quite contradictory theoretical positions. The major theoretical divide has tended to follow the split between "instrumentalists" and "structuralists" (see Gold, Lo, and Wright 1975). But there is no simple demarcation of contending camps; within each general theoretical group there are a variety of contending arguments and positions. Also, there is a recent trend toward theories that integrate elements of seemingly competing positions. Marxists have made important contributions to three specific debates within political sociology: (1) the origins of the New Deal; (2) the extent and methods of business influence over government policy making; and (3) the autonomy of state regulation. Marxist contributions to these debates, as well as recent attempts by Marxists to synthesize competing theories, are discussed below.

The single most important contribution made by Marxists to the pluralist/ elite debate has been to bring in the concept of class (and, by extension, class-based power) as a major explanatory variable. Marxists of all stripes argue that pluralists and elite theorists have neglected the topics of class and class conflict. This having been said, it is clear that most, but not all, Marxists find themselves conceptually closer to elite theory in the debate. Some theorists—for example, G. William Domhoff and Theda Skocpol, whose work is otherwise quite different—are difficult to categorize either as Marxists or elite theorists. Each rejects the Marxist label, but their work has evolved from and addressed debates within Marxist state theory.

Other Marxists, perhaps more surprisingly, seem to show some affinities for the pluralist pole of the debate. The works of some American disciples of Poulantzas—Jill Quadagno, for instance—show an almost pluralist concern with establishing the political field as one of multiple rather than simple determinations. In terms remarkably reminiscent of pluralist rhetoric, Quadagno writes that "the state functions as a mediating body, weighing the priorities of various interest groups with unequal access to power, negotiating compromises between class factions, and incorporating working-class demands into legislation on capitalist terms" (Quadagno 1984:632). The differences with pluralism are clear—the references to "unequal access to power," "class fractions," and "capitalist terms"—but so are the similarities.

The social welfare policies of the New Deal, most especially the Social Security Act of 1935 and the National Industrial Recovery Act of 1933, have been at the center of a long-term debate that has involved a number of prominent neo-Marxist political sociologists (Domhoff 1970, 1986; Skocpol 1980; Skocpol and Ikenberry 1983; Quadagno 1984; Levine 1988; Orloff 1988; Jenkins and Brents 1989). While the specific details are beyond the scope of this chapter (for a review, see Quadagno 1987), in general terms the participants have staked out positions on the scope, timing, and causes of New Deal reforms that roughly correspond to different theories of the state described in the preceding section of this chapter.

For example, Quadagno, Levine, and Quadagno and Meyer (1989) have attempted to develop a Poulantzian analysis of New Deal reforms that emphasizes competing class and class fractional interests and the role of the state in attempting to balance these conflicting pressures. In turn, Domhoff has emphasized the relative consensus of the dominant corporate-liberal sector of monopoly capital and its control of the state in order to explain both the passage and the nature of the reforms. This approach reflects his allegiance to radical elite theory and to more instrumental versions of Marxism.

Of all the participants in the debate, Skocpol and Orloff give the least weight to purely class actors and interests. Instead, they focus on the pressures placed on the state by a variety of class and nonclass actors, the interests of state bureaucrats considered as a separate category, and most important, the constraints created by past policies, the social composition of the Democratic party, and economic conditions in the larger society. Finally, the contributions of Levine, and of Jenkins and Brents, emphasize the role of class struggle and working-class protests in creating the sense of crisis that led to the reforms. In their "class struggle" analysis, they portray New Deal social and industrial policies as resulting from a complex process of protest and struggle on the part of labor, with reform being a state response accepted by a fundamentally divided capitalist class.

While the debate over the New Deal has focused on the federal level of state power, other Marxists have made important contributions to the study of the state at the level of regional and local governments. New Haven, Connecticut, was the site of a famous study by the pluralist Dahl. Then, almost two decades later, New Haven was reexamined by the elite theorist Domhoff. The two studies reached contradictory conclusions. Marxist contributors to this debate have generally agreed with Domhoff that business leaders play a preponderant role in establishing policy at the level of local government.

Just as with New Deal welfare policy, however, there is considerable debate over the relative autonomy of state actors vis-á-vis business elites. Thus, in a comparative analysis of the politics of urban growth, Mollenkopf (1983) concludes that "political entrepreneurs" play the decisive role in formulating urban policy, while Friedland (1983) argues that the impetus behind urban-renewal policies is the political influence of large national business firms. While most Marxists tend to concur with Friedland's position, differences of opinion abound over the degree of internal business unity. On the one hand, Domhoff (1983) found that the elites of New Haven were fundamentally unified, as did Ewen (1978) in her study of Detroit. On the other, Molotch (1976) and Mollenkopf (1978) have emphasized business disunity and the conflicting interests of different capitalist sectors. Still others have emphasized the role of broad-based local business organizations, which mediate intrabusiness conflicts and promote a common business agenda (Whitt 1979, 1984; Ratcliff 1979; Useem 1984; Kleniewski 1987).

Marxist theorists have made significant contributions to our understanding of the ties between the business community and political parties. With the legalization of corporate political action committees (PACs) in the 1970s, a new avenue for business influence in politics emerged. Since 1980, a considerable journalistic literature on business PACs has developed, documenting the increasing importance of business PAC spending in congressional and presidential campaigns (see Drew 1983; Edsall 1984). Marxist sociologists have been primarily interested in using business PAC campaign finance data to answer two questions: Is business political spending unified or divided? Does the record of business campaign spending confirm the "yankee/cowboy" thesis (see Sale, 1976; Davis, 1986) of a fundamental split between the "old" capitalism of the northeastern U.S. and the "new" sunbelt capitalism of the Southwest?

Results have been mixed, with Clawson et al. (1985, 1986) finding a pattern of relatively unified business spending in their two studies of the 1980 campaign (which includes support for both Republicans and Democrats, but in different races) and little support for the yankee/cowboy thesis. But Salt (1989), examining election data for later campaigns, noted an emerging differentiation between eastern capital and a modified capitalist "Sunbelt" that includes midwestern businesses, with Sunbelt industries more conservative than average and more likely to support Republican and New Right candidates. All studies found a high rate of business support for conservative Republican candidates and a corresponding low rate of support for liberal Democrats. These studies of business PACs have been supplemented by an array of Marxist studies of New Right institutions, such as foundations, policy-planning institutes, and think tanks (see Jenkins and Shumate, 1985; Peschek, 1987, 1989). These studies demonstrate how the economic resources of capitalists are used, first, to influence government policy formulation in the think tanks and policy-planning institutes and, then, by influencing who gets elected, to effect the subsequent process of policy making.

Similar theoretical disputes mark Marxist studies of state regulation. Regulation is important for Marxists studying the state because regulatory agencies are the medium through which the state most directly impinges on and acts to promote the accumulation of private capital. Here the debate has centered on questions of who initiates and controls the state regulatory process. In his *Railroads and Regulation* (1965), Gabriel Kolko argued that, contrary to popular belief and liberal pluralist theory, railroad executives were the principal force behind the passage of the 1887 Interstate Commerce Act establishing federal regulation of the railroad industry. They favored regulation because of their inability "to rationalize their increasingly chaotic industry" through voluntary agreements (Kolko 1965:4). The resulting legislation was intended to utilize the coercive power of the state to overcome the destructive effects of intraindustry competition. This interpretation established the basic outlines of the theory of corporate liberalism. This theory underlay many Marxist analyses of the 1960s (see Domhoff 1986), as well as other, more recent "instrumentalist" and "power structure" research on regulation.

As in other areas of political sociology we have examined, the development of more structural models of state power—especially "class struggle" theory (see Esping-Anderson et al., 1976)—and "state-centered" approaches has led to the emergence of competing analyses and interpretations of state regulation. Thus, for example, recent analyses of government regulatory agencies by Skocpol and Finegold (1982) and Hooks (1990) have stressed the autonomy of state managers.

Frietag (1983) examined the composition of federal regulatory commissions from 1887 to 1975 and found little evidence of corporate domination. This finding influenced his subsequent (1985) reexamination of Kolko's study of the Interstate Commerce Act. Frietag concludes that Kolko's "business leaders" were in fact desperate men reeling under a barrage of labor attacks and social criticism. Unlike the more state-centered approaches of Skocpol and Hooks, Frietag emphasizes the structurally limited or "relative" autonomy of the state by noting that in passing regulatory legislation, the state necessarily acted to preserve capitalist-class interests. However, he also indicates that these events occurred in a broader institutional context than Kolko's instrumentalist account would suggest. Like Kolko, Frietag concludes that railroad regulation benefited the railroad industry's owners. But, Frietag argues, the enactment of railroad regulation had, in addition to the goal of creating prosperity for the railroads, the further objectives of accommodating the interests of other sectors of capital and (by regulating labor relations) defusing class conflict between workers and owners in the railroad industry. An unanticipated consequence of this action was to displace conflict between capital and labor from the workplace to the state— a theme developed by other "class struggle" theorists.

In contrast to the two interpretations of state regulation discussed earlier, other theorists (DiTomaso 1978; McGuire 1989) have reiterated the instrumentalist position in studies of the U.S. Department of Labor and of regulation of the electric utility industry at the turn of the century. Some recent studies have attempted to go beyond the conflicting theoretical positions to develop theories that synthesize components of these theories. Thus, while starting from a fundamentally instrumentalist position, McGuire (1989) incorporates elements of class-struggle theory into his account of the origins of electric utility regulation in the United States. He argues that the typical instrumentalist focus on the manipulation of state policy making by capitalist actors needs to be expanded to take account of the ways in which state policy makers attempt to contain challenges from below by transferring economic contradictions into the state apparatus.

Finally, we should note two general trends that we see emerging. First, there have been several attempts to synthesize competing theories by individuals working from various perspectives. Martin (1989) has proposed a "coalition perspective" which suggests a need to recognize state-centered interests while acknowledging the relative power of state actors vis-á-vis class-based groups (1989:216). Amenta and Carruthers offer a different but related argument, which suggests that different theories may explain particular outcomes better and, therefore, each theory should be valued for its particular explanatory capacity (1988:676).

Marxist analysts have occasionally found support for specific propositions of state-centered theory (cf. Miller and Canak 1988), but they continue to emphasize class formations and economic dynamics as the central, if not the determinate, factor shaping state form, function, and action. They have criticized state-centered synthetic approaches for conflating and collapsing levels of analysis, for simply reversing the terms of the instrumentalist problematic, and for ignoring the crucial variable of class (cf. Levine 1988:7–14). More successful Marxist syntheses have involved combining insights from different class-based theories—an approach utilized by Domhoff (1987), Jenkins and Brents (1989), McGuire (1989), and Hooks (1990), among others.

A second recent trend in class-focused theory suggests that the extent of state autonomy and class unity should be conceived as variables to be demonstrated within (historically) specific contexts. This point was made most forcefully by

Preschel (1990:650), but had been offered earlier by Zeitlin (1980, 1984), and Domhoff (1987). This position has suggested the need for further empirical testing. This is a return to the long-standing strength of U.S. sociology (compared to other national traditions). Recent research (by advocates of both state-centered and Marxist theory) has involved testing the explanatory power of theories at the local, regional, national, and even supranational levels. This work has indicated: (1) significant variance in the autonomy of state actors from class domination at various levels of the state; and (2) the ability of the capitalist class to formulate nationwide policy through the mobilization of capacity and enactment of policy from various levels within the state. Marxist sociology, by redefining and expanding the concepts of state and politics, has fundamentally altered American political sociology.

Conclusion

When Jessop surveyed state theories in 1981, he found U.S. theory so under-developed that he essentially ignored it, suggesting that it was only a pale imitation of European theories (1982). In the intervening decade, American Marxists have analyzed and assimilated insights from the European debates. There have been two unique contributions. State-centered theory is unique, although its explanatory ability remains to be demonstrated. Second, the seem-ing universality of direct class influence has repeatedly been demonstrated at various levels in the United States. This may seem an anachronism to those who thought we had superseded the days of control of the state by identifiable business leaders and interests. It is clear that by beginning to analyze state policy making at various levels and by investigating the impacts of class forces on various governmental forms (parliamentary, federalist, republican, absolutist, etc.), U.S. theorists are poised to make a contribution to synthesizing and/or specifying the relevance of state theory.

Marxist state theory also seems to be at a significant turning point that may affect its influence in the larger society as well. The array of available evidence on the limits of state autonomy (especially in the United States) is increasingly impressive. Yet this insight should not signal a return to Leninism. Instead, consistent with the insights of Altvater, Poulantzas, and Bobbio and the contin-ued success of socialist parties in Western Europe and Canada, the existence of some state autonomy and the susceptibility of the state to democratic change may signal a potential for changing the relations of class power in the United States.

To the extent that Marxist and neo-Marxist theories of the capitalist state (1) enlighten us about the contradictions between classes and class fractions, and within the state; (2) identify the crucial elements of class domination; and (3) provide insight into those circumstances when noncapitalist class power was successfully mobilized to enact policy, they may indicate potential courses and methods of action that could guide democratic movements in their efforts to remove such restraints. Using such insights to guide democratic action may help us reverse the setbacks in social, economic, political, environmental, and spiritual life that have occurred in the United States since the 1950s.

References

Altvater, Elmar. 1973. "Notes on Some Problems of State Interventionism." *Kapitalistate* 1:96–116; 2:76–83.

Amenta, Edwin, and Bruce Carruthers. 1988. "The Formative Years of U.S. Social Spending Policies: Theories of the Welfare State and the American States During the Great Depression." *American Sociological Review* 53:661–78.

Aumeeruddy, Aboo, Bruno Lautier, and Ramon Tortajada. 1978. "Labor Power and the State." *Capital and Class* 6:42–66.

Baran, Paul, and Paul Sweezy. 1966. *Monopoly Capital.* New York: Monthly Review Press.

Blanke, Bernhard, Ulrich Jurgens, and Hans Kastendiek. 1978. "On the Current Marxist Discussion on the Analysis of Form and Function of the Bourgeois State." Pp. 108–47 in *State and Capital*, ed. John Holloway and Sol Picciotto. Austin: University of Texas Press.

Block, Fred. 1987. *Revising State Theory*. Philadelphia: Temple University Press.

Bobbio, Norberto. 1987a. *Which Socialism?* Minneapolis: University of Minnesota Press.

———. 1987b. *The Future of Democracy*. Minneapolis: University of Minnesota Press.

Bowles, Samuel, and Herbert Gintis. 1986. *Democracy and Capitalism*. New York: Basic Books.

Burris, Val. 1987. "Business Support for the New Right: A Consumer's Guide." *Socialist Review* 91:33–63.

Carnoy, Martin. 1984. *The State and Political Theory*. Princeton: Princeton University Press.

Clawson, Dan, Allen Kaufman, and Alan Neustadtl. 1985. "Corporate PACs for a New Pax Americana." *Insurgent Sociologist* 13:63–75.

Clawson, Dan, Alan Neustadtl, and James Bearden. 1986. "The Logic of Business Unity: Corporate Contributions to the 1980 Congressional Elections." *American Sociological Review* 51:797–811.

Cunningham, Frank. 1987. *Democratic Theory and Socialism*. Cambridge: Cambridge University Press.

Dahl, Robert. 1961. *Who Governs?* New Haven: Yale University Press.

———. 1967. *Pluralist Democracy in the United States*. Skokie: Rand McNally.

Davis, Mike. 1986. *Prisoners of the American Dream*. London: Verso.

DiTomaso, Nancy. 1978. "The Expropriation of the Means of Administration: Class Struggle Over the U.S. Department of Labor." *Kapitalistate* 7:81–105.

Domhoff, G. William. 1967. *Who Rules America?* Englewood Cliffs: Prentice-Hall.

———. 1970. *The Higher Circles*. New York: Vintage Books.

———. 1978. *Who Really Rules?* Santa Monica: Goodyear.

———. 1986. "Corporate-Liberal Theory and the Social Security Act: A Chapter in the Sociology of Knowledge." *Politics and Society* 15:297–330.

———. 1987a. "Corporal Liberal Theory and the Social Security Act." *Politics and Society* 15:297–321.

———. 1987b. "The Wagner Act and Theories of the State: A New Analysis Based on Class-Segment Theory." *Political Power and Social Theory* 6:159–85.

Drew, Elizabeth. 1983. *Politics and Money*. New York: Macmillan.

Dye, Thomas. 1976. *Who's Running America?* Englewood Cliffs: Prentice-Hall.
Edsall, Thomas Byrne. 1984. *The New Politics of Inequality*. New York: Norton.
Engels, Friedrich. 1978. "The Tactics of Social Democracy." Pp. 556–573 in *The Marx-Engels Reader*, ed. Robert Tucker. New York: Norton.
———. 1973. *The Condition of the Working Class in England*. Moscow: Progress Publishers.
Esping-Anderson, Gosta, Roger Friedland, and Erik Olin Wright. 1976. "Modes of Class Struggle and the Capitalist State." *Kapitalistate* 7:186–220.
Ewen, Lynda Ann. 1978. *Corporate Power and Urban Crisis in Detroit*. Princeton: Princeton University Press.
Friedland, Roger. 1983. *Power and Crisis in the City*. New York: Schocken Books.
Frietag, Peter. 1983. "The Myth of Corporate Capture: Regulatory Commissions in the United States." *Social Problems* 30:480–91.
———. 1985. "Class Conflict and the Rise of Government Regulation." *Insurgent Sociologist* 12:51–65.
Gold, David, Clarence Lo, and Erik Olin Wright. 1975. "Recent Developments in Marxist Theories of the Capitalist State." *Monthly Review* 27:(Oct.)29–43, (Nov.)36–51.
Goldman, Emma. 1923. *My Disillusionment in Russia*. New York: Doubleday.
Gough, Ian. 1979. *The Political Economy of the Welfare State*. London: Macmillan.
Gramsci, Antonio. 1977. *Selections from Political Writings (1910–1920)*. New York: International Publishers.
Habermas, Jurgen. 1975. *Legitimation Crisis*. Boston: Beacon Press.
Held, David. 1987. *Models of Democracy*. Stanford: Stanford University Press.
Hindess, Barry. 1987. *Politics and Class Analysis*. London: Basil Blackwell.
Hirsch, Joachim. 1979. "The State Apparatus and Social Reproduction: Elements of a Theory of the Bourgeois State." Pp. 57–107 in *State and Capital*, ed. John Holloway and Sol Picciotto. Austin: University of Texas Press.
Holloway, John and Sol Picciotto, eds. 1979. *State and Capital: A Marxist Debate*. Austin: University of Texas Press.
Hooks, Gregory. 1990. "From an Autonomous to a Captured State Agency: The Decline of the New Deal in Agriculture." *American Sociological Review* 55:29–43.
Horne, Alistair. 1965. *The Fall of Paris*. New York: St. Martin's.
Jenkins, J. Craig and Barbara Brents. 1989. "Social Protest, Hegemonic Competition, and Social Reform: A Political Struggle Interpretation of the Origins of the American Welfare State." *American Sociological Review* 54:891–909.
Jenkins, J. Craig and Teri Shumate. 1985. "Cowboy Capitalists and the Rise of the 'New Right': An Analysis of Contributors to Conservative Policy Formation Organizations." *Social Problems* 33:130–45.
Jessop, Bob. 1982. *The Capitalist State*. New York: New York University Press.
Kautsky, Karl. 1964. *The Dictatorship of the Proletariat*. Ann Arbor: University of Michigan Press.
Keane, John. 1988. *Democracy and Civil Society*. London: Verso.
Kleniewski, Nancy. 1987. "Local Business Leaders and Urban Policy: A Case Study." *Insurgent Sociologist* 14:33–56.
Kolko, Gabriel. 1965. *Railroads and Regulation, 1877–1916*. New York: Norton.
———. 1967. *The Triumph of Conservatism*. Chicago: Quadrangle Books.
LaClau, Ernesto, and Chantal Mouffe. 1985. *Hegemony and Socialist Strategy*. London: Verso.
Lenin, V.I. 1971. *Selected Works*. New York: International Publishers.
———. 1975. "The Proletarian Revolution and the Renegade Kautsky." Pp. 461–76 in *The Lenin Anthology*, ed. Robert Tucker. New York: Norton.
Levine, Rhonda. 1988. *Class Struggle and the New Deal*. Lawrence: University of Kansas Press.

Luxemburg, Rosa. 1961. *The Russian Revolution and Leninism or Marxism?* Ann Arbor: University of Michigan Press.

McGuire, Patrick. 1989. "Instrumental Class Power and the Origin of Class-Based State Regulation in the U.S. Electric Utility Industry." *Critical Sociology* 16:181–203.

McQuarie, Donald, and Mark Spaulding. 1989. "The Concept of Power in Marxist Theory." *Critical Sociology* 16:3–28.

Martin, Cathie. 1989. "Business Influence and State Power: The Case of U.S. Corporate Tax Policy." *Politics and Society* 17:189–223.

Marx, Karl. 1973a. *The Revolutions of 1848*. London: Penguin Books.

———. 1973b. *Surveys from Exile*. London: Penguin Books.

———. 1974. *The First International and After*. London: Penguin Books.

———. 1975. *Early Writings*. London: Penguin Books.

Miliband, Ralph. 1969. *The State in Capitalist Society*. New York: Basic Books.

———. 1970. "The Capitalist State—Reply to Nicos Poulantzas." *New Left Review* 59:53–60.

———. 1973. "Poulantzas and the Capitalist State." *New Left Review* 82:83–92.

Miller, Berkeley and William Canak. 1988. "The Passage of Public Sector Collective Bargaining in the American State." *Political Power and Social Theory* 7: 249–92.

Mills, C. Wright. 1956. *The Power Elite*. New York: Oxford University Press.

Mollenkopf, John. 1978. "The Postwar Politics of Urban Development." Pp. 117–52 in *Marxism and the Metropolis*, ed. William Tabb and Larry Sawyers. New York: Oxford University Press.

———. 1983. *The Contested City*. Princeton: Princeton University Press.

Molotch, Harvey. 1976. "The City as a Growth Machine: Toward a Political Economy of Place." *American Journal of Sociology* 82:209–32.

O'Connor, James. 1973. *The Fiscal Crisis of the State*. New York: St. Martin's.

Offe, Claus. 1984. *Contradictions of the Welfare State*. Cambridge: MIT Press.

Orloff, Ann. 1988. "The Political Origins of America's Belated Welfare State." Pp. 37–80 in *The Politics of Social Policy in the United States*, ed. Margaret Weir, Ann Orloff, and Theda Skocpol. Princeton: Princeton University Press.

Pannekoek, Anton. 1975. "Workers' Councils." Pp. 384–500 in *Root and Branch*. New York: Fawcett.

Peschek, Joseph. 1987. *Policy-Planning Organizations*. Philadelphia: Temple University Press.

———. 1989. "'Free the Fortune 500!' The American Enterprise Institute and the Politics of the Capitalist Class in the 1970s." *Critical Sociology* 16:165–80.

Poulantzas, Nicos. 1969. "The Problem of the Capitalist State." *New Left Review* 58:67–78.

———. 1973. *Political Power and Social Classes*. London: NLB.

———. 1975. *Classes in Contemporary Capitalism*. London: NLB.

———. 1976. "The Capitalist State: A Reply to Miliband and Laclau." *New Left Review* 95:63–83.

———. 1978. *State, Power, Socialism*. London: NLB.

Preschel, Harland. 1990. "Steel and the State: Industry Politics and Business Policy Formation, 1940–1989." *American Sociological Review* 55:648–68.

Przeworski, Adam. 1985. *Capitalism and Social Democracy*. Cambridge: Cambridge University Press.

Quadagno, Jill. 1984. "Welfare Capitalism and the Social Security Act of 1935." *American Sociological Review* 49:632–47.

———. 1987. "Theories of the Welfare State." Pp. 109–28 in *Annual Review of Sociology*, ed. W. Richard Scott and James Short, Jr. Palo Alto: Annual Reviews.

Quadagno, Jill, and Madonna Meyer. 1989. "Organized Labor, State Structures, and Social Policy Development: A Case Study of Old Age Assistance in Ohio, 1916–1940." *Social Problems* 36:181–96.

Ratcliffe, Richard. 1979. "Capitalist Class Structure and the Decline of Older Industrial Cities." *Insurgent Sociologist* 9:60–74.

Rose, Arnold. 1967. *The Power Structure*. London: Oxford University Press

Sale, Kirkpatrick. 1976. *Power Shift*. New York: Random House.

Salt, James. 1989. "Sunbelt Capital and Conservative Political Realignment in the 1970s and 1980s." *Critical Sociology* 16:145–63.

Serber, David. 1975. "Regulating Reform: The Social Organization of Insurance Regulation." *Insurgent Sociologist* 5:83–105.

Skocpol, Theda. 1980. "Political Response to Capitalist Crisis: Neo-Marxist Theories of the State and the Case of the New Deal." *Politics and Society* 10:155–201.

Skocpol, Theda, and Kenneth Finegold. 1982. "State Capacity and Economic Intervention in the Early New Deal." *Political Science Quarterly* 97:255–78.

Skocpol, Theda, and John Ikenberry. 1983. "The Political Formation of the American Welfare State in Historical and Comparative Perspective." Pp. 87–148 in *Comparative Social Research*, ed. Richard Tomasson. Greenwich: JAI Press.

Sirianni, Carmen. 1982. *Workers' Control and Social Democracy*. London: New Left Books.

Smart, D.A., ed. 1978. *Pannekoek and Gorter's Marxism*. London: Pluto Press.

Strikwerda, Karl. 1991. "Three Cities, Three Socialisms." Pp.185–201 in *Bringing Class Back In*, ed. Scott McNall, Rhonda Levine, and Rick Fantasia. Philadelphia: Temple University Press.

Therborn, Göran. 1977. "The Rule of Capital and the Rise of Democracy." *New Left Review* 103:3–41.

———. 1978. *What Does the Ruling Class Do When It Rules?* London: NLB.

Tudor, H., and J.M. Tudor, eds. 1988. *Marxism and Social Democracy*. New York: Cambridge University Press.

Urry, John. 1981. *The Political Economy of Capitalist Societies*. London: Macmillan.

Useem, Michael. 1984. *The Inner Circle*. New York: Oxford University Press.

von Braunmuhl, Claudia. 1978. "On the Analysis of the Bourgeois Nation State within the World Market Context." Pp. 160–77 in *State and Capital*, ed. John Holloway and Sol Picciotto. Austin: University of Texas Press.

Whitt, J. Allen. 1979. "Can Capitalists Organize Themselves?" *Insurgent Sociologist* 9:51–9.

———. 1984. *Urban Elites and Mass Transportation*. Princeton: Princeton University Press.

Wolfe, Alan. 1977. *The Limits of Legitimacy*. New York: Free Press.

Wright, Erik Olin. 1978. *Class, Crisis, and the State*. London: NLB.

Zeitlin, Maurice. 1980. "On Classes, Class Conflict, and the State: An Introductory Note." Pp. 1–37 in *Classes, Class Conflict, and the State*, ed. Maurice Zeitlin. Cambridge: Winthrop.

———. 1984. *The Civil Wars in Chile*. Princeton: Princeton University Press.

CORPORATIONS AND THE ECONOMY:

MARXIST SCHOLARSHIP AND THE CORPORATE ECONOMY

Davita Silfen Glasberg
and
Kenneth J. Neubeck

The large-scale corporation seems to touch almost every facet of the operation of modern-day capitalist society. Yet the political, economic, and social significance of the corporation is today, as it has been over the past century, a subject of continuing debate and inquiry. The principal critics of capitalism and the role of corporations within it have, until recently, come largely from outside the discipline of sociology. Such critics have included social activists, labor leaders, and academicians from a variety of fields. Many engaged in Marxist analyses that framed theoretical issues on which sociologists have since shed empirical light. Most sociological scholarship dealing with the corporation followed in the wake of path-breaking work by the late C. Wright Mills (1956), who in the mid-1950s warned of the dangers posed to democracy in the United States by concentrated corporate power. Subsequent work in sociology can only be said to have underscored Mills's concerns and provided an additional list of ways in which the exercise of corporate power has grown to be problematic.

Non-Marxist analysts of this new corporate capitalism were prone to ignore its shortcomings in favor of celebrating its successes. In their view, the organization of corporate enterprise was moving in directions that could only be socially beneficial. The response to the unexamined faith that "Capitalism works!" was provided by Marxist analyses, at first from outside sociology and more recently from within. Sociologists have not only focused their attention on industrial corporations, in the tradition of most Marxist analysts; they have also of late been exploring the political, economic and social role of major financial corporations, such as banks. Current research on finance capital has put sociology on the cutting edge of present-day Marxist scholarship on the corporation. The legacy of this scholarship rests with Marx himself, and so it is with him that we open this chapter.

Karl Marx

The life of Karl Marx (1818–83) spanned a unique period of economic change. Machinery transformed not only methods of production but the entire labor process. Industrial capitalism meant a decline in the economic significance of individual artisans and craftspersons; they were supplanted by the small manufacturing firm in which production was brought under one roof. Independent producers became employees, as the relations of production shifted in favor of the owners of capital. It was a world of "free enterprise" in which owners of capital were free to start up a manufacturing endeavor, free to compete in the market with others, free to produce what and how they wanted without state interference, and free to go out of business. It was a world of numerous small entrepreneurs whose strivings constituted the "invisible hand" behind economic progress, to use the words of Adam Smith (Smith 1952).

Marx viewed this world of free enterprise, to which machine technology contributed so much opportunity for increased productivity, as riding on an important set of dynamics (Marx 1967). Production, once under the control of individual craftspersons and artisans, and performed in towns and villages across the countryside, was being relocated. The city-based factory, managed by its owner, was the new locale. Factory production involved segmenting labor into ever more specialized but unskilled activities. Because they were without ownership interests in their place of employment, workers were denied say over the direction, quality, and quantity of work demanded of them.

This social arrangement represented a carefully engineered labor process designed to maximize profits for the owner of the firm (Braverman 1974; Edwards 1979; Clawson 1980). Ironically, as Marx pointed out most fully in *Capital*, when the workers strove to produce more, they enriched not themselves but the capitalist. The owner's profit, or "surplus value," as it accumulated, provided a source of capital that made it possible to expand production further. This effort was often aided by investments in newer technology that reduced the need for labor while expanding the productivity of the firm.

In this world of "free enterprise," individual capitalists found themselves in competition with one another. To win out in this competition, firm owners found it necessary to use increasing amounts of capital to improve, update, and modernize technology so as to minimize costs, maximize productivity, and extract as much surplus value from each worker as was possible. This "revolutionizing of the forces of production" forced down wage rates and increased worker unemployment and alienation (Marx 1974). At the same time it weeded out weaker or less affluent firm owners. The latter process meant that ownership within industrial capitalism would become concentrated in fewer and fewer hands.

Marxist scholars have examined these processes and relationships, generating an enormous array of insights into the role of corporations in the modern-day capitalist political economy. Some of the most recent Marxist research has begun to examine the ascendance of financial institutions as these have become central corporate actors. This new scholarship suggests the need to explore the roles of both financial and nonfinancial corporations in the capitalist political economy.

We begin here by discussing the historic emergence of the corporation and its changing patterns of ownership and control. As we then see, the latter have given rise to debate and subsequent scholarly inquiry in which Marxist analyses have played an important role.

The Development of the Corporate Economy

In the United States, the process of firm growth and concentration of ownership began to take hold after the Civil War. The modern "corporation" was born in the nineteenth century as transportation and communication technology began to make regional and even national markets for manufactured goods possible (Chandler 1977). Free enterprise capitalism—the world of small competitive entrepreneurs—began to give way to "corporate capitalism." A relatively small number of large, heavily capitalized firms would come to dominate most sectors of U.S. manufacturing.

Under free-enterprise capitalism, firm owners were also their managers. Given the small size of such firms and the relative simplicity of the technology involved, this was not a problem. Under corporate capitalism, however, owners found that the demands for worker supervision and the increasing complexity of technology outran their capabilities. The solution was the employment of salaried managers for day-to-day control of corporate operations.

A second development that occurred during the emergence of corporate capitalism was the opening up of opportunities for firm ownership to the general public. Increasingly expensive technology and the pressures to expand markets became too costly for even the most successful firms to support through their own profits. To escalate the rate at which investment capital was generated, owners offered shares of stock in their firms to anyone—including workers—who cared to make the investment. Stockholding was not only an economic activity; owning a share of stock entitled one to a vote on corporate matters at stockholders' meetings. Stockholding thus implied the right to exercise some owner power over firm management; no longer was this right privately monopolized. For many observers, particularly those outside sociology, stockholding also heralded the separation of ownership and control, so that stockholders shared ownership and managers controlled the functioning of the firm (Berle and

Means 1932). This notion was based on the assumption that ownership of shares of stock was dispersed among thousands of small independent shareholders.

Scholars unsympathetic to Marxist thought argued that the separation of ownership and control (proclaimed as the "managerial revolution") put day-to-day managerial decisions in the hands of persons without substantial ownership interests (Burnham 1941). According to this view, salaried managers were thus relieved from pressures for profit maximization, which could and at times had led to abuses of managerial authority vis-á-vis workers. Instead, managers had only to produce the minimum amount of profits it took to satisfy the expectations of investors (Dahrendorf 1957; Cyert and March 1963; Bell 1973). Beyond this, managers were free to be concerned with the needs of workers, consumers, and so on, as well as to plan for the long-run needs of firm development. The managerial revolution having been proclaimed a reality, some of its proponents even began to speak of the emergence of the "soulful corporation," intent on doing good even at the sacrifice of profits (Kaysen 1957). To some, the heart of the modern, socially responsible, capitalist enterprise was its "technostructure"—the highly skilled and educated staff upon whom top corporate managers depended (Galbraith 1967). Their knowledge gave them power in the firm. Since they were salaried and without ownership interests, these members of the technostructure were prone to push their firms in socially responsible directions.

Moreover, said those arguing that capitalism works, we have a system of ownership quite unlike anything Marx envisioned. Far from being a system whose ownership is dominated by a rapacious, exploitative propertied class, modern capitalism is a model of democracy. We have a system more rightfully called "democratic capitalism" or "people's capitalism" (see Perlo 1958; Villarejo 1962 for a description of this). Anyone can own a piece of the capitalist system and benefit from its fruits. Indeed, the harder people work for the system, the more shares of ownership they may be able to purchase in it and the more valuable these shares are likely to become. We do not need a revolution to transfer ownership into workers' hands; such a transfer is already under way. And it is under way because of the success of our capitalist system, not its failures.

Those who have been anxious to dispose of Marx's ideas have also been quick to point out that ours is a two-tier economy in which small business continues to play an important role. Yes, some corporations have risen to dominant, top-tier positions within the capitalist system; but their powers have been mitigated or checked by "countervailing powers" that help to ensure that the needs of society are served (Galbraith 1952). The modern large corporation must attend not only to the demands of stockholders and workers, customers, and suppliers but to the demands of our government as well. Smaller businesses, occupying the lower tier, have their own reasons to be "soulful." The market arenas of small firms are highly competitive, much more akin to the "free-enterprise economy" discussed earlier. The need to please is a constant presence in the life of the small firm. But they do not have the resources available to be as philanthropic as do large corporations. Moreover, the presence of this second sector represents further ownership opportunities for workers. Within our capitalist system, they are free to "be their own boss" and join the ranks of small business owners if they so wish.

In sum, the modern corporation was portrayed by non-Marxist scholars as a benign, even kindly institution that arose to meet people's common needs. In the next section we see how Marxist analysis established a different portrait.

Marxist Critiques of the 'Soulful Corporation' and Managerialism

Beginning in the 1960s, Marxist scholarship began a systematic critique of the underpinnings of the view that capitalism was successful and had a "human face" (Perlo 1957; Kolko 1962). First, the notion of separation of ownership and control, upon which the concept of the soulful corporation largely depends, was attacked. The data available concerning corporate ownership are limited because corporations are not required to disclose their owners on request. Nevertheless, it was clear that corporate managers had ownership interests through mechanisms such as options to buy stock in their own firms at favorable prices (Villarejo 1962; Glasberg and Schwartz 1983). More recent research has demonstrated that, as an occupational group, corporate managers are involved in stock ownership—both in their own firms and in others—to a significant degree (Neubeck and Breslin 1989). Scholars thus questioned the extent to which the separation of ownership and control actually existed, as well as the managerialists' claim that managers could control the firm with as little as 5 percent ownership of its stock. Furthermore, research indicated no difference in profit performance between owner-controlled and manager-controlled firms (Kamerschen 1968; Zeitlin and Norich 1979; Useem 1980). Indeed, the factor that did account for variations in firms' profit performance was barrier to entry: larger corporations posed barriers to newly formed smaller firms' ability to compete and survive in established industries. In this context, the notion of the soulful corporation could be seen only as a public relations ploy designed to mystify the true interests of those who managed modern firms.

The concept of "people's capitalism" was likewise subjected to harsh criticism (Perlo 1958; Lundberg 1968). While it was true that most large corporations had made their stock available for purchase by members of the public, in others, shares of ownership were still privately held. And while millions of members of the public did indeed own stock, most of the shares held by individuals remained in the hands of the most affluent, including the managers of America's largest firms (Zeitlin 1974). The degree to which stock ownership is concentrated in the hands of a few was largely a matter of speculation until recent federal studies of wealth distribution in the United States (Avery 1984; U.S. Department of Commerce 1986).

Marxist analysts also challenged the notion that the modern corporation (and its management) is essentially passive and reacts to the felt needs of "countervailing powers" that constrain and direct its activities (Baran and Sweezy 1966). Instead, the institutional bases of corporate power were explored (Mintz and Schwartz 1985; Schwartz 1987). Three would be seen as particularly important: (1) the development of oligopolies that effectively dominated virtually all major industrial sectors; (2) the presence of interlocking directorates, whereby a director of one corporation sits on the board of one or more other corporations; and (3) the ability of the corporate sector to wrestle concessions from and to influence the state.

First, the development of oligopolies can be seen as the natural outcome of competition among firms operating in an industrial sector. Most domestically produced commodities—from autos to breakfast cereals—are manufactured by a small group of U.S. firms. For the most part these firms still jockey for larger shares of the domestic consumer market (we deal with international interests shortly), but the competition tends not to be based on price. It is "understood" that there are limits to the rules of competition, and tacit understandings allow oligopolistic firms to structure a predictable environment for long-term planning and growth. The power of the large firm thus lies in its ability to use its membership in an oligopoly to reduce risk (Blumberg 1975; Dye 1979; U.S. Senate 1980).

Second, sociologists have begun to recognize the significance of modern corporations' boards of directors. Boards theoretically dictate broad policy guidelines to top managers. But in actuality top managers typically are members of boards of directors. They therefore play a major role in constructing board members' sense of reality when it comes to the day-to-day operations and even long-range needs of the firm. But what is important in our discussion of the bases of corporate power is the interlocking nature of boards of directors (Mizruchi 1982). This interlocking provides large corporations means by which to cooperate with one another as well as exert influence on smaller firms. Interlocking helps firms reduce debilitating competition, work out common problems within a community of shared interests, reduce uncertainty in their environments by increasing their bases of information, and in general helps large corporations in their quest for command positions that will help minimize risk and maximize predictability (Herman 1981; Mintz and Schwartz 1981; Useem 1985).

This above-mentioned quest forces large firms to seek ways to use the state in the interests of profit and growth objectives. While the relationship between capital and the state is explored in another chapter, suffice it to say that many Marxist scholars basically view the state as operating to serve the interests of the capitalist class and as the vehicle that generates its capital. "Instrumentalist" theories of the capitalist state (Domhoff 1967, 1970, 1983; Miliband 1969) point to several factors that help corporations define the agendas within which state decisions are made. These include: (1) the constant presence of corporate members in key decision-making state positions; (2) the ability of firms to influence candidate selection and incumbents' policies through sizeable campaign contributions; and (3) the ideology-generating role of corporate-backed policy formation associations, think tanks, and foundations. "Structuralist" theories of the capitalist state (Poulantzas 1968; O'Connor 1973; Gold, Lo, and Wright 1975; Block 1977) emphasize the dependence of the state on corporate processes such as capital accumulation in order for the state to have access to tax revenues needed to carry out programs that legitimate its existence in the eyes of the mass of workers. This dependence helps to structure an affinity between the expressed needs of the corporate world and state power, albeit an affinity that is often uneasy and even at times difficult to maintain. In the big picture, however, the combination of corporate dominance and structural integration results in a political economy within which the state serves capital, even if at times this is clearly in contradiction to the well-being of the working class.

Several innovations have been introduced into America's capitalist economy that on the surface appear to challenge Marxist analyses of labor-capital relations (Lindenfeld and Whitt 1982). For example, over 250,000 firms in the United States operate with some form of worker profit sharing (based on increases in profits) or gain sharing (based on productivity increases) (Metzger 1974; Frieden 1980). So-called Scanlon Plans are a form of gain sharing that includes worker participation in decision making. Here, innovations in the production process emerge from the shop floor and are sent to management for evaluation, instead of such innovations coming from the top down (Zwerdling 1984). Profits generated this way are shared by the workers (Frieden 1980). The typical profit-sharing arrangement under this plan of worker participation has workers receiving 75 percent of increased profits and the company receiving 25 percent (Ford 1988). These arrangements, begun during the 1930s, exist in an estimated 500 firms in the United States (Frieden 1980).

Employee stock ownership plans (ESOPs) represent a form of profit-sharing through stock ownership. Under this arrangement, corporations allow workers to purchase stock in the firm, thereby facilitating profit sharing in the event that the stock's value increases. While law requires voting rights for stock ownership in publicly traded firms, more than half of the ESOP programs in the U.S. do not provide for workers' voting rights on the basis of such ownership (Ford 1988). As such, ESOPs represent risk sharing but not power sharing. Nevertheless, they pose an interesting potential for altering traditional labor-capital relations in that they may enable workers to buy out a firm when plant shutdowns are threatened. Thus, ESOPs may become a mechanism for worker ownership and may empower labor to have greater control over preserving jobs, even when firms run away to other countries for production.

Labor-management committees, which began during World War II with the War Production Board, facilitate joint decision making. While most of these committees are composed of representatives only from labor and management, some have included community representatives (Ford 1988).

Finally, worker cooperatives represent arguably the most democratic form of worker participation (Rothschild and Whitt 1987). This is because cooperatives are entirely owned and operated by their workers. Workers enjoy voting rights as equal co-owners, based not on number of shares owned but on a one-person, one-vote principle. There are an estimated 800 such worker cooperatives in the United States today (Rosen, Klein, and Young 1986).

With the exception of worker-owned and worker-controlled cooperatives, however, the kinds of innovations described fail to alter radically the relations of production within the firm. This is to say, labor remains—even when sharing in profits or gains, or contributing to decision making—the principal source of surplus value appropriated by the firm's capitalist owners. Only in cases where workers themselves both own and control their firms, as with cooperatives, are the capitalist relations of production within the corporation transformed.

Thus far, the discussion has centered on the role of corporations in the American economy. But Marxists and non-Marxists alike have recognized that corporations and their range of influence are not restricted to a given nation-state. What is the role of the corporate economy in the world system?

The Corporate Economy and the World System

Much of the apologia for U.S. capitalism has celebrated the appearance of yet another development, the massive increase in direct foreign investment by U.S. firms (Magdoff 1969). Since World War II, this investment has grown enormously. While principally directed at Europe and Canada, most controversy around direct foreign investment has been with regard to its effects in the Third World. Some observers have interpreted the postwar proliferation of multinational corporations, based in the United States and Europe but operating around the world, as a positive force. Multinationals have been portrayed as meeting the needs of distant markets, providing employment opportunities for those in need, and in general contributing to the process of economic development in the foreign nations affected (Warren 1973).

Marxist analysts, going back to the concerns of Lenin, who saw imperialism as "the highest stage" of capitalism (Lenin 1917; see also Hilferding 1910; Luxemburg 1955), have rejected the above interpretation. The activities of multinationals have been seen as evidence of the restless need of capital to expand—to exploit new markets, new raw material sources, and new avenues to surplus profit through cheap labor. Research on the effects of multinationals' presence in underdeveloped countries, in fact, reveals that any positive stimuli to development abroad are short run; long-run effects are profoundly negative, impairing development efforts and aggravating inequality both between nations and between elites and the poor within nations (Barnet and Muller 1974; Petras 1978). Furthermore, Marxists have interpreted imperialism as an important means by which U.S. capitalism has stabilized itself: The economic exploitation of other nations by multinationals has helped buttress the economic health of American capitalism. The state has facilitated the multinationals' incursion into and exploitation of other nations. This has been particularly true in the Third World (where rates of return on direct investments tend to be highest), with state policies ranging from diplomacy to war (Kolko 1969). Even indirect threats to investments, such as the civil war in Vietnam, have invited the exercise of state power and, in the case of North Vietnam, almost genocidal violence. The U.S. leadership role in the 1991 war against Iraq was another example of the use of force to protect corporate interests—in this case, access to and control over inexpensive petroleum supplies.

In recent years Marxist scholarship has focused on the internationalization of capital; firms increasingly seem to have little in the way of national identity or loyalty. Capital flight from the United States, for example, has contributed to the process of deindustrialization whereupon literally millions of domestic manufacturing jobs have disappeared permanently (Bluestone and Harrison 1982; Bensmen and Lynch 1987). Corporate decisions have turned the United States increasingly into a "service economy" that is no longer a producer of goods its citizens consume, but an importer of such goods. It is becoming clear that U.S. capitalism is part of an ongoing worldwide economic reordering (Hearn 1988), in which "stronger capitalisms" such as Japan and the European Community are supplanting the dominance of U.S capitalism. U.S. firms are involving themselves in this reordering in a self-serving way that does not bode well for domestic economic health and well-being. One sign of this is the threatened "disappearance" of America's middle class and the polarization of the class structure. This polarization could yet give rise to class-based political movements that question capitalism's basic worth (Newman 1988; Phillips 1990).

In sum, recent developments in the United States being explored by Marxist scholars make a mockery of earlier assertions that "capitalism works" and that its deterioration is a dead issue. U.S. capitalism is undergoing rapid transformation and in doing so is failing to "deliver the goods" to ever increasing numbers of its erstwhile supporters. This reality helps account for the falling rate of confidence in large corporations that has been tracked by public opinion polls since the mid-1960s (Lipset and Schneider 1983).

Up to this point our discussion of the corporation has focused on Marx's principal point of reference, the manufacturing firm. Yet a second strand of Marxist thought also has emerged, concerning the role of financial institutions. The early analyses of the role of financial institutions came from outside sociology, particularly from Hilferding, Lenin, and Rochester. It has become clear in recent years that a richer understanding of the corporation within capitalism requires making a distinction between financial and nonfinancial corporations, since the former have come to command enormous power within contemporary corporate capitalism. It is to this strand of Marxist analysis that we now turn.

Financial Corporations

Marxist literature up until the 1970s focused primarily on manufacturing firms, with a few notable exceptions. Lenin's (1917) analysis emphasized the power of banks over industrialists by virtue of their control over lending decisions (see also Hilferding 1910). Hilferding viewed finance capital as the domination of banks over industrialists, asserting these to be two distinct, separate groups. Lenin, in contrast, defined finance capital as the *fusion* of banks and industrials into a single group. Despite this basic disagreement over the construction of finance capital, both saw banks as an increasingly significant force in capitalist development and relations.

Lenin's analysis emphasized the power of single banks over industrialists by virtue of their control over lending determinations. He noted the concentration of finance capital in a small handful of powerful banks to be common in several countries, including the United States, Great Britain, Germany, France, and Russia, and he believed this magnified banks' power of loan allocation. Rochester (1936) enhanced this European analysis of finance capital in her path-breaking work on American financial institutions. She described how corporations supplanted independent entrepreneurs because the corporate organization provided a mechanism for outside investors to accumulate capital without being involved in the daily management of the firm. While the sale of stocks and bonds provided firms with a second vehicle to raise increasingly important investment capital, it also imposed greater constraints on managers' autonomy. More significantly, the growing importance of both the sale of stocks and bonds and increased borrowing to support rapid industrial expansion promoted the empowerment of financial institutions, particularly a small handful of banks and Wall Street financiers. Rochester noted that, beyond loans, a bank's ability to buy and sell bonds provided financial power. Banks and other financial institutions are typically bondholders, while individuals and groups of individuals more typically own stocks (but not bonds). Bonds carry no right to vote (as do stocks) and therefore do not entitle their holders to participate directly in decisions affecting the internal affairs of a corporation. But they still represent a source of bank power, particularly during periods of corporate crisis. This is because bondholders' claims take precedence over stockholders' claims in bankruptcy proceedings.

Rochester also noted that the central role banks played in corporate affairs was reinforced by interlocking directorates, in which banks were major and frequent participants. Like Lenin, she saw an increasing fusion of industrial and finance capital, in which finance capital dominated. Unlike Lenin, she argued that this fusion came not just from lending relationships but from a combination of lending, stock sales, and interlocking directorates, all of which are dominated by financial institutions.

The observations of Lenin, Hilferding, and Rochester regarding banks' powers challenged Marxist theory's preoccupation with the role of manufacturing firms. They also raised the issue of which (if either) dominated within capitalism: financial or nonfinancial (i.e, industrial and commercial) corporations? This issue was largely ignored until the 1970s, when analysts outside sociology began to examine a variety of sources of contemporary bank power, including loans (Fitch and Oppenheimer 1970; Menshikov 1969; Sweezy and Magdoff 1975); ownership of nonfinancial firms' stock (Fitch and Oppenheimer 1970; Herman 1975); and banks' control of trust and pension funds (Rifkin and Barber 1978). When the question of the role of financial institutions began to attract sociologists, most attention (including the attention of Marxist sociologists) focused on the presence of banks' officers on nonfinancial firms' boards of directors, and the network of interlocking directorates among the very largest corporations their presence created (Gogel and Koenig 1981; Sonquist and Koenig 1975; Mariolis 1975; Mintz 1978). Indeed, banks' central positions in such interlocks were largely assumed to be the source of their power over nonfinancials (see, especially, Mintz and Schwartz 1981a; Mokken and Stokman 1978; Norich 1980).

Yet these interlock studies only demonstrated that individual banks were positioned as the hubs in structures of corporate interlocks; they did not demonstrate that this was, in fact, the principal source of bank power. Morever, little attention was being paid to the possibility that it was not the position of individual banks, but the structural unification of the banking industry as a whole that was important to understand. Recent research establishing this structural unification for the first time allows us to appreciate the enormous (although often hidden) magnitude of power wielded by banks. In the next sections, we explore the bases of this unification, the kinds of powers wielded, and their impacts. As we see, not only are nonfinancial corporations subject to the powers of the banking industry, but its powers extend to encompass local communities, the state, and even whole nations. In order to understand this, we need to examine the structure of the financial community that facilitates such empowerment.

The Structure of the Financial Community

Much of the recent literature concerning the implications of the structure of the banking community developed primarily from the contributions of Marxist sociologists. Together, they have noted several important factors that have combined to empower an organized banking community. We now turn to these factors.

Banks are pivotal actors within capitalism in that they absorb surplus capital and redistribute it through a variety of investments. Their investment decisions determine corporations' and states' access to critical capital resources through loans (Glasberg 1989; Lichten 1986; Delaney 1989); they own or control significant blocks of stocks in corporate America, purchased with the enormous pension and trust funds they administer (Rifkin and Barber 1978; Born 1980); and they are overwhelmingly the most central corporations in networks of interlocking directorates (Bearden et al. 1975; Mizruchi 1982; Mintz and Schwartz 1985). Interlocks can serve as facilitators of informational flows from the firm to the banks, in support of lending and stock purchase decisions. Interlocks can also serve as conduits of power and persuasion from the banks which are lending to the firm, affecting corporate decision making (Glasberg 1987c, 1989). Stock purchases can be used to support firms to which banks have extended significant loans (Herman 1975). Their pivotal position means that banks can collectively monopolize a vital resource: finance capital. State and corporate entities needing finance capital have no resource alternatives or substitutes. Furthermore, finance capital is the only resource that can be used to purchase other resources necessary for economic production and for the administration of state policies. Thus, those who determine the distribution of finance capital can stimulate growth and development of firms and governments by providing access to it, or they can damage such efforts by denying access.

Control of finance capital by single competitive banks could never produce the magnitude of power created by organized banks. Nonfinancial corporations and governments could easily manipulate competition between banks in their attempts to secure advantageous capital arrangements. The critical element in the power of finance capital is the banking community's structural unification. It is based on several factors. First, the Glass-Steagall Banking Act of 1933 restricts individual banks from lending more than 10 percent of their assets to any single borrower. Given this legal restriction, no bank alone can supply the enormous amounts of finance capital corporate and state customers typically seek. Banks must therefore form large lending consortia, in which they pool their

legally limited resources to meet the needs of corporations and states collectively
(see Mintz and Schwartz 1986; Glasberg 1989).

Second, since World War II pension funds have increasingly grown as a
standard feature of labor accords. Labor and corporate management have
negotiated agreements to have a prudent, disinterested third party administer
these "deferred wages," identifying banks as that third party. Pensions are
collectively valued today at approximately $600 billion and grow at an annual
rate of 10 percent. They therefore collectively represent "the largest pool of
private capital anywhere in the world" (Rifkin and Barber 1978:81). Pension
funds, as invested by banks, currently own almost one-fourth of the stock on the
New York and American stock exchanges. Banks often invest these funds in
corporations whose activities are antithetical to labor's interests. For example,
banks invest in U.S. firms that have a significant proportion of their labor force
abroad or are nonunionized (Born 1980). Banks thus can play an important role
in the dynamics of class struggle through pension fund administration.

Third, the contents of trust and pension fund portfolios managed by different
banks bear remarkable similarities. The simultaneous movement of large blocks
of stocks by many banks can therefore be a critical event for corporations.
Business analysts generally assume that movement by major financial institutions into and out of the stock market accounts for dramatic changes in stock
prices. The changes are often compounded by the "herding effect" in the market,
in which smaller investors and banks follow the lead of larger banks into and out
of the market. Smaller institutions assume that the larger banks' presence on
corporate boards and their role as lenders provide them with more adequate
information on which to base their investment decisions. The smaller banks also
follow the lead of the larger ones because they are afraid their holdings in a
corporation will lose value should the large banks dump substantial blocks of that
corporation's stock (*New York Times* December 17, 1976:D2). The herding
effect may stimulate a stampede of purchases, which can create the impression
of a healthy, desirable firm. It may, on the other hand, provoke massive sales of
specific stocks, which can construct the reality of a corporate crisis (Glasberg
1981, 1985).

Fourth, the herding effect and the similarities of bank-managed trust and
pension fund stock portfolios combine with the need to cooperate in lending
consortia to consolidate banks' common interests and reduce competition
between them (Glasberg 1989).

While we have thus far stressed sources of structural unification in the
banking industry, there are several sources of conflict and competition within it:
for example, between large and small banks, regional and major financial banks
in New York City, and commercial and savings and loan banks. Evidence of this
conflict and competition can be seen in the recent spate of takeovers of savings
and loan associations by large commercial banks, facilitated by federal deregu-

lation of the banking industry and the savings and loan bailout legislation. Even the largest commercial banks, which may share broadly defined common interests, are not always unified in their short-run specific interests or in their assessment of strategies to achieve shared goals. Competition among major financial groups has at times materialized, competition that is "sometimes sharp, sometimes muted" (Kotz 1978:85).

Yet, despite evidence of occasional conflict and competition within the banking community, we must not exaggerate the fissures. What is more important are the processes by which financial corporations transcend their differences to produce unity. For example, the larger commercial banks have at times disciplined smaller regional banks during crisis situations, when the small banks recognized the contradictions between their short-run interests and those of the large banks. In those instances, the small banks resisted the strategies of the large banks, only to meet the hostility and the greater resources of the larger institutions on which the smaller ones rely. Such was the case when small banks wanted to resign from participation in the lending consortia for W.T. Grant Company and Mexico. The larger banks threatened the smaller ones with great financial losses and denial of participation in future consortia. In both instances, the smaller banks begrudgingly caved in to the demands of the large banks and remained members in problematic consortia (Glasberg 1987b, 1987c). Major financial groups also often share common membership in lending consortia, which restrains their competitive tendencies and antagonisms.

The process of banking industry structural unification results in *bank hegemony*. Bank hegemony entails a coordinated ability to restrict the decision-making alternatives and discretion of other actors in the political economy. Control of capital flows coupled with bank hegemony increase the probability that the banking community will have its interests met over those of other groups (eg., stockholders, workers, the state, and nonfinancial corporations).

The concept of hegemony as it is used here draws from Marxist theory, which argues that hegemony results from the dominant class's privileged access to the major social and economic institutions. This privileged access empowers the dominant class to reinforce only those values and biases that advocate and legitimate its position. Such access also empowers this class to nullify those interests and viewpoints that seriously challenge its domination (Gramsci 1971; Boswell et al. 1986). In the context of the role of financial corporations in capitalist society, the concept of hegemony refers to the use of a structural monopoly over capital flows to restrict the viable alternative options for action open to corporations, the state, and labor (Patterson 1975; Glasberg and Schwartz 1983). This structural unification works to inhibit conflicts and rifts in the banking industry, producing cohesion instead. Cooperatively organized capital-flow agreements thus mitigate antagonisms among banks by fusing their immediate interests vis-á-vis other actors in the political economy (Mintz and Schwartz 1985; Glasberg 1989).

Bank hegemony does not imply control of individual corporations or the state by individual banks. Instead, bank hegemony research has revealed how banks can *collectively* dominate the corporate community, the state, and labor. Nor does hegemony suggest absolute power. Banks do not always achieve all their goals all the time. In fact, sometimes they are notably unsuccessful in attaining their major objectives. In 1978–79, for example, a consortium of banks failed to force the city of Cleveland to sell its publicly owned utility to a private utility company (Glasberg 1988). At other times, banks may lose large sums of money, as they did when W.T. Grant Company went bankrupt in 1975 (Glasberg 1987c). Sometimes banks must accept unfavorable or undesirable compromises in the process of struggle. For example, a group of banks were involuntarily forced to convert a substantial proportion of Chrysler's debt to equity in their attempts to elicit a congressional bailout of their investment in the auto maker (Glasberg 1987a). Banks' investments and loan repayments may at times be threatened, as they were by the possible formation of a debtor's cartel in Latin America (*Business Week*, December 28, 1987:88–89). There are also times when the larger banks disengage and part company from one another. When the Bank of Boston and Citicorp wrote down portions of troublesome loans to some developing countries, for example, they left the Bank of America overextended. This means that the Bank of Boston kept higher cash reserves as insurance against failure of repayment, so that if the countries defaulted on their loans the bank would not be caught short of cash. In this way, the Bank of Boston broke ranks with other banks in underdeveloped countries' consortia. The Bank of America was forced either to write down its loans as well or continue its greater exposure instead of the shared risk assumed by a unified banking community.

The kinds of problems banks can face are quite real. The point, however, is that financial corporations can collectively confront individual nonfinancial corporations and the state from a structurally organized position because there are factors drawing financial corporations into a unified group. The structural hegemony of the banking industry, coupled with its collective control over capital flows, endows it with power inaccessible to nonfinancial firms, labor, or governments.

Under normal, everyday circumstances, bank hegemony arrangements generally do not produce dramatic consequences for corporations and the state. But, the banking industry can turn its organized position into a weapon when confronted with political or economic threats to its common interests. It is not necessary for the threats perceived by banks to be factual. Once it defines a situation as threatening, the banking industry is able to act collectively on that definition because of its structural unity. The consequences of this definitional process are indeed real. Such was the case with a financially healthy Leasco

Corporation, which in 1969 tried to take over Chemical Bank. Since the banks considered it "sacrilegious" for a nonfinancial firm to take over a bank, they collectively sold substantial blocks of Leasco's stock (called stock "dumping"). Banks are usually presumed to buy and sell stocks on the basis of the financial health of the firm. In this instance, the sales were based on banks' perceptions of a threat of an interloper in their fraternity. The very real consequence of the organized stock dumping was that Leasco's stock price plummeted and has never recovered (Glasberg 1981, 1989). Thus, while there are at times important divergences and antagonisms within the banking community, their significance withers when banks perceive threats to their common interests.

This discussion suggests how organized control of a unique resource—finance capital—empowers banks to constrain both corporate and governmental options, strongly influence their economic and political trajectory, and intrude in political processes and class struggles. Thus bank hegemony can influence the discretion of the state (see, for example, Glasberg 1987a, 1987b; Lichten 1986). Such relations may also pose great consequences for community and regional as well as world-system development. Let us examine these issues.

Bank Hegemony and Community Development

A rich expanding body of sociological literature concerns the relationship between the mobility of finance capital and development. Much of it has been shaped by Marxists' concerns with understanding how capitalism operates. Such studies suggest that banks play a powerful role on the local, national, and international levels of development. For example, Beveridge (1985) demonstrated how the infusion of bank credit stimulated community development in the United States during the early phases of industrialization. Similarly, Ballard's (1983) comparative study of four small communities showed the critical role banks played in stimulating or hindering growth through their ability to determine the direction and magnitude of credit and loan allocation (see also Green 1987; Zey-Ferrell and McIntosh 1987). Glasberg and Glasberg (1991) found a striking pattern of bank disinvestment in southern Illinois, a region that has been plagued by underdevelopment. While the study did not establish a direct causal relationship between bank disinvestment and regional underdevelopment, it did suggest that lack of finance capital was an important factor in the region's inability to promote development and growth. Furthermore, the power to determine placement of investment capital can simultaneously produce uneven patterns of growth and development in one region or sector and decline and underdevelopment elsewhere (see Makler 1979; Neubeck and Ratcliff 1988). These studies demonstrate that financial corporations' investment decisions, like those of developers, affect the direction and content of community and regional development, thereby altering decision making by the state.

Control over loans to cities, communities, and regions is not the only mechanism whereby banks may influence urban development. Mortgage decisions can also significantly affect a city's development and growth. Ratcliff (1979–80 1980) found that urban decline in St. Louis resulted from redlining, a practice whereby whole areas of a city are defined by banks as ineligible or undesirable for mortgage loans. Notably, the areas redlined in St. Louis were not characterized by urban decay or decline prior to the banks' decision to disinvest. This suggests that decay was not the stimulus producing the banks' decision; rather, it was the banks' disinvestment decision that produced the decline. What the redlined communities did have in common was their status as older inner city, working class or poor, and racially integrated neighborhoods (see also U.S. Senate 1975; Bradford and Rubinowtiz 1975).

Redlining can frequently have a racial component to it. This happens, for example, whenever "a variety of agencies, including realtors and financial institutions 'steer' or 'contain' blacks in suburbs that whites no longer find desirable" (Logan 1988:336). Banks reinforce this steering by refusing to give mortgages to blacks for homes in white neighborhoods, and by redlining entire black and interracial neighborhoods. Steering blacks into mortgage-starved communities means that local governments will be unable to raise healthy revenues from property taxes. As such, local schools and services such as police, fire, sanitation, and roads will suffer (see also Leahy 1985; Pearce 1979).

Insurance companies, as members of the financial community, can serve bank disinvestment desires through their own redlining. For example, Squires, DeWolfe and DeWolfe (1979) found that neighborhoods characterized by high concentrations of minority or low-income residents were redlined by insurance companies, which denied the residents access to homeowners' insurance. Banks, of course, will not extend mortgages to borrowers who cannot produce evidence that their new homes will be insured. The researchers noted that the refusal to provide insurance was not related to crime or fire rates. They concluded that insurance redlining was not a response to community decline, but instead contributed to the decline of low-income and minority neighborhoods (see also Squires and Velez 1987). Such studies suggest ways in which coordinated control over capital flows can result in the reinforcement of racial cleavages and economic disadvantage within the working class. This reinforcement may contribute to a racial "divide and conquer" wedge within the working class. As such, coordination among various financial institutions may hinder the development of working-class consciousness. Marxist theory did not quite anticipate this role of finance capital.

Similar relationships of bank hegemony have been found to operate in world-system development processes. We next examine the role of finance capital in this arena.

Bank Hegemony and World-System Development

Bank hegemony processes affect international development, frequently with the participation of official aid agencies such as the International Monetary Fund (IMF). Lending to underdeveloped countries through consortia is an attractive investment opportunity for private banks for several reasons. First, the capital requirements of underdeveloped countries are typically far higher than the legal restrictions on loans to a single borrower within which individual banks in the U.S. operate. Lending consortia thus enable individual banks to have access to this desirable and profitable business. Second, lending consortia spread the risks involved in international lending. Syndicated arrangements such as consortia also augment the profitability of international lending. This is because the banks that organize the consortia can charge the borrowers higher commission fees for organizing and maintaining the consortia. Lending consortia hence empower the banking industry in its relations with underdeveloped countries, since they structurally organize and unify the supply as well as the suppliers of finance capital. This unification mitigates suppliers' competitive tendencies, which borrowers might otherwise exploit to their advantage.

How lucrative is international lending for banks? The ten largest U.S. banks make almost half of their total profits from foreign investments (Moffitt 1983:51). Lichtensztejn and Quijano (1982:203) have noted that "...the international gains of the thirteen principal United States banks amounted to 34.2 per cent of total profits in 1973 and 47.7 per cent in 1975, and it is estimated that roughly 75 per cent of the profits of United States banks in 1976 came from their foreign operations." In addition, the number of banks that function as lead bank (i.e, the bank that organizes and maintains the consortia) and provide loans to underdeveloped countries has dwindled, contributing even further to the structural hegemony of the banks these countries confront. In 1975, for example, almost 40 percent of underdeveloped countries' debt from private banks was organized by only six banks (Dale and Mattione 1983; Lichtensztejn and Quijano 1982).

What are the implications of bank hegemony for development in the world system? The process of increasing concentration of finance capital and its suppliers in the international private capital markets has meant "a worsening of concessional terms of indebtedness: a tendency to an increase in interest rates (plus commissions) and the reduction of maturities" (Lichtensztejn and Quijano 1982:265). This deterioration of concessional terms for underdeveloped countries has exerted tremendous pressures on their balance of payments as a result of the increased burden of debt servicing (OECD 1984; Seiber 1982). The drain of finance capital out of underdeveloped countries to pay nonconcessional interest rates with inflation-ravaged and devalued dollars also leaves few resources to support development efforts in those countries. Their only recourse is to borrow yet more.

The international influence facilitated by bank hegemony often fuses political and economic concerns, so that the provision or denial of loans can dramatically affect underdeveloped countries' political economies. For example, Seidman and Makgetla (1979) described how banks in the United States, England, and West Germany formed an international lending consortium for South Africa during the 1970s. The loans provided by the consortium strengthened the white minority government's ability to resist the challenges from the black majority population within South Africa and from newly independent Mozambique and Angola. At the same time, the loans also provided the capital South Africa required to purchase increasingly expensive imported oil, capital goods for production, and weapons for military expansion. The huge loans needed to fund all these costly expenditures simultaneously could be provided only by a consortium of major banks. That consortium enabled the white South African government to suppress challenges to apartheid while pursuing development priorities compatible with the interests of the capitalist class.

During the 1970s, Jamaica, like many underdeveloped countries, found its balance of payments deteriorating dramatically, in part because of sharp increases in the price of imported oil, global inflation, and recession. Many observers understood the roots of the problem to lie in these international political and economic relationships and crises. Jamaica's banks and the IMF, however, defined the problem as a purely economic one, stemming exclusively from Jamaica's internal dynamics and fiscal mismanagement by a socialist political leadership. In particular, the IMF cited high real wages of labor and excessive government intervention in the market. The collective viewpoint of the IMF and the private banks prevailed. In order for Jamaica to receive the IMF's "Good Housekeeping seal of approval" and qualify for private loans, the country had to accept the IMF's austerity package. That package required severe cuts in wages, devaluations of Jamaican currency, privatization of critical nationalized industries such as bauxite extraction, and sharp decreases in social welfare expenditures. The power of collective purse strings wielded by the banks and the IMF together ensured that the socialist political economy in Jamaica would be forcibly altered to one with a more free-market orientation. Ironically, the result of this IMF-imposed austerity program (which was supposed to return Jamaica to prudent fiscal management and economic health) was not economic stabilization leading to development. Instead, by 1979, the program had aggravated Jamaica's balance-of-payments deficit and further hampered the country's well-being. This was because increasing proportions of the country's gross national product were devoted to foreign debt repayment, leaving very little for development (see Girvan 1984).

Mexico had very similar experiences, largely the product of bank hegemony processes. In 1982, Mexico suffered the deleterious economic effects of increasing global inflation and rising interest rates. It owed $80 billion to a lending consortium of over 1600 banks; 60 percent of that debt was owed to U.S. banks (U.S. House 1982:6–7; U.S. Congress, Joint 1984:46). The consortium combined forces with the IMF to force Mexico to accept the standard austerity package, similar to the one imposed on Jamaica. The results echoed those in Jamaica. Cuts in wages, job layoffs, elimination of government subsidization of food staples, and devaluations of currency forced labor to bear the brunt of the stabilization program. Privatization of nationalized industries, including the banks, meant that the processes of bank hegemony had succeeded in shifting the Mexican political economy from one characterized by substantial state participation to one that was more free-market oriented. Curbs on imports meant that capital goods for production and spare parts for industrial machinery could no longer be purchased, thereby undermining Mexico's industrial sector. And the program's requirement that greater resources be devoted to foreign debt repayment meant sharp decreases in available resources for development (see Glasberg 1987b, 1989).

These cases all illustrate the strong influence bank hegemony structures and processes can have on development in the world system. Lending consortia, coupled with the power of the IMF to impose austerity packages, can inhibit or alter the content of development in underdeveloped countries, particularly during economic crises. Although many of those crises are provoked by international forces beyond the control of individual countries, banks and the IMF frequently define the problem as the product of fiscal mismanagement or "inappropriate" political/economic structures. Their collective control of critical loans enables them to enforce that definition, thereby affecting the structure of the political economy, the range of the state's discretion in decision making, class-struggle processes, and the development of the crisis-stricken nations. This suggests that internationally organized finance capitalists can transcend national boundaries and intrude in national class struggles. They can, in fact, set back progress made by workers in previous class struggles by the power of collective purse strings in ways that a national capitalist class may be unable to accomplish. Thus, class struggles become internationalized.

Conclusion

While Marx's analysis of capitalism followed the startling transition from "free enterprise" to corporate capitalism in an age of industrialization, his principal focus was on the manufacturing firm. In the United States, the rise of the modern corporation, coupled with the alleged separation of ownership and control, and "people's capitalism," led proponents of capitalism to conclude that the system works. Corporate actors were said to be constrained in their power and motivated to serve the needs of society.

Marxist scholars, initially outside sociology, responded critically, empirically demonstrating the bases for corporate power and emphasizing the command role large firms have come to play, both economically and politically. In the classical Marxist tradition, the principal focus remained on the manufacturing firm. Only in the late 1970s did this scholarship begin to probe the distinctions to be made between nonfinancial and financial corporations, both in terms of their respective roles within corporate capitalism and, more important, their power vis-á-vis each other. In the spirit of interdisciplinary scholarship, Marxist sociologists built on and expanded the insights provided by observers outside the discipline.

When the issue of the role of financial institutions was opened up, Marxist scholars were quick to begin peeling away the mysteries surrounding financial corporations. Banks were found to exist in a state of structural unity that gave them power over the flow of finance capital—a resource on which other actors in the political economy were absolutely dependent. The collective power of financial corporations has grown to the point where the destiny of communities, labor, the state, and other countries in the world system now rests heavily on their decisions. The emerging dominance of an organized banking industry has altered the classical Marxian analysis of the meaning of the capitalist class by identifying distinctive and often antagonistic sectors within that class. Bank hegemony processes have also altered class relations between labor and capital. We can see some of these alterations in the management and deployment of pension funds and in loans to nonunionized and runaway or relocating firms. Implications for the role of finance capital in class relations thus remain potent in the struggle over control of pension funds and how these are invested.

The increasing dominance of finance capital also poses challenges to Marxist notions of the relations between capital and the state: collective control of financial resources empowers banks to restrict the state's discretion in decision making, both domestically and abroad. Indeed, the power of banks transcends national boundaries so that it can intrude on class relations and class struggles in other countries. This finding alters traditional Marxist theory's focus on class relations within countries. It extends world-system analyses that emphasized the role of industrial corporations in global development processes. The ascendance of finance capital as the dominating force in capitalist relations has occurred as an extension of the ongoing processes of struggle, increasing concentration of wealth and production, and globalization of production. As such, Marxist theory must now expand its framework to incorporate analyses of the pivotal role of banks as unique corporate forms in capitalist society.

References

Avery, Robert B., et al. 1984. "Survey of Consumer Finances, 1983." *Federal Reserve Bulletin* 70(September):679–92.

Ballard, Chester C. 1983. "Banking Policy in Relation to Small Community Development." *Free Inquiry in Creative Sociology* 11(2):223–26.

Baran, Paul, and Paul Sweezy. 1966. *Monopoly Capital*. New York: Monthly Review Press.

Barnet, Richard, and Ronald Muller. 1974. *Global Reach*. New York: Simon and Schuster.

Bearden, James, William Atwood, Peter Freitag, Carol Hendricks, Beth Mintz, and Michael Schwartz. 1975. "The Nature and Extent of Bank Centrality in Corporate Networks." Paper presented at the annual meeting of the American Sociological Association, San Francisco, August.

Bell, Daniel. 1973. *The Coming of Post-Industrial Society*. New York: Basic Books.

Bensman, David, and Roberta Lynch. 1987. *Rusted Dreams*. New York: McGraw-Hill.

Berle, Adolf, Jr., and Gardiner C. Means. 1932. *The Modern Corporation and Private Property*. New York: Macmillan.

Beveridge, Andrew A. 1985. "Credit and Community Change: A Case Study during Early United States Industrialization." Paper presented at the annual meeting of the American Sociological Association, Washington, DC, August.

Block, Fred. 1977. "The Ruling Class Does Not Rule: Notes on the Marxist Theory of the State." *Socialist Review* 7(May-June):6–28.

Bluestone, Barry, and Benjamin Harrison. 1982. *The Deindustrialization of America*. New York: Basic Books.

Blumberg, Philip I. 1975. *Megacorporation in American Society*. Englewood Cliffs: Prentice-Hall.

Born, Roscoe C. 1980. "Pension Power: Organized Labor Seeks to Wield It More Aggressively." *Barron's*, December 1:4–6ff.

Boswell, Terry E., Edgar V. Kiser, and Kathryn A. Baker. 1986. "Recent Developments in Marxist Theories of Sociology." *Insurgent Sociologist* 13(4):5–22.

Bradford, Calvin P., and Leonard S. Rubinowitz. 1975. "The Urban-Suburban Investment-Disinvestment Process: Consequences for Older Neighborhoods." *Annals of the American Academy of Political and Social Science* 422(November):77–86.

Braverman, Harry. 1974. *Labor and Monopoly Capital*. New York: Monthly Review Press.

Burnham, James. 1941. *The Managerial Revolution*. New York: John Day.

Chandler, Alfred D., Jr. 1977. *The Visible Hand*. Cambridge: Harvard University Press.

Clawson, Dan. 1980. *Bureaucracy and the Labor Process*. New York: Monthly Review Press.

Cyert, R.M., and J.G. March. 1963. *A Behavioral Theory of the Firm*. Englewood Cliffs: Prentice-Hall.

Dahrendorf, Ralf. 1957. *Class and Class Conflict in Industrial Society*. Stanford: Stanford University Press.

Dale, Richard S., and Richard P. Mattione. 1983. *Managing Global Debt*. Washington, D.C.: Brookings Institution.

Delaney, Kevin. 1989. "Control during Corporate Crises: Asbestos and the Manville Bankruptcy." *Critical Sociology* 16(2–3):51–74.

Domhoff, G. William. 1967. *Who Rules America?* Englewood Cliffs: Prentice-Hall.

———. 1970. *The Higher Circles*. New York: Random House.

————. 1983. *Who Rules America Now?* Englewood Cliffs: Prentice-Hall.

Dye, Thomas R. 1979. *Who's Running America?* Englewood Cliffs: Prentice-Hall.

Fitch, Robert, and Mary Oppenheimer. 1970. "Who Rules the Corporations?" Part I. *Socialist Review* 1(4):73–108; Part II 1(5):61–114; Part III 1(6):33–94.

Ford, Ramona. 1988. *Work, Organization, and Power: Introduction to Industrial Sociology*. Boston: Allyn and Bacon.

Frieden, Karl. 1980. *Workplace Democracy and Productivity*. Washington, D.C.: National Center for Economic Alternatives.

Galbraith, John Kenneth. 1952. *American Capitalism*. Boston: Houghton Mifflin.

————. 1967. *The New Industrial Society*. New York: New American Library.

Girvan, Norman. 1984. "Swallowing the IMF Medicine in the 'Seventies." Pp. 169–81 in *The Political Economy of Development and Underdevelopment*, ed. Charles K. Wilber. 3rd ed. New York: Random House.

Glasberg, Davita Silfen. 1981. "Corporate Power and Control: The Case of Leasco Corporation versus Chemical Bank." *Social Problems* 29(2):104–16.

————. 1987a. "Chrysler Corporation's Struggle for Bailout: The Role of the State in Finance Capitalist Society." *Research in Political Sociology* 3:87–110.

————. 1987b. "International Finance Capital and the Relative Autonomy of the State: Mexico's Foreign Debt Crisis." *Research in Political Economy* 10:83–108.

————. 1987c. "Capital Markets and Corporate Behavior: The Case of W.T. Grant's Bankruptcy." *Sociological Forum* 2(2):305–30.

————. 1988. "Finance Capital Mobility and Urban Fiscal Crisis: Cleveland's Default, 1978." *Journal of Urban Affairs* 10(3):249–52.

————. 1989. *The Power of Collective Purse Strings: The Effects of Bank Hegemony on Corporations and the State*. Berkeley: University of California Press.

Glasberg, Davita Silfen, and Clifford L. Glasberg. 1991. "The Politics of Uneven Regional Development: Underdevelopment and Response in Southern Illinois." *The Journal of the Community Development Society* 22(2):118–43.

Glasberg, Davita Silfen, and Michael Schwartz. 1983. "Ownership and Control in Corporations." *Annual Review of Sociology* 9:311–32.

Gogel, Robert, and Thomas Koenig. 1981. "Commercial Banks, Interlocking Directorates and Economic Power: An Analysis of the Primary Metals Industry." *Social Problems* 29(2):117–28.

Gold, David, Clarence Lo, and Erik Olin Wright. 1975. "Recent Developments in Marxist Theories of the State." *Monthly Review* 27:29–43.

Gordon, R.A. 1938. "Ownership by Management and Control Groups in the Large Corporation." *Quarterly Journal of Economics* 52(May):367–400.

————. 1940. "Ownership and Compensation as Incentives to Corporate Executives." *Quarterly Journal of Economics* 54(May):455–73.

Gramsci, Antonio. 1971. *Selections from the Prison Notebooks*. New York: International Publishers.

Green, Gary. 1987. *Finance Capital and Uneven Development*. Boulder: Westview Press.

Hearn, Frank, ed. 1988. *The Transformation of Industrial Organization*. Belmont, Calif.: Wadsworth.

Herman, Edward S. 1975. *Conflicts of Interest: Commercial Bank Trust Departments*. New York: Twentieth Century Fund.

————. 1981. *Corporate Control, Corporate Power*. Cambridge: Cambridge University Press.

Hilferding, Rudolf. 1910 (1981). *Finance Capital: A Study of the Latest Phase of Capitalist Development*, ed. Tom Bottomore, trans. Morris Watnick and Sam Gordon. London: Routledge and Kegan Paul.

Kamerschen, David. 1968. "The Influence of Ownership and Control on Profit Rates." *American Economic Review* 58(3):432–47.

Kaysen, Carl. 1957. "The Social Significance of the Modern Corporation." *American Economic Review* 47(May):311–19.

Kolko, Gabriel. 1962. *Wealth and Power in America*. New York: Praeger.

———. 1969. *The Roots of American Foreign Policy*. Boston: Beacon Press.

Kotz, David M. 1978. *Bank Control of Large Corporations in the United States*. Berkeley: University of California Press.

Larner, Robert J. 1970. "The Effects of Management Control on the Profits of Large Corporations." Pp. 251–262 in *American Society, Inc.*, ed. Maurice Zeitlin. Chicago: Markham.

Leahy, Peter J. 1985. "Are Racial Factors Important for the Allocation of Mortgage Money?" *American Journal of Economics and Sociology*, July, 185–96.

Lenin, V.I. 1917 (1968). *Imperialism: The Highest Stage of Capitalism*. New York: International Publishers.

Lichten, Eric. 1986. *Class, Power and Austerity: The New York City Fiscal Crisis*. South Hadley, Mass.: Bergin and Garvey.

Lichtensztejn, Samuel, and Jose Manuel Quijano. 1982. "The External Indebtedness of the Developing Countries to International Private Banks." Pp. 185–265 in *Debt and Development*, ed. J.C. Sanchez Arnau. New York: Praeger.

Lindenfeld, Frank, and Joyce Rothschild Whitt, eds. 1982. *Workplace Democracy and Social Change*. Boston: Porter-Sargent.

Lipset, Seymour Martin, and William Schneider. 1983. *The Confidence Gap*. New York: Free Press.

Logan, John R. 1988. "Fiscal and Developmental Crises in Black Suburbs." Pp. 333–56 in *Business Elites and Urban Development: Case Studies and Critical Perspectives*, ed. Scott Cummings. Albany: SUNY Press.

Lundberg, Ferdinand. 1968. *The Rich and the Super-Rich*. New York: Lyle Stuart.

Luxemburg, Rosa. 1955. *The Accumulation of Capital*. London: Routledge.

Magdoff, Harry. 1969. *The Age of Imperialism*. New York: Monthly Review Press.

Makler, Harry M. 1979. "Financial Institutions, Credit Allocation and Marginalization in the Brazilian Northeast: The Bahian Case." *Sociologie et Societes* 11(2):145–67.

Mariolis, Peter. 1975. "Interlocking Directorates and Control of Corporations: The Theory of Bank Control." *Social Science Quarterly* 56:425–39.

Marx, Karl. 1967. *Capital*, Vol. I. ed. Frederick Engels. New York: International Publishers.

———. 1974. "Wages, Price and Profit." Pp. 186–229 in *Karl Marx and Frederick Engels: Selected Works*. New York: International Publishers.

Menshikov, S. 1969. *Millionaires and Managers: Structure of the U.S. Financial Oligarchy*. Moscow: Progress Publishers.

Metzger, Bert. 1974. "Profit-Sharing: Capital's Reply to Marx." *Business and Society Review* 11(Autumn):40–41.

Miliband, Ralph. 1969. *The State in Capitalist Society*. New York: Basic Books.

Mills, C. Wright. 1956. *The Power Elite*. New York: Oxford University Press.

Mintz, Beth. 1978. "Who Controls the Corporation? A Study of Interlocking Directorates." Ph.D. dissertation, State University of New York at Stony Brook.

Mintz, Beth, and Michael Schwartz. 1981. "Interlocking Directorates and Interest Group Formation." *American Sociological Review* 46(December):851–69.

———. 1985. *The Power Structure of American Business*. Chicago: University of Chicago Press.

Mizruchi, Mark S. 1982. *The American Corporate Network*. Beverly Hills: Sage.

Moffitt, Michael. 1983. *The World's Money: International Banking From Bretton Woods to the Brink of Insolvency*. New York: Simon and Schuster.

Mokken, Robert J., and Frans N. Stokman. 1978. "Traces of Power: The 1972 Intercorporate Network in the Netherlands." Paper presented at the European Consortium for Political Research, Grenoble, April.

Monsen, R.J., J.S. Chiu, and D.E. Cooley. 1968. "The Effect of Separation of Ownership and Control on the Performance of the Large Firm." *Quarterly Journal of Economics* 82(August):435–51.

Neubeck, Kenneth J., and Dennis D. Breslin. 1989. "What Do Capitalists Own?" Paper presented at the annual meeting of the American Sociological Association, San Francisco, August.

Neubeck, Kenneth J., and Richard E. Ratcliff. 1988. "Urban Democracy and the Power of Corporate Capital: Struggles over Downtown Growth and Neighborhood Stagnation in Hartford, Connecticut." Pp. 299–332 in *Business Elites and Urban Development: Case Studies and Critical Perspectives*, ed. Scott Cummings. Albany: SUNY Press.

Newman, Katherine S. 1988. *Falling from Grace: The Experience of Downward Mobility in the American Middle Class*. New York: Free Press.

Norich, Samuel. 1980. "Interlocking Directorates, the Control of Large Corporations, and Patterns of Accumulation in the Capitalist Class." Pp. 83–106 in *Classes, Class Conflict and the State*, ed. Maurice Zeitlin. Cambridge, Mass.: Winthrop Publishers.

OECD (Organization for Economic Cooperation and Development). 1984. "Patterns of External Financing of Developing Countries' Payments of Balances." Pp. 95–106 in *Foreign Aid and Third World Development*, ed. Pradip K. Ghosh. Westport, Conn.: Greenwood Press.

O'Connor, James. 1973. *The Fiscal Crisis of the State*. New York: St. Martin's.

Patterson, Tim. 1975. "Notes on the Historical Application of Marxist Cultural Theory." *Science and Society* 39(3):257–91.

Pearce, Diana M. 1979. "Gatekeepers and Homeseekers: Institutional Patterns in Racial Steering." *Social Problems* 27(February):325–42.

Perlo, Victor. 1957. *The Empire of High Finance*. New York: International Publishers.

———. 1958. "People's Capitalism and Stock Ownership." *American Economic Review* 48:333–347.

Petras, James. 1978. *Critical Perspectives on Imperialism and Social Class in the Third World*. New York: Monthly Review Press.

Philips, Kevin. 1990. *The Politics of Rich and Poor*. New York: Random House.

Poulantzas, Nicos. 1968. "The Problem of the Capitalist State." Pp. 238–53 in *Ideology in Social Science*, ed. Robin Blackburn. New York: Pantheon.

Ratcliff, Richard E. 1979–80. "Capitalist Class Structure and the Decline of Older Industrial Cities." *Insurgent Sociologist* 9(2–3):60–74.

———. 1980. "Banks and the Command of Capital Flows: An Analysis of Capitalist Class Structure and Mortgage Disinvestment in a Metropolitan Area." Pp. 107–32 in *Classes, Class Conflict and the State*, ed. Maurice Zeitlin. Cambridge, Mass.: Wintrop Publishers.

Rifkin, Jeremy, and Randy Barber. 1978. *The North Will Rise Again: Pensions, Politics and Power in the 1980s*. Washington, D.C.: People's Business Commission.

Rochester, Anna. 1936. *Rulers of America: A Study of Finance Capital*. New York: International Publishers.

Rosen, Carey, Katherine J. Klein, and Karen M. Young. 1986. *Employee Ownership in America: The Equity Solution*. Lexington, Mass.: Lexington Books.

Rothschild, Joyce and J. Allen Whitt. 1987. *The Cooperative Workplace*. New York: Cambridge University Press.

Schwartz, Michael, ed. 1987. *The Structure of Power in America*. New York: Holmes and Meier.

Seiber, Marilyn J. 1982. *International Borrowing by Developing Countries*. New York: Pergamon Press.

Seidman, Ann, and Neva Makgetla. 1979. "Transnational Banks in Southern Africa." *Contemporary Crises* 3(4):365–98.

Smith, Adam. 1952. *An Inquiry into the Nature and Causes of the Wealth of Nations*. Chicago: Encyclopaedia Britannica.

Sonquist, John A., and Thomas Koenig. 1975. "Interlocking Directorates in the Top U.S. Corporations: A Graph Theory Approach." *Insurgent Sociologist* 5(3):196–229.

Squires, Gregory D., Ruthanne DeWolfe, and Alan S. DeWolfe. 1979. "Urban Decline or Disinvestment: Uneven Development, Redlining and the Role of the Insurance Industry." *Social Problems* 27(1):79–95.

Squires, Gregory D., and William Velez. 1987. "Insurance Redlining and the Transformation of an Urban Metropolis." *Urban Affairs Quarterly* 23(1):63–83.

Sweezy, Paul and Harry Magdoff. 1975. "Banks: Skating on Thin Ice." *Monthly Review* 26(9):1–21.

U.S. Congress: Joint. 1984. "International Debt." *Hearings before the Subcommittee on Economic Goals and Intergovernmental Policy of the Joint Economic Committee, Cong. of the U.S.* 98th Congress, 2nd sess. Washington, D.C.: Government Printing Office.

U.S. Department of Commerce. 1986. *Household Wealth and Asset Ownership: 1984*. Washington, D.C.: Government Printing Office.

U.S. House of Representatives. 1982. "International Financial Markets and Related Matters." *Hearings before the Committee on Banking, Finance, and Urban Affairs*. 97th Cong., 2nd sess. Washington, D.C.: Government Printing Office.

U.S. Senate. 1975. "Home Mortgage Disclosure Act of 1975." *Hearings before the Committee on Banking, Housing, and Urban Affairs*. 94th Congress, 1st sess. Washington, D.C.: Government Printing Office.

———. 1980. "Structure of Corporate Concentration." *Hearings before the Committee on Governmental Affairs*. 99th Cong. Washington, D.C.: Government Printing Office.

Useem, Michael. 1980. "Corporations and the Corporate Elite." *Annual Review of Sociology* 6:41–77.

———. 1985. *The Inner Circle*. New York: Oxford University Press.

Villarejo, Don. 1962. "Stock Ownership and the Control of Corporations." *New University Thought* 2(Autumn):33–77; 2(Winter):47–65.

Warren, Bill. 1973. "Imperialism and Capitalist Industrialization." *New Left Review* 8(Sept.–Oct.):3–44.

Zeitlin, Maurice. 1974. "Corporate Ownership and Control: The Large Corporation and the Capitalist Class." *American Journal of Sociology* 79(March):1073–19.

Zeitlin, Maurice, and Samuel Norich. 1979. "Management Control, Exploitation, and Profit Maximization in the Large Corporation: An Empirical Confrontation of Managerialism and Class Theory." *Research in Political Economy* 2:33–62.

Zey-Ferrell, Mary, and William Alex McIntosh. 1987. "Agricultural Lending Policies of Commercial Banks: Consequences of Bank Dominance and Dependency." *Rural Sociology* 52(2):187–207.

Zwerdling, Daniel. 1984. *Workplace Democracy: A Guide to Workplace Ownership, Participation, and Self-Management Experiments in the United States and Europe*. New York: Harper Colophon.

EDUCATION AND KNOWLEDGE:

READING CLASS: MARXIST THEORIES OF EDUCATION

William D. Armaline,
Kathleen S. Farber,
and
Shan Nelson-Rowe

Examining Marx's writings on education, the first thing we notice is the paucity of reading material we have to inspect. For example, in one of the principal edited works, *The Marx-Engels Reader*, only 11 of the 411 pages of text even refer to education (1978a:775). In another, only 7 of 706 pages of text discuss education (1970:792). How, then, can we explain the impressive, almost overwhelming amount of "Marxist" and "neo-Marxist" literature published, especially in the past thirty years, on education and schooling? The explanation is simple. Rather than examine and apply what Marx had to say explicitly about education, contemporary theorists have used Marx's analysis of social dynamics to develop their ideas regarding the role of education in a base/superstructure dialectic.

This chapter begins with a brief explication of Marx's ideas about ideology and social control and uses this base and superstructure relationship to illuminate the role of schooling in society. We then explore the neo-Marxist elaborations of Gramsci and those of theorists from the Frankfurt School of critical theory. Next we address dominant themes from more contemporary theorists (1960–90) who focus primarily on the debate over various forms of reproduction theory in Marxist discourse. We follow reproduction theory with a section on resistance theory as a corrective to the reductionism inherent in reproduction theory. We end our discussion by synthesizing contemporary sociological theory of education (within and outside Marxist thought), suggesting the beginnings of a critical educational theory that draws together a set of interpretive lenses from Marxist, feminist, and poststructuralist writings on schooling in society.

We want to emphasize at the outset that a comprehensive and exhaustive review of Marxist and neo-Marxist thought relative to education and schooling is not within the scope of this chapter. Instead, we intend to draw out major themes and trends in educational sociology discourse. In so doing, we attempt to optimize the degree to which we represent the scope and complexity of Marxist discourse and at the same time avoid producing a text that is so dense as to be impenetrable. We offer this chapter as an invitation to further discourse, an opportunity to engage readers in dialogue over creating a dynamic and critical sociological theory of education.

Marx on Base/Superstructure Dialectics and Education

The key factor in understanding Marx on education is to recognize that his formulation arises from his concept of base and superstructure. In traditional Marxist social analysis, the "lever" that drives society is the aggregate of productive forces—the labor/labor power, raw materials, objects of production, and the productive process itself—existing at any given historical point. Further, the productive forces mesh with the material relations of production—the arrangement of the various productive forces. As the productive forces change as a result of new technologies, the changing availability of resources, or both, there follow concomitant changes in the material relations of production. In addition to the material relations of production, there are the social relations of production—the relations between the owners and nonowners of the means of production—which are supported by custom and law and are highly resistant to change. As the productive forces and the material relations of production change in response to historical circumstances, the social relations of production become external "fetters" on or impediments to historical progress (Marx 1970:182–83).

Classes arise out of the social relations of production, and those classes engage in a struggle for control of the means and processes of production. Tied to this class-based struggle over production is the political struggle for control of the state and state power and the ideological struggle for the hearts and minds of those in the social relations of production (Marx 1970:182–83). Within this ideological and political struggle over the hearts and minds of women and men, education becomes an important and perhaps even determinant factor. As such, Marx sees the importance of education in terms of its relationship to the production and reproduction of labor power and to ideological indoctrination and hegemony. Further, these two aspects of the relationship between education and society are interactive and mutually supportive.

As an illustration of the interaction of the dual concerns of preparation for work and ideological control, Marx criticized capitalist education on a number of grounds, including its failure to train working-class children for skilled work. As for "moral education," capitalist schools were little more than places where "bourgeois principles" could be "drum(med) into the heads" of children (1978b:205). A few months later, in the *Communist Manifesto*, Marx and Engels attacked the ideological character of bourgeois education, claiming that under the communists the values and beliefs of the ruling class would be supplanted by proletarian education (1978c:487).

Similarly, while Marx generally supported the establishment of free public schooling (1978c:490), he was adamant that the state have as little control over schools as possible. In his *Critique of the Gotha Program*, Marx found the call for elementary education by the state to be "altogether objectionable." Government and religion alike, he believed, should be excluded as far as possible from the operation of schools, for each had its own set of interests distinct from those of the working class (1978d:539–40). For public schools to serve the interests of the working class, the working class would need to be in control of the schools.

The problem of education relative to work and ideology also attracted the attention of Russian revolutionaries. Speaking to a gathering of young communists in 1920, Lenin repeatedly stressed two themes. First he condemned the "old schools" as "thoroughly imbued with the (capitalist) class spirit" and geared "to the children of the bourgeoisie." In these schools, he said, working-class children were "trained in such a way as to be useful servants of the bourgeoisie" (1975:663). Second, he argued that a communist education must not consist solely of learning "communist slogans." Instead, Lenin claimed, "You can become a Communist only when you enrich your mind with a knowledge of all the treasures created by mankind" (1975:663–65). For Lenin, education was one means of establishing a proletarian culture, or "Proletcult," in revolutionary Russia. The task of the schools, and the young communists in them, was to acquire and use the knowledge generated in bourgeois society (as well as prebourgeois societies) to revive the country economically. At the same time communist schools would help transmit a communist ethics as a means of undermining the possessive spirit of capitalist morality (1975:666–67).

At a more practical and less theoretical level, socialists in many countries engaged in a variety of educational projects designed to challenge the prevailing capitalist ideology. Between 1890 and 1920, socialists in the United States and Britain established socialist Sunday schools. Although these schools were seldom endorsed by national or local party officials, local activists started dozens of these schools in which song and play were used to teach the basic principles of socialist thought to children (Reid 1966; Teitelbaum and Reese 1983). American socialists were also involved in the creation of "labor colleges" in the 1920s and 1930s. These institutions trained labor organizers, editors, writers, and workers' education teachers, and constituted a radical influence on the American labor movement of this period (Altenbaugh 1990). These socialist Sunday schools and labor colleges reflected an interest in transforming capitalist society by using schools as purveyors of radical thought and in opposition to the dominant ideology.

Neo-Marxist Extensions of Ideology, Hegemony, and Education: Gramsci and the Frankfurt School

The notion that schools are purveyors of ideological control pervades early-twentieth-century Marxist and neo-Marxist writings on education. Yet in these writings we also find the belief that schools hold the potential to be liberating institutions if they can be captured by members and representatives of the working class. Several key neo-Marxists developed theories of education emphasizing the problem of ideology and social control. Beginning with Antonio Gramsci in the 1920s and 1930s and extending through the critical theorists of the Frankfurt School, we find expressed the belief that workers and Marxist intellectuals in capitalist societies must seize control of superstructural cultural institutions such as schools before actually seizing state power and control of the productive forces. This "war of position" would allow radicals to transform the civic culture, gain support for their beliefs, and facilitate a political revolution (Gramsci 1971:206–7). The Gramscian emphasis on ideology and hegemony, echoed by theorists of the Frankfurt School, has provided the theoretical basis for much of the neo-Marxist educational discourse of the past three decades. The breadth, depth, and range of issues and ideas explored by the Frankfurt School also give testimony to the enormous difficulty of the task of identifying class biases and constructing counterhegemonic concepts and positions. This work also showed the tenacity with which the dominant class holds on to power via elements of superstructure.

For Gramsci, schools are a part of "civil society," which he defines as institutions that are not part of the machinery of government. One function of the institutions of civil society is to promote "hegemony," or the "spontaneous consent" of the masses to the rule of the dominant class. Hegemonic control is distinct from the "direct domination" of the political institutions of government, which rule through coercion. By contrast, hegemony works through the prestige and authority accorded to the "dominant group...because of its position and function in the world of production" (1971:12).

As key components of civil society, schools help create the ideological conditions under which the hegemony of the dominant group is maintained. They do this, first, by conveying the belief that individual rights and duties, as defined by the state, are consistent with the natural order. This is not accomplished through morality or civics lectures, though these may take place. Instead, the everyday practices of teachers and students mimic the world of work, where individual rights and duties predominate. Thus, Gramsci argues, in the course of carrying out the daily rituals of schooling, students come to believe in a social system that promotes the dominance of one social group over others (1971:34).

Differentiation among schools also reinforces hegemony by creating the illusion of democratic choice while in reality perpetuating group distinctions. Gramsci was somewhat vague on this matter, but cited the proliferation of vocational schools in the early twentieth century as an example of educational "reform" intended to reproduce social differences among ruling and subordinate groups. This reproduction takes place not because pupils in elite schools "learn how to rule there," nor because elite schools produce more gifted leaders than vocational schools. Instead, the "fact that each social group has its own type of school" leads inexorably to the preservation of cultural differences between ruling and subordinate groups, and these cultural differences reinforce hegemony. Moreover, the existence of varied types of academic and vocational schools "gives the impression of being democratic." This impression arises because a variety of schools encourages diversification among students, students are supposedly able to make their own choices among schools, and all choices are formally open. Yet this formal choice only masks the reality that substantive differences in the social power of ruling and subordinate groups are reinforced through the educational system (Gramsei 1971:40).

Marx had clearly been aware of the stabilizing force of superstructural institutions such as schooling to maintain the status quo. Yet he also had been optimistic about the inevitability of proletarian supremacy and the transition to a classless society. He clearly had given prominence to the base in the base/superstructure dialectic, believing that when the capitalistic social relations of production became fetters on the advancement of the productive forces/material relations of production, those social relations of production and the related class system would be radically changed. Gramsci gives us a more complex and in some ways more enlightening picture of the ideological mechanisms of society. He saw those ideological mechanisms acting as both supports for the dominant social, political, and economic order and as brakes on working-class consciousness by obscuring the oppressive conditions of life under capitalism.

With the concept of hegemony as the process of engineering spontaneous consent of the governed, Gramsci helps us to understand how differentiated labor power is reproduced and the dominant order is maintained without direct use of force and coercion. To extend our analysis of ideological hegemony, we move to the "critical" theorists of the Institute for Social Research, founded in 1923 at the University of Frankfurt and known as the Frankfurt School. These critical theorists (like Gramsci) were affected by the rise to power of fascism in Europe, the apparent resilience of capitalism in Europe and in the United States, and the corruption of socialist ideals by Stalin in the Soviet Union. Hence, as the years progressed, they paid more attention to the reproductive functions of state and cultural institutions that created the conditions of stasis through ideology and hegemony (Jay 1973:21)

The Institute for Social Research was made up of a diverse and changing group of scholars from a wide variety of fields, including sociology, philosophy, social psychology, economics, musicology, psychoanalysis, political science, popular culture, literature, and law. While there was great variability among the orientations, interests, and approaches of the theorists, there was some unity of purpose. As David Held explained:

> They sought to develop a critical perspective in the discussion of all social practices....The motivation for this enterprise appears similar for each of the theorists—the aim being to lay a foundation for an exploration, in an interdisciplinary research context, of questions concerning the conditions which make possible the reproduction and transformation of society, the meaning of culture, and the relation between the individual, society and nature....The critical theorists believe(d) that through an examination of contemporary social and political issues they could contribute to a critique of ideology and to the development of a non-authoritarian and non-bureaucratic politics. (1980:16)

Our purpose is not to address the similarities and differences among individual theorists associated with the Institute. Instead, taken together, we find in a core group of theorists work that advances our understanding of the ways in which superstructural institutions, including schools, operate to maintain conditions of domination and oppression. In particular, these studies focused on two general areas: the nature of authority as it unfolds in modern states, and the phenomenon of mass culture as a mechanism of social control.

With respect to the nature of authority, Critical Theorists had to address "the failure of Marxism to explain the reluctance of the proletariat to fulfill its historical role" (Jay 1973:116). In this regard, the Institute turned away "from material (in the sense of economic) concerns...(and) focused its energies on what traditional Marxists had relegated to a secondary position, the cultural superstructure of modern society." In particular, it looked to psychoanalysis to fill "a gap in the classical Marxist model of substructure and superstructure" (Jay 1973:84–85).

Mass culture posed a particular problem: While on one level it appeared to have a democratic appeal, in reality it was essentially antipopulist. The Frankfurt School suggested that mass culture was produced by the "culture industry" as a means of subjugation, thereby emphasizing its "antipopulist connotations" (Jay 1973:216). Jay saw in their work that

> The notion of "popular" culture...was ideological; the culture industry administered a nonspontaneous, reified, phony culture rather

than the real thing. The old distinction between high and low culture had all but vanished in the "stylized barbarism" of mass culture. Even the most "negative" examples of classical art had been absorbed into what Marcuse was later to call its "one-dimensional" facade. Tragedy, which once meant protest, now meant consolation. The subliminal message of almost all that passed for art was conformity and resignation. (1973:216)

Members of the Institute recognized that the hegemony of the culture industry was far more effective than overt coercion at maintaining oppressive conditions, largely because of its subtlety and resultant ability to "lull its victims into passive acceptance" (Jay 1973:216–17). With the lessening of the socializing role of institutions such as the family and the spread of technology, the culture industry "helped tighten the control of authoritarian governments in Europe. Radio...was to fascism as the printing press had been to the Reformation" (Jay 1973:216–217).

We must realize that the Institute's theorists never really abandoned their concern with economic forces at work in society. In their eyes, however, to understand authority and the phenomenon of mass culture, we need to go beyond economics and into sociocultural and, indeed, psychological investigation. Institute members felt that

the mediating mechanisms between culture and politics were best understood...in psychological terms. Their studies of popular culture were thus connected with the investigation of the authoritarian potential in America that they conducted in the forties. These investigations were cast primarily as psychological analyses, although always based on the broader assumptions of Critical Theory. (Jay 1973:218)

Frankfurt School theorists extended Marx and Gramsci by looking at the changing conditions of the twentieth-century European state and linking technology, cultural production and reproduction, and mass psychology with totalitarian rule. We might infer that since schooling as a superstructural institution tends not to engage students in critically assessing how the culture industry played along with totalitarian political forces, it serves alongside and even as a part of the culture industry as a support for the authority of the dominant order. The role, then, of culture and the lived experience of the masses was raised to a level of importance at least equal to that of economics by the Frankfurt School. In the changing social, economic, and political conditions of the 1930s and 1940s, they saw that traditional Marxist conceptions of the primacy of the economic base were inadequate. Such conceptions could not provide explanations for

> understanding the integration of the working class in the West or the
> political effects of technocratic rationality in the cultural realm....Like
> Gramsci, Adorno and Horkheimer argued that domination had
> assumed a new form. Instead of being exercised primarily through
> the use of physical force (the army and police), the power of the
> ruling classes was now reproduced through a form of ideological
> hegemony; that is, it was established primarily through the rule of
> consent, and mediated via cultural institutions such as schools,
> family, mass media, churches, etc. Briefly put, the colonization of
> the workplace was now supplemented by the colonization of all
> other cultural spheres. (Giroux 1983:23)

Beginning with Marx and moving through Gramsci and the Frankfurt School we find two complementary reproductory roles of schooling in capitalist society: (1) the preparation of people for varying roles in the labor force, and (2) ideological indoctrination and control. In the 1960s and 1970s, this theme of reproduction was taken up and extended by radical educational theorists in educational sociology.

Neo-Marxist Thought: 1960–1990

While it is certainly true that we find variation in Marxist and neo-Marxist explanations regarding the ways in which power relations are maintained in capitalist society, we find agreement on the position that power relations are indeed maintained. The notion of the maintenance and reproduction of power relations lies at the heart of this section. We found in Marx an explanation of the reproduction of power relations rooted primarily in the economic base, in the material and social relations of production. Ideology served as a support for the material and social relations of production arrangement, but it was clearly secondary in importance. The neo-Marxists such as Gramsci and the various theorists of the Frankfurt School also saw power relations as being reproduced, but their explanations focused primarily on the superstructure, on the cultural and ideological mechanisms of hegemony. The concept of "reproduction" and the explanations for its occurrence dominated much of the radical educational discourse from 1960 to 1990. Further, this discourse examined reproduction in three distinct but related forms: economic reproduction, cultural reproduction, and hegemonic-state reproduction (Aronowitz and Giroux 1985). After reviewing these three forms, this chapter proceeds with a section on resistance theory as a critique and extension of reproduction theory and ends with a section on contemporary critiques from feminist and poststructuralist thought.

Economic Reproduction

A distinction made by neo-Marxist theorists from 1960 to 1990 rests on the extent to which the base determines the ideological, legal, and cultural super-structure (including the schooling system as ideology). The conceptual question, What is meant by "determine" and "determination"? is at the heart of this debate.

In "Base and Superstructure in Marxist Cultural Theory," Raymond Williams addressed this point, stating that 'determine' can be seen generally in two ways.

> There is, on the one hand, from its theological inheritance, the notion of an external cause which totally predicts or prefigures, indeed totally controls a subsequent activity. But there is also, from the experience of social practice, a notion of determination as setting limits, exerting pressures. (1973:4)

What Marx "really" meant is not the issue here. What is important is how these two senses of "determination" affect our view of schooling in the American social system.

The strong sense of determination, as controlling superstructure, has been a major focus of radical critiques of education. Perhaps the most significant example of this approach is *Schooling in Capitalist America* by Bowles and Gintis. These radical theorists see schooling as playing two important roles:

> On the one hand, by imparting technical and social skills and apropriate motivations, education increases the productive capacity of workers. On the other hand, education helps defuse and depoliticize the potentially explosive class relations of the production process, and thus serves to perpetuate the social, political, and economic conditions through which a portion of the product of labor is expropriated in the form of profits. (Bowles and Gintis 1976:11)

As such, then, schooling can only function as "a reinforcer of the economic structure of society, act(ing) only to transfer and reproduce the dominant social ideology. This ideology is embedded in the general social consciousness and can be altered only through changing the economic order" (Wood 1982:57). Therefore, Bowles and Gintis assert that the schools are incapable of altering the social order in any fundamental way. But merely emphasizing that schools in and of themselves cannot reform the social order fails to explain why there is so little opposition to obviously unjust social practice. The reasons that the social order, and the schools within, are not opposed by students, parents, teachers, or all three, is that, as a part of the ideological superstructure, schools are a natural outgrowth of the economic base. "This base generates a hegemonic ideology which prevails upon the workers, and ideology posit(s) their roles within the productive system as either ethically acceptable or technically necessary" (Wood 1982:57). Schools act to legitimate an unequal society through curriculum and instruction, social relations in the school, and a lived experience that acts to prevent critical understanding and social cohesiveness among the students.

According to theories of economic reproduction, schools mirror societal economic conditions and structures via practices such as tracking students through the explicit academic curriculum and the "hidden curriculum" of schooling (Dreeben 1968; Jackson 1968; Giroux and Purpel 1983). For example, Anyon (1980) presents ethnographic data showing that the social class of students affects what and how they are taught in schools. In brief, working-class students are exposed to less in the way of academic knowledge, and the knowledge they "get" tends to be valued less by the dominant culture than that of upper-class, and to a lesser extent, middle-class students. With respect to the hidden curriculum, Anyon found that both the teaching and the behaviors and abilities expected of students also differed by class. Students from working-class homes were "taught" to be passive, silent, punctual, deferent to authority, and to follow directions and take down information, which was then to be "learned" by rote. The degree of individual autonomy, creativity, and critical thinking in classrooms increased as one ascended the social-class ladder, with students from affluent, elite schools being much more self-directed, active, and involved in their own education. The hidden curriculum of schooling tended to parallel the expected job requirements of students, based on the social class into which they happened to have been born (see Carnoy and Levin 1985; Simon et al. 1991).

Bowles and Gintis and other reproduction theorists (Katz 1968, 1971; Cohen and Lazerson 1972; Kantor 1982; Hogan 1982, 1985) see the economic base as the determining factor (in the strong sense) affecting the structure of schools. Hence, to change the social order, action must be directed at this economic base. Liberal educational reform is a diversion, misplaced energy that could be put to better use in revolutionary political activity. Pending this revolutionary activity, Bowles and Gintis do suggest meaningful interim action to be taken by socialist educators, however. They state:

> First, revolutionary educators...should vigorously press for the democratization of schools and colleges....Second, the struggle for democratization should be viewed as part of an effort to undermine the correspondence between the social relations of education and the

social relations of production in capitalist economic life....Third, a movement for socialist education must reject a simple authoritarianism and spontaneity as its guiding principles....Fourth, revolutionary educators must be in the forefront of the movement to create a unified class consciousness....Fifth, socialist educators should take seriously the need to combine a long range vision with winning victories here and now. (1976:287)

In conjunction with other workers, then, educators have a significant role to play in preparing the way for a new consciousness that will spring from the ashes of capitalist destruction (Bowles and Gintis 1976:284–88).

Despite Bowles and Gintis's role for socialist educators, Wood claims that there is little or no justification for action within the schools given the theoretical position of the strong determinists. The worker/student joins the process of reproduction out of necessity and plays a very passive role in this process. Because of the "correspondence" (Bowles and Gintis 1976:12) between schooling experience and the world of work, not only are class-based work roles maintained, but so too are aspects of ideological hegemony that transcend work.

What Bowles and Gintis accomplished was to make explicit what was only implicit in Marx and Gramsci. They took the concepts of Marx and Gramsci on ideology and knowledge and formulated a coherent Marxist theory of education. The gains made by the Bowles and Gintis analysis over previous Marxist and neo-Marxist accounts are indeed significant, but the victory may be a pyrrhic one. What we gain in insight we may lose in cynicism bordering on paralysis (Wood 1982). *How* ideology is accepted by the worker/student is of little concern and is given almost no space in the analysis. Additionally, there is no accounting of how some forms of educational change may be driven by the cultural or political concerns of people within the schools. Finally, explaining change in terms of elite domination is problematic and questioned by more recent sociological research.

Julia Wrigley, for example, charts the conflicts between ethnic and religious groups, unionized teachers and educational administrators, labor organizations and business groups, local politicians and social reformers, all of which shaped the transformation of Chicago public schooling between 1900 and 1950. Her research suggests that Chicago's business leaders "were not anxious to fund rapid educational development, and they were somewhat worried about the prospect of an 'overeducated' workforce" (1982:14). These concerns reflect the possibility that schooling can fuel criticism of the status quo just as it may produce compliant, well-socialized workers. Wrigley also shows how business leaders were unable to determine unilaterally the process of educational change. Though business interests were more powerful than others, their relative success reflected onerous lobbying and coalition building combined with superior financial resources. Additional analyses, not all of which are Marxist, have produced similar themes (Katznelson and Weir 1985; Peterson et al. 1985; Karabel 1984; Reese 1986).

Other complementary research emphasized the role of the professional educator as an increasingly influential participant in the educational reform movement. Ray and Michelson (1989, 1990) have shown how the efforts of business leaders to reform local school policies were successfully altered by educational leaders who were able to transform the way in which educational problems were defined. Other research examines the ways in which educational problems were constructed by educational entrepreneurs in revolutionary Iran and Nicaragua (Najafizadeh and Mennerick 1989). Finally, Nelson-Rowe (1988, 1991) explores the impact of professional educators on educational change relative to the rise of vocationalism in American education. By claiming to hold solutions to the problems posed by industrial change, professional educators could demand and ultimately receive greater resources from public and private organizations. The main thrust of this research seems to reflect a revised reproduction theory regarding the effects of various power groups on educational reform.

Delaying further critique for the moment, the economic reproduction position holds schooling responsible for reinforcing differential work roles based on class position. The analyses that follow extend the notion of reproduction beyond the economic sphere and move us toward conceptions of schooling and society that allow for transformative possibilities.

Cultural Reproduction

Where economic theories see the reproductive role of schooling relationships and functions arising out of their correspondence to the relationships and functions experienced in the workplace ("determined" in the strong sense), theories of cultural reproduction emphasize the degree to which the background experience or culture of different groups match the experience of schooling. While these theorists do not deny that there are significant connections between the experience of working-class students and work roles (the shop floor for males and "domestic/clerical" work in and out of the home for females), they assert that schools do not simply mirror the economic conditions of the dominant society. Instead, while the class position of students cannot be denied or ignored, schools are relatively independent of economic and political social structures. They constitute a

> part of a larger universe of symbolic institutions that do not overtly impose docility and oppression, but reproduce existing power

relations more subtly through the production and distribution of a dominant culture that tacitly confirms what it means to be educated. (Aronowitz and Giroux 1985:80)

Hence, the cultural reproduction theorists adopt a weaker, more restricted sense of "determinism" with respect to the base/superstructure dialectic. Two theoretical works are critical to this account. Bernstein (1977) examines the relationship between the cultural/linguistic practices of the formal school curriculum and students' home experience, while Bourdieu and Passeron (1977) illuminate, among other things, the political and socially constructed nature of school knowledge.

In his study of linguistic codes and social class, Bernstein looked at both the structure of language use and the patterns of communicative interaction. He showed that the linguistic code of family life is the starting point for class inequality in the broader social order. Further, schools reinforce these class-based differences, thereby helping to reproduce that inequality. Bernstein argued that families develop communication systems and patterns that emerge from class-based expectations. Working-class family structure tends to be quite traditional relative to interaction and authority patterns, especially in terms of age, sex, and class position. Bernstein saw working-class families operating with a "restricted" linguistic code that assumes commonality with the listener and therefore does not require elaboration to make meaning explicit. What this engenders is a communication pattern that is more of a "shorthand" or closed form.

In opposition to working-class restricted codes, Bernstein saw middle-class families operating with a more open, flexible, and "elaborated" code. This was also quite consonant with class expectations that emphasize individual personality characteristics and personal relationships, rather than the traditional (and often authoritarian) stereotypic role relationships characteristic of working class life (Bernstein 1971:143–69). This elaborated, more universalistic code is necessary because of the negotiated and flexible nature of communication and interaction in middle-class life. The elaborated, universalistic code of middle-class families more accurately approximates the mode of communication engendered and rewarded by schools. Therefore, middle-class children come to school better able to participate in schooling activities and hence do better in school than children from working-class homes. Bennett and LeCompte argue that

> since working class students have less competence in the language of the school (or in Bernstein's words, have limited access to the elaborated codes of the socializing agencies), they often fail to understand exactly what is expected of them, respond inappropri-

ately, perform more poorly, and reap fewer rewards for their efforts. (1990:16)

With differential schooling performance comes differential social and economic rewards, hence the perpetuation of class differences in the social order.

Bourdieu and Passeron (1977) help us extend Bernstein's linguistic analysis to other aspects of working-class versus middle- and upper-class life through the concept of "cultural capital"—those sets of competencies that emerge as a function of class-based family life. They suggested that the distinctive sets of linguistic and cultural competencies characteristic of different social classes transmitted to students through their family life are assigned different values by the school (1977:71–106). In that school setting, upper-class and, to a lesser extent, middle-class cultural capital are legitimated and rewarded at the expense of working-class cultural capital. Further,

> by appearing to be an impartial and neutral "transmitter" of benefits of a valued culture, schools are able to promote inequality in the name of fairness and objectivity. Through this argument Bourdieu rejects both the idealist position, which views schools as independent of external forces, and orthodox radical critiques, in which schools merely mirror the needs of the economic system. (Aronowitz and Giroux 1985:80)

This position of apparent autonomy enables schooling to reinforce class structure while appearing to operate independently of that structure. Domination and subordination are reproduced, but the role played by schooling as a vehicle of culture is mystified and obfuscated. While cultural reproduction theorists such as Bernstein, Bourdieu, and Passeron take us beyond mere economism, they are relatively silent regarding how we might work to reverse the process of reproduction.

Hegemonic-State Reproduction

Many analysts believe that theories of reproduction emphasizing only the economic and the cultural spheres ignore how political factors create the conditions for state intervention into the educational process. Such intervention aids in the reproduction of existent power relations. It is important to recognize that theorists who examine hegemonic-state forms of reproduction disagree about what constitutes the state and how hegemonic reproduction works relative to capital and education. Some questions that arise are summarized by Apple:

Does the state only serve the interests of capital or is it more complex than that? Is the state instead an arena of class conflict and a site where hegemony must be worked for, not a foregone conclusion where it is simply imposed? Are schools—as important sites of the state—simply "ideological state apparatuses" (to quote Althusser), ones whose primary role is to reproduce the ideological and "manpower" requirements of the social relations of production? Or, do they also embody contradictory tendencies and provide sites where ideological struggles within and among classes, races, and sexes can and do occur? (1982a:14)

The task here is not to review and analyze these differences but to give an overview of the hegemonic-state conception of reproduction. This conception begins with Gramsci's notion of hegemony arising out of the civil, as opposed to the political, side of the state discussed earlier.

The Gramscian notion that schools serve as ideological institutions promising the continued hegemony of dominant groups is also taken up by Althusser in his discussion of "ideological state apparatuses." Whereas Gramsci wavers between defining the institutions of civil society, including schools, as being either distinct from the state or encompassed by the state, Althusser clearly views the state as all-encompassing. The definition of state institutions, or apparatuses, rests not on their public versus private character, but instead on whether they fulfill the state function of promoting capitalist reproduction. For Althusser, two major kinds of state apparatuses, repressive and ideological, combine to achieve this outcome. Repressive state apparatuses include the government, police, army, courts, and prisons, and correspond to what Gramsci termed "political society," or in his more restrictive version, the "state." Ideological state apparatuses include religion, education, the family, political parties, trade unions, and the media, and correspond to Gramsci's concept of "civil society" (Althusser 1971:143–44).

The distinction between ideological and repressive state apparatuses is a theoretical one, while in practice all state apparatuses tend to combine the two techniques of domination. Schools, for example, rely on coercive measures such as detentions, expulsions, and sometimes physical violence, as well as ideological measures. Similarly, the police engage in a variety of public relations measures as well as repression to maintain their power. The difference, for Althusser, is that ideological state apparatuses tend to "function massively and predominately by ideology" (1971:149).

According to Althusser, the dominant ideological state apparatus of modern capitalist societies is education, and its importance reflects its role in the reproduction of labor power. Whereas Marx had stressed the importance of technical education for the (re)production of labor power, Althusser emphasized the role of ideological beliefs and values. Technical "know-how" is important, he notes, but schoolchildren also learn the "rules of good behavior" and the attitudes appropriate for various positions in the division of labor. Ultimately, this means that working-class children must also learn to submit to the ruling ideology and that the "agents of exploitation and repression" must learn to "manipulate the ruling ideology correctly" (1971:132–33).

Poulantzas extends and refines Althusser, emphasizing a less deterministic role for the state as a dedicated class actor or agent. While agreeing that schools function as ideological state apparatuses, Poulantzas views the connection between schooling and the reproduction of class relations in somewhat different terms. For Poulantzas, schools reproduce the "mental/manual labour division" by providing different classes of students with an understanding of distinct sets of cultural symbols. "The training of mental labour," he says, "essentially consists, to a lesser or greater extent, in the inculcation of a series of rituals, secrets and symbolisms which are to a considerable extent those of `general culture,' and whose main purpose is to distinguish it from manual labour" (1975:268). People are thus "qualified" for various occupations by their ability to participate in the dominant culture of society. Those who lack the ability to decipher dominant symbol systems or engage in the rituals of middle- or upper-class life are excluded from the world of mental labor. Schools function to promote such practices. This aspect of Poulantzas's framework comes close to the cultural reproduction arguments of Bernstein (1977) and Bourdieu & Passeron (1977).

Unlike Althusser and Gramsci, Poulantzas suggested that schools, like other state apparatuses, were shaped by the activities of subordinate classes as well as the dominant class. In this regard, Poulantzas criticized Althusser for his view of the state as entirely subordinate to the capitalist class. Instead, Poulantzas called for a conception of the state as "relatively autonomous" from the dominant class and thus partially open to manipulation from below. The state, he argued, "acts within an unstable equilibrium of compromises between the dominant classes and the dominated" (1978:31). As a result, specific measures adopted by the state, through apparatuses such as schools, could sometimes represent positive gains enabling subordinate groups to strengthen their position vis-á-vis the dominant class.

We begin to glean in Poulantzas more than in Althusser the possibility that students (and citizens) can participate in, and perhaps resist, the reproductive process. Like the theorists that preceded them, however, theorists of state hegemony place students and citizens in relatively passive positions with respect to the functioning of schools and society. Yet we see the possibility that economic, cultural, and political arrangements are not merely *reproduced* automatically by objectified social mechanisms, but in fact may be *produced* anew by each generation of students/citizens. It is on this distinction between cultural reproduction and cultural production that theories of resistance rest.

Theories of Resistance and Beyond

To this point in our analysis we have traced from Marx, through Gramsci and the Frankfurt School, to the reproduction theorists of the past thirty years a view of the sociology of education that places schools at the center of social and cultural reproduction on two levels. At one level, schools are a primary mechanism for reproducing labor power. And at a more general level, schools represent one of several institutional supports for ideological hegemony and domination. Much of what we have reviewed thus far looks critically at the ways in which institutions such as schools affect the lives of people, especially those of the lower economic classes. What has not been addressed are the complex and multiple ways in which people negotiate space within the institutional structures of education. As Aronowitz and Giroux observed:

> Beneath a discourse primarily concerned with the notions of domi-
> nation, class conflict, and hegemony, there has been a structured
> silence regarding how teachers, students, and others live out their
> daily lives in schools. Consequently, there has been an overempha-
> sis on how structural determinants promote economic and cultural
> inequality, and an underemphasis on how human agency accommo-
> dates, mediates, and resists the logic of capital and its dominating
> social practices. (1985:96)

Resistance theory looks carefully at the lives, thoughts, and actions of the participants of schooling in an attempt to understand how culture is produced and hegemony is maintained.

Resistance Theories in Education

Resistance theory is not singular, unitary, or without internal debate and conflict. An extension and corrective to reproduction theory, it interjects students and teachers, among others, as actors in the interplay of schooling events. Resistance theory overlaps with reproduction theory in at least two ways. First, they coexist temporally in the educational discourse of the 1960s to 1990s. While reproduction theory is more common in the first half of this period, resistance theory gains prominence in the latter half. Second, many theorists began in a reproductive mode and moved into resistance theory (and in some cases beyond) over time. The work of Michael Apple, one of the most influential critical educational theorists of the period, is a good example of this shift. In his early work (*Ideology and Curriculum*, 1979) Apple adopts a relatively mechanistic conception of reproduction that he criticized and problematized in his later works (*Education and Power*, 1982a; *Cultural and Economic Reproduction*, 1982b; *Teachers and Texts*, 1988).

Resistance theory also draws its origins from the "new sociology of education" in the United Kingdom (Young 1971). According to Karabel and Halsey (1977), the new sociology of education was rooted in the early work of cultural reproduction theorists such as Bernstein. It focused on microanalysis and interpretation of classroom interactions relative to the social construction of knowledge (Berger and Luckmann 1967), analyzing the various forms and meanings that knowledge takes and the ways in which knowledge is distributed. This interest in the phenomenological study of schooling experience interacted with critical reproduction positions and spawned a number of ethnographic studies of schooling and student experience. These ethnographic studies of education in the United States and the United Kingdom have added insight into the complex ways in which oppressed people resist oppressive conditions and, often at the same time, participate in their own oppression (see Willis 1977; McRobbie 1978; McLeod 1987; Fine 1991; Fordham and Ogbu 1986; McLaren 1989; Weiler 1988).

Resistance theory was also affected by the ground-breaking work of the Brazilian educator Paulo Freire. His efforts at empowering illiterate peasants with a pedagogy connecting indigenous culture with the social and collective construction of knowledge has had a major influence on radical educational discourse since the early 1970s (see Freire 1970, 1985; Freire and Macedo 1987).

Resistance theory recognizes that participants in schooling are not merely objects of the machinations of the economic, cultural, or political order, but rather are active subjects in the process of creating and operating society. In other words, social arrangements are not merely reproduced by the culture, they are actively constructed, produced anew, with each passing generation of actors in the world. Further, the identities and worldviews of students are crucial to understanding their actions and the resultant effects on the social order.

Perhaps the earliest and most influential of these ethnographies is Paul Willis's *Learning to Labour: How Working Class Kids Get Working Class Jobs* (1977). He studied a group of working-class males in the context of their participation in a working-class school in an industrial city in the United Kingdom. In his study, Willis not only observed certain students—the lads—in real opposition to the hegemonic system of schooling; he also discovered the extent to which this opposition is mediated and controlled by the hegemonic apparatus of the school. An unmistakable conclusion derived from Willis's work is that a real possibility exists for the development of a counterhegemony and the raising of working-class consciousness. This insight became the impetus for much of the critical educational writing in the 1980s and 1990s that addressed the role of the teacher and school, a literature whose emphasis was increasingly directed toward the concept of cultural production as opposed to cultural reproduction.

What Willis adds to our brief history of Marxist and neo-Marxist thought applied to schooling is evidence that the possibility exists for the creation and development of a counterhegemony of the working class in contemporary society. The lads, in their informal group, do penetrate the nature of the educational exchange within the institution. That their penetrations do not transfer into an articulation of working-class consciousness is owed *not* to the inevitable determination of their social-class position through the social relations of production but to the limitations and divisions growing to a large extent out of their own class experiences.

In a more recent ethnographic account, Fine documents the experience of eventual dropouts from a New York City high school and calls into question both the individualist belief that they were victims of learned helplessness and (implicitly) the notions undergirding reproduction theory that they lived out their plight because of class position. Instead, she found these young people to be very bright and astute regarding the functioning of schooling. For example, they were more likely than their peers who stayed in school to recognize and speak out against injustice, especially if it were engaged in by teachers. Also, they were less depressed than their peers who stayed in school (Fine 1991).

There is a cruel irony at work in both the Willis and Fine accounts. Students who are capable of challenging and questioning the dominant ideology of schooling often do so in such a way that they doom themselves to the very reproductive process that gives rise to their unjust circumstances. As Willis's title suggests and as Fine bears out, there is nothing automatic in the process of working-class kids getting working-class jobs, but the limits of student resistance often doom those very students to the unequal outcomes that have come to characterize late capitalism.

There are a number of problems, in Willis's study in particular and in resistance theory in general. First, all nonconforming behaviors in which students engage are not resistance. Resistance suggests some level of conscious political action, whereas some of the things that students do are simply "oppositional" (Aronowitz and Giroux 1985). McRobbie's (1978) study of British working class teenage girls makes this point quite clearly. These girls oppose schooling sanctions against tight clothing, sloppiness, assertiveness, and anything that is not "feminine" by such actions as asserting their sexuality in the dating of older boys and carving the names of their boyfriends in desktops. Their actions are not liberating; instead, they remain trapped in oppressive sexist conditions in which their sense of self is dependent on their relationship, especially sexual, to a male: "Obviously, the fact that these young women are acting collectively and attempting to define for themselves what they want out of life contains an emancipatory moment. But in the final analysis, this type of opposition is informed by a dominating, rather than liberating, logic" (Aronowitz and Giroux 1985:100).

Another weakness in resistance theory, as well as in reproduction and critical theory that preceded it, is the failure to take into consideration issues of race and gender as equal and interactive variables in social dynamics. Patriarchy, as a phenomenon that cuts across class lines and mediates class position, is seldom interrogated in the works of resistance theorists, especially before 1980. Similarly, while Ogbu (1978), for example, examined the intersection of race and class in education, the ways in which race differentially affects class *and* gender experience is only now being fully explored.

Despite these problems with resistance theory, it nonetheless provides the foundation for much of the work in educational theory captured by the phrases critical, emancipatory, and liberatory pedagogy (Apple 1988; Weiler 1988; Lather 1991; Giroux 1988a, 1988b, 1991a, 1991b). The thrust of this work lies in the belief that teachers can indeed use the opportunities offered by students' resistance to the dominant ideology to enhance their insights and at the same time expose and question the limitations of their resistant behavior. In other words, teachers can act as "transformative intellectuals" (Giroux 1988a) and engage students in an active investigation of the systematic nature of oppression, expose the ways in which they participate in their own oppression, and develop ways of connecting curricular content to the lived experience of students to avoid both the "deskilling" of the teacher (Braverman 1974; Apple 1982a; Weiler 1988) and the alienation of students. With the notions of resistance and cultural production, educational theorists have added a "language of possibility" to the "language of critique" developed out of Marxist and neo-Marxist thought (Aronowitz and Giroux 1985; Giroux 1988a, 1988b).

The concept of teachers as transformative intellectuals is not without problems, however, and these problems go to the root of realizing a language of possibility (Ellsworth 1989). To complete our exploration of Marxist and neo-Marxist sociological thought in education, we must recognize and integrate critical perspectives injected into the discourse by feminist and poststructuralist theorists.

Beyond Resistance Theory

Mouffe succinctly laid the groundwork for moving beyond resistance theory by noting:

Modern citizenship was formulated in a way that played a crucial role in the emergence of modern democracy, but it has become an obstacle to making it wider and more pluralistic. Many of the new rights that are being claimed by women and ethnic minorities are no longer rights that can be universalized. They are the expression of specific needs and should be granted to particular communities. Only a pluralistic conception of citizenship can accommodate the specificity and multiplicity of democratic demands and provide a pole of identification for a wide range of democratic forces. The political community has to be viewed, then, as a diverse collection of communities, as a forum for creating unity without denying specificity. (Mouffe 1989:7)

How can we extend our discussion of Marxist and neo-Marxist theory to embrace Mouffe's conception of a political community marked by both unity and specificity? This final section addresses critiques from feminist and poststructuralist thought applied to the educational context. We must say at the outset that the orientations of many people listed under the "resistance theory" label underwent transformation in the late 1980s and 1990s. The greatest forces behind that transformation seem to have come from feminism and poststucturalism. Giroux and Apple, for instance, are theorists who trace their work to the earlier forms of economic, cultural, and hegemonic-state reproduction theory. But their later work moves through resistance theory and into a new critical sociological theory informed by feminist and poststructuralist discourse (Apple 1988, 1991; Giroux 1991a, 1991b). They are joined by a number of others, including Lather (1991), Wexler (1992) Britzman (1991), Ellsworth (1989), hooks (1989, 1990), and Fine (1991), in a spirited and contested debate over the future directions of critical sociological theory in education. In this section we outline some of the main concerns of feminist and poststructuralist thought that have been used to modify and reframe the Marxist and neo-Marxist theories of education. We then frame a series of questions that seem to emerge from that dialogue.

From Marxist and neo-Marxist critical theory, including reproduction and resistance theory, we have been able to see that society is made up of conflicting groups in contention for finite resources and power. Further, power is maintained in the hands of a dominant group not by sheer force and coercion but by the process of engineered consent and participation of the governed (hegemony). Schooling helps maintain power relations by working to reproduce labor power (albeit in complex interaction with the subjectivity of students and teachers) and, more generally, by working with other social institutions to reinforce ideological hegemony. Critical theorists engage in an ideological critique of the functioning of society and through that critique explain how power relations are reproduced through social institutions (such as the school) in manners that are disadvantageous to the vast majority of the population. Where does this analysis fall short? What additionally needs to be questioned and analyzed to allow for a deeper and more inclusive look at critical educational sociology?

One very difficult problem addressed in current discourse on educational sociology is the degree to which critical, liberatory, or emancipatory pedagogy actually serves to subjugate. How is it, in other words, that in our very efforts to liberate (students and/or teachers), we might be perpetuating relations of domination and oppression? Feminist and poststructuralist theorists respond in at least two ways. First, feminism and poststructuralism offer both a critique and extension of Marxist and neo-Marxist critical theory applied to educational practice. From a feminist/poststructuralist perspective, critical theory substitutes one form of oppression for another—that of a white male working-class for the elitism of traditional capitalism (Ellsworth 1989; Lather 1991). Second, the role of the critical pedagogue (as transformative intellectual, for example) assumes a position of superior knowledge and privileged discourse that can be silencing and oppressive (Lewis and Simon 1986; Lather 1991; Ellsworth 1989). While we do not have to fall victim to rampant epistemological relativism, feminist and poststructuralist critics would have us problematize the privileged position of the teacher in educational discourse. This would add complexity to the question of power differentials beyond class position.

An alternative might be to "shift the role of critical intellectuals *from* being universalized spokespersons to acting as cultural workers whose task is to take away the barriers that prevent people from speaking for themselves" (Apple 1991:ix). According to Apple, feminism can be particularly helpful because it "has had long experience in self-reflexivity and in making (the) commonsense problematic." Therefore, it can "provide the basis for the development of practices of self-interrogation and critique" (Apple 1991:x).

As an additional problem, critical theory maintains a Eurocentric worldview and cultural orientation. According to much feminist and poststructuralist writing, what is needed is a view that does not obscure the lives and histories of individuals and groups not captured by the "master narrative" of class analysis. Feminists and poststructuralists focus on the idea that reality is constructed by a multiplicity of voices and lived experiences, many of whom are marginalized and silenced by such overarching analyses. While there are differences of opinion within each orientation and between feminist and poststructuralist writers, the struggle to situate the individual within a social, political, and cultural context is at the root of much feminist/poststructuralist thought (hooks 1989, 1990; Fraser & Nicholson 1988; Nicholson 1990).

Feminists and poststructuralists also see in critical theory an extension of binary or dichotomous forms of thinking. Binary forms of thinking lead to oppositions and the formation of hierarchies in which one pole is valued over the other. By pitting working class against capitalist, for example, we are precluded from viewing conflict in terms of multiplicity. By emphasizing variety and individuality within class, and by recognizing that other factors such as race, gender, ethnicity, sexuality, and age affect the nature and degree of oppression one experiences, feminists and poststructuralists add needed complexity to critical analyses of society (Moi 1985; Farber 1992).

Additionally, and in a somewhat different vein, poststructuralists see the construct of class being "essentialized" in much of the writings in critical educational theory (Britzman 1992). Rather than assume that there is some essential quality of being working or middle class; female or male; homosexual or heterosexual; African American, Native American, Asian American, Hispanic, or White; we must recognize the ways in which we construct our identity through the active interplay of forces that certainly relate to our "groupings," but only as we invest those groupings with meaning through our lived experience. Further, we must critically assess the ways in which differing experience is represented in schools, both in terms of the formal curriculum and in terms of the ongoing patterns of discourse among teachers and students (Ellsworth 1989; Britzman 1991, 1992; Lather 1991).

While there are certainly other feminist and poststructuralist concepts that are useful to a critique of Marxist and neo-Marxist sociological thought applied to education, the above serves as a framework from which to begin a reconstructive conversation. Ultimately, we are struggling to find meaning in Marxist and neo-Marxist thought, given a changing historical, social, and intellectual context. Lather is worth quoting at length on this point.

The "crisis of Marxism" is nothing new. The Frankfurt School responded to an earlier version with an internal critique of its fundamental categories. Feminist theory has long been suspicious of Marxism's category systems and vanguard politics. Long-noted problems include the failure of actually existing socialisms, inadequate concepts of base/superstructure, power/politics, and the relation between structure, action and consciousness as well as the epistemological issue of the scientific status of Marxism.

Poststructuralism positions Marxism as a movement of controlling, labeling, and classifying which denies its complicity and investment in dichotomy at the expense of the Other. Transforming difference into dichotomous oppositions, it reduces multiplicities and plurality into a single oppositional norm. Hence, the crisis of Marxism is not only of effectivity, organization and popular appeal, but of theory in terms of claims to truth, will to knowledge, and the primacy of reason. Overly cognitive in its conception of the dynamics of subordination and emancipation, ensnared in phallocentric and logocentric assumptions, it relegates practice to an object of theory, history to a teleology where each age is a stepping stone for the next, agency and structure to dualistic categories, and strategy to the masculinist myth of "the One Big Revolution." (Lather 1991:23–24)

The challenge, according to Lather, is that educational sociology should struggle to reposition Marxism as a discourse with a great deal to share regarding the role and function of schooling within the broader society. But it can no longer function as a totalizing discourse. Are we prepared to rethink basic Marxist assumptions about emancipation, subordination, and social progress? Is the recognition of particularity and partiality of experience able to coexist with class dynamics as mechanisms for explaining social phenomena? Can we interrogate the theoretical advances of neo-Marxist theory, such as the role of the critical pedagogue or transformative intellectual, in ways that attend to critiques from feminism and poststructuralism regarding maintenance of power hierarchies, albeit in new forms? What would a poststructural Marxism look like? Is such a notion even imaginable, or is it oxymoronic?

Quoting Lather again, we find the struggle is underway.

In this post-Marxist space, the binaries that structure liberatory struggle implode from "us versus them" and "liberation" versus "oppression" to a multi-centered discourse with differential access to power. Here, nothing is innocent. As Foucault (1980) makes clear, overtly oppositional work, while at war with the dominant systems of knowledge production, is also inscribed in what it hopes to transform....(Patton) sees the renewal of Marxism as accompanied by its dispersal. Given its pretention to unify the field of oppositional politics, "the difference crisis" challenges its very status as the center of leftist discursive practices. What Campioni and Grosz (1983:140) point out as the claim to difference as a strategy of defense against a levelling process decenters the call to unity upon which Marxist practice is based. (Lather 1991:26)

Lather argues that the "decentering" process repositions Marxism from being the "dominant discourse of opposition" to being one of several potentially liberating ways of viewing the world (1991:26). She emphasizes that Marxism needs to be seen as operative within a changed and changing context. Further, as contexts change, so too must the discourses we use to understand and analyze those contexts. We must view Marxism as a discourse that changes and works in conjunction with other discourses.

Conclusion

We have explored major themes in Marxist and neo-Marxist discourse in the sociology of education. While we have included work from a variety of fields and disciplines, the Marxist and neo-Marxist writings affecting the sociology of education arise from two distinct branches—the sociology of education in the discipline of sociology and the sociology of education in the field of education. *Sociology of Education* and other sociology journals that pay attention to the topic of education have published articles by Marxist scholars, but the number of such articles has been small. The influence of Marxist and neo-Marxist thought on the mainstream academic literature of the sociology of education in sociology has been less evident than is the case for the field of education. The most recent *Handbook of Sociology* (Smelser 1988) has a chapter on the sociology of education (Bidwell and Friedkin 1988), but in it there is no mention of Marx's influence and only oblique references to Marxist and neo-Marxist research. The principal focus of Marxist and neo-Marxist work on education in the discipline of sociology has been to extend and refine aspects of reproduction theory regarding the ways in which power elites influence the curriculum and structure of schooling (Wrigley 1982; Katznelson and Weir 1985; Peterson et al. 1985; Karabel 1984; Reese 1986; Ray and Michelson 1989; Nelson-Rowe 1988, 1991).

In contrast, the sociology of education in the field of education has given rise to a rich and contested debate over Marxism as a means for understanding and transforming schooling. The emphasis has been largely on exposing and overcoming ideology and on developing a liberatory and transformative pedagogy out of theoretical and empirical research. Additionally, the Marxist and neo-Marxist discourse itself has been challenged and made problematic by feminist and poststructuralist writers.

At the risk of overgeneralizing, we would say that the sociology of education in sociology has been principally involved in examining macro-level structures and large-scale changes, with empirical studies focusing on aggregate analyses. The sociology of education in education has been typically more interested in micro-level classroom analyses and grounded in practice, with empirical studies more often taking the form of case studies. The result has been multitude of conflicting approaches and findings, with the two bodies of Marxist scholars sometimes seeming to be talking past one another.

At one level, it might seem that Marx will be lost in the confusion and contestation that has been engendered. But we do not think so. We see a necessary and productive conversation/struggle that helps us to understand better the complexities of schooling in the context of an increasingly diverse population. As Lather points out, we would do well to "heed Foucault's prophecy that, 'It is clear, even if one admits that Marx will disappear for now, that he will reappear one day'" (1991:26). In creating this chapter as a part of a book on Marx, we have helped Marx to reappear. Yet how he reappears in our construction is not "innocent" (Lather 1991:26); by constructing this chapter we have entered into the discourse. We take this opportunity to capture as much of the discourse as we can and to engage readers in extending and continuing that discourse.

References

Altenbaugh, Richard J. 1990. *Education for Struggle: The American Labor Colleges of the 1920s and 1930s*. Philadelphia: Temple University Press.

Althusser, Louis. 1971. "Ideology and Ideological State Apparatuses." Pp. 127–86 in *Lenin and Philosophy*. New York: Monthly Review Press.

Anyon, Jean. "Social Class and the Hidden Curriculum of Work." *Journal of Education* 162(1):67–92.

Apple, Michael. 1979. *Ideology and Curriculum*. Boston: Routledge and Kegan Paul.

———. 1982a. *Education and Power*. Boston: Routledge and Kegan Paul.

———, ed. 1982b. *Cultural and Economic Reproduction in Education*. Boston: Routledge and Kegan Paul.

———. 1988. *Teachers and Texts*. New York: Routledge and Kegan Paul.

———. 1991. "Series Editor's Introduction." In Patti Lather, *Getting Smart*. New York: Routledge and Kegan Paul.

Aronowitz, Stanley, and Henry Giroux. 1985. *Education under Siege*. South Hadley, Mass.: Bergin and Garvey.

Bennett, Kathleen, and Margaret LeCompte. 1990. *The Way Schools Work*. New York: Longman.

Berger, P.L., and T. Luckmann. 1967. *The Social Construction of Reality: A Treatise in the Sociology of Knowledge*. New York: Anchor Doubleday.

Bernstein, Basil. 1971. *Class, Codes and Control. Vol. I: Theoretical Studies towards a Sociology of Language*. London: Routledge and Kegan Paul.

———. 1977. *Class, Codes and Control. Vol. III: Towards a Theory of Educational Transmission*. London: Routledge and Kegan Paul.

Bidwell, Charles, and Noah Friedkin. 1988. "The Sociology of Education." Pp. 449–71 in *Handbook of Sociology*, ed. Neil Smelser. Newbury Park, Calif.: Sage.

Bourdieu, P., and J. Passeron. 1977. *Reproduction in Education, Society and Culture*. London: Sage.

Bowles, Samuel, and Herbert Gintis. 1976. *Schooling in Capitalist America: Educational Reform and the Contradictions of Economic Life*. New York: Basic Books.

Braverman, Harry. 1974. *Labor and Monopoly Capital*. New York: Monthly Review Press.

Britzman, Deborah. 1991. *Practice Makes Practice: A Critical Study of Learning to Teach*. Albany: SUNY Press.

———. 1992. "Beyond Rolling Models: Gender and Multicultural Education. Draft of chapter in *Yearbook for the National Society for the Study of Education*, ed. S. Bilken and D. Pollard. Forthcoming.

Carnoy, Martin, and Henry Levin. 1985. *Schooling and Work in the Democratic State*. Stanford: Stanford University Press.

Cohen, David, and Marvin Lazerson. 1972. "Education and the Corporate Order." *Socialist Revolution* 2:47–72.

Dreeben, Robert. 1968. *On What Is Learned in School*. Reading, Mass.: Addison-Wesley.

Ellsworth, Elizabeth. 1989. "Why Doesn't this Feel Empowering? Working through the Repressive Myths of Critical Pedagogy." *Harvard Educational Review* 59(3):297–324.

Farber, Kathleen. 1992. "Feminist Criticism and the Reconceptualization of Critical Thinking." *Journal of Thought*, In Press.

Fine, Michelle. 1991. *Framing Dropouts*. Albany: SUNY Press.

Fraser, Nancy, and Linda Nicholson. 1988. "Social Criticism without Philosophy: An Encounter between Feminism and Postmodernism." Pp. 83–104 in *Universal Abandon! The Politics of Postmodernism*, ed. A. Ross. Minneapolis: University of Minnesota Press.

Freire, Paulo. 1970. *Pedagogy of the Oppressed*. New York: Continuum.

———. 1985. *The Politics of Education*. South Hadley, Mass.: Bergin and Garvey.

Freire, Paulo, and Donaldo Macedo. 1987. *Literacy: Reading the Word and the World*. South Hadley, Mass.: Bergin and Garvey.

Fordham, Signithia, and John Ogbu. 1986. "Black Students' School Success: Coping with the 'Burden' of 'Acting White'." *Urban Review* 18(3):176–206.

Giroux, Henry. 1983. *Theory and Resistance in Education*. South Hadley, Mass.: Bergin and Garvey.

———. 1988a. *Teachers as Intellectuals*. Granby, Mass.: Bergin and Garvey.

———. 1988b. *Schooling and the Struggle for Public Life: Critical Pedagogy in the Modern Age*. Minneapolis: University of Minnesota Press.

———, ed. 1991a. *Postmodernism, Feminism, and Cultural Politics*. Albany: SUNY Press.

———. 1991b. *Border Crossings: Cultural Workers and the Politics of Education*. New York: Routledge.

Giroux, Henry, and David Purpel, eds. 1983. *The Hidden Curriculum and Moral Education*. Berkeley: McCutchan.

Gramsci, Antonio. 1971. *Selections from the Prison Notebooks*. New York: International Publishers.

Held, David. 1980. *Introduction to Critical Theory*. Berkeley: University of California Press.

Hogan, David. 1982. "Making It in America: Work, Education, and Social Structure." Pp. 142–79 in *Work, Youth, and Schooling*, ed. Harvey Kantor and David Tyack. Stanford: Stanford University Press.

———. 1985. *Class and Reform: School and Society in Chicago 1880–1930*. Philadelphia: University of Pennsylvania Press.

hooks, bell. 1989. *Talking Back: Thinking Feminist, Thinking Black*. Boston: South End Press.

———. 1990. *Yearning: Race, Gender, and Cultural Politics*. Boston: South End Press.

Jackson, Philip. 1968. *Life in Classrooms*. New York: Holt, Rinehart and Winston.

Jay, Martin. 1973. *The Dialectical Imagination*. Boston: Little, Brown.

Katznelson, Ira, and Margaret Weir. 1985. *Schooling for All: Class, Race, and the Decline of the Democratic Ideal*. Berkeley: University of California Press.

Kantor, Harvey. 1982. "Vocationalism in American Education: The Economic and Political Context 1880–1930." Pp. 14–44 in *Work, Youth, and Schooling*, ed. Harvey Kantor and David Tyack. Stanford: Stanford University Press.

Karabel, Jerome. 1984. "Status-Group Struggle, Organizational Interests, and the Limits of Institutional Autonomy: The Transformation of Harvard, Yale, and Princeton 1918–1940." *Theory and Society* 13:1–40.

Karabel, Jerome, and A.H. Halsey, eds. 1977. *Power and Ideology in Education*. New York: Oxford University Press.

Lather, Patti. 1991. *Getting Smart: Feminist Research and Pedagogy with/in the Postmodern*. New York: Routledge.

Lenin, V.I. 1975. "The Task of the Youth Leagues." Pp. 661–74 in *The Lenin Anthology*, ed. Robert C. Tucker. New York: Norton.

Lewis, Magda, and Roger Simon. 1986. "A Discourse Not Intended for Her: Learning and Teaching within Patriarchy." *Harvard Educational Review* 56(4):457–72.

McLaren, Peter. 1989. *Life in Schools*. New York: Longman.

McLeod, Jay. 1987. *Ain't No Makin' It: Leveled Aspirations in a Low-income Neighborhood* . Boulder: Westview Press.

McRobbie, Angela. 1978. "Working Class Girls and the Culture of Femininity." Pp. 96–108 in *Women Take Issue: Aspects of Women's Subordination* , ed. the Women's Study Group, Center for Contemporary Cultural Studies. London: Hutchinson.

Marx, Karl. 1964. *The Economic and Philosophic Manuscripts of 1844* . New York: International Publishers.

———. 1967. *Capital*. Vol. I. New York: International Publishers.

———. 1970. "Preface to *A Contribution to the Critique of Political Economy* ." Pp. 181–85 in *Karl Marx and Frederich Engels: Selected Works* . New York: International Publishers.

———. 1972a. *The Grundrisse*. New York: Harper & Row.

———. 1978a. *The Marx-Engels Reader*, ed. Robert C. Tucker. New York: W.W. Norton.

———. 1978b. "Education for the Worker." P. 205 in *The Essential Marx: The Non-Economic Writings*, ed. Saul Padover. New York: Mentor.

———. 1978c. "The Communist Manifesto." Pp. 473–500 in *The Marx-Engels Reader*, ed. Robert C. Tucker. New York: Norton.

———. 1978d. "Critique of the Gotha Program." Pp. 525–41 in *The Marx-Engels Reader*, ed. Robert C. Tucker. 2nd ed. New York: Norton.

Marx, Karl, and Frederich Engels. 1972b. *The German Ideology*. New York: International Publishers.

Mouffe, Chantal. 1989. "Toward a Radical Democratic Citizenship." *Democratic Left* 17(2): 6–7.

Moi, Torvil. 1985. *Sexual/Textual Politics*. New York: Methuen.

Najafizadeh, Mehrangiz, and Lewis Mennerick. 1989. "Defining Third World Education as a Problem: Education Ideologies and Education Entrepreneurship in Nicaragua and Iran." Pp. 283–315 in *Perspectives on Social Problems*, vol. 1, ed. James Holstein and Gale Miller. Greenwich: JAI Press.

Nelson-Rowe, Shan. 1988. "Markets, Politics and Professions: The Rise of Vocationalism in American Education." Ph.D. dissertation, State University of New York at Stony Brook, Department of Sociology.

———. 1991. "The Social Construction of Educational Change and the Origins of Vocational Education in the United States." Paper, Department of Social Sciences, Fairleigh Dickinson University.

Nicholson, Linda, ed. 1990. *Feminism/Postmodernism*. New York: Routledge.

Ogbu, John. 1978. *Minority Education and Caste: The American System in Cross-Cultural Perspective*. New York: Academic Press.

Peterson, Paul E., et al. 1985. *The Politics of School Reform 1870–1940* . Chicago: University of Chicago Press.

Poulantzas, Nicos. 1975. *Classes in Contemporary Capitalism*. New York: Verso.

———. 1978. *Political Power and Social Classes*. New York: Verso.

Ray, Carol Axtell, and Roslyn Arlin Michelson. 1989. "Business Leaders and the Politics of School Reform." *Politics of Education Association Yearbook*, 119–35.

———. 1990. "Corporate Leaders, Resistant Youth, and School Reform in Sunbelt City: The Political Economy of Education." *Social Problems* 37(2):178–90.

Reese, William. 1986. *Power and the Promise of School Reform: Grassroot Movements during the Progressive Era*. Boston: Routledge and Kegan Paul.

Reid, F. 1966. "Socialist Sunday Schools in Britain: 1892–1939." *International Review of Social History* 11:29.

Simon, Roger, Don Dippo, and Arleen Schenke. 1991. *Learning Work: A Critical Pedagogy of Work Education*. New York: Bergin and Garvey.

Smelser, Neil, ed. 1988. *Handbook of Sociology*. Newbury Park, Calif.: Sage.

Teitelbaum, Kenneth, and William J. Reese. 1983. "American Socialist Pedagogy and Experimentation in the Progressive Era: The Socialist Sunday School." *History of Education Quarterly* 23(Winter):429–54.

Weiler, Kathleen. 1988. *Women Teaching for Change*. South Hadley, Mass.: Bergin and Garvey.

Wexler, Philip. 1992. *Becoming Somebody: Toward a Social Psychology of School* . Washington, D.C.: Falmer Press.

Williams, Raymond. 1973. "Base and Superstructure in Marxist Cultural Theory." *New Left Review*. 82:3–16.

Willis, Paul. 1977. *Learning to Labour: Why Working Class Kids Get Working Class Jobs* . Westmead, England: Saxon House, Teakfield.

Wood, Allen. 1981. *Karl Marx*. Boston: Routledge and Kegan Paul.

Wood, George. 1982. "Beyond Radical Educational Cynicism." *Educational Theory* 32(2):55–71.

Wrigley, Julia. 1982. *Class Politics and Public Schools: Chicago 1900–1950* . New Brunswick: Rutgers University Press.

Young, Michael F.D. 1971. *Knowledge and Control: New Directions for the Sociology of Education* . London: Collier-Macmillan.

MEDICINE AND PUBLIC HEALTH:

A STUDY OF THE HEALTH CARE SYSTEM: THE MARXIST CRITIQUE OF A DOMINANT PARADIGM

Beth Mintz
and
Charley MacMartin

A survey of Marxist literature on health care contrasts sharply with the application of Marxist tools of analysis in other important fields. Specifically, the volume of Marxist work on health is considerably more limited than is the study of other topics. This is as true in recent decades as in the early years of Marxist scholarship and is particularly ironic because, as Conrad and Kern (1990:1) note, "the social and political struggles over health and medical care have become major social issues."

In addition, Marxist contributions to the study of health are not well integrated into the mainstream of debate over medicine and medical technology. While a Marxist literature is certainly present—note the existence of the explicitly Marxist *International Journal of Health Services*—the role continues to be a critical voice from the margin, rather than the pivotal critique at center stage.

At the same time, Marxism provides a crucial starting point in framing the debate over health by emphasizing the distinction between the study of medicine and that of health care. Medicine defines a discrete topic within the broader issue of health care: the contending methods of preventing illness and treating the sick. The study of health care, in contrast, especially within a Marxist framework, uses as a point of departure the observation that health and illness are as much—if not more—social as biological. The dimension of class and the historical context of particular systems of knowledge emerge as central to the study of health. This chapter, therefore, emphasizes health care as opposed to medicine and explores the broader social-structural setting within which the contemporary health-care delivery system has developed.

Historical Development of the Marxian Analysis

Marxist scholars produced very little on medicine during the last half of the nineteenth and first half of the twentieth centuries. What literature there is falls under two basic rubrics of debate. The first is the struggle with bourgeois social scientists over the very concept of health, the early stages of which culminated in the 1912 Flexner report, initiating the current period of "scientific medicine."

The second issue flows from the first. As capitalist forces in the United States secured their position in the conflict with and domination over labor, medical institutions reflected this imbalance. These institutions emerged as a second rubric of critique and evaluation in the Marxist literature.

Health and the Working Class

Initial Marxist writings on health and medicine place us back in mid-nineteenth-century England. Frederick Engels wrote his *Condition of the Working-Class in England in 1844* with two objectives in mind. He catalogued the statistical misery of the great majority of English and immigrant workers of the time, and he documented the afflictions of the day—including typhoid, tuberculosis and rickets (Hobsbawm 1962). He also reported on cases of young people working in the cotton and flax-spinning mills and detailed the growth deformities, contraction of the aorta, and anaemic complications suffered by women workers in factories and mines.

Engels (1952) described the lack of access to health care for workers and their families. And as has been pointed out, medical care brought little relief when it was made available (Frazer,1950:30; Marcus,1974:206). He focused as well on occupational hazards. Both acutely dangerous and debilitating through time, the conditions of work in the coal mines of Britain produced a myriad of occupational health hazards including the "black spittle" disease particularly prevalent in Scotland.

Engels's second objective, though, was his distinguishing one. His particular etiology explicitly linked the conditions of health with the conditions of work. In particular, Engels argued that physical disease is a symptom of workers' chief ailment: lack of control over their work. In capitalism, the owner is legally allowed to pay the worker less than the value of the product the worker fabricates, creating surplus value. Owners demand control over the workplace so as to organize production and successfully extract this value. The legal lack of control, or powerlessness, of the worker stands as a necessary precondition for "successful" capitalist production.

From this condition—capitalist social relations of production—Engels (1952:vii) suggests, flows all subsequent social and physical ills. The central problem, then, is not a particular set of ailments: "The cause of the miserable condition of the working-class is to be sought, not in these minor grievances, but in the Capitalistic System itself."

Engels's approach staked out the radical position within the "anti-contagion movement" of the late eighteenth century (Berliner and Salmon 1979; Ackerknecht 1948). In doing so, Engels distanced himself both from the elite proponents of the contagion approach to public health (Snow 1936; Simon 1890) and from liberal anticontagionists (Chadwick 1887; Mitchell 1859; Ringen 1979) who opposed quarantine and expanding state bureaucracies in favor of sanitary reform (Berliner and Salmon 1979:32–33).

But as Engels makes manifestly clear, such reform remains doomed as long as the social relations of capitalism persist. Public health measures and "police regulations have been plentiful as blackberries," Engels (1952:viii) explains. But the "system itself" remains intact. As Engels (1887:44) argues, in an article for the Leipzig Volksstaat on housing conditions, "the capitalist order of society reproduces again and again the evils which are to be remedied with such inevitable necessity."

Marxist Etiology and Medical Reform

Engels's radical etiology had a profound influence on a young Prussian student of medicine, Rudolf Virchow, who was assigned by the government to investigate the outbreak of a typhus epidemic in Upper Silesia, an economically depressed Prussian province. Virchow viewed the social conditions of the province as the decisive factor in bringing about the epidemic of the winter of 1847–48. He detailed the lack of education, poor housing conditions, and concentrated landownership in his report and, in response, called for no less than the economic and social liberation of the Polish minority living in the province (Taylor and Rieger 1984). This approach, with its concentration on the social, political, and economic factors of disease, foreshadowed the development of the historical materialist epidemiology of the next century (Eyer and Sterling 1977; Turshen 1977).

The experience in Upper Silesia prompted Virchow to promote his concept of the social roots of illness through a journal he edited, *Medical Reform*. His ideas—along with those of other like-minded physicians—that disease was as much a social issue as a medical one did not win them favor from conservative governments (Ackerknecht 1953; Riese 1953). Nevertheless, by today's standards, the social component of illness was defined rather narrowly. Marxist and other social critics of the time paid little attention, for example, to women's health issues. Aside from the writings of Engels (1952), one must depart from professional journals and search the popular literature of the era to get a full picture of both the particular health issues of women (Wright 1889; Gilman 1975) and the dimension of power between a woman and her physician (Gilman 1973; Cott 1972).

Early work on women and health did include a feminist critique of protective employment legislation (Eastman 1976). And birth control, as an issue of both health and power, emerged as a central concern by the early twentieth century in the writings of socialist feminists and other social critics (Wiesen Cook 1978; Sanger 1929; Goldman 1934).

Additional dimensions absent from the early Marxist literature include colonial relations and imperialism; an analysis of colonialism and health did not fully emerge until the twentieth century (Turshen 1984). The analytical category of racism, and its implications for the study of power, provided insight into the ideological uses of medicine and health (Elling 1981; Doyal and Penel 1976). And the experiences of Third World liberation movements in addressing health crises clarified the analytical links between health and global capitalist structures (Waitzkin 1983b).

Medicine and Capitalism: U.S. Style

In the United States at the turn of the century, the rapid concentration of wealth and corporate power (Weinstein 1968:163) produced social contradictions that extended to public health. U.S. capitalists responded to the general unrest of the period and secured their position through repression, reform, and co-optation (Weinstein 1968; Kolko 1968). As part of this process, the medical theories and literature congruent with ruling interests were elevated into the arena of public debate. Dissenting views were filtered out or more forcibly removed from the realm of acceptable debate (Therborn 1976).

In the context of this struggle and consolidation, Frederick T. Gates, chief aide to John D. Rockefeller on the latter's philanthropic interests, encouraged Rockefeller to fund what became known as the Flexner Report (1912). Ostensibly, the document—named after its chief writer and researcher, Abraham Flexner—examined the future direction of medical education and research. It encouraged the national adoption of four-year medical schools, the placement of clinical research more centrally in medical training, and the moving of medical schools into the framework of the universities (Berliner 1975; Brown 1979).

The Flexner Report resulted in the closing of many medical schools, including all programs catering to predominantly black and female populations, thus constricting the number of graduates and simultaneously accentuating the exclusive, class nature of medical education. The impact of the report, though, went much further. It endorsed the biomedical, clinical approach to health and disease prevention. This view had been expounded in an earlier work which greatly influenced Gates: William Osler's 1897 piece, *Principles and Practice of Medicine*. Osler built on an individualist conception of societal disorders found in germ theory (Berliner and Salmon 1979) and prevalent among the "contagionists" of the nineteenth century (Ackerknecht 1948). In this view, individual disease reflects a physiological dysfunction that required interventionist—that is, clinical—treatment.

It is easy to see the ideological value of this approach to U.S. ruling interests. Disease, like social problems, could now be understood as an "invasion" by external pathogens and not the result of the conditions in which disease flourishes (Brown 1979:119–20; Wartofsky 1975). Thus, the biomedical approach offered the foundation for attempts at engineered solutions to disease (Markowitz and Rosner 1973:86; Renaud 1975:559) that became a model for problem solving in the social arena (Brown 1979:121).

The Literature of Social Medicine in the United States

Importantly, the Flexner Report was only part of the literature—albeit the dominant part—during the first part of the century. In 1931, Henry Sigerist came to the United States and to Johns Hopkins as a visiting lecturer bringing with him the European tradition of social medicine (Terris 1975; Galdston 1954). His writings (Sigerist 1934, 1937, 1946) pointed towards two basic reforms for health care in the United States.

First, he argued, health care should be a service provided to all citizens. Fee for service corrupted, he pronounced; "those whose minds are on riches had better join the stock exchange." Recognizing the bleak prospects for a national health service in the United States in the 1930s, however, he pushed for national health insurance as a compromise solution.

Second, Sigerist argued for a new kind of medical school (Terris 1975:505). Physicians, he suggested, should incorporate the view of social medicine into their work: "We need a social physician who...considers himself in the service of society. There is no point in training doctors primarily for city practice among the upper middle class."

The influence of Sigerist extended further. His four functions of medicine—promotion of health, prevention of illness, restoration of the sick, and rehabilitation—went beyond the professional purview of physicians when he outlined them in a lecture before the American Philosophical Society in 1946 (Terris 1975). In addition, his view of health as "not simply the absence of disease" (Sigerist 1941:100) became the cornerstone of the World Health Organization (WHO) later that same decade.

Thus the social basis of disease, introduced by Engels and embraced by Vichow, was articulated in the American example most clearly by Sigerest. However, against the power and financing of the Carnegie Foundation, which underwrote the Flexner Report, Sigerist's message had comparatively less immediate impact (Brown 1979). Nevertheless, the most recent tradition of Marxist health-care scholarship is rooted in Sigerist's writings, and it is this emphasis on the social that has framed current Marxist thinking in the field.

Debates within Marxism: The Contemporary Era

Unlike some subfields of sociology, the study of health care has experienced little in the way of vigorous theoretical debate within the Marxist community, either within the academic world or between academic and nonacademic theorists. Although there are, of course, analytic differences and emphases among authors, Marxist analyses of the health-care system are relatively few, and the major focus of available work has been the development of a critique of the dominant view.

At the same time, when we examine the Marxist literature on health care, we find that we are not limited to the contributions of sociologists but can look at the work of the academic left in general, including economists, public health policists, and radical health-care practitioners. Taken together, the body of work includes many of the same general topics that are debated in sociology; rather than detailed discussions within the left, however, on questions about the role of state, the proletarianization of health-care professionals, the contours of class structure and class struggle, or the details of the labor process, these topics are applied to the health-care example with major theoretical developments debated under other disciplinary rubrics. This makes an exploration of Marxist debate within health care less valuable than in other fields. Therefore, instead of emphasizing alternative perspectives, in this section we outline the kinds of questions that have guided Marxist inquiry on health-care issues.

Although Marxist critiques of traditional approaches to the study of health and illness constitute a tiny proportion of the literature of the field, in the past thirty years Marxists have produced a systematic body of work identifying a series of core concerns. Several theoretical overviews of this literature have been presented, most importantly by sociologist Howard Waitzkin (1978, 1989, 1990) and Vincente Navarro (1985) of the Johns Hopkins School of Public Health. While some of our categories overlap with theirs, we concentrate on those topics which are most central to the concerns of the Marxist sociologist as opposed, for example, to the Marxist health care provider.

The Political Economy of Health Care:
The Case of Monopoly Capital

Until fairly recently, health-care delivery in the United States was highly decentralized and characterized by individual physician practitioners who accessed institutional resources through their affiliations with local hospitals.

The transition from solo fee-for-service practice to the medical group and salaried physician of the 1990s has been analyzed as an example of the typical progression of capitalist industry. Viewing the individual practitioner as a major component of a petty bourgeois mode of production (Salmon 1977), the Marxist literature has analyzed contemporary changes as part of the transformation of health care to its monopoly stage.

The growth of technological medicine drastically changed the scale of capital requirements within the health-care sector, necessitating larger and more concentrated capital investments in plant and equipment. Doctors, performing as small scale producers, are brought together in centralized workplaces (hospitals) increasingly controlled by owners of capital (Himmelstein and Woolhandler 1984). As part of this process, health care has become subject to the structural prerequisite of capitalism: the need to realize an acceptable rate of profit, thereby transforming a cottage industry into a capitalist enterprise (McKinlay 1975). This has led to the maldistribution of health resources that has severely limited patient access and, ultimately, to the health-care crisis of the 1990s.

The (New) Medical-Industrial Complex

Flowing directly from the Marxian analysis of capital's invasion of health care is the examination of industry's role as an organizing element within the modern health system. Originally used in reference to the role of major corporations as supplier to health care providers, the term "medical-industrial complex" referred to pharmaceutical houses, hospital equipment manufacturers, the nursing home industry, providers of financial services, construction firms, and the like.

The logic of capitalist expansion, however, predicts the development of the *new* medical-industrial complex in which the corporate presence begins to permeate all facets of medical care from hospital supply to direct delivery of services (Salmon 1984). We discuss this development in detail in the next section; here it is important to note that the assumptions implicit in the Marxian analysis of monopoly capital enabled us to predict this expansion. Moreover, this framework, as Navarro (1976:135) points out, allows us to understand "how the shape and form of the health sector...is determined by the same economic and political forces shaping the political and economic system of the United States...."

The Public, the Private, and the More
General Role of the Capitalist State

As Waitzkin (1981) notes, an important focus of Marxist work on the health-care system is an analysis of the contradiction between the public and private sectors and the extent to which the private uses public resources to generate profit. Researchers have explored the ways in which public funding of Medicaid and Medicare contributed to the private appropriation of health-care dollars (Waitzkin and Waterman 1974; Waitzkin 1983a); how the proliferation of the private hospital, with its tendency toward patient dumping—that is, targeting the most profitable patients while leaving the uninsured and the unprofitable to others—has created a crisis for public hospitals, which are now the major providers of health care for the unemployed, the underemployed and the uninsured (Schiff et al. 1984, Kennedy 1984, Whiteis and Salmon 1987); how the health insurance industry and Health Maintenance Organizations (HMOs) have skimmed the most profitable patient market, again dumping the highest risks on the public sector (Bodenheimer et al. 1974; Bodenheimer 1990; Mintz 1991).

In addition, explicit in the Marxist critique of U.S. health delivery is a general discussion of public responsibility for the nation's health. As more and more Americans—31 million as of 1988 (*Statistical Abstracts of the United States* 1988)—find themselves without health insurance, the notion of a system in crisis has become a part of the public agenda. Even Medicare, designed to provide for the health needs of the elderly, now covers only about 40 percent of those costs (Terris 1990). This has led to increasing discussion of state-sponsored health-care services, with the Canadian health program gaining much attention as a model to explore. While in the United States, more than 11 percent of the gross national product—over $500 billion a year—is spent on health care, Canada, using under 9% of its GNP, has managed to cover its entire population (Terris 1990).

Marxist scholars and activists have been in the forefront of calls for system reform, emphasizing state responsibility to guarantee care to all citizens. Recently, solutions to the health-care crisis have been debated by a wide range of groups including the business community and the American Medical Association. And while questions of access including calls for a national health program dominate the discussion, the left has maintained its interest in the public-private contradiction in relation to occupational health and safety, pollution control, and the broader issues of prevention.

The more theoretical consideration of the relationship between the public and the private uses the Marxist theory of the state, with its emphasis on the importance of reproducing class relations and facilitating the accumulation process as an analytic framework. Vincente Navarro (1976, 1986) has written extensively on the role of the state in the health-care domain, and while the general topic of the capitalist state has been discussed in detail in other chapters of this volume, Navarro makes two specific points that should be noted here. First, he suggests that the state plays an important role in reproducing power relations within health care and that these are embodied in the *practice* of medicine itself (1986:252–53). This suggests that changes in the *culture* of medical practice will not alter those power relations. Second, he argues that the general functions of the state cannot be ignored in creating alternative delivery systems, but its role of reproduction and its interest in accumulation must be understood in order to build progressive alternatives to the current health-care system. Thus, the more general theory of the state has implications for the field of health care, and organizing for improved access and system reorganization must recognize the significance of the larger state agenda.

Class Structure and Class Conflict

Social class as an analytic tool for studying health care has concentrated on three areas: class relations in the control of health-care institutions, class conflict as a force for social change, and the proletarianization of professional work. In addition, the implications of stratification systems on health status have been explored in detail. Here we briefly review the questions most relevant to these analyses.

Emphasizing that it is the *function* and not the composition of the state that establishes it as capitalist, Navarro (1976) argues that the class composition of decision makers nevertheless remains important since this group reflects the class nature of the state. And while numerous studies have documented the class origins of political actors (see Domhoff 1983), additional work has explored the social location of hospital trustees as well as the institutional links which connect hospitals to the larger medical-industrial complex. In reviewing the literature on hospital boards, Landau (1977) reports that the average trustee is a business owner or a professional business manager; Bale (1985) documents the merger of institutional and family capital by his investigation of the corporations and the family fortunes profiting most from health care expansion. And in Canada, Ornstein (1988) found that hospitals exchange institutional links with those corporate sectors most important in the consolidation of the corporate class.

Within sociology, the study of social class includes both the stratification model of Max Weber and the Marxian theory of class as an analytic tool for investigating social change. While the former is used to describe the distribution of resources or attributes among different strata of a society, the latter examines the relationship between the bourgeoisie and the proletariat, suggesting that conflict between these two primary classes is the moving force of history. In studying health care, both approaches have been used, and the stratification model has documented the higher morbidity and mortality rates of lower-class people for almost every illness, as well as the persistence of this trend over time (Syme and Berkman 1990).

The Marxist analysis, with its focus on social change and its emphasis on conflict between classes, is often used to explore the process by which expansion of health services is won, both in the United States and in Europe. Over the years, demands by poor and working class people for adequate health care have resulted in expanded coverage and significant changes in the availability of health services. Successes include the employer-sponsored health-care programs institutionalized in the United States during World War II, the introduction of Medicare and Medicaid in the 1960s, and the development of National Health Services in Great Britain and Canada.

Most important in understanding these struggles is the dialectical nature of change within capitalist societies; victories are won in the context of a larger system of class relations and can be implemented in a manner that may lay the foundation for future losses. In the United States, the expansion of medical services by Medicare and Medicaid provided resources to many patients in need. At the same time, the organization of the program, including the fee-for-service reimbursement system it continued, contributed to the health-care crisis of the 1990s (Mintz 1991). This does not suggest that organizing for increased services is not an important priority. Instead, the Marxist analysis of class conflict emphasizes the interaction between working-class demands and the capitalist setting in which they are implemented. Thus, strategies for change must consider these constraints.

Finally, the changing nature of professional work is addressed in the literature on health care in the context of the proletarianization of the physician. We discuss this in detail in the next section, but here it is important to note that this fits squarely into writings on class structure and into the ongoing Marxist consideration of the role of the middle class in advanced capitalist society.

The Nature of Work

The workplace is important in the study of health care in two different contexts: the general conditions of work as it has an impact on worker health and safety, and the structure of work within the health delivery system. For the former, studies have investigated specific occupational diseases (e.g., Smith 1982; Seltzer 1977 on black lung disease among coal miners), as well as the broader occupational health and safety movement (Berman 1977). Navarro (1986) has presented a theoretical analysis of workplace relations and its impact on health issues.

Some very interesting writing is available on the nature of work within health care. Kennedy and Aries (1990), for example, explore changes in health care occupations tying the class nature of job distribution—women and minorities dominate in bottom levels—to the changing technological requirements of modern medicine. The drive toward technological innovation is not clear cut, however, and the relationship between control of work, profitability and the general needs of capitalist enterprise, including deskilling, are under investigation. A cross-section of this work can be found in Daly and Willis (1989), McKinlay and Stoeckle (1988), and Navarro (1986).

Gender, Race, and Class

While the feminist literature has explored the relationship between health, the larger health-care system, and women's position in society in detail (Rodriguez-Trias 1984; Boston Women's Health Book Collective 1984), the questions of gender and race have not been well integrated into the Marxian discussion of health care. Important exceptions include studies of gender hierarchies within health-care occupations (Butter et al. 1987; Brown 1983), racism and sexism within the medical industry (Weaver and Garrett 1978), occupational health hazards of women's work (Chavkin 1984), case studies of women's health issues (Rindfuss et al. 1983; Weiss 1983), and comparison of the policy implications of Marxist and non-Marxist theories of women's position as applied to health care (Fee 1975).

The Impact of Marxism on the Study of Health Care

While Marxist scholarship has left its mark on most fields within sociology, its influence has not been recognized in all specialties. This is particularly true in the study of health care where, as Navarro (1986:208) points out, an authoritative study of "The State of the Art on Medical Sociology" (Twaddle 1982) did not contain a single Marxist reference. Nevertheless, while in some cases, two literatures—a Marxist and a non-Marxist—stand side by side with few mainstream references to Marxist work, the Marxian critique has had an impact on the ways in which health care has been studied and the questions that have become important in the field.

Since 1960, the study of health care in sociology moved from an emphasis on microscopic investigations of the doctor-patient relationship to an increasing interest in the institutional structure of health delivery systems. Left critiques of the traditional literature, although not all Marxist, have played an important role in the refinement of an institutional approach.

In his classic book, *The Coming of Post Industrial Society,* Daniel Bell (1973:313) included the medical sector in his prediction of the continuing subordination of economic activity to the "political order," suggesting that the effect on health care would be the end of the solo practitioner and the "increasing centrality of the hospital and group practice" (1973:154). While changes in physician practice and increased hospital centrality did in fact occur, Bell's broader analysis of changes within the health-care system came under fire from a number of perspectives, both Marxist and non-Marxist. Alford's (1975) work, while addressing Bell's thesis only briefly, marked an important change in the wider perspective on health care institutions.

Exploring the role of "dominant structural interests" within the health-care sector, Alford (1975:6) argued that neither the "corporate rationalizers" (bureaucratic reformers), the "professional monopolists" (physicians and voluntary hospitals), nor the health-care advocates could accomplish significant change in relation to health-care organization because these forces "do not challenge any of the institutional roots from which the power...derives." This analysis of barriers to change leads Alford to reject Bell's optimism about broader changes in both medical delivery and the organization of society more generally. As important, he locates system defects in the very structure of health care organization.

For Marxists, analyses of structures and power are necessary but insufficient for understanding the process of, and the obstacles to, change. While acknowledging the insights on power provided by Alford and others (Freidson 1970; Ehrenreich and Ehrenreich 1970; Marmor 1973), Marxists offered a critique, using as a point of departure the centrality of class.

Navarro (1976, 1985) and McKinlay (1978), for example, emphasized that the role of corporate "power groups" are themselves constrained by the unequal terrain shaped by the social relations of capitalism. Moreover, Marxism emphasizes the complexity of class and the resultant power dynamics within the provision of health care in a class society. Navarro and McKinlay thus rejected both the optimism of Bell (1973) and the simplicity of instrumentalist theories that (ironically) Marxists themselves were accused of espousing (Starr 1982:17) since both positions assumed that powerholders could mold the system to their needs, thus failing to consider the structural constraints generated by the system itself. Medicine as an institution, then, is not simply an instrument of control but indeed is itself a social relation in contradiction (Navarro 1983, 1985).

The Marxist approach revealed, as well, the limitations of other important non-Marxist studies. Starr (1982), for example, in his award-winning *The Social Transformation of American Medicine*, focused on the political behavior of key players in the evolution of U.S. medicine. Using a structural analysis to identify the underlying patterns that explain both the rise of physician's power and their role in shaping the medical delivery system, Starr emphasized the need to analyze the larger social structure in which medicine is embedded. This approach enabled him to recognize the "coming of the corporation," or the growth of the new medical-industrial complex and to note the policy implications of this process.

Under the lens of Marxist analysis, however, Starr's history is incomplete because it assumes that the major location of decision making is the legislature or polling booth. That is, Starr's analysis addresses only part of the political reality of modern society. Organizational behavior, class relations, the manufacturing of consent, and the state's role in shaping the political agenda—all of these are necessary dimensions in a more complete analysis of the contemporary health-care system (Navarro 1985). And it is Marxist thought that inserts these ideas into the broader discussion of health provision.

The Corporatization of the American Health-Care System

One area now part of the mainstream literature on health care of particular interest to Marxist scholars is the study of the corporatization of health delivery systems. The Marxian analysis of current trends stems directly from the monopoly capital framework discussed earlier. While the issue has been part of the left analysis since the mid-1970s (Navarro 1976; Salmon 1977; McKinlay 1978), corporate participation was introduced into traditional arenas of debate in 1980 by Arnold Relman, editor of the respected *New England Journal of Medicine*, in his article "The New Medical-Industrial Complex." Since that time, the following topics have dominated the larger discussion of corporate participation within the health-care sector: the proprietization of health delivery, the proletarianization of health-care providers, and the role of institutional purchasers in the restructuring of health care.

We begin with the issue of proprietization. Numerous studies have documented the trend toward proprietization or the private ownership of health-care facilities, including the growth of investor-owned multiunit hospital systems, privately held long-term-care facilities, home health-care agencies, health maintenance organizations, hemodialysis providers, free-standing emergicare centers, and diagnostic labs. By 1983, nearly 10 percent of all hospital beds in the United States were owned by private investors, and the four largest companies—Humana, Hospital Corporation of America, American Medical Enterprise, and American Medical International—owned or managed 75 percent of those (Ermann and Gabel 1986). The penetration of capital into the hospital industry replaced previously paternal labor practices of the hospital with a more corporate model of labor relations. The increased organizing and militancy of hospital worker unions, such as New York City Local 1199, emerged in the 1970s amid these changing conditions.

Concern with the implications of the private ownership of health-care facilities is not limited to Marxists; within the larger literature, fear has been voiced that the growth of the for-profit hospital threatens the survival of the voluntary community hospital, results in cuts in staffing ratios, encourages patient dumping, and raises overall system costs (Washington Report on Medicine and Health, June 6 1983). The Marxist analysis of capital expansion and the structural requirements of capitalist enterprise, however, have not been part of the broader discussion of the invasion by the private sector. As Navarro (1986) points out, this leaves capital's entrance into health-care markets as a surprise and encourages a focus on the corporation as one additional group competing for power and influence within the field.

It is within the debate on the proletarianization of health-care professionals where the Marxist analysis of class and work relations has influenced the wider discussion of proprietization and corporatization within health care most directly. While Relman (1980) brought legitimacy to the question of the changing role of corporate actors within health care, Paul Starr's (1982) discussion of the implications of corporate expansion for the nature of physicians' work marked mainstream recognition of the Marxist argument on the proletarianization of professional work.

Arguing that proletarianization "suggests a total loss of control over the conditions of work," a change that he saw as highly unlikely, Starr (1982:446) responded directly to the developing literature on professional autonomy. His broader emphasis on the reciprocal relationship between the physician and the corporation, and his organizational rather than class analysis of big business's entrance into the health-care sector reflects the traditional disagreement between Marxists and non-Marxists on the role of professional work. Whereas the former have explored the class position of managers and professionals in advanced capitalism and investigated the extent to which this group is capable of organized collective action, the latter have emphasized the antagonistic relationship between the requirements of professional work and the needs of the bureaucratic organization. Freidson (1984) illustrates this nicely when he contrasts the theory of proletarianization with the literature describing conflict between professional control and bureaucratic requirements.

Nevertheless, the controversy over proletarianization has been an interesting one, and the class versus bureaucratic perspective has led to some innovative analyses of the nature of bureaucracy. In the past several years, a series of articles in the *International Journal of Health Services* has debated these questions in detail. This interchange began with an article by McKinlay and Arches (1985:161), who defined proletarianization as "the process by which an occupational category is divested of control over certain prerogatives...of its task activities and is thereby subordinated to the broader requirements of production under advanced capitalism." McKinlay and Arches argue that although physicians were able to postpone and minimize this process, they are now undergoing proletarianization. And while bureaucratic growth is the suggested causal factor in this, the authors suggest that bureaucratic organization itself has developed as part of the accumulation process and therefore as a tool of capitalistic expansion.

Reactions to this analysis came from both Marxist and non-Marxist scholars, with responses ranging from basic disagreement with the proletarianization thesis (Relman 1986) to detailed investigation of the historical circumstances that would explain why proletarianization is occurring at the present time (Chernomas 1986). Subsequent work continues to study the process of professional decline with proletarianization contrasted to theories of restratification within the profession (see Freidson 1986; Annandale 1989), suggesting that the tension between a class and an organizational analysis of the nature of physician's work remains alive.

As the cost of health care continues to rise and as expenses in this sector persist in outpacing inflation, the larger corporate community has become more involved in the question of cost containment. As a group, employers in the United States purchase health insurance for about 40 million workers, and this gives capitalists a direct interest in the nature of health delivery (Leyerle 1984).

The issue of rising costs and the corresponding response of institutional purchasers is attracting more attention in the literature, and several themes can be identified. Interest has been expressed in the role of institutional purchasers in the restructuring of health care as well as in splits within the corporate community over the continuing expansion of health delivery.

Institutional purchasers of health care include the federal government with its Medicare and Medicaid programs as well as the insurance companies and employers of the private sector. Government attempts to control the cost of medical care have attracted much attention, but the cost containment strategies of capitalists have been much less visible. While companies have been trimming their employee health-care benefit packages for some time (Staples 1989), corporate commitment to large-scale health-cost reform is at least as important, and several studies have explored this involvement in detail.

Leyerle (1984), for example, traces business organization on health-care issues back to the early 1970s, identifying as their agenda the restructuring of the delivery system. Similarly, Bergthold (1990) analyzes business involvement in health policy formation from 1969 to 1988, documenting successes while recognizing corresponding failures. Implicit in these works is the Marxist assumption of shared interests of capital in maximizing profit on the general level. Note, however, that different fractions of capital have different interests in terms of individual profitability and, therefore, the health-care example illustrates a contradiction in the accumulation process: Some sectors may become particularly profitable at certain times, at the expense of others. Thus, while capital in general is threatened by soaring health care costs, some companies— Humana and Hospital Corporation of America, mentioned earlier, for example—are profiting greatly from health expansion. This has led to investigations of splits within the capitalist community over health-care expansion.

Consistent with theoretical discussions on the internal differentiation of capital, Himmelstein and Woolhandler (1988, 1990) have distinguished between corporate providers' interest in increasing revenues and corporate purchasers' need for cost containment. They suggest that the broader strategy of capitalists has taken both interests into account and that recent developments away from fee-for-service (physician and hospital reimbursement based on each procedure performed) medicine reflect a compromise between the class fractions.

Other work has recognized the potential conflict between those firms profiting from health-care expansion and those paying through the purchase of health insurance for their workers, but, thus far, only Marxists have framed this development as part of the larger historical process of capitalist development (see Reinhardt 1987; Mintz 1991). As conflict between institutional purchasers and corporate providers increases, the Marxian framework will stand in increasingly sharper contrast to mainstream investigations of intercorporate rivalry. Therefore, we expect this issue—and this debate—to be of increasing interest in the broader health-care literature.

Conclusion

The study of health care from a Marxist perspective emphasizes the social basis of health and illness and analyzes the health-care system as part of the larger social and economic environment in which it developed. Put more forcefully, a Marxist analysis of health takes as primary the assumption that the health-care system is a product of the same political and economic forces shaping the larger society and subject to the same constraints.

This starting point leads directly to disagreement with non-Marxist social scientists about the very concept of health, and this disparity explains why Marxists criticize the mainstream literature's failure to distinguish between health care and medicine. This is also reflected by the different questions of interest to Marxist and non-Marxist scholars; issues of concern to the former often flow from a political economy perspective and pay particular attention to a class analysis. In those cases when a problem is considered by both groups, their orientations typically diverge. Analyses of the proletarianization of health-care professionals, for example, are explored by nonMarxists from an organizational perspective while class relations provide the framework for the Marxist investigation.

Marxists, of course, do not speak with one voice, and within the broader scheme of shared assumptions, analytic differences remain. Nevertheless, Marxists usually agree on which issues are most salient, and at the present time it is clear that the Marxist contribution to health-care scholarship and activism lies most importantly in the question of a national health plan. While more and more actors in health-care policy reform are taking the possibility of a national plan seriously, Marxist health-care investigators are prepared to analyze and critique competing recommendations and offer progressive proposals which emphasize universal coverage.

Physicians for a National Health Program (Himmelstein and Woolhandler et al. 1989) and the National Association for Public Health Policy (Terris et al. 1988) have presented well-developed plans stressing comprehensive benefits, the elimination of financial barriers, an emphasis on prevention, and changes in the structure of health-care organization and administration. Although their plans differ in details—and some of these differences are not trivial—both are guided by a Marxist understanding of economic and political relationships. As the fight for a national health-care plan develops over the next few years, that understanding will provide the basis for influencing and evaluating the direction of change. And in this arena Marxist theorists, activists, and providers will make their most important contribution to the U.S. health-care system.

References

Ackerknecht, Erwin H. 1948. "Anti-contagionism between 1821 and 1967." *Bulletin of the History of Medicine* 22:562–93.
———. 1953. *Rudolf Virchow: Doctor, Statesman, Anthropologist.* Madison: University of Wisconsin Press.
Alford, Robert R. 1975. *Health Care Politics.* Chicago: University of Chicago Press.
Annandale, E. 1989. "Proletarianization or Restratification of the Medical Profession? The Case of Obstetrics." *International Journal of Health Services* 19:611–34.
Bale, Tony. 1985. "The Great American Health Fortunes 1984." *Health/Pac* 16(3):29–34.
Bell, Daniel. 1973. *The Coming of Post-Industrial Society: A Venture in Social Forcasting.* New York: Basic Books.
Bergthold, Linda. 1990. *Purchasing Power in Health: Business, the State, and Health Care Politics.* New Brunswick: Rutgers University Press.
Berliner, Howard. 1975. "A Larger Perspective on the Flexner Report." *International Journal of Health Services* 5:573–92.
Berliner, Howard, and J. Warren Salmon. 1979. "The Holistic Health Movement and Scientific Medicine: The Naked and the Dead." *Socialist Review* 9(1):31–52.
Berman, D. 1977. "Why Work Kills: A Brief History of Occupational Health and Safety in the United States." *International Journal of Health Services* 7(1):63–87.
———. 1978. *Death on the Job.* New York: Monthly Review Press.
Bodenheimer, Thomas. 1990. "Should We Abolish the Private Health Insurance Industry." *International Journal of Health Services* 20:199–220.
Bodenheimer, Thomas, Steven Cummings and Elizabeth Harding. 1974. "Capitalizing on Illness." *International Journal of Health Services* 4:583–98.
Boston Women's Health Book Collective. 1984. *The New Our Bodies Ourselves.* New York: Simon and Schuster.
Brown, C. 1983. "Women Workers in the Health Service Industry," Pp. 105–16 in *Women and Health: The Politics of Sex and Medicine*, ed. Elizabeth Fee. Farmingdale, N.Y.: Baywood Publishing.
Brown, E. Richard. 1979. *Rockefeller Medicine Men.* Berkeley: University of California Press.

Butter I., E. Carpenter, B. Kay, and R. Simmons. 1987. "Gender Hierarchies in the Health Labor Force." *International Journal of Health Services* 17:133–49.

Chadwick, Edwin. 1887. *The Health of Nations*, ed. B.W. Richardson. London: Longmans, Green.

Chavkin, Wendy. 1984. *Double Exposure*. New York: Monthly Review Press.

Chernomas, R. 1986. "An Economic Basis for the Proletarianization of Physicians." *International Journal of Health Services* 16:469–77.

Conrad, P., and R. Kern. 1990. *The Sociology of Health and Illness: Critical Perspectives*. New York: St. Martin's.

Cott, Nancy F. 1972. *Root of Bitterness: Documents of the Social History of American Women*. New York: Dutton.

Daly, J. and Evan Willis. 1989. "Technological Innovation and the Labour Process in Health Care." *Social Science Medicine* 28:1149–57.

Derber, C., W. Schwartz and Y. Magrass. 1990. *Power in the Highest Degree: Professionals and the Rise of a New Mandarin Order*. New York: Oxford University Press.

Domhoff, G.W. 1983. *Who Rules America Now?* Englewood Cliffs: Prentice Hall.

Doyal, Lesley and Imogen Pennell. 1976. "Pox Brittanica: Health, Medicine and Underdevelopment." *Race and Class* 18:155–72.

Eastman, Crystal. 1976. "Equality or Protection." Pp. 112–14 in *Toward the Great Change: Crystal and Max Eastman on Feminism, Antimilitarism, and Revolution*, ed. Blanche Wiesen Cook. New York: Garland.

Ehrenreich, Barbara, and John Ehrenreich. 1970. *The American Health Empire*. New York: Random House.

Elling, Ray H. 1981. "The Capitalist World-System and International Health." *International Journal of Health Sciences* 11:21–51.

Engels, Frederick. 1887. *The Housing Question*. New York: International Publishers. Originally published in 1872.

———. 1952. *The Condition of the Working-Class in England in 1844*. London: George Allen and Unwin. Originally published in 1845.

Ermann, Dan, and Jon Gabel. 1986. "Investor-Owned Multihospital Systems: A Synthesis of Research Findings." Pp. 474–91 in *For-Profit Enterprise in Health Care*. Washington D.C.: National Academy Press.

Eyer, Joseph, and Peter Sterling. 1977. "Stress-Related Mortality and Social Organization." *Review of Radical Political Economics* 9:1–44.

Fee, Elizabeth. 1975. "Women and Health Care: A Comparison of Theories." *International Journal of Health Services* 5:397–415.

Flexner, A. 1912. *Medical Education in the United States and Canada*. New York: Carnegie Foundation for the Advancement of Teaching, Bulletin No. 4.

Frazer, W.M. 1950. *A History of English Public Health 1834–1939*. London: Bailliere, Tindall and Cox.

Freidson, E. 1970. *Professional Dominance*. New York: Atherton Press.

———. 1984. "The Changing Nature of Professional Control." *Annual Review of Sociology* 10:101–20.

———. 1986. *Professional Powers: A Study of the Institutionalization of Formal Knowledge*. Chicago: University of Chicago Press.

Galdston, Iago. 1954. *The Meaning of Social Medicine*. Cambridge: Harvard University Press.

Gilman, Charlotte Perkins. 1973. *The Yellow Wallpaper*. Old Westbury, N.Y.: Feminist Press.

———. 1975. *The Living of Charlotte Perkins Gilman: An Autobiography*. New York: Harper Colophon.

Goldman, Emma. 1934. *Living My Life*. New York: Garden City Publishing.

Himmelstein D. and S. Woolhandler. 1984. "Medicine as Industry: The Health-Care Sector in the United States." *Monthly Review*, April, 13–25.

———. 1988. "The Corporate Compromise: A Marxist View of Health Maintenance Organizations and Prospective Payment." *Annals of Internal Medicine* 109:494–501.

———. 1990. "The Corporate Compromise: A Marxist View of Health Policy." *Monthly Review* 42(1):14–29.

Himmelstein D., S. Woolhandler, and the Writing Committee of the Working Group on Program Design. 1989. "A National Health Program for the United States: A Physicians' Proposal." *New England Journal of Medicine* 320:102–08.

Hobsbawm, E.J. 1962. *The Age of Revolution.* New York: World Publishing.

Illich, I. 1976. *Medical Nemesis: The Expropriation of Health.* New York:Pantheon.

Kennedy, L. 1984. "The Losses in Profits: How Proprietaries Affect Public and Voluntary Hospitals." *Health/Pac Bulletin*, Nov.-Dec., 5–13.

Kennedy, L., and N. Aries. 1990. The Health Labor Force: The Effects of Change." Pp. 195–206 in *The Sociology of Health and Illness: Critical Perspectives*, ed. P. Conrad and R. Kern. New York: St. Martin's.

Kolko, Gabriel. 1968. *The Triumph of Conservatism*. New York: Free Press.

Landau, David. 1977. "Trustees: The Capital Connection." *Health/Pac Bulletin*, Jan.–Feb., 1–23.

Leyerle, Barbara. 1984. *Moving and Shaking American Medicine: The Structure of a Socioeconomic Transformation.* Westport, Conn.: Greenwood Press.

McKinlay, J. 1975. "On the Medical-Industrial Complex." *Monthly Review* 27(5):38–42.

———. 1978. "On the Medical-Industrial Complex." *Monthly Review* 30(5):38–42.

McKinlay, J., and J. Arches. 1985. "Towards the Proletaianization of Physicians." *International Journal of Health Services* 15:161–95.

McKinlay, J., and J. Stoeckle. 1988. "Corporatization and the Social Transformation of Doctoring." *International Journal of Health Services* 18:191–205.

Marcus, Steven. 1974. *Engels, Manchester, and the Working Class.* New York: Random House.

Markowitz, Gerald E., and David Karl Rosner. 1973. "Doctors in Crisis: A Study of the Use of Medical Education Reform to Establish Modern Professional Elitism in Medicine." *American Quarterly* 25:83–107.

Marmor, Ted. 1973. *The Politics of Medicare.* New York: Aldine.

Mintz, B. 1991. "The Role of Capitalist Class Relations in the Restructuring of Medicine." Pp. 65–82 in *Bringing Class Back In*, ed. Scott McNall, Rick Fantasia and Rhonda Levine. Boulder: Westview.

Mitchell, J., W. Stason, K. Calore, M. Freiman, and H. Hewes. 1987. "Are Some Surgical Procedures Overpaid?" *Health Affairs* 6(2):121–31.

Mitchell, J.K. 1859. *Five Essays by John Kearsley Mitchell*. Philadelphia: Lippincott.

Navarro, V. 1976. "Social Class, Political Power and the State and Their Implications in Medicine." *Social Science and Medicine* 10:437–57.

———. 1980. "Work, Ideology, and Science: The Case of Medicine." *Social Science and Medicine* 14:191–205.

———. 1983. "Radicalism, Marxism, and Medicine." *International Journal of Health Services* 13:179–202.

———. 1985. "U.S. Marxist Scholarship in the Analysis of Health and Medicine." *International Journal of Health Services* 15:525–45.

———. 1986. *Crisis, Health and Medicine: A Social Critique.* New York: Tavistock.

Ornstein, Michael. 1988. "Corporate Involvement in Canadian Hospital and University Boards 1946–1977." *Canadian Review of Sociology and Anthropology* 25:365–88.

Osler, William. 1984. *Principles and Practice of Medicine*. 21st ed. Norwalk, Conn.: Appleton-Century-Crofts. Originally published in 1897.

226   FROM THE LEFT BANK TO THE MAINSTREAM

Reinhardt, U. 1987. "Resource Allocation in Health Care: The Allocation of Lifestyles to Providers." *Milbank Memorial Fund Quarterly* 65:157–76.
Relman, A. 1980. "The New Medical-Industrial Complex." *New England Journal of Medicine* 303:963–70.
———. 1986. "Proletarianization of Physicians or Organization of Health Services?" *International Journal of Health Services* 168:469–71.
Renaud, Marc. 1975. "On the Structural Constraints to State Intervention in Health." *International Journal of Health Services* 5:559–72.
Riese, Walter. 1953. *The Conception of Disease*. New York: Philosophical Library.
Rindfuss, R., J. Ladinsky, E. Coppock, V. Marshall, and A. Macpherson. 1983. "Convenience and Occurence of Births: Induction of Labor in the United States and Canada" Pp. 37–58 in *Women and Health: The Politics of Sex and Medicine*, ed. E. Fee. Farmingdale, N.Y.: Baywood.
Ringen, Knut. 1979. "Edwin Chadwick, the Market Ideology, and Sanitary Reform." *International Journal of Health Sciences* 9:107–20.
Rodriguez-Trias. 1984. "The Women's Health Movement: Women Take Power." Pp. 107–26 in *Reforming Medicine: Lessons of the Last Quarter Century*, ed. V. Sidel and R. Sidel. New York: Pantheon.
Salmon, J. 1977. "Monopoly Capital and the Reorganization of the Health Sector." *Review of Radical Political Economy* 9:125–33.
———. 1984. "Organizing Medical Care for Profit." Pp. 143–186 in *Issues in the Political Economy of Health Care*, ed. J. McKinlay. New York: Tavistock.
Sanger, Margaret. 1929. *Laws Concerning Birth Control in the United States*. New York: Goldstein and Goldstein.
Schiff, G., K. Angus, and S. Razafinarivo. 1984. "The Base of the Iceberg: Outpatient Dumping in Chicago." *Health/Pac Bulletin*, Nov.-Dec., 14–16.
Seltzer, C. 1977. "Health Care by the Ton." *Health Pac/Bulletin* 79:1–33.
Sigerist, Henry E. 1934. *American Medicine*. New York: Norton.
———. 1937. *Socialised Medicine in the Soviet Union*. New York: Norton.
———. 1941. *Medicine and Human Welfare*. New Haven: Yale University Press.
———. 1946. *The University at the Crossroads, Addresses and Essays*. New York: Henry Schuman.
———. 1956. *Landmarks in the History of Hygiene*. London: Oxford University Press.
Simon, John, Sir. 1890. *English Sanitary Institutions*. London: Cassell. Originally published in 1856.
Smith, B. 1982. "Black Lung: the Social Production of Disease." *International Journal of Health Services* 12:343–59.
Snow, John. 1936. "On the Mode of Communication of Cholera." Pp. 1–139 in *Snow on Cholera*. New York: Commonwealth Fund. Originally published in 1849.
Staples, C. 1989. "The Politics of Employment-Based Insurance in the United States." *International Journal of Health Services* 19:415–31.
Starr, Paul. 1982. *The Social Transformation of American Medicine*. New York: Basic Books.
Syme, S., and L. Berkman. 1990. "Social Class, Susceptibility, and Sickness." Pp. 28–34 in *The Sociology of Health and Illness: Critical Perspectives*, ed. P. Conrad and R. Kern. New York: St. Martin's.
Taylor, Rex, and Annelie Rieger. 1984. "Rudolf Virchow and the Typhus Epidemic in Upper Silesia: An Introduction and Translation." *Sociology of Health and Illness* 6:201–17.
Terris, Milton. 1975. "The Contributions of Henry E. Sigerist to Health Service Organizations." *Health and Society* 53:489–530.
———. 1990. "Lessons from Canada's Health Program." *Technology Review* 93:27–34.
Therborn, Goran. 1976. *Science, Class and Society*. London: New Left Books.
Turshen, Meredeth. 1977. "The Political Ecology of Disease." *Review of Radical Political Economics* 9:45–60.

———. 1984. *The Political Ecology of Disease in Tanzania.* New Brunswick: Rutgers University Press.

Twaddle, A. 1982. "The State of the Art on Medical Sociology." Pp. 227–251 in *Sociology: The State of the Art*, ed. T. Bottomore, S. Nowak, and M. Sokolowska. Beverly Hills: Sage.

Waitzkin, H. 1978. "A Marxist View of Medical Care." *Annals of Internal Medicine* 89:264–78.

———. 1981. "A Marxist View of Medicine." Pp. 72–108 in *Political Economy: A Critique of Amercian Society*, ed. Scott McNall. Glenview, Ill.: Scott, Foresman.

———. 1983a. *The Second Sickness: Contradictions of Capitalist Health Care*. New York: Free Press.

———. 1983b. "Health Policy and Social Change: A Comparative History of Chile and Cuba." *Social Problems* 31:235–48.

———. 1989. "Marxist Perspectives in Social Medicine." *Social Science and Medicine* 28: 1099–1101.

———. 1990. "Discrimination in Social Science and Medicine." *International Journal of Health Services* 20:525–31.

Waitzkin, H., and B. Waterman. 1974. *The Exploitation of Illness in Capitalist Society*. Indianapolis: Bobbs-Merrill.

Wartofsky, Marx. 1975. "Organs, Organisms, and Disease: Human Ontology and Medical Practice" Pp. 67–83 in *Evaluation and Explanation in the Biomedical Science*, ed. H.T. Engelhardt and Stuart Sicker. Boston: D. Reidel.

Washington Report on Medicine Health. 1983. "Hospitals: A proprietary interest." *Perspectives*, June 6. Washington D.C.: McGraw-Hill.

Weaver, J., and S. Garrett. 1978. "Sexism and Racism in the American Health Care Industry: A Comparative Analysis." *International Journal of Health Services* 8:677–703.

Weinstein, James. 1968. *The Corporate Ideal in the Liberal State, 1900–1918*. Boston: Beacon Press.

Weiss, K. 1983. "Vaginal Cancer: An Iatrogenic Disease?" Pp. 59–75 in *Women and Health: The Politics of Sex and Medicine*, ed. E. Fee. Farmingdale, N.Y.: Baywood.

Whiteis, D., and J. Salmon. 1987. "The Proprietarization of Health Care and the Underdevelopment of the Public Sector." *International Journal of Health Services* 17:47–64.

Wiesen Cook, Blanche. 1978. *Crystal Eastman on Women and Revolution.* New York: Oxford University Press.

Wright, Carrol D. 1889. *The Working Girls of Boston.* Boston: Wright and Polter.

RELIGION:

MARXIST-CHRISTIAN DIALOGUES: THE LIBERATION OF THEOLOGY

Milagros Peña

When Karl Marx and Friedrich Engels first published their ideas on religion, scientific rationalism was in its heyday and Darwinism was emerging. Both challenged religious myths with scientific reasoning. Marx and Engels's critique of religion went beyond the science versus mythology debate of the era. Reflecting a reliance on the materialist dialectic, Marxist analysis declared religion anathema to the revolutionary goals of socialism and communism. They critiqued theology for its sentimental idealism, which they claimed deceived the oppressed masses rather than liberated them. Marx and Engels also dismissed Christian socialism as mere petty bourgeois socialism. In the *Manifesto of the Communist Party* (1973) they declared religion was "the holy water with which the priest consecrates the heart-burnings of the aristocrat." The aristocrats and the church hierarchy were one and the same, and religious ideology was an extension of their vested interests.

Marx and Engels's bold assertions were never fully embraced by the larger socialist movement. By 1905 many Social Democrats in Europe, including K. Kautsky, E. Vandervelde, A. Pannekoek, and others, declared religion a private matter (Bociurkiw 1987:116). While holding this position, they also cautioned that "from the moment when the priests use the pulpit as a means of political struggle against the working class, the workers must fight against the enemies of their rights and their liberation" (Luxemburg 1970:152).

Building on this more tolerant and open approach to religion, some Christians began regularly engaging in formal talks with Marxists during the 1950s. These exchanges have influenced a host of groups interested in achieving a progressive and liberating convergence on many important political and economic issues. These dialogues permeated the intellectual communities of Europe, North America, and, by the early 1960s, Africa, Asia, and Latin America (Metz and Jossua 1977; Piediscalzi and Thobaben 1985).

First and Third World religious groups and Marxists met to discuss the possibilities of a synthesized religious-political social ethic (Piediscalzi and Thobaben 1985; Torres and Fabella 1978). Popular insurgencies in the Third

228

World created the climate and urgent need to expedite dialogues and create fruitful results. Given the political and economic realities of Third World nations, many theologians saw the need for analyzing capitalism as a socially oppressive system and began pondering the idea of a Marxist-religious ethic. As these linkages were made, theologians began turning to the social sciences for their methods of analyses, which gave them the opportunity to study the Marxist critique of capitalism. This synthesis has been hotly debated by the Catholic church, in particular, and by Marxists who remain critical of dealing with religious institutions.

To assess the transformations that took place among theologians influenced by Marxist analysis, one has to turn to Europe, where Marxism made its debut. Marxist Christians had nurtured dialogues through their political activism in Catholic worker movements, particularly in France, Belgium, and Italy. These worker movements were initially inspired by Catholic Action ideology, popular in the 1920s and 1930s, and reflected the Catholic stance on labor of that era. The Catholic church's official position at the time called for a wholistic concern for workers, but rejected political solutions to their problems. According to Whyte (1981), despite its ostensibly nonpolitical nature, Catholic Action had a political impact. After the Great Depression, many of the Catholic worker movements began to fizzle politically, but the political linkages between pockets of radical Christians and the left grew. By 1959, a group of French communists and French Jesuits began informal and unofficial discussions on the relationship between Marxist theory and Roman Catholic doctrine (Kirk 1980:54). In a sense, the Catholic Action years were the cocoon for the metamorphosis that many churches later experienced. As churches moved into more serious dialogues with Marxists, their official positions on Marxism began shifting. One of the more public shifts in this direction came from an unlikely source—the Vatican.

With the election of Pope John XXIII came a new liberalism in the Catholic church, a liberalism expressed in the convocation of the Second Vatican Council, and in papal encyclicals (letters to Catholics stating the church's official social teachings) that followed from those meetings. These meetings were only the second time in the history of the Catholic church that all of the church's leaders met to reflect on and debate church policy and direction. When the Second Vatican Council convened (1963–65), the impetus for Marxist-Christian dialogue was given new life. The church support for dialogue with Marxists was made official by the 1965 encyclical *Gaudium et Spes* (Pastoral Constitution on the Church in the Modern World) (Flannery 1984:903–1014).*Gaudium et Spes* cautiously admitted the possibility of legitimate revolutions, recognized that the present world economic system causes inherent injustices and that property had a social end, and it encouraged dialogue with people who professed atheism, even while rejecting it (Flannery 1984:968–82).

These institutional gestures within Catholic and Protestant churches created a wide range of network opportunities. Theologians and Marxists used these approvals to legitimate and organize their meetings. For example, by 1964 Accion Popular, a Latin American leftist Christian organization that had its roots in Catholic Action groups, regularly used Marxist analysis for much of its basic critique of society (Gotay 1981:50). People in each geographic region began to initiate dialogues focusing on their own regional concerns. The socioeconomic conditions specific to the Third World made the issue of economic exploitation a pressing concern. By the 1970s, "the great religions had to face the fact that socialism was the form of society in one-third of the world, in Asia, Europe, and Latin America, and was being consciously sought in Africa" (Aptheker 1970:18). This emerging political reality shaped the future of the social and cultural meaning of religion, and Marxism was coming to play a significant role in these changes.

This overview of Marxism and the theological dialogues primarily focuses on Marxist-Christian encounters. This focus arises from historical concerns— the initial Marxian critique of Christianity and the response of those churches to Marxism—and because it was these conflicts and dialogues that have been a subject of inquiry for American sociologists. There have been attempts by some revolutionary Islamic groups to incorporate Marxism as part of their nationalist revolutionary programs. It is difficult to assess the particular theologizing that has taken place, in part because of a lack of translated materials. The course of some of the Islamic revolutions and insights of Islamic political leaders such as President Leopold Senghor of Senegal suggest that the emergence of an Islamic-Marxist perspective has begun (Thomas 1985). Nonetheless, given the limitations already mentioned, this overview centers primarily on the Marxist-Christian debates and emerging tradition of dialogue.

Understanding how Marxism came to be a convergent factor in both First and Third World religious movements presupposes an awareness of the historical processes that led to the writings and usefulness of Marxism to revolutionary and liberation theologies. Therefore, it is important to focus on the development of these theologies in their sociohistorical context. Such an analysis lays the foundation for an understanding of the themes and general character of Marxist-religious encounters and debates.

To develop an understanding of the historical events that foreshadowed the Marxist-Christian encounters, of Marxist theory, and of its relevance to the emergence of dialogue, this paper is divided into three time frames. The first focuses on the specific writings of Karl Marx and Friedrich Engels on religion. Particular emphasis is placed on those aspects of their critique of religion that led to significant religious institutional changes and those that reflected critically on the meaning of spirituality and its relation to the human condition. In the second period, European Social Democrats, and later the Italian theorist Antonio

Gramsci, are given credit for their support of religious freedom, which was not characteristic of Marxism-Leninism. This period helps explain how and why radical Christians could begin pursuing a politically based religious ethic. The implications of these breakthroughs are then detailed in the third (post-1960) period. Religious activists, particularly those with a liberationist perspective, have synthesized their religious ethic for human justice with political visions for social change. Their actions illustrate how Marxist critiques of religion have affected both theology and Marxism, resulting in new understandings of the role of religious ideas in revolutionary societies. The chapter concludes with examples of ideological breakthroughs that can be credited to advocates and practitioners of a Marxist-religion synthesis. It also points out that there are some who remain skeptical that such a synthesis is possible.

Marxist Critiques of Religion: 1840–1960

The development of the Marxist critique of society had a profound impact on debates concerning of labor, production, and capitalism in general. It also transformed the way in which social theorists thought about ideology, culture, and other social institutions linked to the capitalist worldview. The harshest of these critiques focused on religious institutions as a cornerstone of antirevolutionary traditionalism. This critique was not exclusive to Marxism. But it was Marxism that emerged as the enemy or the antithesis of religion, particularly as it linked the churches to the historical immiseration of the oppressed classes. Marx and Engels critiqued religious institutions for playing an important part in the alienation of individuals from themselves and their human condition. These points are critical to understanding the course of Marxist-Christian debates including the development of liberation and revolutionary theologies in the 1960s and 1970s.

In Marx and Engels's view, religion was a by-product of human estrangement created by capitalism. Estrangement and alienation were based on the idea of a "self" acted on by history rather than having a hand in transforming it: Marx observed:

> On this premise it is clear that the more the worker spends themselves, the more powerful the alien objective world becomes which they create over-against themselves, the poorer they—their inner world—becomes, the less belongs to them as their own. It is the same in religion. The more humanity puts into God, the less they retain for themselves. The worker puts their life into the object; but now their life no longer belongs to them but to the object....the life which they

have conferred on the object confronts them as something hostile and alien. (1978a:72)

In other words, Marx and Engels understood that overcoming alienation was critical to creating the process through which individuals become aware of the source of their own oppression—that is, to develop a class consciousness. Religion, according to Marx and Engels (1978a), is the tool through which the ruling classes pacify the oppressed masses. "Religion is the self-consciousness and self-feeling of man who has either not yet found himself or has already lost himself again" (Marx 1972:37). In his "Theses on Feuerbach," Marx noted: Feuerbach does not see that the "religious sentiment" is itself a social product and that the abstract individual whom he analyzes belongs in reality to a particular form of society (Marx 1973:14). It is also a mechanism with which the powerful thwart revolutions, thereby stunting social change: "Religion is the sigh of the oppressed creature, the heart of a heartless world, just as it is the spirit of a spiritless situation. It is the opium of the people" (Marx 1978b:38). In Marx's view, people turn to gods, shrines, and churches for relief of their social sufferings—expecting and praying for change. Therefore, religion becomes the object whereby individuals give up control of their own destiny and thereby become enslaved by their own fears and superstitions.

It was his recognition of the individualistic focus of religion and its disinterest in social impacts that unmasked religion for what it was—a tool for elites to rationalize their power:

The production of notions, ideas and consciousness is from the beginning directly interwoven with the material activity and the material intercourse of human beings, the language of real life. The production of man's ideas, thinking, their spiritual intercourse, here appear as the direct efflux of their material condition. (Marx and Engels 1972:65)

Here Marx's emphasis on dialectical materialism as the basic tool for understanding society underscores the Marxist critique of religion—that is, to view religion as a mere product of capitalist interests. That is why there is a tendency to view Marxism as inherently atheistic and opposed to all forms of religious expression as an opiate of the people. This is a pivotal part of why most of the world religions have seen themselves as incapable of even coexisting with Marxism. Marx and Engels also detailed how organized churches were an intrinsic part of the capitalist state and were major property owners (Engels 1979:297–302). Therefore, not surprisingly, they argued that religion participates in and is a product of capitalist production. It would seem that religion as a participant in, and product of capitalist production, is an irreconcilable problem.

The legacy of Marx and Engels led in many directions, and many of their inheritors emerged as orthodox proponents of their critical attitude toward religion. V.I. Lenin fell into this tradition, echoing much of Marx and Engel's critique of religion:

> Religion is one of the forms of spiritual oppression that everywhere weighs on the masses of the people, who are crushed by perpetual toil for the benefits of others, and by want and isolation. The impotence of the exploited classes in the struggle against the exploiters engenders faith in a better life beyond the grave....Religion is a kind of spiritual gin in which the slaves of capital drown their human shape and their claims to any decent human life (1943:658).

Lenin wrote very little on religion, and his writings on the subject largely consisted of articles, speeches, letters and notes, which fell into several stages separated by the revolutions of 1905 and 1917 (Bociurkiw 1987:107). He focused primarily on the importance of atheism and based his observations on the effect of religiosity on Russian society (Bociurkiw 1987:108). He targeted the Russian Orthodox church, and much of his dealings on religion were characterized by a staunch anticlericalism. This was an important period because in his vision of Russian socialism he came to adopt the orthodox Marxist position on religion. Lenin's socialist program had little room for the church.

Yet it is also important to note that both the Roman Catholic and Russian Orthodox churches have published official documents rejecting socialism in all its forms and have persecuted their members for embracing its ideas. Responding to the Russian Revolution of 1917, and subsequent confiscation of its properties and limits on its activities, the Russian Orthodox church condemned socialism. In a message to his followers, the Patriarch Tikhon (1959:36) wrote: "The open and secret enemies of the Truth of Christ have begun to persecute it and are striving to destroy Christ's Cause by sowing everywhere, in place of Christian love, the seeds of malice, hatred and fratricidal strife." He openly refused to recognize the Soviet government. In 1923, the Soviet government declared religion a private matter as long as the church did not interfere in state matters. Tikhon and several other religious leaders then recanted their opposition so that they might continue proselytizing. Meanwhile, the Vatican repeatedly sent telegrams to Lenin condemning his actions against the Russian Orthodox church and staunchly rejecting the socialist program (Tikhon 1959:49–53).

As early as 1891, Pope Leo XIII in his papal encyclical *Rerum Novarum* (On the Condition of Labor) argued against the greed of competition (1948:2), but was firm in his rejection of socialism (1948:7). Forty-three years after the first appearance of the 1848 *Manifesto of the Communist Party*, Pope Leo XIII described socialists as "crafty agitators who constantly make use of disputes to pervert men's judgments and to stir up the people to sedition" (1948:2). He further charged: "The main tenet of socialism, the community of goods, must be utterly rejected; for it would injure those whom it is intended to benefit, it would be contrary to the natural rights of mankind, and it would introduce confusion, and disorder into the commonwealth" (1948:7). In commemorating *Rerum Novarum* forty years later, Pope Pius XI, in his encyclical *Quadragesimo Anno* (On Reconstruction of the Social Order), recognized that in the more moderate sections of socialism, "its programs often strikingly approached the just demands of Christian social reformers" (1948:156). But he was also firm in his rejection of what he cited as the two communist objectives: "Merciless class warfare and complete abolition of private ownership" (1948:155). Where Leo XIII emphasized that capitalist greed could be controlled by simply appealing to moral conscience, Pius XI called for alms giving and volunteerism as all that was required to redress social inequities. It had been this kind of religious reasoning that had prompted Marx and Engels to reject religion.

While Lenin's attitude toward religion emphasized the Marxist-atheist position, there was already debate among socialists over the role of religion in society. Bociurkiw observed:

> By 1905, the problems of the relationship between religion and socialism, and of the advisability of mixing atheism with anti-religious propaganda, had become subjects of a spirited public debate with Western and Russian social democracy; while in Russia, the 1905 revolution awakened a growing interest in religion and religious philosophy in the ranks of the intelligentsia, once solidly alienated from the church. (1987:116)

Among those mentioned as a member of this new religious intelligentsia was Nikolai Berdyaev, a former Marxist. Berdyaev's position came to reflect what is today the basic challenge to Marxists—"the knowledge of God requires continual purifying, and purifying above all from servile sociomorphism" (Berdyaev 1944:82). Berdyaev was critiquing the tendency of religious institutions to accommodate the interests of the ruling classes and emphasized the importance of continual institutional self-criticism as a way to combat the capitalists' manipulation of religious ideology. It would be several decades before theologians would seriously address Berdyaev's critiques and concerns.

Berdyaev was one of several individuals echoing the need for greater tolerance of religion by Marxists. In 1902, *Le Mouvement Socialiste* polled leading Social Democrats on the attitude of their national parties toward religion. Kautsky, Vandervelde, and other Western socialists took the stand that religion was a private matter for Social Democrats (Bociurkiw 1987:116). In a brief article entitled *Socialism and Religion* (1905), Lenin rejected this notion arguing "against all religious stultification of the workers. For us therefore the ideological fight is not a private affair but a general affair of the Party and the proletariat" (Lenin 1943:660). Antonio Labriola, an Italian Marxist, later cautioned against making too much of the tolerant attitude of the Social Democrats. The statement "religion is a private matter" merely meant that the socialists were "too busy with more useful and serious work" (1980:149). In fact, Luxemburg (1970:151), who favored tolerance, also cautioned against priests found "organizing the workers and founding 'Christian' trade unions." In her view, the Christian trade unions were fronts that misdirected the focus of social democracy. Labriola argued that the Social Democrats were merely making a practical concession (Labriola 1980:149).

In his work *Foundations of Christianity* (1953), Karl Kautsky offered an additional dimension to the debates. His comparison of early Christian communism to modern communism anticipated what some analysts have viewed as potentially useful converging points in this debate. He cited important similarities and differences between the utopian socialism of theologians and modern socialism.

Cornel West has critiqued Kautsky and others because he felt they viewed cultural and religious issues in a crude reductionist manner. According to West, the only major antireductionist voices in this deterministic wilderness were those of the Italian Marxist Antonio Labriola and the Irish Marxist James Connolly (1984:11). But while Labriola remained critical of religion, James Connolly separated the actions of the religious hierarchy from the religion itself (Connolly 1988:57–117). Connolly globalized the basic tenets of the world religions into what is essentially the socialist program and argued:

> The day has passed for patching up the capitalist system; it must go. And in the work of abolishing it the Catholic and the Protestant, the Catholic and the Jew, the Catholic and the Freethinker, the Catholic and the Buddhist, the Catholic and the Mahometan will co-operate together, knowing no rivalry but the rivalry of endeavor towards an end beneficial to all. For, as we have said elsewhere, Socialism is neither Protestant nor Catholic, Christian nor Freethinker, Buddhist, Mahometan, nor Jew; it is only Human. We of the Socialist working class realize that as we suffer together we must work together that we may enjoy together. (1988:117)

Thus Connolly perceived the human need for religious expression as posing no threat to socialist goals as long as the religious person could be made to see the difference between the ideals of religion and the practice of its institutions.

Though West classified Kautsky as a reductionist, Kautsky found in the socialism of Thomas More a philosophy consistent with the ideals of modern socialism. In his work *Thomas More and His Utopia*, Kautsky commented:

At a time when the capitalist mode of production was in its infancy, he (Thomas More) mastered its essential features so thoroughly that the alternative mode of production which he elaborated and contrasted with it as a remedy for its evils, contained several of the most important ingredients of modern socialism....Despite the immense economic and technical transformations of the last three hundred years, we find in *Utopia* a number of tendencies which are still operative in the Socialist Movement of our time. (1959:161)

Even so, Kautsky concluded, "sympathy with the poor does not make one a socialist, although without that sympathy no one is likely to become a socialist" (1959:163).

Religion, Mass Mobilization, and Social Change

Kautsky et al. were tolerant but did not actively engage in dialogue with religious leaders or seek to integrate religion as part of a class-based theory of liberation. As West (1984) argued, the possibilities for dialogue between Marxists and religious intellectuals opened up when Marxists began to take the cultural sphere more seriously. Though Marxists have sometimes viewed oppressed people as political or economic agents, they have rarely viewed them as cultural agents (West 1984:17). Antonio Gramsci was one of the first to treat the oppressed as cultural agents. According to West (1984:12): "For the first time, a major European Marxist took with utter seriousness the cultural life-worlds of the oppressed....Gramsci understood culture as a crucial component of class capacity." This section focuses on Gramsci's concept of traditional and organic intellectuals and examines their impact on both political and religious protest movements.

Gramsci provided a new analytical framework in which intellectuals were seen as important contributors to the revolutionary process. Accordingly, he argued:

Every social group, coming into existence on the original terrain of an essential function in the world of economic production, creates together with itself, organically, one or more strata of intellectuals which give it homogeneity and an awareness of its own function not

only in the economic but also in the social and political fields. (1987:5)
It was not until Gramsci developed the concept of organic and traditional intellectuals that Marxists began to appreciate the role of the peasantry in the revolutionary process. As Gramsci noted:

> The experience of many countries...has shown that, if the peasants move through "spontaneous" impulses, the intellectuals start to waver; and, reciprocally, if a group of intellectuals situates itself on a new basis of concrete pro-peasant policies, it ends up by drawing with it ever more important elements of the masses....The peasant party generally is achieved only as a strong current of opinion, and not in schematic forms of bureaucratic organization. However, the existence even of only a skeleton organization is of immense usefulness, both as a selective mechanism, and for controlling the intellectual groups and preventing caste interests from transporting them imperceptibly onto different ground. (1987:74–75)

Gramsci's broad view of the role of peasants in the political process led to a more tolerant understanding of religion. He expressed disdain toward the provincial Catholicism of his day and the general tendency in religion toward traditionalism. But he admired the fact that in the Roman church there was always a struggle to make the world of intellectuals and that of lower classes one and the same (Gramsci 1987:328–29). Gramsci's concern over the dichotomization of interests between the rural masses and traditional intellectuals (party types included) provided an opening toward a dialogue with support for revolutionary and liberation theologies by the left.

This cultural sensitivity on the part of Gramsci was an important factor in the development of an affinity by many Italian Christians for Marxism. The Italian Communist Party changed its platform and accommodated religious Marxist members based on concrete evidence of their commitment to the political causes of Italian communism. As Grace explained:

> The ability of Italian Christians to join the Communist Party and to serve in positions of leadership may be traced in part to the founding of the Unifying Cooperative Party in 1941 and the Catholic Communist Party in 1942....During World War II these people were imprisoned along with Marxist Communists by the Fascists, and they also fought side by side with Communists in the Resistance Movement. These experiences, which occurred basically during the period from 1937 to 1945, taught both Italian Christians and Marxist Communists that there was more that united than separated them. This lesson

eventually moved the Italian Communist Party to declare itself "secular" and "nonideological" thereby removing the acceptance of Marxist ontology as one of the party's membership requirements. (1985:19)

This historical overview highlights why and under what circumstances dialogues between Marxists and Christians were initiated.

Gramsci's distinction between traditional and organic intellectuals, and his emphasis on understanding the political and intellectual life of the proletariat laid the basis for the revolutionary and liberation theologies in the Third World. Between the 1950s and 1980s, Third World revolutions included a politically active and sometimes insurgent popular mass. According to Levine, the term "popular" involves some notion of subordination and inequality, pointing to "popular" groups or classes—a definition that recognizes the political importance of peasants in the revolutionary process (1986:6). In fact, when you examine the revolutionary history of Asia, Latin America, and Africa, you find that the peasantry has played a pivotal role in the revolutionary process.

Included in many political characterizations of the "popular" is an awareness of religious culture and its reformulation into a liberation process. Liberation theology is one expression of this cultural transformation. Before this transformation, the case studies on the role of peasants in religious revolutions had tended to focus on millenarianism (Bricker 1981; Cohn 1970; Tai 1983). (Millenarian revolutionary movements view devotional piety and collective violence as two ends of the same salvationist spectrum of response—Tai 1983:viii.) The social circumstances of outbreaks of revolutionary millenarianism, in which old prophecies about the "last days" have become the basis for mass mobilization, have in fact been quite uniform (Cohn 1970:53). With the developments of liberation and revolutionary theologies, however, there is a growing awareness that millenarianism is only one manifestation of the revolutionary religious voice. Liberation and revolutionary theologies represent two different forms of religious response. Some liberationists are less radical than others, which reflects the changes that have occurred in the shift from revolutionary to liberation theology in the early 1960s. The revolutionary theologians represented the position that armed struggle was a viable option in the revolutionary process. Religious leaders, therefore, both as subjects and proponents of revolutionary and liberation theologies, can be dynamic forces of change—creating change through a political process.

The access to religious power can also be the source of social power, whether for change or stability (McGuire 1981:202). The clergy in Third World nations, for example, have been able to challenge the political and economic powers of their countries because they are members of religious organizations with both an influential national and international base. Their connection to this source of power and to the larger popular insurgent base makes them formidable opponents whether they are politically on the left or right. The relationship between these insurgent religious types and the politically organized progressive mass base has given Marxist-Christian dialogues their impetus.

Ventures by the Left into Marxist-Christian Dialogues, (1960 to the Present)

Most agree that revolutionary theologies and theologies of liberation are in some way a call to socialism (with an emphasis on the small*s* that was present in the character of Christian communities in the first centuries. Most theologians who have looked to incorporate Marxism in their liberation theologies have concluded that Marxism provides an analytical tool with which to see the historical roots of oppression. Gutiérrez, a noted Latin American liberation theologian, spoke for many when he concluded: "The class struggle is a part of our economic, social, political, cultural, and religious reality. Its evolution, its exact extent, its nuances, and its variations are the object of analysis of the social sciences and pertain to the field of scientific rationality" (1973:273). For liberation theologians, understanding the human condition presupposes an awareness of historical processes, social institutions, social systems, and the belief systems that reproduce them, and Marxism was the key to gaining that awareness. Nonetheless, it took several decades for some Marxists and theologians to trust each other's agendas.

The implications of Marxism for theologians and political activists have led to a rethinking of the religious ethical ideal of socialism and the communitarian dimension embedded in the Marxian formula. Gutiérrez put the argument as follows:

> It was becoming more evident that the Latin American people would not emerge from their present status except by means of a profound transformation, a social revolution, which would radically and qualitatively change the conditions in which they lived. The oppressed sectors within each country were becoming aware of their class interests and of the painful road which must be followed to accomplish the breakup of the status quo. (1973:88)

In Latin America, these realizations created a forum for dialogue between Marxists and Christian activists.

The growing awareness of class interests by oppressed groups, not limited to Latin America, helps one understand the historical context and the proliferation of Marxism (and Marxist-religious dialogue) in revolutionary societies. As

Aptheker stated, "religions have recognized that scores of millions of peoples in countries not yet socialist have adhered to a more or less avowedly Marxist perspective" (1970:18).

In assessing the analytical theological transformation that emerged during this time, credit must go to Reinhold Niebuhr. He briefly emerged as one who, early in the 20th century, began to pursue the social importance of Marxism in his work *Moral Man and Immoral Society* (1932). He integrated Marxist critiques of religion with "God talk" about the meaning of human suffering, social inequality, and sin. For Christianity, these formulations laid the foundation for the theological break from the Augustinian and Thomist traditions, which saw sin as individual alienation from God. In other words, Niehbuhr and those who followed him came to view sin as a social product with social implications and solutions. More precisely, they began to emphasize "this worldly" rather than "otherworldly" solutions to social problems, an approach that anticipated liberation theology.

This focus on religion as a source and a response to alienation would later become the basis for the emergence of Marxist-Christian dialogues. In the Christian tradition, alienation from one's self and one's environment has been the basis for constructing mythologies about the human condition. People create gods to explain what they do not understand. But more important, and critical to this discussion, was how concepts of sin have evolved in religious myths. Sin was explained as individual failure, and atonement was to be made to a being outside the self. Atonement, in this traditional concept of religion, does not focus on the person impacted by the sin. Sin, therefore, is not viewed as social sin. Individuals are led to see their human condition as an individual problem, not as a collective one where wrongs are corrected in communities and where inequities are viewed as collective responsibilities. One of the major leaps made by liberation theologians has been their focus on communal atonement—eliminating the inequalities that alienate and injure others.

In both the Augustinian and Thomist traditions, redemption or atonement is based on a being or existence outside the self. The Brazilian theologian Leonardo Boff described the potential outcome of these ideas as a church entrenched in tradition, official and orthodox in its theological formulas (1985:2–3). The consequences of this theological formulation have led orthodox groups to organize their activities around what is religious and what is sacred. In a strict sense, "the Pope, the bishops, and the general hierarchical structure constitute the organizational axis for this understanding of the Church. It is an essentially clerical Church, for without the clergy nothing decisive can happen within the community" (Boff 1985:3). The institutionalization of the Augustinian and Thomist traditions, therefore, has led to two basic problems: (1) a rejection of the material condition of human existence and its relation to the socio-political; and

(2) an institutional replication within the Church of the power relations between society's power elites and the general masses.

The Marxist critique of religious traditionalism has argued convincingly for an accounting of the abuses of power by religious institutions. Jose Miranda has attempted to correct what he perceived as a misrepresentation of Marx's overall view of religion by orthodox Marxists. Miranda convincingly argues for a rereading of Marx on what has been the tendency of Orthodox Marxists to dismiss religion altogether:

> Of course, the communist effort of the primitive Christian commu-
> nity (Acts 2:44 and 4:32) did fail. However, that fact does not strip
> the primitive communism of the early church of its normative
> character vis-á-vis the essence of Christianity. Instead we must ask
> ourselves why it failed and eradicate the causes for that failure.
> According to Marx, it failed because the primitive Christians ne-
> glected the political struggle. In the midst of a world based upon
> commodity production and private property, an isolated community
> cannot avoid the penetrating influence of money and anti-commu-
> nist factors. Centuries later Christians would betray the cause by
> asserting that the elimination of private property is not an obligation
> but a way to higher perfection. (1980:200)

Liberation theologies have begun to bridge what Miranda has called "the essence of Christianity" with a Marxist analytical framework. The Marxist-Christian dialogues have been a key component of this synthesis. Aptheker put it wisely when he wrote that "discussions make for clarification and hopefully we learn from the process" (1970:21).

Analyzing black liberation theology, Cornel West has provided some critical insights into the central points of convergence between liberation theology and Marxism:

> Marxist thinkers, like black theologians, employ a dialectical meth-
> odology in approaching their subject matter. But they do so con-
> sciously and their subject matter is bourgeois theories about capital-
> ist society. The primary theoretical task of Marxist thinkers is to
> uncover the systematic misunderstanding of capitalist society by
> bourgeois thinkers; to show how this misunderstanding, whether
> deliberate or not, supports and sanctions exploitation and oppres-
> sion in this society; and to put forward the correct understanding of
> this society in order to change it. (1982:110)

West then criticized black liberation theology for its lack of an overall economic analysis as a basis for understanding racism. He argues:

> Black theologians all agree that black liberation has something to do with ameliorating the socioeconomic conditions of black people. But it is not clear what this amelioration amounts to. There is little discussion in their writings about what the liberating society will be like. The notion and the process of liberation are often mentioned, but, surprisingly, one is hard put to find a sketch of what liberation would actually mean in the everyday lives of black people, what power they would possess, and what resources they would have access to. (1982:111; see also Leech 1988)

Historical Encounters between Marxists and Religious Radicals

It is this kind of challenge that has created new possibilities for Marxist-religious encounters. We turn now to a review of the forms these encounters have taken around the world.

Europe

Marxist-Christian encounters in the 1950s, as stated earlier, focused on critiques of theology and a push to incorporate Marxist analysis into a Christian ethic. By the 1960s, such encounters had evolved into a regular forum for dialogue and attempts to reshape theology. Two noted theologians, Johann-Baptist Metz and Jurgen Moltmann, both Europeans, were central figures in this process of change. They developed a "political theology" and a "theology of hope." They emphasized four basic items, the needs to:

1. overcome present social and economic contradictions and sufferings;

2. see beyond existing perspectives for change (thereby creating a basis for constructing a new image of society which will challenge the claim that present society has reached a harmonious state);

3. focus on a purely factual, technical analysis of present reality as an inadequate basis for change;

4. understand people's alienation and oppression as part of the economic forces which dominate them (Kirk 1980:62). One author describes Metz and Moltmann as "seeking to rescue theology from the individualistic morass of existentialism, and to turn it into a critical, disciplined analysis of trends in society in dialogue with current utopias" (Kirk 1980:66).

Opportunities for Marxist-Christian dialogues emerged as new groups created forums for debates. The first of these meetings took place in Salzburg in 1965 (Boutin 1985:41). The Paulus-Gesellschaft (The Society of Paul), founded by Erich Kellner, began conducting seminars (Boutin 1985:41). These seminars began the formal dialogues, and they quickly inspired other groups to do the same. Arbeloa Muru and Estéfani y Robles explained:

> From 1967 onwards, Christians took part in the "Weeks of Marxist Thought" in Paris and Lyons, and Marxists attended seminars of Catholic intellectuals in Paris....The meetings were not attended by Soviet representatives nor by representatives from those countries whose dogma remained faithful to the ruling orthodoxy of Moscow. On the other hand, there was an abundance of Italian, French, Polish and Czech Communists and these were the years of influence of Garaudy, Lombardo Radice, Mury, Luporini, di Marco, Machovec and others. (1977:30).

Among the more notable European Marxists to pursue a dialogue with Christians was Roger Garaudy. In "De l'anathéme au dialogue" (From Anathema to Dialogue), a conference paper presented in Salzburg in 1965, Garaudy declared openly that the thesis proclaiming that religion has always acted as the opium of the people has never been a thesis of Marx's (Garaudy 1966). Momjan (1974) and other orthodox Marxists rejected this view and criticized Garaudy and others for their deviant positions. Yet among pursuants of the Marxist-Christian dialogues, Garaudy's writings have been much admired. His ideas have influenced "a growing number of adherents, including a sizeable number of 'democratic' socialists in the United States, Europe, and Latin America, together with Christian socialists who claim that certain aspects of Marxism, separable from official Communist ideology, are quite compatible with Christianity" (McGovern 1981:50).

North America

Gregory Baum provides an excellent assessment of Christian socialism in Canada. He argues that the creation of the Cooperative Commonwealth Federation (CCF), "modelled largely upon the British Labour Party, was a pragmatic union of several radical and progressive movements" (Baum 1977:13). Led predominantly by Protestant groups, the Canadian social gospel movement provided the ideological impetus for a broader understanding of socialism.

> Between 1914 and 1924 the Canadian social gospel, derived from British and American sources yet expressed in terms of the historical, social movements in Canada, inspired churchmen of various denominations, especially Methodists, to promote a radical social Christianity, to form labour churches in various parts of Canada, and to exercise leadership among the oppressed farmers and workers in the West. (Baum 1977:15)

As ministers began to synthesize their social gospel interpretation with a more secular political position, they often found themselves at odds with their more conservative denominations. But these radicalized Christians of the CCF found renewed support for their position during the Great Depression. By the 1930s, "in close association with the League for Social Reconstruction, the Canadian equivalent of the British Fabian Society, a group of Christian theologians in Toronto and Montreal began to interpret the Christian gospel in the light of a socialist analysis of society" (Baum 1977:16).

Among Canadian Catholics, there were groups that became members of CCF. But the papal condemnation of socialism in the 1931 encyclical *Quadragesimo Anno* forbade Catholics to join socialist organizations, which made Catholic participation in the CCF less significant than that of Protestants. The strong opposition to the CCF by Canadian bishops in Quebec, for example, was one reason why the CCF had a limited impact in Catholic Quebec. The Catholic tension with the CCF was at the heart of Quebec's concern over "the centralizing trend of Canadian socialism" because Catholics saw the CCF as a "secular political movement with a certain Protestant evangelical flavour" (Baum 1977:19). While these factors tended to minimize the participation of Catholics in the CCF, they were by no means decisive. Catholics joined the CCF in Saskatchewan, British Columbia, Northern Ontario, and Cape Breton. And the strained relationship between Canadian Catholics and the CCF did not deter later Marxist-Christian dialogues. In fact, "a group of Catholics, including workers and intellectuals, called Politisés Chrétiens, are presently pursuing the meaning and power of Marxist socialism from the Catholic faith-perspective" (Baum 1977:21).

In the United States, there were some early efforts to construct utopian Christian communities, such as the Oneida Community, the Christian Socialist Institute, and the Christian Socialist Fellowship, but these usually ended within a few years in disorder and mutual recrimination (Symes and Clement 1972:8, 204, 232). The first successful attempts at Christian socialism in the United States came during the Great Depression. Dorothy Day, a journalist, social worker, and erstwhile communist, began the Catholic Worker movement in the early 1930s (Abell 1963). Aroused by the taunts of communists that Catholics had no love for the poor, Day resolved late in 1932 to devise ways to personalize

Catholic sympathy for the victims of the Great Depression, especially the homeless and unemployed (Abell 1963:246). While Catholic Action and its inspired worker movements provided a forum for individuals to question social inequities, these movements never produced formal dialogues between Marxists and Christians. Catholic Worker movements paralleled the publication of the encyclical *Quadragesimo Anno*, which was staunchly antisocialist. Catholics everywhere were cautioned by bishops against membership or associations with Marxists and socialists. Catholic Worker movements were important because, even though these movements eventually fizzled, they provided a forum for initial moves toward a Christian socialism (Whyte 1981).

One of the few movements incorporating a socialist Christian slant without papal interference during the 1920s and 1930s in the United States incorporated the ideas of A.J. Muste. Muste was an ordained minister in the Dutch Reformed Church, active in labor movements and renowned for his antiwar stance (Muste 1940; Hentoff 1967:1–43). Once a staunch Marxist-Leninist renouncing all religion as the opiate of the people, he returned to his religion finding that movements of prophetic religion, social reform and revolution, and democracy "are...each...largely bound up with that of the other two" (Muste 1940:2–11). Like Day, Muste belonged to a generation of Christian activist writers who flirted with socialism, but whose ideas (along with those of the theologian Niebuhr) never really produced formal Marxist-Christian dialogues.

Such dialogues in the United States did not begin until the 1960s. They were initiated by Gus Hall, leader of the Communist party/USA, in response to Pope John XXIII's encyclical (1963) on peace. According to McGovern, the first encounter occurred in July 1965 at a Christian summer camp in cooperation with Herbert Aptheker's then newly established American Institute of Marxist Studies (AIMS). "It brought together several well-known U.S. Marxists and Christians, including Aptheker and Howard Parsons on the Marxist side, and Father Quentin Lauer, S.J., Harvey Cox, and others from a Christian perspective" (McGovern 1985:64). Eventually these encounters became more frequent, leading to an openness between marxists and christians never before experienced in U.S. history. Michael Harrington, for example, posed the question: "What, as a conclusion to all of this, can socialism contribute and what stance might a Christian take?" McGovern, in considering the question, posits that

> what follows is not an argument for "the" correct strategy Christians in the United States should follow. It is perhaps a 'philosophy of social change' which dovetails with Michael Harrington's strategy of long-range vision and immediate tasks....Socialism points to an important alternative possibility, and offers a needed critique of capitalism. For a Christian to work for a democratic socialism would seem a perfectly justifiable option. The very uncertainties about

socialism might be all the more reason for Christians to be part of the movement, to help shape its directions and values. (1981:323)

Added to these debates, which are shaping the Socialist Democratic movement in the United States today, are issues of race and gender.

James Cone's black theology of liberation (1970) emerged out of the Black Power tradition and focused on religion and race. His work added a new perspective to U.S. theology and eventually to dialogues with socialists. Cone had not sought a dialogue with Marxists, but saw his work as an extension of the evolving history of the black church and the Black Power movement in the United States. At the same time, Gustavo Gutierrez and other Latin American liberation theologians began publishing their own versions of liberation theology, grounding themselves in a Marxian analysis. The Latin Americans did not examine or integrate considerations of race or gender oppression. Cone, who opened dialogue between U.S. black and Latin American theologians, criticized them for omitting issues of race at the 1975 Theology in the Americas Conference. Among the most incisive works from this time were those produced by Cornel West—a socialist Christian. His synthesis of religion and Marxism was especially important because he represented a bridge to the black churches in the United States, the work of James Cone, and a call to the black church to engage its activism and analysis of race in the context of a broader Marxist perspective. Because the Latin Americans had already developed a paradigm for the applications of Marxist analysis to theology along class lines, the Theology in the Americas conference became a forum in which liberation theologians were challenged to address class and race issues.

Initially, there was no serious incorporation of gender issues. Not until the works of Mary Daly, Elizabeth Fiorenza, Rosemary Reuther, Elsa Tamez, Beatriz Melano Couch, Delores Williams, and others had come to the forefront of theological debate did gender issues became important. Major women theologians and writers have not seriously incorporated Marxism into their critique—this omission has led to their work being challenged by women in the Third World and women of color in the United States. Women theologians have started to rethink liberation theology in terms of their own struggles, many of them articulating the economic and patriarchal aspects of oppression as a central issue in their theology. No one theologian has synthesized gender, race, and class issues in a manner that would offer a more wholistic liberation theology.

The Third World

The late 1960s to mid-1980s was a time of renewal for the Latin American church. Revisions inspired by the Second Vatican Council and the Latin

American Episcopal Council's (CELAM) meeting in Medellin, Colombia (1968) set the tone for renewal. For many activists in the church, this period of radical change in the church became their moment for redefining the goals of the institution, by creating and supporting their own versions of Christianity. Consequently, they formed their own Christian communities, often known as Base Christian Communities, some of them inspired by the particular vision of the leftist Brazilian educator Paulo Freire. As Berryman has argued:

> The Freire method provided a model of work in which outsiders—that is, people who were not themselves poor—could go to the Popular classes in a nonpaternalistic way. As a method, it gave church people, social workers, and organizers a sense of what to do, whether directly in literacy classes, or in using the "concientizacion" (the process by which one becomes conscious of one's oppression) approach, to help the community come together, articulate its needs, and become organized. They can be what Antonio Gramsci called "organic intellectuals." (1987:36)

The 1960s gave birth to both reformist and revolutionary religious groups. Camilo Torres, who became known as the "guerrilla priest," was not only a priest but a Marxist who believed in armed struggle. Torres was a founder of revolutionary theology—using direct action to do God's work. Those associated with liberation theology were seen as reformists because they opted to work within the limits set by their churches. Torres died in guerrilla combat in 1966, and interest in revolutionary theology shifted to the liberationist perspective. Liberation theology provided the ideological impetus for social reform in Latin American while maintaining ties to its church institutions.

These events led to the creation of a number of organizations, many of which sought dialogue with the Marxist left. Even Fidel Castro recognized the progress that had been made. In January 1968, Castro addressed fifteen hundred intellectuals gathered in Havana for an International Cultural Congress. Hageman and Deats noted: "After reading a statement prepared by priests attending the Congress, he acknowledged changes in the posture of some segments of the church and questioned dogmatic Marxist perspectives on religion" (1985:179). In his January 1968 speech, Castro commented:

> It is unquestionable that we are before new facts, before new phenomena....Marxism needs to develop itself, to come out of a certain stiffening of the joints, to interpret today's realities in an objective and scientific sense, to act as a revolutionary force and not as a pseudo-revolutionary church. These are the paradoxes of history. How, when we see sectors of the clergy transformed into

revolutionary forces, are we going to resign ourselves to see sectors of Marxism transforming themselves into ecclesiastical forces. (1971:139)

In a 1985 interview conducted by Father Frei Betto, Castro further elaborated his stance on religion (Betto 1987). These views on religion began to be shared by those in other Third World nations who were staging Marxist revolutions.

In December 1962, President Leopold Senghor of Senegal invited African political leaders to Dakar for the Colloquium on Policies of Development and African Approaches to Socialism. The vague contours of what is known as African socialism emerged, in which "nationalism, Pan-Africanism, and socialism were woven together to create an overall African ideology of modernization" (Thomas 1985:135).

Rejecting Marx's assessment of religion as "the opiate of people," Senghor found no conflict between the utopian visions of his mentors Karl Marx and Teilhard de Chardin, a French Jesuit philosopher. Senghor not only found no conflict between Marxism and Christianity, but, according to Thomas, his ecumenical posture focused on the universal values of Christianity and Islam. He considered both faiths to be revolutionary because they introduced universal values useful in assimilating the values of socialism to those African cultural values, which he termed *Negritude* (Thomas 1985:136). Senghor's views were not exceptional; others in Zambia, Zimbabwe, and Ghana saw no conflict in a Marxist-religious synthesis.

A similar synthesis was developed in India via people like Father Vadakkan, who was attracted to the Communist party in India because of his desire to achieve justice for the poor and the oppressed in Kerala (Mathew 1985:159). This perspective was also a central theme in other countries developing versions of liberation theology, including the Philippines and Korea. Each of the encounters underscored one fundamental belief: "that work for development and liberation implies commitment to bring about a radical change in the structures of society, and this calls for radical changes in the Church as well" (Amalorpavadass 1978:147).

Marxist-religious encounters have been a common theme in this global effort toward radical political changes. Wherever theologians have become part of the political process in their individual national contexts, they have been challenged to rethink the traditional roles played by their religious institutions in quieting the masses. This challenge has encouraged the reformulation of religious ideology, making it both relevant and useful to the insurgent masses.

Among First World nations, the process has been slower. Lacking a ripened revolutionary sociopolitical environment, the convergences in the First World have tended to be more of an intellectual encounter. Nevertheless, the international impetus for dialogue has created a context for a global rethinking of the political importance of cultural expressions—including religion.

Voices of Dissent among Critical Theorists

This chapter has provided an overview of the debates in Marxist theory over the role of religion in society and an overview of the uses of Marxist theory in the religious sphere. While the debates have produced a Marxism more sensitive to religious issues, it is also fair to challenge whether this synthesis can be reconciled with Marxist theory at all. Taking a negative tone, the critical theorist Horkheimer argued that to the extent that Christianity becomes the bedfellow of the state, its ideas remain an illusion. In the end, "when the authoritarian state seems to engage in a historic conflict with religion, the essential issue is whether the two shall compete, be coordinated, or go their separate ways" (Horkheimer 1972:130). The role of theology, therefore, has been simply "to reconcile the demands of the Gospel and of power" (Horkheimer 1974:36). Furthermore, religious ideology, in the form of theology, simply mediates class conflicts that in the end favor the interests of the rich. In the end, theology provides no real social transformation—at best, it is an illusory appeal to moral conscience.

Extending this argument, István Mészáros, a former student of the Hegelian Marxist Georg Lukács, argues that "Judaism and Christianity are complimentary aspects of society's efforts to cope with its internal contradictions. They both represent attempts at an imaginary transcendence of these contradictions, at an illusory 'reappropriation' of the 'human essence' through a fictitious supersession of the state of alienation" (1986:30). Mészáros underscores the position of the critical theorists—the fundamental task of Marxism is to abolish the need for theology. In their view, theology perpetuates false consciousness. In quoting Marx, Mészáros notes that the criticism of theology is transformed into the criticism of politics, when philosophy unmasks human self-alienation in its sacred form (1986:74). These theorists therefore challenge that there is anything fruitful in a Marxian-Christian synthesis.

The Vatican decision to censor liberation theology for its use of Marxist analysis suggests that this kind of theologizing is limiting as long as those who profess it remain within church institutions. There have been a hundred years of debate over the relevance of Marxist analysis to religious values. Yet in his commemorative encyclical, *Centesimus Annus* (1991), Pope John Paul II reaffirmed what had been stated in *Rerum Novarum* (1891), underscoring that the Roman Catholic church rejects the infusion of Marxism into theology.

These developments suggest that a fully developed Marxian-Christian synthesis may be impossible. Perhaps Horkheimer was correct in his observation that "even if it involves hardship the church must ultimately see that its own social position depends on the continued existence of the basic traits of the present system. If these were to change, the church would lose all and gain nothing" (Horkheimer 1972:130). Yet despite these objections, sociologists have turned their interests to what they see as a more balanced analysis of the role of religion in society.

Marxist Scholarship and the Sociology of Religion

In her assessment of the relation between Marxist sociology and the sociology of religion, Barbara Hargrove noted some significant changes. In the 1960s, Marxist sociology had "written religion off as a negative factor in society" (Hargrove 1989:11). Political theologies and liberation theology changed all that. In American sociology, for example:

> The rise of liberation theology in the southern hemisphere has brought about, in mostly Catholic circles, something like a renewal of the cooperation between sociology and the Social Gospel movement of North American Protestantism, where the study of society is linked with a movement for social change anchored in religious ideology and emerging religious institutions. (Hargrove 1989:13)

Marxist sociology and the sociology of religion have also benefited from the works of theologians, philosophers, and others who have brought to the social sciences what is viewed as a new understanding of religious revolutionary potential.

Marxist scholarship now takes into account the religious factor when analyzing social movements or revolutions. Because "persons in opposition to the 'establishment' have not had to decry religion...as their oppressor, but could and did form new religious groups to free themselves for social change" (Hargrove 1989:13), it has had an impact on the way some Marxists have come to view both religion and culturally diverse societies. As Hargrove explains:

> Most of the movements in the periphery are tied to a rising nationalism, a demand for respect for the culture and identity of particular peoples in the face of processes of modernization that tend to homogenize all cultures. It is often difficult to distinguish the relative importance of religion and politics in these movements. Some observers say that the religious rhetoric is only used to cover political issues. That may be the case in some instances, but the problem is usually that of the modern observer who assumes greater separation of religion from the rest of the culture than is true in many societies whose culture is less affected by modernity. (1989:312)

A combined Marxist analysis of class, race, gender, and theology has also liberated theologians to link the religious factor with the political. In this manner, Marxists have provided theologians with analytical tools for understanding oppression and critiquing society. Regardless of whether it will prove fruitful in the end, liberation theologians have succeeded in reformulating Marxist thinking on the subject of religion.

The emergence of liberation theology and its use of Marxist analysis has opened a new era for students of religion. In her seminal text*Religion: the Social Context*, McGuire argues that

> Marxian thought has, especially in recent years, emphasized the relative autonomy of religion. This school strives to study religious belief systems in themselves, locating them in a larger social-historical context. These theorists retain the insights of Marx and especially Engels but focus on the complex reciprocal influences between religion and social structure. By treating the relationship as complex, this latter Marxian approach identifies both the passive and active, conservative and revolutionary elements in religion. (1981:185)

McGuire credited Maduro (1977) and Mayrl (1976) for their insights in unraveling the Marxism-religion question. Addressing U.S. sociologists, Maduro summarized the new Marxist approach to religion as follows:

> (1) Religion is not a mere passive effect of the social relations of production; it is an active element of social dynamics, both conditioning and conditioned by social processes; (2) religion is not always a subordinate element within social processes, it may often play an important part in the birth and consolidation of a particular social structure; (3) religion is not necessarily a functional reproductive or conservative factor in society; it often is one of the main (and sometimes only) available channels to bring about social revolution. (1977:366)

In a recent edition of her work *The Sociology of Religion*, Hargrove (1989) has included a section titled "The Response of the Marginalized," which attests to the proliferation of the new Marxist approaches in the study of religion. Specialized studies using a Marxist framework have emerged as well. For example, Billings analyzes the oppositional movements of coal miners and textile workers in the U.S. South after World War I and concludes that "in the case of class-based oppositional movements, religion may figure as a significant dimension of the politics of class formation." This insight leads Billings to conclude that "Gramsci's thoughts on the historicity of class relations, which included a stress on the open-endedness of class phenomena as they are lived and experienced, stands in sharp contrast with conceptions of class as an objective configuration of interests" (1990:27).

The visible role played by religious institutions in protest movements in Africa, Asia, Latin America, and North America has demonstrated that the assumption that religion is only a functional stabilizing agent is at best one-sided. And sociologists, including U.S. scholars, have come to recognize this development and have begun to incorporate the Marxist analytic framework and methodology into their work.

Summary

Wherever class interests are mirrored in social institutions, such as religion, they contain both the quieting and transforming potentials that characterize class struggles. It has been argued here that religion can play both roles, depending on the political uses to which it is put.

The influence of Marxist analysis in the transformation of religious concepts and institutions has taken several decades to develop, but that it has happened is now apparent. Oddly enough, the Marxist critique of religion has played a significant role in these changes, particularly as Marxism became the ideological paradigm for many modern revolutions. Within this context of revolution, a synthesis developed between the political and the cultural expressions of the insurgent masses. While the Social Democrats had long opted to tolerate religion as a "private matter," more orthodox Marxists began to rethink the role of religion only when Marxist Christians became active in official leftist organizations. Gradually, this tendency became a global pattern. As more and more political activists saw no contradictions between their political agenda and their religious convictions, the opportunities for dialogue became more prevalent.

Crucial to understanding the transitions within the religious communities are a similar slow process of decades of slowly emerging theological interest in the challenges posed by Marxism. Nevertheless, only when activist groups—and peasant worker organizations and church councils—began pressing their churches for tolerance toward Marxism did the impetus for dialogue become an important concern for the major religious sects. The Second Vatican Council and Third World organizations became beacons for pronounced shifts in support of dialogues. The popular demand for changes in the traditional affiliations of the churches with oppressive structures produced new liberation and revolutionary theologies, now popular among these radical groups. The political persistence of this revolutionary sector has recruited religious intellectuals to its cause, and the result has been the creation of a synthesis of theology with Marxist analysis.

Marxists have also begun to rethink their orthodox positions on religion. Many in the New Left have come to recognize and to witness the commitment of religious activists who apply Marxist analysis to their political ethic. Castro, Senghor, and others, have publicly supported those efforts. While some in the New Left, particularly critical theorists, still remain firm in their atheism, others have supported efforts at dialogues. Unlike many of the orthodox Marxists of the early period, those in the New Left who support dialogue have inherited what many identify as the fruitful outcomes of the Marxist debates on religion. The underlying basis for convergence remains on the economic and political levels, which is why liberation and revolutionary theologies are particularly compelling. There also remains a commitment to revolution and the transformation of society. Of the theologians willing to engage in dialogue, those who remain open to these possibilities are also the ones at the center of dialogues with Marxists.

The liberationist perspectives have, in many instances, looked to Marxism for historical and economic analyses of the human condition. Religious ideology, like political ideology, helps members communicate their ideas and beliefs, and these beliefs create a sense of their moral unity within the group and support for their causes. Thus the dialogues that have emerged between Marxists and religious groups were based on the discovery of common political and moral goals. While the methods may be different, and the analyses particular to material or spiritual rationalism, the ethics driving the collective vision were sufficiently similar that it opened the possibility for convergence.

Marxism has developed out of its own particular historical conditions and political trajectory. If Marx and Engels were guilty of being too harsh in their attack on religion, they did so at a time when their particular critique had historical merit. If theologians and Marxists have found grounds on which to engage in dialogue, it has been possible because of an ongoing historical transformation of the institutions once critiqued for their exclusive association with the ruling classes. Fidel Castro's advocacy of these changes signifies a new era of understanding, even if it is just a practical understanding of convenience and political necessity. Neither Marxists nor theologians assume the other to have reformulated the basic principles on which each stand—but each has recognized the other's revolutionary potential. Both traditions have been strengthened by various popular cultural traditions. In turn, these cultural expressions have given Marxist theorists, theologians, and sociologists an opportunity to question their own positions.

References

Abell, Aaron I. 1963. *American Catholicism and Social Action: A Search for Social Justice* . Notre Dame: University of Notre Dame Press.

Amalorpavadass, D.S. 1978. "The Indian Universe of a New Theology." Pp. 137–56 in *The Emergent Gospel: Theology from the Developing World*, ed. Sergio Torres and Virginia Fabella, M.M. New York: Orbis Books.

Aptheker, Herbert. 1970. *The Urgency of Marxist-Christian Dialogue*. New York: Harper and Row.

Arbeloa Muru, Víctor Manuel, and José María González-Estéfaniy Robles. 1977. "Socialists and Christians: Confrontation and Dialogue." Pp. 23–34 in *Christianity and Socialism*, ed. Johann-Baptist Metz and Jean-Pierre Jossua. New York: Seabury Press.

Baum, Gregory. 1977. "Canadian Socialism and the Christian Church." Pp. 13–22 in *Christianity and Socialism*, ed. Johann-Baptist Metz and Jean-Pierre Jossua. New York: Seabury Press.

Berdyaev, Nikolai. 1944. *Slavery and Freedom*. New York: Scribner.

Berryman, Phillip. 1987. *Liberation Theology: Essential Facts about the Revolutionary Movement in Latin America and Beyond*. New York: Seabury Press.

Betto, Frei. 1987. *Fidel and Religion: Castro Talks Revolution with Frei Betto*. New York: Simon and Schuster.

Bigo, Pierre. 1977. *The Church and Third World Revolutions*. New York: Orbis Books.

Billings, Dwight B. 1990. "Religion as Opposition: A Gramscian Analysis." *American Journal of Sociology* 96:1–31.

Bociurkiw, Bohdan R. 1987. "Lenin and Religion." Pp. 107–34 in *Lenin: The Man, the Theorist, the Leader—A Reappraisal*, ed. Leonard Schapiro and Peter Reddaway. Boulder: Westview Press.

Bock, Kim Yong, ed. 1981. *Minjung Theology: People as the Subjects of History*. Singapore: The Commission on Theological Concerns (The Christian Conference of Asia).

Boff, Leonardo. 1985. *Church: Charism and Power*. New York: Crossroad Publishing.

Boutin, Maurice. 1985. "Austria and West Germany." Pp. 41–58 in *Three Worlds of Christian-Marxist Encounters*, ed. Nicholas Piediscalzi and Robert G. Thobaben. Philadelphia: Fortress Press.

Bricker, Victoria. 1981. *The Indian Christ, The Indian King*. Austin: University of Texas Press.

Castro, Fidel. 1971. *Religion in Cuba Today: A New Church in a New Society*, trans. Alice L. Hageman and Philip E. Wheaton. New York: Association Press.

Cohn, Norman. 1970. *The Pursuit of the Millennium*. New York: Oxford University Press.

Cone, James. 1970. *A Black Theology of Liberation*. Philadelphia: Lippincott.

Connolly, James. 1988. *James Connolly: Selected Writings*, ed. P. Berresford Ellis. London: Pluto Press.

Engels, Friedrich. 1979. *The Condition of the Working-Class in England*. London: Grenada.

Fierro, Alfredo. 1977. *The Militant Gospel: A Critical Introduction to Political Theologies*. New York: Orbis Books.

Flannery, Austin, ed. 1984. *Documents of Vatican II*. Detroit: William B. Eerdmans.

Garaudy, Roger. 1966. *From Anathema to Dialogue*. New York: Herder and Herder.

Gotay, Samuel Silva. 1981. *El Pensamiento Cristiano Revolucionario en America Latina*. Salamanca: Ediciones Sigueme.

Grace, Edward J. 1985. "Italy." Pp. 19–40 in *Three Worlds of Christian-Marxist Encounters*, ed. Nicholas Piediscalzi and Robert G. Thobaben. Philadelphia: Fortress Press.

Gramsci, Antonio. 1987. *Selections from the Prison Notebooks*. New York: International Publishers.

Gutiérrez, Gustavo. 1973. *A Theology of Liberation*. New York: Orbis Books.

Hageman, Alice L. and Paul Deats. 1985. "Cuba." Pp. 173–192 in *Three Worlds of Christian-Marxist Encounters*, ed. Nicholas Piediscalzi and Robert G. Thobaben. Philadelphia: Fortress Press.

Hargrove, Barbara. 1989. *The Sociology of Religion*. Chicago: Harlan Davidson.

Hentoff, Nat, ed. 1967. *The Essays of A.J. Muste*. Indianapolis: Bobbs-Merrill.

Horkheimer, Max. 1972. *Critical Theory: Selected Essays*. New York: Seabury Press.

———. 1974. *Critique of Instrumental Reason*. New York: Seabury Press.

Kautsky, Karl. 1953. *Foundations of Christianity*. New York: S.A. Russell.

—————. 1959. *Thomas More and His Utopia*. New York: Russell and Russell.

Kirk, J. Andrew. 1980. *Theology Encounters Revolution*. Champaign: InterVarsity Press.

Labriola, Antonio. 1980. *Socialism and Philosophy*. St. Louis: Telos Press.

Leech, Kenneth. 1988. *Struggle in Babylon: Racism in the Cities and Churches of Britain*. London: Sheldon Press.

Lenin, V.I. 1943. *Selected Works*. Vol. 11. New York: International Publishers.

Leo XIII, Pope. 1948. "Rerum Novarum." Pp. 1–30 in *Five Great Encyclicals*. New York: Paulist Press.

Levine, Daniel H. 1986. "Religion, the Poor, and Politics." Pp. 3–23 in *Religion and Political Conflict in Latin America*, ed. Daniel H. Levine. Chapel Hill: University of North Carolina Press.

Luxemburg, Rosa. 1970. *Rosa Luxemburg Speaks*. New York: Pathfinder Press.

McGovern, Arthur F. 1981. *Marxism: An American Christian Perspective*. New York: Orbis Books.

—————. 1985. "United States." Pp. 59–77 in *Three Worlds of Christian-Marxist Encounters*, ed. Nicholas Piediscalzi and Robert G. Thobaben. Philadelphia: Fortress Press.

McGuire, Meredith. 1981. *Religion: the Social Context*. Belmont, Calif.: Wadsworth.

Maduro, Otto. 1977. "New Marxist Approaches to the Study of Religion." *Sociological Analysis* 38:359–67.

—————. 1982. *Religion and Social Conflicts*. New York: Orbis Books.

Marx, Karl. 1973. "Theses on Feuerbach." Pp. 13–15 in *Selected Works in Three Volumes*. Moscow: Progress Publishers.

—————. 1978a. "Economic and Philosophic Manuscripts of 1844." Pp. 66–125 in *The Marx-Engels Reader*, ed. Robert C. Tucker. New York: Norton.

—————. 1978b. "On the Jewish Question." Pp. 26–52 in *The Marx-Engels Reader*, ed. Robert C. Tucker. New York: Norton.

Marx, Karl, and Friedrich Engels. 1972. *On Religion*. Moscow: Progress Publishers.

—————. 1973. "Manifesto of the Communist Party." Pp. 108–37 in *Selected Works in Three Volumes*. Moscow: Progress Publishers.

Mathew, George. 1985. "India." Pp. 155–71 in *Three Worlds of Christian-Marxist Encounters*, ed. Nicholas Piediscalzi and Robert G. Thobaben. Philadelphia: Fortress Press.

Mayrl, William. 1976. "Marx's Theory of Social Movements and the Church-Sect Typology." *Sociological Analysis* 37:19–31.

Meszaros, Istvan. 1986. *Marx's Theory of Alienation*. London: Merlin Press.

Metz, Johann-Baptist, and Jean-Pierre Jossua. 1977. *Christianity and Socialism*. New York: Seabury Press.

Miranda, Jose. 1980. *Marx Against the Marxists*. New York: Orbis Books.

Momjan, Hachik Nishanovich. 1974. *Marxism and the Renegade Garaudy*. Moscow: Progress Publishers.

Muste, A.J. 1940. *Non-Violence in an Agressive World*. New York: Harper and Brothers.

Niebuhr, Reinhold. 1947. *Moral Man and Immoral Society*. New York: Scribner.

Piediscalzi, Nicholas, and Robert G. Thobaben, ed. 1985. *Three Worlds of Christian-Marxist Encounters*. Philadelphia: Fortress Press.

Pius XI, Pope. 1948. "Quadragesimo Anno." Pp. 125–68 in *Five Great Encyclicals*. New York: Paulist Press.

Schapiro, Leonard, and Peter Reddaway, ed. 1987. *Lenin: The Man, the Theorist, the Leader—A Reappraisal*. London: Westview Press

Symes, Lillian, and Travers Clement. 1972. *Rebel America: The Story of Social Revolt in the United States*. Boston: Beacon Press.

Tai, Hue-Tam Ho. 1983. *Millenarianism and Peasant Politics in Vietnam*. Cambridge: Harvard University Press.

Tamez, Elsa. 1987. *Against Machismo*. Chicago: Meyer Stone Books.

Thomas, Norman E. 1985. "Black Africa." Pp. 135–53 in *Three Worlds of Christian-Marxist Encounters*, ed. Nicholas Piediscalzi and Robert G. Thobaben. Philadelphia: Fortress Press.

Tikhon, Patriarch. 1959. "Anathematizing the Soviet Regime, of February 1, 1918." Pp. 36–37 in *The Russian Revolution and Religion: A Collection of Documents Concerning the Suppression of Religion by the Communists*. Notre Dame: University of Notre Dame Press.

Torres, Sergio, and John Eagleson. 1976. *Theology in the Americas*. New York: Orbis Books.

Torres, Sergio, and Virginia Fabella. 1978. *The Emergent Gospel: Theology from the Developing World*. New York: Orbis Books.

West, Cornel. 1982. *Prophesy Deliverance: An Afro-American Revolutionary Christianity*. Philadelphia: Westminster Press.

———. 1984. "Religion and the Left: An Introduction." *Monthly Review* 36(July-August):9–19.

Whyte, John H. 1981. *Catholics in Western Democracies*. New York: St. Martin's.

CRIME AND LAW:

REDISCOVERING CRIMINOLOGY: LESSONS FROM THE MARXIST TRADITION

Michael J. Lynch

Criminology is a conservative field; it generally maintains and legitimizes existing values and generates repressive policies of social control. Criminology's conservative nature can be explained by its origins in biology and positivism during the late eighteenth century (Vold and Bernard 1986). The primary concern of biological-positivist criminology was to demonstrate how*individual characteristics* could be used to explain criminal tendencies objectively. This concern dominated criminology through the 1930s when it was replaced by a more sociologically oriented (but still conservative) perspective. Given criminology's historical context, primary objectives and focus on the individual, and a conservative social and academic environment (especially in the United States, as evidenced by such occurrences as the "Red Scare" during the 1950s), it is easy to understand why the Marxist tradition had little impact on criminology until the 1970s.

The dramatic social changes of the 1960s, the increasing viability of Marxist regimes in Eastern Europe, and the liberalization of academia (see Beirne 1979; Meier 1976; Shichor 1980) all contributed to the development of a radical criminology (Lynch and Groves 1989:1–4). The term "radical criminology" implies criminological theory that has its roots in Marx's materialism (Lynch and Groves 1989:vii–ix). This tradition has a number of varieties (Lynch and Groves 1989:4; Bohm 1982; Milovanovic 1990), and has been employed to: (1) challenge the class and race biases embedded in traditional criminology and its preference for individualistic explanation; (2) examine systematic class bias in the criminal justice system and law; (3) direct greater attention to crimes of the powerful; and (4) address how power and inequality affect criminal labelling processes.

The goal of radical criminology is to explain crime within definite economic and social contexts and to expose the connection between the nature of class society, crime and social control. In so doing, a few criminologists discovered Marx, and along the way, rediscovered criminology. The remainder of this chapter provides a brief overview of the development of this ever-changing radical perspective on crime.

Early Marxist Explanations of Crime

Marx wrote little about crime (Lynch and Groves 1989:3), and what he did write is scattered throughout his numerous works (Phillips 1980; Greenberg 1983; Hirst 1975; e.g., *Theories of Surplus Value*, Part I, Appendix, 1905; "Capital Punishment," 1853; "Population, Crime and Pauperism," 1859; "Debates on Law and the Theft of Wood," 1842). Marx's discussions of crime focused upon the role social, economic, political and bureaucratic *structures* and *inequality* play in generating crime.

For example, in "Population, Crime and Pauperism," Marx focused on crime as the product of law-enforcement policies. His approach, reminiscent of labelling theory (Phillips 1980:165; Greenberg 1983:102), implicates social structure as a cause of crime: "There must be something rotten in the very core of a social system which increases its wealth without diminishing its misery, and increases in crime even more rapidly than in numbers" (Marx 1971:92). Marx's structural and contextual approach is evident in his response to Adolphe Quetelet (1831), who performed the first statistical study of crime and employed his findings to comment on the regularity of crime: "It is not so much the particular political institutions of a society as the fundamental conditions of modern bourgeois society in general which produce an average amount of crime in a given national fraction of society" (Marx and Engels 1975:151). Marx's position emphasized the connection between crime and structural conditions, but more importantly that between rapid increases in crime and the social and economic institutions of capitalism. This connection became a major theme for radical criminologists in the 1970s (e.g., Quinney 1979, 1980a; Platt 1974 1978; Chambliss 1975).

These few examples demonstrate how Marx applied the materialist approach to explain crime. He did not, however, develop a penetrating or extensive theory of criminal behavior. A more unified materialist approach to crime emerged in the writings of Engels, particularly in his *The Condition of the Working-Class in England* (1973). It was here that Engels discussed how structural forces contributed to crime among the working class, and he critiqued criminal law and the criminal nature of capitalist society (see also Engels 1964:219–20).

Speaking of law and the administration of justice, Engels (1973:317–18) noted that:

> legislation...protect[s] those that possess property....Laws are necessary only because there are persons...who own nothing;...this is

directly expressed in...laws...against vagabonds and tramps, in
which the proletariat as such is outlawed....The partisanship of the
Justice of the Peace...surpasses all description....And the conduct of
the police corresponds to that of the Justices of Peace. The bourgeois
may do what [they] will..., but the proletariat is roughly, brutally
treated; his poverty...casts...suspicions of every sort of crime upon
him and cuts him off from legal redress against any caprice of the
administrators of the law; for the [proletariat]...protecting forms
of...law do not exist....

Engels questioned the definition of crime as an act of the individual. Instead,
he depicted society as the criminal and claimed that society threatened the lives
of the proletariat daily, deprived them of necessities (1973:134); placed them in
brutal, unsafe work environments (1973:135–71, 173–222, 226–48); and generated deaths as violent as those by the "sword or bullet" (1973:134). Yet such acts,
though equally as harmful as legally defined "crimes," were not treated as
crimes. The structure and ideology of capitalism established conditions in which
the abuses of the working class were disguised, commonplace, and acceptable.
Under these conditions, "no man sees the murderer,...[and] the death of the
victim seems...natural" (1973:135). In short, Engels argued that the powerful
and their acts are hidden, not exposed by the law.

In addition to these observations, Engels set forth a theory of working-class
crime. His main premise was that the competitive and demoralizing nature of
capitalism ensured that workers' moral, educational, physical, and psychological needs were not met (1973:153). Workers, in effect, were cast out and ignored
by the structure of capitalist society and treated like brutes. And because they
were treated like brutes, they acted like brutes (1973:153), sometimes resorting
to crime. Once reduced to brutes and pauperized by the progress of capitalism,
"law [has] no further terrors for [the workers]; why should he restrain his desires?
What inducement has the proletarian not to steal?...Want leaves the working-
man the choice between starving slowly, killing himself speedily, or taking what
he needs" (1973:154).

In this view, the working class occupied an insecure position, living from
hand to mouth, that was a direct consequence of its role in capitalist society. This
lifestyle, which "makes a proletarian of him" (1973:155), is a direct consequence
of capitalism and its need to produce and constantly expand profit or surplus
value. One way surplus value is expanded is by replacing human labor with
machine labor. As machine labor replaces human labor, a larger and larger
percentage of the working class finds itself unemployed or turned into a surplus
population—they are, as contemporary Marxists claim, marginalized. In Engels's
own words, the production of surplus value meant that "every improvement in
machinery throws workers out of employment, and the greater the advance [of

technology], the more numerous the unemployed; each great advance produces...upon a number of workers the effect of a commercial crisis, creates want, wretchedness, and crime" (1973:173). This idea has influenced the work of many modern-day radical criminologists (e.g., Spitzer 1975; Lynch 1988a; Lynch and Groves 1989:63–64).

Engels, like Marx, argued that the working class is condemned to work, owning nothing but their labor power, which they must sell to the capitalist in order to survive. While voluntary work is "the highest enjoyment...compulsory toil is the most cruel, degrading punishment" (Engels 1973:157). The need to labor combined with capitalism's competitive and demoralizing nature *created* in society a war of all against all; of workers against workers, and workers against capitalist (Engels 1973:171; 1964:219–20, 224). It is not surprising, Engels argued, that crime arises under such circumstances.

In sum, Engels argued that the brutality capitalism visits on the working class turns the worker into a "thing without volition,...subject to the laws of Nature....Hence with the extension of the proletariat, crime has increased in England, and the British nation has become the most criminal in the world" (1973:168). Crime, in this view, is a form of rebellion, although its least fruitful and most primitive form (1973:250–51). The protest of the criminal, of the single individual against the brutal conditions of capitalism, is easily crushed by the superior force of society (1973:251). But crime could not always be conceptualized as rebellious behavior, since capitalists and the middle classes also resorted to crime (Engels 1964:224; 1981:49). Ultimately, Engels believed that crime resulted from the social and economic organization of capitalism, which affected all classes equally. The difference in the criminality of different classes was their political and economic power: those with political and economic power were able to escape criminal sanctions and labelling while the powerless could not.

These themes reappeared in the work of Willem Bonger (1916), the first scholar to make extensive use of a materialist framework to study crime. While imperfect, Bonger's important application of Marxian analysis to crime draws "the attention of criminologists to social conflict, class struggles, power, interests, economic conditions and exploitation as possible determinants of crime" (Barlow 1990:64). It remains the most often cited work of Marxist criminology (Seigle 1989:228–29), and thus a closer examination of Bonger's assumptions are warranted.

In *Criminality and Economic Conditions* (1916) Bonger's goal was twofold: first, to explain why capitalist societies of his day had higher crime rates than other societies, and second, to explain why the working class appeared to commit more crime than other social classes. The obvious explanation was that capitalist societies created a more crime-prone environment than other forms of social organization. Further, capitalist forms of social organization were particularly debilitating for members of the working class. In fleshing out this connection, Bonger argued that the competitive nature of capitalist society promoted social conditions that generated individualism and self-interest. These forces were evenly spread among social classes. Bonger labelled this force "egoism," and charged that capitalist societies, more so than other societies, promoted egoism. Societies with low crime rates, however, appeared to promote altruism or social responsibility and social equality.

Given Bonger's claim that egoism is evenly spread among social classes, how do we account for the fact that individuals from the working class, rather than individuals from other social classes, are more likely to be labelled criminal? Bonger argued that the answer could be located in the unequal distribution of power and resources promoted by capitalism. In short, those with power could use their resources and positions to avoid criminal prosecution and labelling—an argument that both Marx and Engels and modern-day radicals rely on. Bonger's argument implied that members of the working class, while possibly facing life conditions such as poverty that would increase their chances of committing specific crimes, were no more egoistic than members from other social classes; they simply lacked the resources and power that could be used to avoid negative labels or influence the content of law.

Having reviewed early work in this area, let us consider some controversies that emerged during the height of this field's development during the 1970s and 1980s.

Controversies in Radical Criminology 1970–90

Over the past two decades several controversies have emerged in this relatively new criminological perspective. These controversies include the debate over positivism, the nature of the state, and the nature of criminal behavior. These issues are important because they are the primary debates among radical criminologists. Before reviewing these debates, let us turn to the ultimate debate: whether or not a radical or Marxist criminology is possible.

The Debate over Marxist Criminology

From its inception as a specialized field of study, there have been those who question the possibility of creating a truly Marxist criminology (Hirst 1972, 1975, 1979; Mugford 1974; Bankowski et al. 1977; O'Malley 1988). This argument hinges on the observation that crime was not a central feature of either Marx's or Engels's theory of society, and therefore the application of this perspective to crime is a "stretching" of theory to concerns that are not within the realm of Marxian analysis.

In response, some argue that Marx's and Engels's theory was not fully developed at the time of their deaths and that there is no reason, on these grounds, to rule out Marxian analyses of crime (Greenberg 1981:20–21). Additionally, while it is true that neither Marx nor Engels developed a "complete" theory of crime, law or justice, they did, from time to time, investigate these issues (Greenberg 1981:21). Further, even if Marx or Engels had never said a single word about crime, law, or justice, this does not mean that their approach could not be applied to these issues in new and innovative ways. In fact, precisely because Marxian analysis is a historically situated structural explanation, we must expect that the theory as well as the issues this theory deals with will be revised and adapted to emerging historical circumstances (Lynch and Groves 1989:17–18). Thus there is little reason to believe that Marxist assumptions cannot be fruitfully applied to the study of crime, law, and justice. The rapid growth and transformation of radical criminology are surely signs that a Marxian perspective in criminology is possible and viable. In short, this debate appears to have been settled, not by way of sound arguments or theoretical justifications, but through increased interest in applying Marx's and Engels's insights to criminology.

The Debate over Positivism

There has also been a long-standing debate concerning the relationship of Marxism and positivism (generally see Horkheimer 1974; Marcuse 1964; Benton 1983:382–83; on criminology, see Groves 1985; Greenberg 1981). Early radical criminologists neglected (and some rejected) the use of quantitative methods of theory testing in an attempt both to distance themselves from traditional criminology and to provide a critique of it. This circumstance, coupled with radicals' preference for qualitative and historical analysis (e.g., Chambliss 1964; Quinney 1974, 1980a; Balbus 1973), radical critiques of positivism (Taylor et al. 1973:31–66; Quinney 1970, 1979) and the "objectivity of science" (e.g., Quinney 1979, 1980a; Irvine et al. 1979), and radicals' rejection of "technocratic knowledge" (Garofalo 1978:18), led to a general understanding that radical criminology was antiempirical (Nettler 1978:209, 213–16; Akers 1979, 1980; Klockars 1979, 1980) and unscientific (Turk 1979).

This conclusion was drawn by traditional criminologists and was based on critiques of radical criminology that cited its lack of empirical support (Schichor 1980; Sparks 1980). The traditionalists' view of radical criminology was, however, legitimized by radical writings that argued in favor of humanistic, subjectively oriented concerns and against positivism (Taylor et al. 1973;

Quinney 1970, 1979, 1980a). Thus the depiction of radical criminology as antiempirical and unscientific was not without standing, given that a few vocal members of the radical community did indeed reject positivist methods on the grounds that they were "bourgeois" in nature and replicated "bourgeois" social order. Nevertheless, radicals such as Richard Quinney, who was heavily criticized for his rejection of empirical methods, have often been misinterpreted. Quinney and others argue that statistical data can be "fruitfully" used but must ultimately be "understood in their political context" (Quinney 1979:53). This amounts to a critical understanding of data, rather than an outright rejection of data and data analysis as inappropriate to the radical position (Groves 1985).

In the 1980s a number of important empirical investigations by representatives of the radical approach began to emerge (e.g., Groves and Corrado 1983; Hagan et al. 1987, 1985; Hagan and Albonetti 1982; Lizotte et al. 1982; Lynch 1988a). These studies, along with theoretical arguments claiming that radical criminology and, more generally, Marxist theory was not antiquantitative (Groves 1985; Lynch 1987; Greenberg 1981; Mugham 1980), have made empirical studies by Marxist criminologists more acceptable within and outside radical circles. Thus, for the time being, the debate has subsided and empirical studies consistent with the theoretical premises of Marxist theory (but not necessarily positive criminology; see Lynch 1987) are more common and acceptable.

The Debate over the Nature of the State

In its formative years, radical criminologists relied heavily on an instrumental interpretation of the state (Quinney 1970, 1974, 1979). Instrumental Marxism (e.g., Miliband 1969) captures specific insights from Marx's and Engels's claim that "the executive of the modern state is but a committee for managing the common affairs of the whole bourgeoisie" (1955:11–12). As a result, instrumental Marxists view the state as the "handmaiden" or tool (instrument) of the capitalist class. In this view, the state fulfills the needs, wants, and desires of the capitalist class because it is directed to do so by the capitalist class. In fact, many instrumentalists claim that the state and the capitalist class are one and the same thing. A number of studies have examined this claim, and have demonstrated a close connection between the state and the capitalist class—that is, state officials also tend to be members of the capitalist class (Domhoff 1967, 1970, 1984; Kolko and Kolko 1972).

The same basic ideas have been applied to criminology. Here the argument is made that law (criminal and civil) and criminal justice mechanisms are designed, controlled, and used by the ruling class to repress the lower classes and maintain the power of the upper class (Quinney 1974, 1979). In this view, the state uses every opportunity to defend the interests of the capitalist class (Quinney 1974:95), turning law and criminal justice mechanisms into tools of class struggle wielded by the powerful. This view of the state has been legitimized by Quinney's (1974, 1971) investigation of the class composition of national crime commissions during the 1960s (see also Platt 1971).

Instrumentalism, however, contains several limitations. First, law and criminal justice do not *always* operate in the interest of the ruling class (Friedrichs 1980; Greenberg 1981); sometimes state decision making and interests are directed by working-class or other groups' concerns (e.g., consumer interests). Second, an instrumental view is conspiratorial and inconsistent with a radical preference for examining "impersonal structural influences" (Lynch and Groves 1989:24). Third, instrumentalism also exaggerates the cohesiveness of the ruling class (Bernard 1981; Chambliss and Seidman 1982). In other words, there are conflicts within the capitalist class (Spitzer 1980; Hagan and Leon 1977), and what is in the best interest of one segment of the capitalist class is not necessarily in the best interest of all capitalists. Thus, capitalists are divided and must fight among themselves to be represented by the state. And finally, not all state officials are capitalists.

Ultimately, instrumentalism, while an important explanation of law, crime, and justice in particular historical eras (Chambliss and Seidman 1982), is currently viewed as an extreme, inflexible, and reductionist misinterpretation of existing social practices and conditions (Lynch and Groves 1989:24, 25–26). Given these deficiencies, radical criminologists currently adhere to various versions of structuralism (Gold et al. 1975a, 1975b; Althusser and Balibar 1977; Chambliss and Seidman 1982; Poulantzas 1973). A significant variation on this theme is an emerging post-Frankfurt, critical perspective (see Groves and Sampson 1986).

Structural Marxists argue that the state is not an instrument of the capitalist class but is relatively autonomous (acts relatively independently) from the capitalist class. The state, and therefore law and justice, act to maintain the long-term interests of the capitalist class (Friedrichs 1980). In this view, the interests of the state and the capitalist class often converge, given that the survival and power of both groups depend on the continuation of the status quo. But the state also has legitimation concerns (Habermas 1975), which dictate that it appear "fair and neutral" in its decision making. This means that the state cannot invariably favor the capitalist class, since doing so would undermine its legitimacy (Wolfe 1977; Milovanovic 1981a, 1981b). In the structuralist view, the state is not a tool of class struggle, but an arena in which class struggle is fought. This approach acknowledges that capitalists do not always win and explains why laws protecting noncapitalist interests sometimes emerge (O'Connor 1973; Milovanovic 1984; Chambliss and Seidman 1982).

In short, structural Marxism examines how the social forces that operate in a capitalist system determine the agenda of society independently of the efforts of individuals. But this approach is also not entirely accurate because it ignores the fact that individuals and interest groups often have a great deal to do with legal decision making (Chambliss and Seidman 1982; O'Connor 1973). Even with this shortcoming, most radical criminologists argue that structuralism is a better explanation of the state than instrumentalism.

The Debate over the Nature of Criminal Behavior

This debate can be traced to Marx's (1977:643) assertion that criminals were part of the lumpenproletariat (Greenberg 1981:11, 62–63). By this, Marx implied that criminals existed outside capitalist social relationships and consequently had little class consciousness, meaning that they were not part of the revolutionary class. As Greenberg (1981:63) notes, such a conceptualization "displays scorn for the people so described...[and] may interfere with analysis rather than advance it."

Despite Marx's "scorn" for criminals, early radical criminologists took the reverse path and attributed revolutionary potential to criminal behavior: criminals were viewed as rebels of a sort. Such a claim may have been influenced by Engels's (1973:250–51) discussion of the nature of criminal behavior as primitive rebellion. Quinney (1980a:57–58), for example, argued that some criminals committed crimes of resistance. These were crimes of conscious political rebellion that could be engaged in by workers who smashed or sabotaged machinery as a reaction against alienating working conditions; or they could be the acts of political "terrorists" and reformers who acted outside the law to dismantle capitalist economic and social relationships.

Such a conceptualization of the criminal is currently widely rejected by radicals (Powell 1990:7; Schwartz 1989; Lea 1987; Young 1987; Matthews 1987; Beirne and Messerschmidt 1991:499; Michalowski 1990). The typical criminal is hardly a revolutionary, as Quinney also realized, and radicals must be careful not to "romanticize" the behavior of criminals (Balkan et al. 1980:79). The realization that most criminals were not revolutionaries gave rise to the idea that certain crimes were acts of accommodation that arose in response to the oppressive nature of life in capitalist societies (Quinney 1980a:54–55). These acts include predatory crimes such as robbery, burglary, assault, larceny, and even murder. Today, radical criminologists view crime as a response to life chances presented to different classes within capitalist societies (Groves and Frank 1987; Lynch and Groves 1989), thus avoiding the tendency to romanticize and politicize criminal behavior.

The debate over the nature of criminal behavior has, however, yet to be fully settled. While radical criminologists have attended to discussions of the revolutionary potential of criminal behavior, they have not sufficiently analyzed its other properties, such as class consciousness and rationality. Some radicals (Quinney 1980a; Greenberg 1981, 1977), have taken a position on rationality and crime by viewing crime as a rational response to conditions of life presented by capitalism. A minority (and admittedly ambiguous) opinion questions whether crime is a rational response for the working class (Lynch 1988a, 1988b). Still, the connection between class consciousness, rationality, and crime has not been as central to radical criminology as it has been for other radical enterprises (Lukacs 1985). Such a discussion is sorely lacking from the radical criminological literature. Having reviewed some of the major debates in this area, we turn to a consideration of the current state of radical theories of criminal behavior.

The Current State of Radical Theories of Crime

To begin, let us briefly define what we mean by radical criminology. This definition is suggestive and imprecise given the breadth of this area and the fact that radical criminology is constantly changing and emerging in new forms.

Radical criminologists analyze crime, criminal behavior, law, criminal justice mechanisms, the ideology of crime, law and justice, and public opinion on crime (i.e., crime-related phenomena) from a materialist perspective. To do so, they establish theoretical (and sometimes empirical) connections between historically specific economic conditions, class relations, the political context, and the crime-related phenomena noted above. The goal is to place crime-related phenomena within existing and definite social contexts that arise from material conditions of life and social organization.

A radical perspective on crime gives rise to ever-changing notions about crime since social life, class relationships, justice mechanisms, definitions of crime, and criminal motivations and opportunities vary historically. As the material structure of society changes, its responses to crime, laws, and the kinds and amount of crime that occur in society also change. Thus the theories that explain these phenomena must also change.

As a result, radical explanations of crime are historically situated macro-level or structural explanations that seek to explain trends in crime. Radical explanations of crime thus provide a sharp contrast to traditional theories of crime that attempt to explain why specific individuals commit crime. As Mills (1959) argued, however, structural explanations are incomplete unless they can be linked to the biography and troubles of real individuals. This, in a nutshell, is what radical criminology is about: explaining the causes, opportunities, and reactions to crime in a historically specific, materialist context that addresses the life chances of real people becoming victims of crime, or becoming or being labelled as criminals. To illustrate these concerns, let us review the basic elements of radical theories of crime and provide a few examples of how these concerns have been addressed. We restrict this discussion to capitalist society, since most radical research has focused on this society.

Basic Premises of Radical Criminology

Capitalism is characterized by a fundamental structural inequality between those who own and those who work the means of production. Consequently, society is stratified into social classes, each possessing different amounts of wealth, power, and status. These classes include the capitalist, bourgeoisie or owning class; the petty bourgeoisie, those who manage corporate, legal, and criminal justice systems; the working class, which constitutes the bulk of the population in capitalist societies; and marginal or surplus populations of underemployed, low-wage, and unemployed workers. The common assumption made by radical criminologists is that people in these classes face different life chances and opportunities for success and failure that has an impact on their chance of committing crime, being labelled as criminals, or being victims of crime (Lynch and Groves 1989:52–54). These basic assumptions have been used to investigate crime in a variety of ways.

Explaining Crimes of the Powerful

Radical criminologists use Marxian assumptions to investigate the types of crimes that the powerful, by virtue of their class position, have both the opportunity and the motivation to commit. Included in this list of crimes are white-collar, corporate, and governmental crimes. Edwin Sutherland, though not a radical, popularized the study of white-collar crime in the late 1930s. He argued that these crimes could be committed only by persons of high social status in the course of a legitimate occupation (Sutherland 1949). Radicals, such as Quinney (1980a), called these behaviors "crimes of domination and repression" to indicate that these acts are committed by the upper class to maintain their power and simultaneously exploit the rest of the population. Others, like Michalowski (1985:314), claim that these acts "arise from the ownership or management of capital or from occupancy of positions of trust in institutions designed to facilitate the accumulation of capital" and should be called "crimes of capital."

Regardless of how they label these acts, radicals argue that "crimes of the powerful" are socially injurious behaviors that cause more physical and financial harm than street or ordinary crimes (Reiman 1990; Nalla et al. 1989; Messerschmidt 1986; Kramer 1985; Michalowski 1985). Yet the general public fears street crime more than it fears crime by the powerful. This fear appears misplaced, since American citizens are more likely to die from work-related diseases and injuries that result from corporate violations of law than from street crime (Michalowski 1985; Reiman 1990; Frank and Lynch 1992). To put this claim in perspective, Messerschmidt (1986:100) argued that while homicides take a life every twenty-eight minutes, unsafe working conditions take a life every three minutes. And Michalowski (1985:325) concluded that work-related deaths from unsafe working conditions are six times more likely than homicide.

Reiman (1990) argues that our perceptions of crime and lack of suspicion of the upper class is created by the criminal justice system and the media—by the ideology of crime. The criminal justice system and the media focus on lower-class criminals who steal little and cause less physical harm than upper-class criminals. In doing so, they create a criminal stereotype and an ideology of crime that diverts our attention from the upper-class criminal (Reiman 1990). As a result of these ideological mechanisms and the power of those who engage in upper-class crime, the harmful activities of the powerful are not often treated as crimes by the legal or criminal justice system, nor are they perceived as crimes by the vast majority of the population. Radicals have done much to expose this bias that favors the rich and discriminates against the poor (Balkan et al. 1980; Box 1984; Chambliss 1984; Hagan and Parker 1985; Krisberg 1975; Pearce 1976).

Crimes of the powerful can be explained in various ways, the goal being to suggest how the economic and social context creates conditions conducive to committing these crimes. Most radical criminologists would agree that crimes of the powerful emerge for two reasons. First, capitalist societies place great stress on material success, the lesson being "more is always better." Consequently, even the well-to-do feel the need to have more. If they cannot achieve more legitimately, they can use their class position and occupational locations to access specific illegitimate opportunities. In short, the drive for success instilled in individuals by the structure of capitalist socialization creates the motivation for powerful individuals to engage in illegal activities, while their location in the class structure provides them the opportunity. Second, law and law enforcement are overwhelmingly focused on the crimes the lower class are most likely to commit. Thus the chance of an upper-class individual being caught, and if caught being punished for committing a corporate, white-collar, or governmental crime is greatly diminished (Reiman 1990).

For years, traditional criminologists, while acknowledging the need to study crimes of the powerful, criticized radicals for their preoccupation with these crimes and their neglect of ordinary or street crimes. Responding to these criticisms, radicals began to produce a number of explanations concerning ordinary crime during the 1980s.

Explaining Ordinary or Street Crimes

Radical explanations of street crime are similar to their explanations of the crimes of the powerful: Both result from structurally induced pressures to succeed, the inculcation of individualism, the severing of bonds to the social and economic order, and the criminal justice system's focus on lower-class behaviors (Lynch and Groves 1989:72–81). Some early radical criminologists carried this argument to its extreme and claimed that capitalism was a cause of crime (Quinney 1979; Gordon 1971, 1973). But it became clear that noncapitalist nations also experienced crime, even if to a lesser extent. Thus the question became: "What is it about the social and economic organization of capitalism that increases the crime rate?" Again, there are a variety of answers to this question.

Blau and Blau (1982) suggested that visible inequality in urban areas that arises in a highly class-stratified society undermines social cohesion, generating alienation and feelings of relative deprivation that contribute to rising rates of violent crime in American cities. Groves and Sampson (1987) make a similar claim when they argue that capitalism's structural imbalances destroy the ability of lower-class communities to satisfy human needs, bond individuals to the social order, and prevent crime through informal social control. This same argument is found in Spitzer's (1975) claim that a person's structural or class location affects his or her degree of commitment to the social system. All these analyses point out how macro-level structures impinge on and restrict the effectiveness of intermediary social forces that have a direct impact on the life chances and choices of people occupying different class locations.

Others (Colvin and Pauly 1983; Hagan et al. 1987, 1985, 1979; Singer and Levine 1988; Hill and Atkinson 1988) tie social structure to family socialization patterns through parents' workplace location. For Colvin and Pauly, parents' workplace experiences and location affect the type of discipline they employ in the home. Those parents whose jobs promote stability, consistent disciplinary routines, and attachment to work promote these same practices and values at home. Lower-class parents, however, are exposed to inconsistent coercive workplace controls, replicate these practices in the home, and produce children with an inconsistent value structure. This argument could also be extended to marginal or surplus populations. Having been cut off from full economic participation, marginal groups are not socialized into specific routines, experience unstable work relationships (or none at all), are more likely to come into contact with extremely repressive forms of social control (e.g., police, courts), and consequently may be more likely to reproduce inconsistent and very repressive or no social control over children.

Hagan et al. extend this argument to gender, arguing that gender-specific forms of social control vary with a family's social-class position and the role that both mothers and fathers play in the workplace (Hagan et al. 1987:791–92). Hagan et al.'s "power-control theory" states that in unbalanced (traditional) households, fathers have more authority than mothers as a result of their differential location in the economic sphere. In unbalanced households, mothers have less control over sons, providing sons with a greater chance to deviate than daughters, who are raised in the tight, traditional control of the mother. Balanced households, where both parents hold economic positions of relatively equal importance, generate equality in parental control, which diminishes differences in criminality between males and female children raised in these circumstances (for an excellent alternative argument related to gender and capitalism, see Messerschmidt 1986).

Other explanations of crime focus on the structural production of marginal populations and the effect marginality has on individuals who find themselves cut off from legitimate economic employment. These insights are drawn directly from Marx's (1974) discussion in *Capital* that describes how capitalist economic systems produce surplus populations of unemployable workers. The argument is as follows:

As a system of production, capitalism is based on the ability of the capitalist class to extract surplus value from the laboring class. To do so, capitalists rely on production techniques that intensify labor, such as mass production, labor specialization, and technology. These techniques reduce the amount of human labor needed to manufacture commodities and produce; with each increase in the use of these techniques, there is an ever-expanding marginal or surplus population of low-wage, part-time, and unemployable workers. Thus some radical criminologists argue that the economic structure of capitalism generates unemployed populations whose only rational alternative for survival is crime (Quinney 1979, 1980a; Greenberg 1977). Others (Spitzer 1975) suggest that powerless marginal populations, because they represent a threat to conventional order, are more likely to be the focus of formal social control and criminal labelling. In addition, it is likely that marginality reduces the commitment of marginalized workers to the conventional order and increases the likelihood that they will resort to crime (Spitzer 1975; Lynch 1988a). This position has been supported by empirical studies demonstrating a connection between unemployment and crime (Box 1987; Box and Hale 1983a, 1983b; see Chiricos 1987 for review; see Bohm 1985 for critique), and the rate of surplus value and crime (Lynch 1988a).

Recent Developments

One of the most recent developments in radical criminology, "left realism," appeared in England during the late 1980s and soon spread to Canada and Europe. "Realist criminology understands crime as a political process, historically located within a patriarchal society divided along the lines of race, class, and gender" (Currie 1990:4). The founders of this perspective (Young 1986, 1987, 1988; Lea 1987; Matthews 1987; Lea and Young 1986; Matthews and Young 1986), argue that crime results from relative deprivation experienced by the working class and leads to reactionary, selfish responses to disorganization in working-class communities. It is against this context that left realists seek to develop alternative crime-control strategies and evince a deep commitment to praxis and voicing the concerns of the working class with respect to crime.

Left realists claim to reject empiricism or positivism, yet much of their work is grounded in public opinion surveys of working-class concerns about crime. Left realism has been criticized as ahistorical (Michalowski 1990), a claim its supporters reject (Currie 1990). It also appears to be weakly grounded in a theory explaining how the material context affects public opinion. Left realism does contain the advantage of connecting social structure to individual concerns— another recent development in radical theory (see Groves and Lynch 1990; Mills 1958). There is currently much debate over left realism, and the issue of its importance has yet to be completely settled.

Other current trends include critical semiotics, postmodernism, and deconstruction (see Manning 1990, 1989; Milovanovic 1989, 1988, 1986; Hunt 1990; Thomas and O'Malchoatha 1989). These perspectives focus on critical analysis of communication and language in legal codes, regulations, and rules in relation to class, race, and gender biases (Manning 1989:7; Milovanovic 1988:125; Thomas 1988; Milovanovic and Thomas 1989). The idea is that any form of language, including legal language, is value laden and embedded with the same inequalities that appear in economic forms. Material concerns and inequalities thus structure and influence the content and actions of law (Milovanovic 1988:127–28). In a capitalist society, where all things are treated as commodities (Milovanovic 1981b), law, legal language, and skills are not evenly distributed but are distributed on the ability to pay for these forms of communication. In short, justice is for sale to the highest bidder (Lynch and Groves 1989:97–100). These are just a few of the simpler issues raised by postmodern radical theorists, and this brief discussion does not do this emerging perspective justice. We are sure to see much more postmodern, semiotic, and deconstructive radical criminology in the future (see Thomas and Malchoatha 1989; Schwartz 1989).

There are several other interesting trends which we do not have the space to review, such as socialist-feminist criminology (Cain 1989; Messerschmidt 1986), peacemaking criminology (Quinney 1980b, 1988, 1990), the focus on homeless crime and victimization (Barak 1990, 1991; Barak and Bohm 1989), the critical (Frankfurt School) orientation (Groves and Sampson 1986), and even "green criminology," a blend of radical criminology and the green environmental movement (Lynch 1990). These trends have revitalized the radical perspective and have made it the most rapidly growing and evolving area in criminology.

Conclusion

This brief review of radical criminology reveals only the tip of the iceberg; many areas escape this synopsis. We have tried to emphasize radicals' commitment to analyzing crime, law, and criminal justice in a material and contextual fashion that relates these issues to structured inequality and the problems real people face in their daily lives. Given this focus, most radicals argue that the way to remedy these ills is through actions that minimize or eliminate structured inequality (e.g., economic, sexual, or racial). We still have a long road to travel in our attempts to fulfill this mission. To do so requires that radical criminologists begin to build a political platform that reaches the people and affects their understanding of crime (Lynch 1990). To do less reduces radical criminology to academic rhetoric. A large portion of this challenge lies ahead, and it is up to future generations to take up the cause of combating injustice and inequality.

References

Akers, Ronald. 1979. "Theory and Ideology in Marxist Criminology: Comments on Turk, Quinney, Toby and Klockars." *Criminology* 16:527–43.
———. 1980. "Further Critical Thoughts on Marxist Criminology." In *Radical Criminology: The Coming Crisis*, ed. J. Inciardi. Beverly Hills: Sage.
Althusser, Louis, and E. Balibar. 1977. *Reading Capital*. Paris: Francois Maspero.
Balkan, Sheila, Ronald Berger, and Janet Schmidt. 1980. *Crime and Deviance in America*. Belmont, Calif.: Wadsworth.
Bankowski, Zenon, Geoff Mungham, and Peter Young. 1977. "Radical Criminology or Radical Criminologist?" *Contemporary Crises* 1(1):37–51.
Barak, Gregg. 1990. "The Violent Nature of Homelessness." *Critical Criminologist* 2(2):7–8, 11, 13.
———. 1991. *The Violence of Homelessness in America*. New York: Praeger.
Barak, Gregg, and Robert Bohm. 1989. "The Crimes of the Homeless or the Crime of Homelessness? On the Dialectics of Criminalization, Decriminalization and Victimization." *Contemporary Crises* 13(3):275–288.
Barlow, Hugh. 1990. *Criminology*. Boston: Little, Brown.
Beirne, Piers. 1979. "Empiricism and the Critique of Marxism on Law and Crime." *Social Problems* 26:373–85.
Beirne, Piers, and James Messerschmidt. 1991. *Criminology*. San Diego: Harcourt Brace Jovanovich.
Benton, Ted. 1983. "Positivism." In *A Dictionary of Marxist Thought*, ed. T. Bottomore et al. Cambridge: Harvard University Press.

Bernard, Thomas. 1981. "The Distinction between Conflict and Radical Criminology." *Journal of Criminal Law and Criminology* 72(1):362–79.

Blau, Judith, and Peter Blau. 1982. "The Cost of Inequality: Metropolitan Structure and Violent Crime." *American Sociological Review* 47:114–29.

Bohm, Robert. 1982. "Radical Criminology: An Explication." *Criminology* 19(4):565–89.

————. 1985. "Beyond Unemployment: Toward a Radical Solution to the Crime Problem." *Crime and Social Justice* 21–22:213–22.

Bonger, Willem. 1969 [1916]. *Criminality and Economic Conditions*. Boston: Little, Brown.

Box, Steven. 1984. *Power, Crime and Mystification*. London: Tavistock.

————. 1987. *Recession, Crime and Punishment*. Totowa, N.J.: Barnes and Noble.

Box, Steven, and Chris Hale. 1983a. "Liberation or Economic Marginalization: The Relevance of Two Theoretical Arguments to Female Crime Patterns in England and Wales 1951–1980." *Criminology* 22(4):473–97.

————. 1983b. "Liberation and Female Criminality in England and Wales Revisited." *British Journal of Criminology* 22:35–49.

Cain, Maureen. 1989. "New Directions in Feminist Criminology." *Critical Criminologist* 1(4):3–4.

Chambliss, William. 1964. "A Sociological Analysis of the Law of Vagrancy." *Social Problems* 12:67–77.

————. 1975. "Toward a Political Economy of Crime." *Theory and Society* 2(2):149–70.

————. 1984. "White Collar Crime and Criminology." *Contemporary Sociology* 13:160–62.

Chambliss, William, and Robert Seidman. 1982. *Law, Order and Power*. Reading, Mass.: Addison-Wesley.

Currie, Dawn. 1990. "Realist Criminology, Women and Social Transformation in Canada." *Critical Criminologist* 2(2):3–4, 12.

Domhoff, G. William. 1967. *Who Rules America?* Englewood Cliffs: Prentice-Hall.

————. 1970. *Higher Circles*. New York: Random House.

————. 1984. *Who Rules America Now?* Englewood Cliffs: Prentice-Hall.

Engels, Friedrich. 1964 [1844]. "Outlines of a Critique of Political Economy." In K. Marx, *The Economic and Philosophic Manuscripts of 1844* , ed. D.J. Struck. New York: International.

————. 1973 [1845]. *The Condition of the Working Class in England*. Moscow: Progress.

————. 1975 [1878]. *Anti-Duhring*. Moscow: Progress.

————. 1981. "The Demoralization of the English Working Class." In *Crime and Capitalism*, ed. D. Greenberg. Palo Alto, Calif.: Mayfield.

Friedrichs, David O. 1980. "Radical Criminology in the United States: An Interpretive Understanding." In *Radical Criminology: The Coming Crisis* , ed. J. Inciardi. Beverly Hills: Sage.

Gold, David C., C.Y.H. Lo, and Eric O. Wright. 1975a. "Recent Developments in Marxist Theories of the Capitalist State, Part I." *Monthly Review* 27(5):29–43.

————. 1975b. "Recent Developments in Marxist Theories of the Capitalist State, Part II." *Monthly Review* 27(6):36–51.

Gordon, David. 1971. "Class and the Economics of Crime." *Review of Radical Political Economy* 3(3):51–72.

————. 1973. "Capitalism, Class and Crime in America." *Crime and Delinquency* 19:163–86.

Greenberg, David, ed. 1981. *Crime and Capitalism*. Palo Alto, Calif.: Mayfield.

————. 1983. "Crime." Pp. 100–102 in *A Dictionary of Marxist Thought*, ed. T.B. Bottomore et al. Cambridge: Harvard University Press.

Groves, W. Byron. 1985. "Marxism and Positivism." *Crime and Social Justice* 23:129–50.

Groves, W. Byron, and Charles Corrado. 1983. "Culture as Metaphysics: An Appraisal of Cultural Models." *Crime and Social Justice* 20:99–120.

Groves, W. Byron, and Michael J. Lynch. 1990. "Reconciling Structural and Subjective Approaches to the Study of Crime." *Journal of Research in Crime and Delinquency* 27(4):348–75.

Groves, W. Byron, and Robert J. Sampson. 1986. "Critical Theory and Criminology." *Social Problems* 33(6):s58–s80.

———. 1987. "Traditional Contributions to Radical Criminology." *Journal of Research in Crime and Delinquency* 24(3):181–214.

Habermas, Jurgen. 1975. *Legitimation Crisis*. Boston: Beacon Press.

Hagan, John, and Celesta Albonette. 1982. "Race, Class and the Perception of Criminal Injustice in America." *American Journal of Sociology* 88:329–55.

Hagan, John, A.R. Gillis, and J. Sampson. 1979. "The Sexual Stratification of Social Control: A Gender Based Perspective on Crime and Delinquency." *British Journal of Criminology* 30:25–38.

———. 1985. "The Class Structure of Gender and Delinquency: Toward a Power-Control Theory of Common Delinquent Behavior." *American Journal of Sociology* 90(6):1151–78

———. 1987. "Class in the Household: A Power-Control Theory of Gender and Delinquency." *American Journal of Sociology* 92:788–816.

Hagan, John, and J. Leon. 1977. "Rediscovering Delinquency: Social History, Political Ideology and the Sociology of Law." *American Sociological Review* 42(4):457–598.

Hagan, John, and P. Parker. 1985. "White-Collar Crime and Punishment: The Class Structure and Legal Sanctioning." *American Sociological Review* 50(3):302–16.

Hill, G.D., and M.P. Atkinson. 1988. "Gender, Family Control and Delinquency." *Criminology* 26(1):127–47.

Hirst, Paul. 1972. "Marx and Engels on Law, Crime and Morality." *Economy and Society* 1:28–56.

———. 1975. "Marx and Engels on Law, Crime and Morality." In *The New Criminology*, ed. I. Taylor, P. Walton, and J. Young. London: Routledge and Kegan Paul.

———. 1977. "The Marxism of the New Criminology." *British Journal of Criminology* 13(4):396–98.

———. 1979. *On Law and Ideology*. Atlantic Fields, N.J.: Humanities Press.

———. 1983. "Marxist Criminology in the 1970s: Clarifying the Clutter." *Crime and Social Justice*, Summer, 65–74.

Horkheimer, Max. 1974 [1947]. *Eclipse of Reason*. New York: Seabury Press.

Hunt, Alan. 1990. "Postmodernism and Criminology." *Critical Criminologist* 2(1):617–18.

Klockars, Carl. 1979. "The Contemporary Crisis of Marxist Criminology." *Criminology* 16:477–515.

———. 1980. "The Contemporary Crisis of Marxist Criminology." In *Radical Criminology: The Coming Crisis*, ed. J. Inciardi. Beverly Hills: Sage.

Kramer, Ronald. 1984. "Corporate Crime: The Development of an Idea." In *Corporations as Criminals*, ed. E. Hochsteadler. Beverly Hills: Sage.

Kolko, Joyce, and Gabriel Kolko. 1972. *The Limits of Power*. New York: Harper & Row.

Lea, John. 1987. "Left-Realism: A Defence." *Contemporary Crises* 11:357–70.

Lea, John, and Jock Young. 1986. "A Realist Approach to Law and Order." In *The Political Economy of Crime: Readings for a Critical Criminology*, ed. B. MacLean. Englewood Cliffs: Prentice-Hall.

Lukacs, Georg. 1985. *History and Class Consciousness*. Cambridge: MIT Press.

Lynch, Michael J. 1987. "Quantitative Analysis and Marxist Criminology: Old Answers to a Dilemma in Marxist Criminology." *Crime and Social Justice* 29:110–27.

———. 1988a. "The Poverty of Historical Analysis in Criminology: A Review Essay." *Social Justice* 15(1):173–85.

———. 1988b. "Surplus Value, Crime and Punishment: A Preliminary Examination." *Contemporary Crises* 12:329–44.

———. 1990. "The Greening of Criminology: A Perspective on the 1990s." *Critical Criminologist* 2(3):3–4, 11–12.

Lynch, Michael J., and W. Byron Groves. 1989. *A Primer in Radical Criminology*, 2nd ed. New York: Harrow and Heston.

Manning, Peter. 1989. "Critical Semiotics." *Critical Criminologist* 1(4):7–8, 16, 18.

———. 1990. "Critical Semiotics: Part II." *Critical Criminologist* 2(1):5–6, 16.

Marcuse, Herbert. 1964. *One-Dimensional Man*. Boston: Beacon Press.

Marx, Karl. 1971 [1859]. "Population, Crime and Pauperism." In K. Marx and F. Engels, *Ireland and the Irish Question*. Moscow: Progress.

———. 1974 [1867]. *Capital*. Vol. I. New York: International.

Marx, Karl, and Frederick Engels. 1975. *On Britain*. Moscow: Progress.

Matthews, Roger. 1987. "Taking Realist Criminology Seriously." *Contemporary Crises* 11:371–401.

Matthews, Roger, and Jock Young, eds. 1986. *Confronting Crime*. Beverly Hills: Sage.

Meier, Robert F. 1976. "The New Criminology: Continuity in Criminological Theory." *Journal of Criminal Law and Criminology* 67:461–69.

Messerschmidt, James. 1986. *Patriarchy, Capitalism and Crime*. Totowa, N.J.: Rowman and Littlefield.

Michalowski, Ray. 1985. *Order, Law and Crime*. New York: Random House.

———. 1990. "Niggers, Welfare Scum, and Homeless Assholes: The Problems of Idealism, Consciousness and Context in Left-Realism." *Critical Criminologist* 2(3):5–6, 17–18.

Miliband, Ralph. 1969. *The State in Capitalist Society*. New York: Basic Books.

Milovanovic, Dragan. 1981a. "Ideology and Law: Structuralist and Instrumental Accounts of Law." *Insurgent Sociologist* 10(4):93–8.

———. 1981b. "The Commodity-Exchange Theory of Law: In Search of a Perspective." *Crime and Social Justice* 16:41–9.

———. 1984. "Autonomy of the Legal Order, Ideology and the Structure of Legal Thought." In *Humanistic Perspectives in Crime and Justice*, ed. M. Schwartz and D. Friedrichs. Hebron, Conn.: Practitioner Press.

———. 1986. "Juridicio-Linguistic Communicative Markets: Toward a Semiotic Analysis." *Contemporary Crises* 10:281–304.

———. 1988. *A Primer in the Sociology of Law*. New York: Harrow and Heston.

———. 1989. "Critical Criminology and The Challenge of Post-Modernism." *Critical Criminologist* 1(4):9–10, 17.

———. 1990. "Radical Criminology: A Descriptive Typology." *Critical Criminologist* 2(3):7–8, 18–19.

Milovanovic, Dragan, and Jim Thomas. 1989. "Overcoming the Absurd: Prisoner Litigation as Primitive Rebellion." *Social Problems* 36(1):48–60.

Mugford, S.K. 1974. "Marxism and Criminology: A Comment on the Symposium 'Review of the New Criminology.'" *Sociological Quarterly* 15:591–96.

Mungham, Geoffrey. 1980. "The Career of Confusion: Radical Criminology in Britain." In *Radical Criminology: The Coming Crisis*, ed. J. Inciardi. Beverly Hills: Sage.

Nalla, Mahesh, Michael J. Lynch, and Graeme R. Newman. 1989. "Crime in the U.S.: From the Streets to the Suites." *Justice Profession* 4(2):223–56.

Nettler, Gwynn. 1978. *Explaining Crime*. New York: McGraw-Hill.

O'Connor, James. 1973. *The Fiscal Crisis of the State*. New York: St. Martin's.

O'Malley, Pat. 1988. "The Purpose of Knowledge: Pragmatism and the Praxis of Marxist Criminology." *Contemporary Crises* 12:65–79.

Pearce, F. 1976. *Crimes of the Powerful: Marxism, Crime, and Deviance*. London: Pluto Press.

Phillips, Paul. 1980. *Marx and Engels on Law and Laws*. New York: Barnes and Noble.

Platt, Anthony. 1971. *The Politics of the Riot Commission*. New York: Macmillan.

———. 1974. "Street Crime: A View from the Left." *Crime and Social Justice* 9:26–34.

———. 1978. "Prospects for a Radical Criminology in the U.S." *Crime and Social Justice* 1:2–10.

Powell, Chris. 1990. "Left-Realism: Neither Left nor a Contender." *Critical Criminologist* 2(1):7.

Poulantzas, Nicos. 1973. *Political Power and Social Classes*. New York: Schocken.

Quetelet, Adolphe. 1984 [1831]. *Research on the Propensity for Crime at Different Ages*. Cincinnati: Anderson.

Quinney, Richard. 1970. *The Social Reality of Crime*. Boston: Little, Brown.

———. 1971. "National Commission on the Causes and Prevention of Violence: Reports." *American Sociological Review* 36:724–27.

———. 1979. *Criminology*. Boston: Little, Brown.

———. 1980a. *Class, State and Crime*. New York: Longman.

———. 1980b. *Providence*. New York: Longman.

———. 1988. "Crime, Suffering, Service: Toward a Criminology of Peacemaking." *The Quest*, Winter, 66–75.

———. 1990. "Oneness of All: The Mystical Nature of Humanism." *Critical Criminologist* 2(3):1–2, 11.

Reiman, Jeffrey. 1990. *The Rich Get Richer and the Poor Get Prison*. 3rd ed. New York: Macmillan.

Schwartz, Marty. 1989. "U.S. as Compared to British Left-Realism." *Critical Criminologist* 2(2):5–6, 12.

Siegel, Larry. 1989. *Criminology*. New York: West.

Shichor, David. 1980. "The New Criminology: Some Critical Issues." *British Journal of Criminology* 20(1):1–19.

Singer, S., and M. Levinve. 1988. "Power-Control Theory, Gender and Delinquency: A Partial Replication with Additional Evidence on the Effects of Peers." *Criminology* 26(4):627–48.

Sparks, Richard. 1980. "A Critique of Marxist Criminology." In *Crime and Justice: An Annual Review of Research*, ed. N. Morris and M. Tonry. Chicago: University of Chicago Press.

Spitzer, Steven. 1975. "Toward a Marxian Theory of Deviance." *Social Problems* 22:638–51.

———. 1980. "Left-Wing Criminology—An Infantile Disorder?" In *Radical Criminology: The Coming Crisis*, ed. J. Inciardi. Beverly Hills: Sage.

Sutherland, Edwin H. 1949. *White-Collar Crime*. New York: Holt, Rinehart and Winston.

Sweezy, Paul. 1942. *The Theory of Capitalist Development*. New York: Monthly Review Press.

Taylor, Ian, Paul Walton, and Jock Young. 1973. *The New Criminology*. New York: Harper & Row.

———, eds. 1975. *Critical Criminology*. London: Routledge and Kegan Paul.

Thomas, Jim. 1988. *Prisoner Litigation: The Paradox of the Jailhouse Lawyer*. Totowa, N.J.: Allen and Littlefield.

Thomas, Jim, and Aogan O'Malchatha. 1989. "Reassessing the Critical Metaphor: An Optimistic Revisionism View." *Justice Quarterly* 6:143–72.

Turk, Austin. 1979. "Analyzing Official Deviance: For a Non-Partisan Conflict Analysis in Criminology." *Criminology* 16(3):459–76.

Vold, George, and Thomas Bernard. 1986. *Theoretical Criminology*. New York: Oxford University Press.

Wolfe, Alan. 1977. *The Limits of Legitimacy: The Political Contradictions of Contemporary Capitalism*. New York: Free Press.

Young, Jock. 1987. "The Task Facing a Realist Criminology." *Contemporary Crises* 11:337–56.

———. 1988. *Realist Criminology*. Beverly Hills: Sage.

———. 1986. "The Failure of Criminology: The Need for Radical Realism." In *Confronting Crime*, ed. R. Matthews and J. Young. Beverly Hills: Sage.

URBAN AND REGIONAL SOCIOLOGY:

VIEWS OF THE CITY:
URBAN AND REGIONAL SOCIOLOGY

Nancy Kleniewski

The questions and concerns of urban sociology arose from the same source that spawned sociology. Both were responses to the Industrial Revolution, which was accompanied by massive urbanization and social change. The upheavals that occurred in Europe during the late eighteenth and early nineteenth centuries prompted Marx, Weber, Durkheim, and other classical sociologists to examine the consequences of the social, economic, and political changes that characterized their times. The growth of cities, the relationship of cities and towns to rural areas, the migration of people moving from farm work to factory work, the changing relationships of social classes to one another, and the nature of life in urban settings were some of the important questions they examined. These concerns still influence contemporary urban research, although some of the specific characteristics of cities have changed over the years.

In contemporary cities, even those that are "booming" economically, we observe the movement of middle-class families to the suburbs, the loss of jobs from central cities, growing urban concentrations of poor people and racial minorities, and high crime rates. At the same time, city governments are increasingly unable to respond to the requirements of urban life by providing adequate schools, housing, sanitation, recreational facilities, transportation, and police protection for their residents. Although cities are increasingly intertwined with the regions around them and even with cities in different parts of the world, political boundaries (especially in cities of the United States) separate communities from one another and discourage cooperation.

For at least a century, analysts have asked questions about why cities are the way they are, why one city is different from another, and what people can do to shape urban life. Many disciplines other than sociology have contributed to the study of cities and regions, including history, geography, planning, economics, political science, and social work. Thus, the "urban sociology" we are discussing in this chapter is really interdisciplinary, with a somewhat heavier emphasis on writers who call themselves "sociologists" than on those who identify as members of other disciplines. As for the "Marxist" part of the project, we examine the work of some people who explicitly consider themselves to be

277

Marxist scholars and some who do not. The authors have been selected because of their contributions to furthering the dialogue on the important urban questions, regardless of the number of times they use Marxist terminology or refer to Marx's works in their writing. The writers we consider to be in "the spirit of Marx" analyze the effects of capitalism on people and cities, even though they may have derived their analysis from Weber (or from other theorists) as well as from Marx.

Unfortunately, Marx gave us very little basis in his writings for studying urban structure or urban social patterns. Aside from a brief discussion of the division of labor between town and country in *The German Ideology* (Marx and Engels 1977), he made no systematic statements on the nature of cities. Since his time, however, many urbanists have applied his more general economic and social concepts in their work. Some of the most important of Marx's concepts that have been used in urban analysis are the distinction between use and exchange value, the falling rate of profit, the theory of rent, the different circuits of capital, exploitation in the class structure, and the contradictions produced by the capitalist system.

The work of Engels, particularly *The Condition of the Working Class in England*, but also to a lesser degree *The Housing Question*, provides a more direct application of Marxist theory to urban issues than does the work of Marx. Engels's vivid descriptions of Manchester and the other "great towns" of industrial Britain provide both a critique of the social conditions brought about by class exploitation and an analysis of the geographic patterns of capitalist industrial cities. Engels describes the workers' housing conditions, the rudimentary city planning of his time, and the ineffectiveness of the authorities' attempts to protect public health and safety. He points out the spatial arrangements by which the bourgeoisie dominates desirable locations on the main streets, while the workers are confined to the smaller, meaner, and virtually invisible back streets. In short, Engels shows how the growth, layout, and social relations of the city are all shaped by the process of production.

Few urban social scientists followed up on the works of Marx and Engels immediately. In fact, it took over a century (well into the 1970s) for an explicitly Marxist urban studies to appear in the university. During the interim, however, a number of radicals, urban critics, social workers, and political figures wrote, spoke, and acted in ways that contributed to our understanding of urban phenomena. Although they were not always accepted by the social scientists of their times, these "ancestors" of Marxist urban sociology laid important groundwork for the researchers who followed them.

Ancestors of Marxist Urban Sociology

One of the most famous ancestors was Henry George, author of *Progress and Poverty* (1938). George thought that urban poverty was caused by the operation of the urban land market. He argued that property owners acted as speculators, driving up land prices and in effect controlling the lives of propertyless working people. He was critical not only of the gap between the rich and the poor but also of the obvious maldistribution of good and bad physical locations in cities. George's policy solution was to eliminate all income taxes, which mainly tax people's labor, and institute only a single tax—on land. By shifting taxes away from labor and onto land (minus the value of its improvements), he thought that the unjustified rewards of landownership would be done away with and that the widening gap between the rich and the poor would be narrowed.

Although Henry George's analysis was not incorporated into academic theories, it proved to be enormously popular with the general public, both in the United States and abroad. The "single tax" proposal became the center of a social movement aligned with organized labor and antimonopoly groups. George's times, the 1880s, were a turbulent period in which the struggles between labor and capital frequently erupted into pitched battles in the streets. Radical and reformist movements for social change gained great influence among the voting public. Socialists and single-taxers were elected mayors of several large cities; Henry George himself came in second in a New York City mayoral race, defeating Theodore Roosevelt (Edel 1977).

From Victorian England came another important source of social thought on cities. Novelists such as Charles Dickens had already begun describing the inequalities and frightful conditions of Victorian cities. By the end of the nineteenth century, a group of social reformers set about to document urban poverty in a more scientific and policy-oriented way than the earlier fictional presentations. Led by Charles Booth, these Victorian social critics conducted surveys of urban areas, mapping out in exact detail the conditions in different districts and using their survey findings to make recommendations for public policy on housing, public sanitation, and education. They were very influential both as researchers on social conditions and as advocates for change. Over thirty years, most of the reforms they proposed were enacted, and Booth's survey methodology became well established among social researchers (Glass 1968).

The survey work of Booth and his colleagues had an impact on urban research in the United States through Booth's follower Jane Addams. Addams had become acquainted with the realities of slum life in London while traveling in Europe after her college graduation. She learned about Booth's social survey methodology and also about the settlement house movement (the latter led by Christian Socialists, then a prominent group in England). When Addams returned to the United States, she founded Hull House in Chicago as a settlement house and trained social workers to do surveys of the Chicago slums, following Booth's pattern.

Although her work was derived from socialist movements in England, Addams publicly disavowed belief in any "social faith," including socialism and the single-tax movement. She feared that in the increasingly conservative 1920s, progressive social change could too easily be derailed by opponents charging that the changes were "too radical." In *The Second Twenty Years at Hull House*, Addams (1930:154) complained that the political atmosphere had changed so dramatically after World War I (with its attendant "Red Scare" after the Russian Revolution) that "to advance new ideas was to be a radical, or even a bolshevik." This conservative political atmosphere, she thought, prevented social workers in the United States from pushing for social reform as strongly as they did in Europe.

Addams's work had an important, though generally unacknowledged influence on the fledgling field of urban sociology. Her Hull House surveys of Chicago slums provided a model for the field surveys of the pioneer urban sociologists at the University of Chicago. One reason that Addams's work is not more widely known among sociologists is that the disciplines of sociology and social work were becoming more distinct in the United States, while in England they were much more closely intertwined. Observers have commented that as sociology became an established discipline in universities, sociologists distanced themselves from their roots in feminism, populism, and social work. To become more respectable, sociology had to become more scientific, and to become more scientific, it had to avoid the appearance of intervening in social problems. Thus sociologists increasingly derided "uplift" of the poor, defining it as a moral endeavor, to be avoided in the attempt to retain "scientific objectivity" (Deegan 1988; Lee 1988).

Some early sociologists nevertheless used the social survey as a scientific methodology in urban areas of the United States. One was W.E.B. Du Bois. Through his training, at Harvard and in Europe, he had been prepared for an empirical study of social inequalities (Baltzell 1967). As a young assistant professor, Du Bois studied the most concentrated area of black settlement in Philadelphia, the Seventh Ward, and published his findings as The *Philadelphia Negro: A Social Study* (1967). His work included detailed mapping of the social, economic, religious, and political characteristics of the black population of the Seventh Ward, showing the spatial relationships between the races. While whites and blacks lived in close physical proximity, whites tended to occupy the larger houses on the "front" streets, while the vast majority of the blacks were confined to poorly constructed alley, or "back street," housing, often with entire families occupying one room.

Du Bois also addressed the causes of black poverty and its relationship to other social inequalities, concluding that the "kernel of the Negro problem...[was] the narrow opportunities afforded Negroes to earn a decent living" because of racial discrimination by the white population (1967:394). An important contribution that he made to the sociological literature was to raise the question that we now know as "race versus class." Du Bois was careful to point out the existence of class divisions within the black population, contradicting the widespread belief among whites that blacks constituted a homogeneous mass of equally poor individuals. He also pointed out the economic progress that whites from "inferior" backgrounds had made over the years, rising above their hereditary lower-class standing. In drawing attention to the class-based nature of the status of poor blacks and their possibilities for rising into the middle class, he was implicitly arguing against the hereditarian view of black inequality previously advanced by some leading sociologists. Du Bois, however, clearly did not think that "the Negro problem" was simply a problem of class standing and economic exploitation. He identified racial discrimination and prejudice of the white population as a major source of the problem, noting that many whites were actively opposed to the meager progress blacks had made since the Civil War.

By the 1920s and 1930s, the framework for urban and community studies in the United States was being set. The University of Chicago in the 1920s had produced the most active and influential sociology department in the country, and its specialty was urban sociology. While urban sociology in England meant for the most part the study of urban poverty, in the United States it increasingly meant the search for laws supposedly governing urban life and behavior. The so-called Chicago School, which soon became the mainstream of American urban research, used a natural science approach for the study of the city. Calling themselves "human ecologists," the urban researchers self-consciously modeled their methods on botanical studies of plant ecology, looking for regularities and natural laws governing human behavior. Social scientists such as Robert Park, Ernest Burgess, and R.D. McKenzie (1925) at first mapped out "natural areas" of cities (e.g., "gold coasts," "vice areas," and "slums") and then tried to show geographic relationships and regularities among the different areas. The early focus was on the physical structure of the city and its relationship to the social groups living there. Later, human ecologists made the argument that all of social behavior was derived from the natural or subsocial relationships that tied human populations to territory the way that plants were tied to the land.

Human ecologists were materialists in the sense that they thought that the material basis of life—territory, living space, and so on—influenced the other social levels, the "moral order" as they called it, of norms and social interaction. But, despite some similarities with the work of Engels, they never referenced his work. Instead, Emile Durkheim and Georg Simmel (and, to a lesser extent, Max Weber) were their inspirations. As the subdiscipline of urban sociology grew, human ecology became the dominant approach, and (as we later see) the critique of its limitations became an important starting point for the development of a more radical or Marxist approach.

While the human ecologists were studying the physical form and the distribution of social areas of the city, other sociologists turned to the study of social-class patterns in communities. These works, which today we call "community" studies, had more of a radical overtone than the research of the human ecologists. Probably the most famous of these was *Middletown* by Robert and Helen Lynd, a study of Muncie, Indiana, in the 1920s. The Lynds had gone to Muncie to study the role of religion in the community, but they soon found that the most important fact of social life in the town was the division between social classes, including pervasive class conflict. The Lynds restudied Muncie ten years later to see the effects of the Great Depression on the town and published their sequel as *Middletown in Transition.* In the 1930s, they found that social-class divisions were even more dominant but that, as in the 1920s, people of the community were reluctant to speak openly of the class divisions they implicitly recognized. While the ideological consensus of the town was that "business and labor are partners," the business class was critical of the working class and did all in its power to prevent union organizing (Lynd and Lynd 1937). Besides its analysis of the class structure of a community, the most important contribution of the *Middletown* research was to document the impact that economic changes could have on the overall shape of community life, including work, politics, religion, education, and family life.

During the 1920s and 1930s, as sociologists studied the impacts that industrialization, the depression, and urbanization were having on city life, city planners were beginning to investigate ways of managing those impacts. The field of planning was a hybrid, applying not only social science but also art, architecture, and engineering to urban life. Planners, like urban sociologists, investigated the interplay between the layout of physical spaces and human social interaction. Unlike sociologists, however, they were often connected to government bodies that made decisions about how cities would be structured. That is, planners were more closely tied to the policy-making process than were sociologists. This gave them the ability to influence policy but also often constrained them, restricting the range of proposed policies to those that were politically acceptable. Some planners, reacting to these political constraints, became more visionary, acting as social critics rather than nuts-and-bolts implementers of policy.

One of the most important visionary planners was Lewis Mumford, who wrote extensively on urban life and form between the 1920s and the 1960s. Mumford drew on British and American sociology, architecture, and planning literature to examine the history and nature of city life. In his landmark volume *The Culture of Cities,* (1970), Mumford began with the classic question of the impact of industrialization and urbanization on social life. Unlike most other urbanists, however, he pushed beyond that initial question to the more funda-mental (from a Marxist point of view) question of the impact of capitalism on social life and urban patterns.

Mumford perceived that the "machine age" of industrial growth had already passed its peak by the 1930s, and he foresaw that the industrial cities were on the verge of decline. His solution to the problems of the industrial cities lay in creating smaller, more human-scale communities in which people would live with, rather than against, nature. In addition to his critique of industrialism, Mumford strongly opposed many aspects of capitalism. He criticized capitalism's tendency to encourage every individual to think only of accumulating for himself or herself. He decried capitalist exploitation of people and natural resources. He criticized private property for its tendency to separate people from one another and to foster competitiveness. In contrast, Lewis Mumford proposed ideas for communities in which people could feel connected to others, rather than separated in their individual spheres, for example, through public and cooperative ownership of housing and retail shops. Mumford did not limit his critique of urban life to capitalism; instead, he saw inhumane mechanization and bureaucracy as problems of all industrial societies.

One additional influence on Marxist urban sociology was the work of the community power researchers, best exemplified by Floyd Hunter's *Community Power Structure* (1953). After World War II, government at all levels in Europe and the United States was beginning to intervene in urban problems, from building highways to rebuilding the cities destroyed by war (as in Europe) or by a lack of investment capital (as in the United States). Hunter, in a variation of the classic community study, interviewed business and civic leaders in Atlanta to determine who had influence on the many policy issues facing the city. The information he received from his informants provided the basis for mapping the structure of power in Atlanta. Hunter argued that power was a function not only of particular individuals' influence but also of ongoing relationships among organizations in the community. He showed that the issues of most concern to the leaders of the business community inevitably dominated the policy agenda of the city government.

The Emergence of Marxist Urban Sociology

A truly Marxist urban sociology began to emerge gradually in the 1960s from a shared sense among urbanists that the intractability of urban problems revealed a lack of theoretical understanding of basic urban social, economic, and political phenomena. In searching for a more systematic explanation of the connections between urban problems and other societal patterns, social scientists in Europe and the United States eventually turned to Marx and Engels. Two sources prompted the search for new answers to the urban questions: (1) the appearance of new and ever greater urban crises; (2) social scientists' frustration at the limits of human ecology. We briefly examine each of these and then show how they affected the emergence of Marxist urban sociology in France, Britain, and the United States.

Changes in international economic structures after World War II had major impacts on cities in the United States and Europe. By the 1960s, massive demographic changes were under way, with the growth of communities of nonwhite people in major cities in the United States, Great Britain, and France. Racial differences overlay and combined with social-class differences to create complex patterns of urban social divisions. At the same time, political institutions were changing. New social movements were emerging in many localities, challenging existing relationships of power. In the United States, the civil rights movement, neighborhood and workplace organizing, and the anti-Vietnam war movement tied into the themes of political participation and empowerment for ordinary people. Ghetto race riots were a more chaotic but still related response to the same problems. In France, the domestic political upheavals of 1968 and negative reactions to the Algerian war politicized the society and forged connections between student intellectuals and manual workers, who united under radical slogans for change.

Government actions to try to solve urban problems often seemed more like part of the problem than true solutions. An example of a policy that many critics questioned was urban renewal. In the United States and France (and, later, Britain) government agencies were created to rebuild parts of cities that had deteriorated because of a lack of private capital investment in urban areas. One result of these programs was that in the attempt to eliminate slums, much low-cost housing was destroyed and its residents displaced from their neighborhoods. After a while, residents of urban-renewal areas began to resist these programs by rioting, refusing to move, and other disruptive means, causing additional problems for local governments. Another example of failed urban policy was regional planning to shut down "nonviable" towns and neighborhoods. In Britain, many older industrial and mining towns had lost their employment bases as a result of the movement of industry to other areas (a process known as *capital mobility*). The British government responded to this problem by empowering planning agencies to indicate which towns should grow and which ones should shrink. Some urban planners in the United States similarly argued that the less prosperous and less populated sections of the major cities should be emptied out. In both countries, these policies of "planned shrinkage" prompted political resistance from the residents of the areas planned to shrink.

In the light of these increasingly severe urban problems, many social scientists were disappointed by the failure of their research tools to allow them to address problems seriously. Urban sociologists were struggling toward a replacement for the theory of human ecology, whose adequacy had been questioned for decades (see, for example, the critiques by Alihan 1938; Firey 1945; Form 1954; Abu-Lughod 1968; Wilhelm 1973). They saw that the human ecology approach had supported policies that created more problems, such as the unplanned and uncontrolled growth of the suburbs. The urban crisis of the 1960s provided a new research agenda of questions to answer, and many sociologists began to explore Marxist theory as a framework within which to address them.

Urbanists joined their colleagues in other disciplinary areas who had begun to discuss more radical directions for their work. The late 1960s saw the emergence of a sustained body of Marxist scholarship in the United States, building on a tradition established somewhat earlier in Europe. As a result, several explicitly Marxist or radical journals were founded in the 1960s, including *New Left Review* (1960), *Review of Radical Political Economics* (1968), and *Antipode* (1969). Within the next decade, new journals devoted to urban studies in a Marxist (or critical) perspective were founded, including *Comparative Urban Research* (1975) and the *International Journal of Urban and Regional Research* (1976).

It is a tribute to the comparative and international nature of Marxist urban studies that its two most important early statements published in the United States were written by Europeans. The first was David Harvey's *Social Justice and the City* (1973), and the second was Manuel Castells's *The Urban Question* (1977). While the books are very different, both include as a main point of departure a critique of traditional approaches to urban social science.

Social Justice and the City is a deliberate attempt to initiate a scientific revolution in thought on urban issues. Harvey, an English geographer, reframes the classic questions of urban research, such as the locations of different land uses and social-classes' residences, by using Marx's concepts. He questions the assumptions that guided urbanists for a century, such as the "fact" that ghettos are the result of competitive bidding for land and thus are unavoidable. Harvey points out that the simplest way to solve the problem of ghetto formation is to make its assumptions untrue, that is, to eliminate competitive bidding for land by establishing social control over both land allocation and the housing market. He goes on to point out that older housing, which does not command a very high price on the market (has little *exchange value*), is still habitable (has *use value*). In a capitalist land market, however, owners would write it off as useless, not because people cannot live in it, but because it is not profitable to rent out (1973:137–38). Thus it becomes useless, and a slum is created. For the most part, Harvey discusses patterns familiar to traditional urban social scientists, but he reinterprets them. He argues that current patterns are not inevitable laws; instead, they are the result of the current social and economic arrangements, in this case, the capitalist housing market.

The Urban Question by Manuel Castells was published in France in 1972 but was not translated for English-speaking readers until 1977. When Harvey wrote *Social Justice and the City*, he did not even know of it, although the two books contain some striking similarities. Castells criticizes the analysis of traditional urban sociologists because they take for granted rather, than question, the structure of the economy underlying the patterns of urban areas. Castells argues that what urbanists are really studying is not "the city" but the urban aspect of industrial capitalism. He thus examines the urban crisis in the United States as a crisis of a particular form of urban structure important for a number of elements of capitalism:*capital accumulation* (profit-making), the organization of *social consumption* (providing for collective social needs such as education and transportation of the working population), and *social reproduction* (providing opportunities for individual needs of the working population, such as housing). Castells argues that the postwar city was produced in its particular form by the needs of capital but that it then created certain *contradictions* that presented further problems for capital. An example he gives is that urban-renewal programs were implemented to "save" central cities, yet they disrupted poor and minority communities, causing them to riot, and creating more problems for authorities (1977:393–95).

The first indigenous American statement of a Marxist urban studies came from a conference of urbanists associated with the Union for Radical Political Economics (URPE). Edited by William K. Tabb and Larry Sawers, the book resulting from the conference was titled *Marxism and the Metropolis* (1978). Although the theoretical perspectives of the authors range from Marxist to mildly liberal, the one thing they all share is a critique of the traditional approaches to the field. The editors note that Engels had done a better job of describing and explaining features of cities such as spatial distributions of classes and the impact of urban-renewal programs than had human ecologists writing fifty years later. Tabb and Sawers argue that mainstream economic analysts attribute the urban crisis to the way economic markets operate, which in turn is ultimately determined by consumers' preferences and choices. The policy implication of such analysis is either *laissez-faire* (i.e., no government action at all) or limited and isolated programs to solve specific problems that the market cannot address. Marxist analysts, in contrast, assume that since problems are a result of the economic system itself, fundamental changes to the economic system are necessary to solve them.

The main focus of the Marxist urbanists was and continues to be the analysis of the contradictions of capitalism as they are manifested in cities. Speaking of one branch of Marxist urban sociology (Althusserian structuralism), sociologist Ivan Szelenyi commented that it

offered a macrosociological perspective for urban sociological research, and guaranteed that urban sociology addressed itself to some of the central questions of sociological theory in the last decade (the theory of the state, class analysis, the problems of fiscal and legitimation crisis, the analysis of social movements, black and women's liberation, dependency and world system theory, etc.). (Szelenyi 1981:1)

While the Marxist urbanists have agreed broadly on their critique of traditional urban methods of analysis and their focus on the contradictions of capitalism, they have debated many other specific points about urban theory. If all of urban sociology could be reduced to a single question, *"What makes cities the way they are,"* then Marxist urbanists might be grouped into one of three categories, depending on how much attention they pay to each of three factors: *(1) the mode of production, (2) class conflict, and (3) the state.* Within each of the "answers" to the question are different positions that urbanists have taken. We briefly survey the main positions and summarize the most prominent debates within each one (for other overviews and interpretations, see Zukin 1980; Lebas 1982; Procter 1982; Jaret 1983; Gottdiener,1985).

One approach to analyzing cities from a Marxist point of view has emphasized the particular *mode of production* within which the city is located. Larry Sawers (1975), for example, argues that the form of cities in the United States in the twentieth century is a reflection of the prevailing mode of production: advanced industrial capitalism. He shows how the growth of suburbs and the creation of the metropolis (as opposed to the single town or city) can be attributed to features of monopoly capitalism, such as the growth of the auto industry and its preemption of mass transit, the movement of firms to the suburbs to make higher profits, and the high degree of inequality among households creating a highly segmented housing market. In contrast, Sawers argues, cities in socialist modes of production (e.g., the USSR, Cuba, and China) have attempted to avoid the overgrowth of metropolitan areas and the separation between town and country that Marx said were products of capitalism. In order to prevent that separation, according to Sawers, socialist planners have stressed decentralization of industry in small "new towns," limitations on migration into the large cities, and improving the standard of living in rural areas. The assumption that a socialist mode of production produces different settlements than those produced by capitalist modes of production has been questioned by other authors, including Castells (1977) and Szelenyi (1978).

Even within the capitalist mode of production, evolutionary changes in the economy affect urban form. Building on the work of Piore and Sabel (1984), A.J. Scott (1988) shows how industrial capitalism has changed in the past thirty years, and how that change has affected cities. Within a mode of production such as capitalism, different strategies for making profits, called *regimes of accumulation,* can exist. In the early part of the twentieth century, the dominant regime of accumulation was characterized by large enterprises that mass-produced durable goods in rationally organized workplaces and paid high wages to a stable workforce. Today we call this regime "Fordism" after the company that made it an international symbol. Since the 1950s, however, the Fordist regime has been gradually replaced by a new form (variously called "Post-Fordist" or "the regime of flexible production"), one characterized by smaller enterprises producing many different kinds of products with a less stable workforce. The new regime's most important characteristic is *flexible production,* meaning that machinery can be adapted to produce different products from one day or even hour to the next. The shift from Fordism to flexible production has had a major impact on communities in the industrialized countries. While Fordism brought with it the development of huge firms in concentrated industrial regions (the Great Lakes area of the United States and the Ruhr of Germany), flexible production has spurred the development of small firms in generally nonindustrialized areas such as inner cities, rural farming communities, and small towns outside the established industrial belts. Thus the urban growth and decline configurations are being changed in major industrial countries, especially Italy, but also the United States, Great Britain, and France. Urbanists are currently debating whether these changes are positive or negative and whether cities and regions can do anything to shape the process of industrial transformation (see, e.g., Logan and Swanstrom 1990).

Another way of looking at the impact of the mode of production on cities is through the needs of capitalists to make profits on their investments, the so-called accumulation function. David Harvey (1978) analyzes urban processes as the result of different possibilities for capital investment. Those investments directly related to producing products (e.g., machines) are part of the *primary circuit of capital*. Other kinds of investments including buildings, roads, and so on, that are only indirectly related to producing products (the "material infrastructure" of capitalism, the bulk of which is located in cities) form the *secondary circuit*. Harvey points out that there is a tendency toward *overaccumulation* in the primary circuit when too many investors invest their capital at the same time, causing profits to fall. At such times, investors are likely to redirect their capital into the secondary circuit, adding to the "built environment" rather than to machinery and equipment.

While such investments are necessary to production, they also place limits on future profit making (when, for example, certain factories, offices, etc., become outmoded). Harvey argues that capitalists resolve this contradiction by systematically destroying the value of the past investments they have made (e.g., by abandoning a building and writing it off on the company's books). He says there is "a perpetual struggle in which capital builds a physical landscape appropriate to its own condition at a particular moment in time, only to have to destroy it, usually in the course of a crisis, at a subsequent point in time" (1978:122). Thus, deterioration of property is not a simple "problem" of modern cities but is part of the very nature of the investment process within a capitalist mode of production. Several theorists, including Francois Lamarche (1976), have analyzed the role of an identifiable fraction of capital, namely, property capitalists, in reshaping urban areas by producing and managing the built environment for other capitalists.

The second general approach to why cities are the way they are is that they are shaped by *class conflict*. David Gordon (1977), for example, has analyzed the different community structures found in the United States during different historical periods as responses by capitalists to their employees' struggles to organize. He argues that employers began to move plants away from the centers of towns in the late nineteenth century partly to remove manual workers from the political support during labor disputes they would have had from their neighbors, who were members of other social classes. Gordon sees a contradiction in this action. By moving industrial workers to their own isolated neighborhoods, capitalists inadvertently strengthen the internal solidarity of their workers and provide the conditions for more successful strikes. In recent times, manufacturers have tended to move their plants from industrial cities to rural areas and to the Sunbelt, where workers are more dispersed and easier to control.

A great deal of the analysis of class conflict and the city revolves not around the direct struggles involved in production (i.e., workplace issues) but in the indirect class conflict involved in the sphere of *reproduction* (i.e., the distribution of housing, education, and other goods necessary to reproduce the workforce). Manuel Castells (1977, 1972) began this kind of analysis by examining social movements outside the workplace as an aspect of class conflict. He identifies neighborhood issues as struggles over *collective consumption*, that is, the goods and services that workers receive from local government. Although capitalists need to have the labor force reproduced, they are reluctant to pay for it in higher wages. Collective consumption is thus actually a wage "paid" to workers indirectly by their local government, rather than directly by their employer. In contemporary urban areas, although residents have many different employers, they can unite and form social movements around the neighborhood issues they have in common. Castells argues that local political struggles about seemingly isolated issues are actually a form of class conflict played out in the community, rather than the workplace.

So far, we have looked at the first two sets of answers to the question "What makes cities the way they are?" These have concentrated on the capitalist mode of production and on class conflict. Theorists concentrating on these two explanations for urban form can be grouped together as exponents of *political economy*, a framework that, in crude terms, stresses the needs of capital, the needs of labor, and their interplay in affecting the outcome of specific historical events. While there is a consensus among Marxist urbanists that capital's needs help shape cities, the extreme version of this position can result in a teleological argument (that the outcome is determined in the beginning by the needs or requirements of capital). Thus this school of thought is sometimes called *capital logic* (as in "the logic of capital" requires that...) and is criticized for circular reasoning and the exclusion of human action from the analysis. For example, David Harvey has accused some writers of seeing spatial organization as "a mere reflection of the processes of accumulation and class reproduction" (1982, quoted in Logan and Molotch 1987). Both Harvey and Castells have tried to avoid this problem by bringing other factors into their analysis in very complex ways, showing interplays among capital, labor, and the state.

Let us now turn to the third set of answers, those analyzing the role of the *state* (which includes government bodies and other related political and administrative forms) in relationship to the economy. In the postwar period, states have grown tremendously, have taken on additional tasks, and have become increasingly intertwined in the economies of their countries through planning, regulation, and state-run enterprises. While this has been a pattern in all industrialized capitalist countries, it has happened more dramatically in France than elsewhere, prompting French researchers to take an early theoretical interest in the state (Lebas 1983).

The first state theory to be discussed in the urban sociology literature was the *state monopoly capital* (SMC) thesis, which held that a new stage of capitalism was emerging. The analysis of the shift from competitive capitalism, with many small, competing firms, to monopoly capitalism, in which economies were dominated by large, monopolistic enterprises, had long been discussed in the literature. SMC theorists argued that the economies of the industrialized nations were moving toward state monopoly capitalism, in which these large enterprises were increasingly intertwined with a huge state apparatus. This position, which was the official doctrine of the French Communist party in the 1960s, was applied to urban phenomena by Jean Lojkine (1976) and other theorists. They stressed the role played by the state (including the state at the local level) in protecting capital from a falling rate of profit. The chief way this was accomplished, SMC theorists argued, was by restructuring space through planning and urban-renewal programs. The SMC theory in general and its urban application were criticized on the grounds that state apparatuses did not consistently favor the interests of capital, especially at the local level, but were often effective avenues of protest or organization against capitalist interests.

Structuralism, the second theory of state involvement in urban areas, grew out of that criticism. Following the French philosopher Louis Althusser (1970), a number of urbanists, including Castells, argued that state structures are neither part of capital (as the SMC theorists hold) nor completely independent from it but are relatively autonomous. Structuralists argue that the state plays an important role for capital, namely, that of resolving those problems and conflicts that capitalists are unable to resolve for themselves. Two such mechanisms are state economic planning and state funding of collective consumption, the costs of maintaining an urban workforce that the capitalists as individuals are unwilling to fund. But, structuralists argue, contradictions result from this arrangement. More and more of the costs of reproduction (e.g., housing and health care) and social investment (e.g., transportation and infrastructure) are being borne by the state. Capitalists resist both paying higher wages to fund these items directly and increasing their taxes to fund them indirectly. Thus, the resulting problem for states is recurrent *fiscal crises* in which state expenditures increase far faster than tax revenues. Several theorists in the United States, including O'Connor (1971),

Hill (1978), and Tabb (1982), profitably applied structuralist theory to the analysis of urban fiscal crises.

Structuralism was an important advance in theoretical development, and for a while it dominated not only urban theory but Marxist sociology in general. Over time, however, several criticisms were raised that allowed its analytical power to be questioned. Ivan Szelenyi (1981) summarized these, as they applied to urban studies, with the charge that structuralism was too rigid and too narrow. It was too rigid because it analyzed every urban phenomenon as the result of one of the requirements of capital accumulation. This criticism was similar to that leveled at the "mode of production" theorists. It was too narrow in that it concentrated on only the most advanced industrial nations, rather than on cities in Third World, socialist, or other kinds of societies. Szelenyi called for more comparative and empirical work to understand urban patterns in different societies. Structuralism was also widely criticized for focusing on abstract "structures," rather than people as the agents of history. Castells himself (1983) has even joined the critics of structuralism by arguing that cities are structured by people, not by contradictions. The general response to this debate among urbanists has been to adopt a "constrained actor" point of view; in other words, while capitalism sets certain general boundaries of activity, individuals and groups have a number of possible responses they can make. This line of reasoning follows Marx in the idea that people make history, but they do not make it just as they please.

Contributions to Urban and Regional Studies

Marxist thought has had major impacts on the field of urban and regional sociology. Some aspects of Marxist theory are now the accepted wisdom in urban sociology. For example, Marxist analysis has forced urbanists to step back from the description of empirical patterns in individual cities and to investigate the more remote causes of these patterns. Urban sociologists can no longer simply describe how neighborhoods change; they now must understand the causes and consequences of those changes in the economy, politics, and society. One example of a book that provides this wider focus is Sharon Zukin's *Loft Living* (1982), which shows how manufacturing, real estate, and art have together reshaped the patterns of land use in lower Manhattan. Zukin argues that the social movement of artists' loft living could not have come about without previous economic and political changes.

Another important Marxist contribution is the emphasis on how changes in industrial structure are linked with changes in city form. It is now part of mainstream sociology to examine the impact of global economic restructuring on cities and regions, as was pioneered by Susan Fainstein et al. (1983). Both Manuel Castells (1985) and Mike Davis (1990) have shown how the urban landscapes of California cities have been affected by the industrial changes in the high-tech industries and the service sector. Saskia Sassen's *The Mobility of Capital and Labor* (1988) provides an even broader scope, showing how international flows of capital have affected migration and immigration patterns, which in turn have affected the nature of the labor market in cities such as New York and Los Angeles, changing the industrial structures of those cities. Sassen explores the immigrant communities of those cities by going "backward" to see why they immigrated and "forward" to see how they help create new economic possibilities for capital in the cities they now inhabit.

A related focus of urban research to which Marxist sociologists have contributed is the study of the "informal economy" of unpaid or unrecorded work, such as house painting, babysitting, drug dealing, sewing at home, hairdressing, and selling homemade products. Marxists have not been alone in discovering this sector; urban anthropologists have long documented it, and neo-Weberians such as Ray Pahl (1980) have been insistent on its importance for some time. Marxists have been able to put it into the context of post-Fordist regimes of accumulation, however, linking the growth of the informal sector of the economy with reductions in the size of manufacturing firms and the severing of many workers' permanent connections to the paid labor force. Mainstream sociologists, economists, and geographers continue to see the problem of inner-city poverty as simply a "geographic mismatch" between where new jobs are being created and where unemployed workers are located, but Marxist urbanists argue that this geographic pattern is not a coincidence but an outgrowth of structural changes in the nature of advanced capitalism (see, for example, Walker and Storper 1981, on attempts of business to control labor by locating plants away from stable communities of workers).

Another way in which Marxist urbanists have forced the discipline to look beyond surface patterns is in the question of mechanisms by which space is structured. Both human ecologists and mainstream economists assume that urban space is structured by the free competition of different subgroups for living or working space. Many Marxist urbanists, in contrast, argue that a specific class of people, called property capitalists, or *rentiers*, structure urban space. This analysis is controversial; some Marxists deny the existence of a class of *rentiers* in contemporary cities. The debate, however, has worked its way into the mainstream sociology literature (Jaret 1983). Discussions such as those by Marxists Francois Lamarche (1976) and Joe Feagin (1982) of property capital-ists and urban real estate speculators have have influenced the way urbanists look at land use. A good example is Harvey Molotch's (1979) article analyzing the impact of capital on urban neighborhoods and how it is mediated by *rentiers*.

Marxist writings have contributed to sociology by giving sociologists a better understanding of the contradictions of capitalist development. This way of thinking has particularly influenced work on the causes of urban deterioration and slum formation. Harvey's analysis has shown how the destruction of property, as much as investment in it, is intrinsic to the nature of capitalism. The notion of contradiction also applies to such phenomena as the fiscal crisis, which even mainstream urbanists have had to admit is not simply a result of city governments' overspending but actually a structural problem they face, with an ongoing tendency toward smaller incomes and larger expenses for government bodies (Congressional Budget Office 1975).

Besides their infusion of new ideas into the sociological literature, another way in which Marxist urbanists have influenced the field of urban sociology is by revitalizing and refocusing existing scholarly debates. The question Castells asked, "Is There an Urban Sociology?" (1976) is actually an old question (see Pahl 1970, chap. 10). Castells revived and refocused the argument, changing the meaning from "Is urban sociology simply the study of anything that happens in cities?" to "Is urban sociology studying cities, or rather, the urban aspect of capitalism?" Similarly, the "structure-agency" debate is an old one, asking whether the "movers" of society are social structures or human actors. For decades, sociologists have debated these two approaches (see, for example, Molotch 1967). According to Mark Gottdiener (1985), the advantage of the current Marxist approach is that it is both historic and humanist. It traces the development of social phenomena over time, rather than search for unvarying laws, and it studies what humans do, rather than concentrate solely on abstract structures.

One perplexing question still being debated within the Marxist arena as well as in the mainstream is the relationship between the different levels of economic development among nations, regions within nations, and communities within regions. For example, it is unclear whether the causes of the distribution of wealth and poverty in the Third World are similar to the causes of the same distribution in the inner cities of the advanced capitalist nations. While Doreen Massey (1978) stresses the differences between international patterns and those within the cities of the advanced capitalist nations, Neil Smith (1984) stresses the similarities. The contribution that the debate has had on the understanding of urban poverty in any location, however, is that it has drawn scholarly attention away from the individual attributes of poor people as a cause of poverty and has highlighted the importance of investment patterns for the wealth or poverty of particular communities.

Another area that has been affected by the Marxist approach to urban sociology is the emergence of a feminist urban studies. In the 1960s, Marxist and radical thought had inspired a revival of feminist thought about politics and culture (Evans 1979). Later it inspired a new wave of feminist thinking about the city, particularly about housing. Dolores Hayden's *Redesigning the American Dream* (1984) discusses the sexist assumptions underlying the design of the single-family home: the insularity of the nuclear family, the separation of home life and work life, the needs of the "working" father and "nonworking" mother, the division of interior space into "male" and "female" preserves, and so on. Hayden shows the interconnections between family, work, home, and community that industrial capitalist society has tended to segment into different spheres. The British collective Matrix (1984) further probes the connections between capitalism, gender relations, and space in communities.

In making their presence felt within urban sociology, Marxist urbanists have sparked many debates and have generated many critics. Some of these are "friendly critics," analysts whose own works are close to the positions of the Marxists but who differ from them in some significant ways. A number of the most influential urban sociologists writing today are friendly critics of Marxist analysis. For example, John Logan and Harvey Molotch recently received the American Sociological Association's award for the best book in sociology, *Urban Fortunes* (1987), which is a critique of both Marxist and classical theories of the city. The "Marxism" that Logan and Molotch criticize, however, is the rigid and controversial (even among Marxists) school that analyzes every urban phenomenon as existing to meet the needs of capital. In contrast, *Urban Fortunes* forthrightly uses many Marxist concepts such as use value and exchange value, capital mobility, and commodification. The authors' overall approach, which they call "political economy," is heavily influenced by the writings of Marxist scholars.

Another set of "friendly critics" are the urban power-structure researchers such as G. William Domhoff, author of *Who Rules America Now?* (1983). Domhoff also criticizes "Marxists," meaning structuralists, and has debated structuralist theorists about whether there is a ruling class that directly governs communities in the United States or whether the capitalist class rules indirectly through government structures set up to favor it. Some Marxists have called Domhoff (who writes in the tradition of C. Wright Mills and Floyd Hunter) an "instrumentalist" because they say he sees individual political leaders as instruments of capital (see Gold et al. 1975). Despite that sometimes acrimonious debate, Domhoff's assumptions are compatible with the main thrust of a Marxist approach: that there is a capitalist class, that it is class conscious, and that it often unites to act in its own interests. One important outcome of this debate on power is that sociologists and political scientists have now moved beyond the pluralist-elitist debate of the 1960s in search of new explanations for urban power structures. Sociologists like Whitt (1982) have developed more complex explanations, looking at both the unifying and fragmenting tendencies within capitalist elites.

A final set of "friendly critics" with whom Marxist urbanists have had much fruitful dialogue is a group usually referred to as "neo-Weberians." This group tackles many of the same problems as the Marxists (and sometimes comes to surprisingly similar conclusions) but without as much theoretical reliance on

Marx. Two of the leading neo-Weberians, John Rex and Ray Pahl, are also critics of mainstream sociology, engaged in a search for more powerful analytical tools with which to understand changing cities. Rex, for example, has studied race relations in British cities and has developed a new way of looking at class relations among urban residents. Rather than simply seeing class as one's relationship to the means of production, he has followed Weber's suggestion that class is a market phenomenon. Thus, he says, a group with the same relation to the means of production (i.e., all workers) may vary on their access to housing, forming different "classes" where housing is concerned (Rex 1973). This helps us understand why urban patterns vary from one "working class" neighborhood to another. Pahl makes the same argument about the other services that cities offer: that the spatial distribution of education, health care, and so on available to people differs by their residence somewhat independently of their position in the occupational structure (Pahl 1970). Rex and Pahl have been discussing in different terms some of the same phenomena that Marxists such as Castells and Lojkine discuss as part of "collective consumption."

Naturally, not all critics of Marxist urban sociology have been friendly. There has been a tendency among some human ecologists and neoclassical economists to reject the Marxist critique of urban sociology and to counterattack. The most important debate has centered on the role of markets in structuring space. Mainstream theorists such as Berry and Kasarda (1977) and Peterson (1981) argue that cities are shaped by the sum of individuals' choices in the market, based on their tastes and preferences. They hold that the market itself is impersonal and its effects are benign, since it allows individuals to maximize their choices of location. Although there is competition for space, they say, class conflict is minimal; cities are not class stratified, merely "functionally differentiated." Marxists have answered in several ways. First, they argue that changes in investment patterns shape individual tastes, rather than vice versa (Smith 1979). Second, they hold that the "free market" is not really free but is molded by various powerful groups, both capitalists and government (Feagin 1988). Finally, they contend that social groups and institutions, rather than individual consumers and producers, are the most important influences on cities (Gottdiener 1985).

Conclusion

Although Marx wrote very little about cities, his work provided important theoretical cues that urban sociologists have developed since the late 1970s. Unlike the previously dominant theory of human ecology, Marxist urban sociology locates the sources of urban problems in the set of economic, political, and social institutions existing in advanced capitalist societies. Additionally there is now some analysis of urban processes in Third World countries and of the relationships between cities in the two kinds of societies.

Marxist urban sociologists view cities as shaped by the processes of economic production and social reproduction of the labor force within a context of capital accumulation. Urban form and urban social patterns are shaped by the mode of production, by conflicts over the distribution of resources both within and outside the workplace, and by actions of the state, which are usually but not always in the interests of capital. Actions taken by capitalists (or by the state on their behalf) often produce contradictions that generate new problems and sometimes generate crises requiring significant changes in the direction of either capitalism or state policies.

In the early stages of development, Marxist urban sociologists, like the previously dominant human ecologists, were engaged in a quest for universal laws and regularities in urban patterns. Some Marxist pioneers tended to rely on Marx's more deterministic phrasings such as the "law" of uneven development. These rigid approaches to urban phenomena have now been criticized and replaced with a more historicist view, one that traces developments in urban processes without assuming that they will be uniform in all respects. The tendency to look for laws may have been an outgrowth of the analysts' desire to generate scientifically based political programs that would foster social change. Their early analyses, however, were often subject to the same critique as the mainstream sociologists' work: They were too abstract, were irrefutable, and used circular logic. Manuel Castells has alerted us to this difficulty by pointing out that "academic Marxism can be as formalistic and useless as functionalism was in the past." He challenges all sociologists to "cast light on the real world, instead of codifying it into the obsolete categories of the academic establishment" (1980:127).

Marxist urban sociology was, in part, a long-overdue reaction to the difficulties and finally the exhaustion of the mainstream paradigm of human ecology in particular and functionalist sociology in general. Like other radical sociologists, Marxists have been concerned with *praxis*, or the practical application of their knowledge in the real world. Richard Flacks (1988) has indicated the significance of this kind of social science. As a direct attack on not only the substantive theories but also on the "value-free" perspective of mainstream sociology, radical sociology has become a threat to the "establishment." Not surprisingly, Flacks continues, the establishment initially counterattacked in many ways; among others, by denying the Marxists university positions and barring them from sociological organizations. In less than twenty years, however, Marxist urban sociology has had an enormous influence on the fields of urban sociology and urban studies. Marxist, neo-Weberian, and other compatible perspectives are now accepted within the sociological community as valid approaches to understanding the nature of cities.

Some sociologists (e.g., Gottdiener and Feagin 1988) argue that Marxism has already replaced human ecology as the dominant paradigm (or theoretical framework) in urban sociology. Whether or not this is the case, urban sociology will continue to be influenced by Marxist analysis in the future. It seems improbable that the trends and problems of the past twenty years, namely, racial and class antagonisms, job loss, increasing poverty and economic dislocation, immigration, and the fiscal crisis, will disappear. Furthermore, links will continue to be created among cities in different parts of the world. The value of Marxist urban sociology is that it has established a framework for studying those and other phenomena as part of an entire system, rather than as fragmented problems.

References

Abu-Lughod, Janet. 1968. "The City Is Dead-Long Live the City: Some Thoughts on Urbanity." In *Urbanism in World Perspective*, ed. S. Fava. New York: Crowell.

Addams, Jane. 1930. *The Second Twenty Years at Hull House*. New York: Macmillan.

Alihan, Milla. 1938. *Social Ecology: A Critical Analysis*. New York: Columbia University Press.

Althusser, Louis. 1970. *For Marx*. London: New Left Books.

Baltzell, E. Digby. 1967. "Introduction to the 1967 Edition." In *The Philadelphia Negro* by W.E.B. Du Bois. New York: Schocken Books.

Berry, Brian, and John D. Kasarda. 1977. *Contemporary Urban Ecology*. New York: Macmillan.

Castells, Manuel. 1972. *City, Class and Power*. New York: St. Martin's.

———. 1976. "Is There an Urban Sociology?" In *Urban Sociology: Critical Essays*, ed. C.G. Pickvance. New York: St. Martin's.

———. 1977. *The Urban Question*. Cambridge: MIT Press.

———. 1980. "Cities and Regions Beyond the Crisis." *International Journal of Urban and Regional Research* 4:127–29.

———. 1983. *The City and the Grassroots*. Berkeley: University of California Press.

———. 1985. "High Technology, Economic Restructuring and the Urban-Regional Process in the U.S." In *High Technology, Space, and Society*, ed. M. Castells. Beverly Hills: Sage.

Congressional Budget Office. 1975. *New York City's Fiscal Problem: Its Origins, Potential Repurcussions, and Some Alternative Policy Responses*. Washington, D.C.: Government Printing Office.

Davis, Mike. 1990. *City of Quartz*. London: Verso.

Deegan, Mary Jo. 1988. *Jane Addams and the Men of the Chicago School 1892–1918*. New Brunswick, N.J.: Transaction Books.

Domhoff, G. William. 1983. *Who Rules America Now?: A View for the '80s*. Englewood Cliffs, N.J.: Prentice-Hall.

Du Bois, W.E.B. 1967 [1899]. *The Philadelphia Negro*. New York: Schocken Books.

Edel, Matthew. 1977. "Rent Theory and Working Class Strategy: Marx, George, and the Urban Crisis." *Review of Radical Political Economics* 9(Winter):1–15.

Engels, Freidrich. 1954. *The Housing Question*. Moscow: Progress Publications.

———. n.d. *The Condition of the Working-Class in England*. Moscow: Progress Publishers.

Evans, Sara. 1979. *Personal Politics: The Roots of Women's Liberation in the Civil Rights Movement and the New Left*. New York: Vintage Books.

Fainstein, Susan, N. Fainstein, R.C. Hill, and M.P. Smith. 1983. *Restructuring the City: The Political Economy of Urban Redevelopment*. London: Longman.

Feagin, Joe. 1982. "Urban Real Estate Speculation in the U.S.: Implications for Social Science and Urban Planning." *International Journal of Urban and Regional Research* 6:35–60.

———. 1988. *Free Enterprise City: Houston in Political and Economic Perspective*. New Brunswick, N.J.: Rutgers University Press.

Firey, Walter. 1945. "Sentiment and Symbolism as Ecological Variables." *A merican Sociological Review* 10:140–48.

Flacks, Dick. 1988. "The Sociology Liberation Movement: Some Legacies and Lessons." *Critical Sociology* 15:9–18.

Form, William H. 1954. "The Place of Social Structure in the Determination of Land Use: Some Implications for a Theory of Urban Ecology." *Social Forces* 32:317–23.

George, Henry. 1938 [1882]. *Progress and Poverty*. New York: Modern Library.

Glass, Ruth. 1968. "Urban Sociology in Great Britain." In *Reading in Urban Sociology*, ed. R.E. Pahl. London: Pergamon Press.

Gold, D.A., C.Y.H. Lo, and E.O. Wright. 1975. "Recent Developments in Marxist Theories of the Capitalist State." Parts I and II. *Monthly Review* 27(5,6):29–43, 36–51.

Gordon, David. 1977. "Class Struggle and the Stages of American Urban Development." In *The Rise of the Sunbelt Cities*, ed. D. Perry and A.J. Watkins. Beverly Hills: Sage.

Gottdiener, Mark. 1985. *The Social Production of Urban Space*. Austin: University of Texas Press.

Gottdiener, Mark and Joe Feagin. 1988. "The Paradigm Shift in Urban Sociology." *U rban Affairs Quarterly* 24(2):163–87.

Harvey, David. 1973. *Social Justice and the City*. Baltimore: Johns Hopkins University Press.

———. 1978. "The Urban Process Under Capitalism: A Framework for Analysis." *I nternational Journal of Urban and Regional Research* 2:101–31.

Hayden, Dolores. 1984. *Redesigning the American Dream*. New York: Norton.

Hill, Richard Child. 1978. "Fiscal Collapse and Political Struggle in the Decaying U.S. Central City." In *Marxism and the Metropolis*, ed. W. Tabb and L. Sawers. New York: Oxford University Press.

Hunter, Floyd. 1953. *Community Power Structure: A Study of Decision Makers*. Chapel Hill: University of North Carolina Press.

Jaret, Charles. 1983. "Recent Neo-Marxist Urban Analysis." In *Annual Review of Sociology*, vol. 9, ed. R.H. Turner. Palo Alto, Calif.: Annual Reviews.

Lamarche, Francois. 1976. "Property Development and the Economic Foundations of the Urban Question." In *U rban Sociology: Critical Essays*, ed. C.G. Pickvance. New York: St. Martin's.

Lebas, Elizabeth. 1982. "Urban and Regional Sociology in Advanced Industrial Societies." *C urrent Sociology* 30:1–264.

———. 1983. "The State in British and French Urban Research, or the Crisis of the Urban Question." In *Urban Social Research: Problems and Prospects*, ed. V. Pons and R. Francis. London: Routledge and Kegan Paul.

Lee, Alfred McClung. 1988. "Steps Taken toward Liberating Sociologists." *C ritical Sociology* 15(2):47–60.

Logan, John, and Harvey Molotch. 1987. *Urban Fortunes: The Political Economy of Place*. Berkeley: University of California Press.

Logan, John, and Todd Swanstrom, eds. 1990. *B eyond the City Limits: Urban Policy and Economic Restructuring in Comparative Perspective*. Philadelphia: Temple University Press.

Lojkine, Jean. 1976. "Contribution to a Marxist Theory of Capitalist Urbanization." In *U rban Sociology: Critical Essays*, ed. C.G. Pickvance. New York: St. Martin's.

Lynd, Robert and Helen Lynd. 1929. *M iddletown*. New York: Harcourt, Brace.

———. 1937. *Middletown in Transition*. New York: Harcourt, Brace.

Marx, Karl, and Frederick Engels. 1977 [1846]. *The German Ideology*. New York: International Publishers.

Massey, Doreen. 1978. "Regionalism: Some Current Issues." C *apital and Class* 6:106–25.

Matrix. 1984. *Making Space: Women and the Man-Made Environment*. London: Pluto.

Molotch, Harvey. 1967. "Toward a More Human Human Ecology." *Land Economics* 43:336–41.

———. 1979. "Capital and Neighborhood in the U.S.: Some Conceptual Links." *Urban Affairs Quarterly* 14:289–312.

Mumford, Lewis. 1970 [1938]. *The Culture of Cities*. New York: Harcourt Brace Jovanovich.

O'Connor, James. 1973. T *he Fiscal Crisis of the State*. New York: St.Martin's.

Pahl, R.E. 1970. W *hose City?* London: Longman.

———. 1980. "Employment, Work, and the Domestic Division of Labour." *International Journal of Urban and Regional Research* 4(1):1–20.

Park, Robert E., E.W. Burgess, and R.D. McKenzie, eds. 1925. *The City*. Chicago: University of Chicago Press.

Piore, Michael, and Charles Sabel. 1984. T *he Second Industrial Divide: Possibilities for Prosperity*. New York: Basic Books.

Procter, Ian. 1982. "Some Political Economies of Urbanization and Suggestions for a Research Framework." *International Journal of Urban and Regional Research* 6:83–98.

Rex, John. 1973. *Race, Colonialism, and the City*. London: Routledge and Kegan Paul.

Sassen, Saskia. 1988. T *he Mobility of Labor and Capital*. New York: Cambridge University Press.

Sawers, Larry. 1975. "Urban Form and the Mode of Production." R *eview of Radical Political Economics* 7:52–68.

Scott, A.J. 1988. "Flexible Production Systems and Regional Development: The Rise of New Industrial Spaces in North America and Western Europe." *International Journal of Urban and Regional Research* 12(2):171–86.

Smith, Neil. 1979. "Toward a Theory of Gentrification." *Journal of the American Planning Association* 45:538–48.

———. 1984. *Uneven Development*. New York: Basil Blackwell.

Szelenyi, Ivan. 1978. "Class Analysis and Beyond: Further Dilemmas for the New Urban Sociology." *Comparative Urban Research* 4:86–96.

———. 1981. "Structural Changes of and Alternatives to Capitalist Development in the Contemporary Urban and Regional System." *International Journal of Urban and Regional Research* 5:1–14.

Tabb, William K. 1982. *The Long Default: New York City and the Urban Fiscal Crisis*. New York: Monthly Review Press.

Tabb, William, and Larry Sawers, ed. 1978. M *arxism and the Metropolis*. New York: Oxford University Press.

Walker, Richard, and Michael Storper. 1981. "Capital and Industrial Location." P *rogress in Human Geography* 5:473–509.

Whitt, J. Allen. 1982. *Urban Elites and Mass Transportation: The Dialectics of Power*. Princeton: Princeton University Press.

Willhelm, Sidney. 1973. "The Concept of the Ecological Complex: A Critique." In T *he Sociology of the City*, ed. S. Halebsky. New York: Scribner.

Zukin, Sharon. 1980. "A Decade of the New Urban Sociology." T *heory and Society* 9:575–601.

———. 1982. *Loft Living: Culture and Capital in Urban Change*. Baltimore: Johns Hopkins University Press.

BIOGRAPHIES

William D. Armaline is Assistant Professor of Educational Theory and Social Foundations at the University of Toledo. He publishes in the area of urban education, reflectivity, and critical educational theory.

Kathleen S. Farber is Assistant Professor of Educational Foundations and Inquiry at Bowling Green State University. She publishes in the areas of urban education, reflectivity, and feminist pedagogy.

James A. Geschwender is Professor of Sociology at SUNY-Binghamton and 1990–91 President of the Society for the Study of Social Problems. His early work on African Americans included *Racial Stratification in America* (W.C. Brown, 1977) and *Class, Race, and Worker Insurgency* (Cambridge University Press, 1978). His recent work has analyzed racial stratification in Hawaii and Canada and has examined the social construction of gender within racial and ethnic groups.

Davita Silfen Glasberg is Associate Professor of Sociology at the University of Connecticut-Storrs. She has published extensively on issues of bank hegemony, the state in financial capitalism, and political economy, including *The Power of Collective Purse Strings* (University of California Press, 1989).

Arthur Jipson is a doctoral student in the Department of Sociology at Bowling Green State University. His professional interests include the sociology of labor and work, sociological theory, and the structure of the music industry. His 1991 Master's thesis was "Actors and Activists: The 1934 Electric Auto-Lite Strike."

Howard Kimeldorf is Associate Professor of Sociology and Director of the Center for Research on Social Organizations at the University of Michigan. He is coeditor of the journal *Political Power and Social Theory*. He authored *Reds or Rackets* (University of California Press, 1988) and has published articles in *Social Forces*, *Labor History*, and elsewhere. He is currently studying class formation in the United States during the interwar period.

Nancy Kleniewski is Associate Professor and Chair of the Department of Sociology at SUNY-Geneseo. She is coauthor of *Urban Problems in Sociological Perspective* (Waveland Press, 1991) and *Philadelphia: Economic Transformation and Social Inequality* (Temple University Press, 1992). Her current research examines social inequality and urban policy.

300

Jerry Lembcke teaches sociology at Holy Cross College. He is an associate editor of *Critical Sociology* and is the author of *Capitalist Development and Class Capacities* (Greenwood Press, 1988). Currently he is working on a book on working-class formation and capital mobility, tentatively entitled *Time, Space, and Class Power.*

Rhonda F. Levine is Associate Professor of Sociology at Colgate University. She is the author of *Class Struggle and the New Deal* (University of Kansas Press, 1988), a coeditor of *Recapturing Marxism* (Praeger, 1987), *Radical Sociologists and the Movement* (Temple University Press, 1990), and *Bringing Class Back In* (Westview Press, 1991).

Michael J. Lynch is Assistant Professor in the Program in Criminal Justice at the School of Criminology and Criminal Justice, Florida State University. He is coauthor of *A Primer in Radical Criminology* (Harrow and Hestin, 1989). He has published papers in several journals, including *Crime and Social Justice, Contemporary Crises,* and *Critical Criminologist.*

Patrick McGuire is Associate Professor of Sociology at the University of Toledo. His work has appeared in *Sociological Quarterly, Critical Sociology, Social Science Quarterly* and elsewhere. With Mark Granovetter and Michael Schwartz, he is completing a book tentatively titled *The Social Construction of Industry* (Cambridge University Press, 1994).

Charley McMartin is currently a graduate student in history at Columbia University. He has published recent essays in *The Texas Observer, Covert Action Information Bulletin,* and *The Guardian* (New York).

Scott G. McNall is Dean of Arts and Sciences at the University of Toledo and is a past President of the Midwest Sociological Society. He is the author of *The Greek Peasant* (American Sociological Association, 1974); *Career of a Radical Rightist* (Kennikat Press, 1975); and *Road to Rebellion* (University of Chicago Press, 1988). He is the coeditor of *Bringing Class Back In* (Westview Press, 1991) and coauthor of *Plains Families* (St. Martin's, 1983) and *Sociology* (Prentice-Hall, 1992).

Donald McQuarie is Director of Graduate Studies and Professor of Sociology at Bowling Green State University. He is the editor of *Marx: Sociology, Social Change, Capitalism* (Quartet, 1978) and *Readings in Contemporary Sociological Theory* (Prentice-Hall, 1994). He has published papers in *Critical Sociology, American Sociologist, Sociological Quarterly,* and *Social Science Quarterly.* His current research interest is municipal socialism in Ohio at the turn of the century.

Beth Mintz is Professor of Sociology at the University of Vermont. Her recent publications include *The Power Structure of American Business* (with Michael Schwartz—University of Chicago Press, 1985), "The United States," in Bottomore and Brym, eds. *The Capitalist Class* (Harvester, 1989), and "The Role of Capitalist Relations in the Restructuring of Medicine," in McNall et al., eds. *Bringing Class Back In* (Westview, 1991). Her current research focuses on splits among capitalists regarding issues of health-care cost containment.

Marietta Morrissey, Associate Professor and Chair of the Department of Sociology, University of Toledo, is the author of *Slave Women in the New World* (University of Kansas Press, 1989). Her work has previously appeared in *Social Forces, Review of Radical Political Economics, Latin American Perspectives,* and *Studies in Comparative International Development*

Martin J. Murray is Professor of Sociology and Director of Undergraduate Studies at SUNY-Binghamton. He is the author of *The Development of Capitalism in Colonial Indochina 1870–1940* (University of California Press, 1980); *South African Capitalism and Black Political Opposition* (Schenkman, 1981); and *South Africa* (Verso, 2nd Ed., 1992). He is the coeditor of *Radical Sociologists and the Movement* (Temple University Press, 1990).

Shan Nelson-Rowe is Assistant Professor of Sociology at Fairleigh Dickinson University. His research focuses on the connection between schooling and the economy. He recently published "Corporation, Schooling, and the Labor Market at General Electric" in *History of Education Quarterly* (1991).

Kenneth J. Neubeck is Associate Professor of Sociology at the University of Connecticut-Storrs. He is the author of *Corporate Response to Urban Crisis.* He has contributed to numerous anthologies and has published articles in *Social Problems, Social Policy,* and *Teaching Sociology.* He is currently studying consumer and investment behaviors of American families.

Milagros Peña is Assistant Professor of Ethnic Studies and Sociology at Bowling Green State University. She has done extensive field research in Peru on the Catholic church, contrasting theologies as part of an analysis of the role of ideas in social movements. She has published articles in *Sociological Analysis* and the *Journal for the Scientific Study of Religion,* and has a forthcoming book *Theologies and Liberation* (Temple University Press, 1994).

Randy Stoecker is Assistant Professor of Sociology and Research Associate in the Urban Affairs program at the University of Toledo. He has published articles on critical theory, social movements, and participatory research in journals including *Berkeley Journal of Sociology, Sociological Review,* and *Perspectives on Social Problems,* and he is the author of *Defending Community: The Struggle for Alternative Redevelopment in Cedar-Riverside* (Temple University Press, 1994).

INDEX